The Revolutions of 1688

D1712965

THE REVOLUTIONS OF 1688

The Andrew Browning
Lectures
1988

EDITED BY
ROBERT BEDDARD

CLARENDON PRESS · OXFORD
1991

Barry University Library
Miami, FL 33161

Oxford University Press, Walton Street, Oxford OX2 6DP

Oxford New York Toronto
Delhi Bombay Calcutta Madras Karachi
Petaling Jaya Singapore Hong Kong Tokyo
Nairobi Dar es Salaam Cape Town
Melbourne Auckland

and associated companies in
Berlin Ibadan

Oxford is a trade mark of Oxford University Press

Published in the United States
by Oxford University Press, New York

© *The Contributors, 1991*

All rights reserved. No part of this publication may be reproduced, stored in a retrieval system, or transmitted, in any form or by any means, electronic, mechanical, photocopying, recording, or otherwise, without the prior permission of Oxford University Press

British Library Cataloguing in Publication Data
The Revolutions of 1688—(The Andrew Browning lectures)
1. Great Britain. Political events 1685–1702
I. Beddard, Robert
941.067
ISBN 0–19–822920–8

Library of Congress Cataloging in Publication Data
The Revolutions of 1688: the Andrew Browning lectures, 1988 /
edited by Robert Beddard.
p. cm.
Includes index.
1. Great Britain—History—Revolution of 1688.
2. Revolutions—History—17th century.
I. Beddard, Robert. II. Title: Andrew Browning lectures, 1988.
DA452.R48 1991 941.06'7–dc20 90–42401
ISBN 0–19–822920–8

Typeset by Hope Services (Abingdon) Ltd.
Printed and bound in
Great Britain by Biddles Ltd.
Guildford and King's Lynn

DA
452
.R48
1991

209167

Contents

List of Contributors

Dr Robert Beddard, Fellow of Oriel College, Oxford

K. G. Davies, former Fellow of New College, Oxford, and retired Professor of History, Trinity College, Dublin

Dr Mark Goldie, Fellow of Churchill College, Cambridge

Dr Simon Groenveld, Department of History, University of Leiden

Patrick Kelly, Department of History, Trinity College, Dublin

Bruce P. Lenman, Department of History, University of St Andrews

Professor J. G. A. Pocock, Johns Hopkins University, Baltimore

Dr John Stoye, Emeritus Fellow of Magdalen College, Oxford

Introduction: The Protestant Succession

ROBERT BEDDARD

In November 1688 William Henry, hereditary Prince of Orange and *Stadhouder* of the Dutch Republic, invaded England with a powerful army. He came at the invitation of a group of James II's Protestant subjects: seven dissident noblemen and gentlemen—five Whigs and two Tories—who wished to check the king's unpopular catholicizing policies, but felt themselves unequal to the task without the prince's active 'protection to countenance their rising' against the promoters of Popery at home. Their appeal for outside help—itself an admission of native despair in the face of a strong and wilful Catholic monarch—sprang from a deep-rooted dissatisfaction 'with the present conduct of government', not from an overpowering desire to pull down the monarchy or to switch kings. The absence of a sitting parliament (none had met since November 1685), and their exclusion from royal favour (increasingly monopolized by their opponents), denied them any alternative means of bringing pressure to bear on King James and his ministers to get them to abandon their unacceptable measures. Their aim in calling in the Prince of Orange was to preserve the lawful Protestant Establishment in Church and State from what they feared was the threat of imminent Catholic subversion. They sought to reassert the laws of the land 'in relation to their religion, liberties, and properties', all of which, they believed, had been 'greatly invaded', and to remove, by force if necessary, the king's 'evil counsellors', foremost of whom they reckoned the hated Papists and their fellow-travellers, the ultra-Tory prerogative men.[1] In this enterprise to reverse royal policy they cast William of Orange in the role of Protestant deliverer. It was, of course, a role for which his high birth and international character as a sovereign prince pre-eminently suited him.

[1] PRO SP 8/1, pt. 2, fos. 224–7: Earls of Danby, Shrewsbury, and Devonshire, Bishop Compton, Edward Russell, and Henry Sidney to William of Orange, 30 June 1688.

William was the grandson of Charles I, England's revered martyr king, and the great-grandson of William the Silent, the admired champion of Dutch Protestantism. Moreover, by his marriage into his mother's family, he was the husband of James II's elder daughter, Princess Mary, long regarded as the Protestant heir to the three kingdoms of England, Scotland, and Ireland.[2] To close kinship with the ruling Stuart dynasty William added his own, impeccably Protestant, personal record. While he owed his sovereign status to the tiny and remote Principality of Orange, a dependency of the House of Nassau in southern France, he had come to the forefront of European politics as the heroic saviour of the Dutch Republic. Ever since 1672, when in an act of unprovoked aggression France had invaded the United Provinces, he had assumed the militancy of his Calvinist ancestors and the leadership of his country.[3] Since then he had waged an unremitting war—diplomatically, politically, and ecclesiastically, as well as militarily—against the might of Louis XIV's France: the power which, above any other, menaced the peace and stability of Europe by challenging the legal rights and overthrowing the settled frontiers of its continental neighbours.[4] As if he had not received enough firsthand experience of the assertiveness of 'the most Christian barbarian', the occupation of the Principality of Orange in 1682 and subsequent *dragonnade* of its Protestant inhabitants underlined the French Crown's blatant disregard for princely and confessional liberties.[5] It is hardly surprising that William's identification of the objectives of the Bourbon monarchy,

[2] N. Japikse, *De Geschiedenis van het Huis van Oranje-Nassau* (2 vols., The Hague, 1937), ii. 45–8; J. K. Oudendijk, *Willem Stadhouder van Holland Koning van Engeland* (Amsterdam 1954), 111–15; A. Browning, *Thomas Osborne, Earl of Danby* (3 vols., Glasgow 1944–51), i. 248–54; S. B. Baxter, *William III* (1966), 148–50, 165, 167, 201.

[3] P. Hazard, *La Crise de la conscience européenne 1680–1715* (Paris 1961), 74; N. Japikse, *Prins Willem III De Stadhouder–Koning* (2 vols., Amsterdam 1930–3), i. 318 ff.; L. André, *Louis XIV et l'Europe* (Paris 1950), 124; M. van der Bijl, 'Willem III, stadhouder–koning: pro religione et libertate', in W. F. de Gaay Fortman *et al.* (eds.), *Achter den tijd: Opstellen aangeboden aan G. Puchinger* (Haarlem 1986), 155–82.

[4] P. O. Hoynck, *Frankreich und seine Gegner auf dem Nymwegener Friedenskongress* (Bonn 1960), 73–88, 95 ff.; P. Sonnino, 'Louis XIV and the Dutch War', in R. Hatton (ed.), *Louis XIV and Europe* (1976), 155 ff.

[5] For Lt.-Gen. de Montanegue's occupation and *dragonnade* of the Principality, see *Verbalen Van't gepasserde in de Stadt; Ende het Prinsdom van Oranje* (1682); *The History Of The Persecutions Of The Protestants By The French King, In The Principality of Orange, From the Year 1660, to the Year 1687* (1689), 8, 12.

as the establishment of French domination and the eradication of Protestantism in Europe, should have been confirmed.

From the tentacles of French diplomacy not even the island politics of England were safe. In repeated efforts to enhance their master's reputation, successive French ambassadors had indifferently hugged and squeezed both Court and country, but with markedly different results.[6] Despite the often cordial friendship felt for their Catholic cousin of France by the Stuart brothers, Charles II and James II, their Protestant subjects conceived a growing aversion to the dictatorial policies of Louis *le Grand*.[7] For all their contempt for the insidious cult of the 'Sun King', and their hatred of Catholic France, not even the most intransigent of Louis's parliamentary critics could ignore the unpalatable fact that he was rapidly becoming the 'Master of all Christendom'. The combination of uninterrupted French aggrandizement in Europe and unrelenting French diplomacy in London convinced many patriots that he had designs on Protestant England. That was the considered opinion of Sir William Coventry, an informed observer of the international scene. In April 1679 Coventry warned parliament that, 'considering the spirit of the *French* King, all set upon glory nothing will fill his sails with more glory [than] the accession of such a spot of ground as this to the Catholic Religion'.[8] He also understood, as did countless other parliament men, that the robust Protestantism of the English people meant that, for French ambitions to succeed, England's reconciliation to the Church of Rome could only come about through Louis's encouragement of Stuart susceptibility to the old faith: the faith of their ancestors. The alarming waywardness of Charles II's ecclesiastical policy since the Restoration had taught Church of England Protestants that he was not to be trusted.[9] But, for them, worse—far worse—was in store.

The unexpected conversion to Catholicism of Charles's heir, James Duke of York, in 1669—a conversion which was blamed on the malign influence of his deceased mother, Henrietta Maria

[6] M. Lee, *The Cabal* (Urbana, Ill. 1965), 11, 83–9, 93, 95–6, 98–9, 100–4, 107 ff.

[7] J. R. Jones, *The First Whigs* (1961), 150–1, 160, 195; K. H. D. Haley, *The First Earl of Shaftesbury* (Oxford 1968), 406–7, 412–13, 502–3.

[8] A. Grey, *Debates Of The House of Commons, From the Year 1667 to the Year 1694* (10 vols., 1769), vii. 107–8. Cited below as *Debates*.

[9] R. A. Beddard, 'The Restoration Church', in J. R. Jones (ed.), *The Restored Monarchy 1660–1688* (1979), 159–72.

of France—marked a watershed in dynastic and national fortunes: one which Protestants at the time instinctively believed presaged the 'ruine of this poore Nation'.[10] It strengthened the impression, which had been gaining ground for years, that the royal family was itself the source of rising Popish ambition within England. In October 1680 Sir Henry Capel, a Cavalier's son who had turned Whig, declared: 'In the descent of four Kings, still the Parliaments have been troubled with Popery. Laws have been made against it, and all fail. Sometimes Popery is in the Ministers of State, and in another state too, the Clergy; and now, to our misfortune, we find it in the Heir presumptive of the Crown.' In joining in the Whig party's demand for James's exclusion from the throne, as a Papist, Capel not only stressed the need to preserve the monarchy and parliament as the guarantors of English Protestantism, but also urged his fellow MPs to consider 'the safety of all *Christendom*, and the safety of that part especially that is not willing to be under the French Government'.[11] Whig advocates of the Protestant Succession at home sensed a community of interest with France's enemies abroad, particularly the Dutch Republic, which had so long been the butt of Louis's displeasure. In consequence, they steadily focused their aspirations for the future welfare of the monarchy and nation on the Protestant Princess of Orange, as the entail of the Second Exclusion Bill made perfectly plain in November 1680.[12]

As Francophobia and anti-Popery became ever more closely linked with one another in the mind of the nation, they constituted key elements in the 'opposition' which in the 1670s and 1680s was directed against a Court that was increasingly regarded as Frenchified and 'Popishly affected'; first by the Whigs under Charles II, and later by the Tories under James II.[13] The prerogative-minded cleric Samuel Parker, whom James made Bishop of Oxford in 1686, noted the quite extraordinary and baneful hold that these passions had over contemporary Englishmen. 'There were', he wrote, 'two inchanting terms, which at the first pro-

[10] R. A. Beddard, *A Kingdom without a King* (Oxford 1988), 9–10, 27.

[11] Grey, *Debates*, vii. 360.

[12] *HMC, 11th Report, Appendix, pt. ii: House of Lords MSS, 1678–1688* (1887), 196–7.

[13] K. H. D. Haley, '"No Popery" in the Reign of Charles II', in J. S. Bromley and E. H. Kossman (eds.), *Britain and the Netherlands*, v: *Some Political Mythologies* (The Hague 1976), 102–19.

nunciation could, like Circe's intoxicating cups, change men into beasts; namely, *Popery*, and *the French Interest.*' In the House of Commons these had but to be mentioned for 'all serious counsels' to be turned 'into rage and clamour' and men, 'otherwise sober', to be raised 'to a degree of madness'.[14] Popular fear and dread of France and Popery reached its zenith in the years that followed Louis XIV's revocation of the Edict of Nantes in 1685, which let loose a flood of French Protestant refugees into London and the counties of the South-East, as it did into Amsterdam and Holland.[15] The fleeing Huguenots carried with them terrifying tales of Catholic persecution. Such a conspicuous display of Catholic and royal intolerance, which heralded the high tide of the Counter-Reformation in Europe, helped to undermine James's efforts to advance religious toleration at home by exposing his sincerity to intense Protestant questioning—a point that was fully exploited by Orangist propaganda in Holland and in England.[16]

Economic discontent and political anxiety reinforced the fears released by religion. Charles II's controversial support for France in the Dutch crisis of 1672—the year which saw the king's most sustained bid for monarchical independence from the constraints of Cavalier Anglicanism—had awakened influential sections of English public opinion, including the ultra-Protestant merchant community of London, to the importance of denying Louis the

[14] *Bishop Parker's History Of His Own Time*, trans. T. Newlin (1727), 379–80.

[15] [E. Benoît], *Histoire de l'Édit de Nantes* (5 vols., Delft 1693–5), v. 959–60; cf. ibid. iv. 491–3; J. Orcibal, *Louis XIV et les Protestants* (Paris 1951), 107–26; R. L. Poole, *A History of the Huguenots of the Dispersion* (1880), 45–62, 78–9; H. P. H. Nusteling, 'The Netherlands and the Huguenot Émigrés', in H. Bots, G. H. M. Posthumus Meyjes, and F. Wieringa (eds.), *Vlucht naar de vrijheid: De Hugenoten en de Nederlanden* (Amsterdam 1985), 17–34; F. R. J. Knetsch, 'Les Églises réformées des Pays-Bas et la Révocation', in *Tricentenaire de la Révocation de l'Édit de Nantes: La Révocation et l'extérieur du royaume* (Montpellier 1985), 173–92; E. S. de Beer, 'The Revocation of the Edict of Nantes and English Public Opinion', *Proceedings of the Huguenot Society of London*, 18 (1947–52), 292–310; R. D. Gwynn, *Huguenot Heritage* (1985), ch. 8.

[16] For a translation of Jean Claude's influential *Les Plaintes des Protestants*, see *An Account Of The Persecutions And Oppressions Of The Protestants In France* (Printed in the Year 1686). It was ordered to be burnt by Secretary Sunderland. PRO SP44/56, p. 333: 3 May 1686. William granted Claude a pension. Gwynn, *Huguenot Heritage*, 141. See also *An Edict Of The French King, Prohibiting all Publick Exercise of the Pretended Reformed Religion in his Kingdom . . . To which is added . . . A Brief and True Account of the Persecution* (Printed by G.M. Anno Dom. 1686); G. H. Dodge, *The Political Thought of the Huguenots of the Dispersion* (New York 1947), 40.

benefit of England's assistance in European affairs. Burdened by the 'unfavourable balance' of trade between the two nations, the City appreciated the harm which unrestricted French access to international markets and to Whitehall politics could cause.[17] Furthermore, the long-standing English equation of Popery with arbitrary government bolstered the determination to maintain native freedoms by keeping French and Popish influence at bay. Englishmen feared the political no less than the religious tyranny of the Counter-Reformation. 'From Popery came the notion of a standing Army and arbitrary power,' claimed Sir Henry Capel in the Parliament of 1679, 'but lay Popery flat, and there's an end of arbitrary Government and Power. It is a meer chimæra, or notion, without Popery.'[18] The worried merchants of London and anxious parliamentarians of Westminster were not alone in their distrust of a Popish alliance between Stuart and Bourbon. During *het Rampjaar*—the year of disaster in 1672—the young Prince of Orange had been made aware of the cardinal significance of obtaining an active English alliance, as the hinge on which the success or failure of an effective Dutch and European strategy against France turned.[19] Yet, sadly for him, neither his enormously popular marriage to the Princess Mary in 1677,[20] nor the reciprocal terms of the Anglo-Dutch Treaties of 1678,[21] secured

[17] M. Priestley, 'Anglo-French Trade and the "Unfavourable Balance" Controversy, 1660–1685', *Economic History Review*, 2nd ser., 4 (1951–2), 37–53; 'London Merchants and Opposition Politics in Charles II's Reign', *Bulletin of the Institute of Historical Research*, 29 (1956), 205–19.

[18] Grey, *Debates*, vii. 149. For the most famous contemporary treatment of the theme, see Andrew Marvell, *An Account of the Growth of Popery And Arbitrary Government in England* (Amsterdam 1677).

[19] N. Japikse (ed.), *Correspondentie van Willem III en van Hans Willem Bentinck, eersten Graaf van Portland* (5 vols. in 2 pts., Rijks Geschiedkundige Publicatiën, The Hague 1927–37), II. i. 41, 48; [Jean Paul, Comte de Cerdan], *L'Europe esclave si Angleterre ne rompt ses fers* [Rotterdam ? 1677]; K. H. D. Haley, *William of Orange and the English Opposition 1672–1674* (Oxford 1953), 5–6, 10–11, 48–50, 81, 122, 185; M. A. M. Franken, 'The General Tendencies and Structural Aspect of the Foreign Policy and Diplomacy of the Dutch Republic in the Latter Half of the Seventeenth Century', *Acta Historiae Netherlandica*, 3 (1968), 1–43.

[20] *Commons Journal*, ix. 427–8: 28 and 29 Jan. 1678. The marriage occasioned an upsurge of Protestant dynastic sentiment, see R. A. Beddard, 'Wren's Mausoleum for Charles I and the Cult of the Royal Martyr', in J. Newman (ed.), *Design and Practice in British Architecture: Studies in Architectural History Presented to Howard Colvin* (1984), 37–8.

[21] C. L. Grose, 'The Anglo-Dutch Treaty of 1678', *English Historical Review*, 39 (1924), 349–72, 526–51; K. H. D. Haley, 'The Anglo-Dutch Rapprochement of 1677', ibid., 73 (1958), 614–48.

him the whole-hearted backing that he wanted (and thought that he deserved) from his uncle, Charles II. The accession of another uncle, his father-in-law James II, to the British throne in February 1685 made little practical difference to his position and did nothing to retrieve the situation in Orange.[22] Preoccupied with their internal concerns—Charles with defeating Exclusion and James with boosting Catholicism—the later Stuart kings preferred to remain in self-imposed isolation.

True to form, James held aloof in the summer of 1686 from the League of Augsburg: a defensive alliance formed by the Empire, Spain, Sweden, Bavaria, and a cluster of minor German states, who agreed to support each other in the event of a French attack, and (having accepted Louis's annexation of Strasburg and Luxemburg in 1684) to resist the eastward expansion of France.[23] Though James kept clear of European entanglements, the quickening pace of his catholicizing policy at home gave cause for concern in Rome and Vienna, and his obstinate neutrality abroad was widely, though unjustly, interpreted as covert support for France.[24] If Louis had been unable to engage England on his side, he was credited with having obliged her 'to stand neuter, and to be an idle, unconcerned spectator of the horrid tragedy the French king acts upon the theatre of Europe'.[25] Fear of French domination was spreading among the European powers, great and small, Catholic and Protestant, and was no longer confined to the Prince of Orange and his Dutch partisans. Even among the republican *regenten* of Amsterdam, who had so often been opposed to William's foreign policy in the past, there was a decided shift in favour of resisting French encroachment in the

[22] R. E. Clark, *Sir William Trumbull in Paris 1685–1686* (Cambridge 1938), 26, 60, 65, 68, 77–8, 85–6, 91, 97–8, 102, 105, 180–2.

[23] O. Klopp, *Der Fall des Hauses Stuart und die Succession des Hauses Hannover* (7 vols., Vienna 1875–88), iv. 181, 192, 446–7; B. Erdmannsdörffer, *Deutsche Geschichte vom Westfälischen Frieden bis zum Regierungsantritt Friedrichs des Grossen, 1648–1740* (2 vols., Berlin 1892), i. 716–18; M. Immich, *Geschichte des europäischen Staatensystems von 1660 bis 1789* (Munich 1905), 125; André, *Louis XIV et l'Europe*, 226–8; Hazard, *La Crise de la conscience européene*, 75–81; Baxter, *William III*, 213–14.

[24] B. Neveu, 'Jacques II médiateur entre Louis XIV et Innocent XI', *Mélanges d'archéologie et d'histoire*, 79 (1967), 694–764; C. Gérin, *Innocent XI et la révolution anglaise de 1688* (Paris 1876), *passim*; Klopp, *Der Fall des Hauses Stuart*, iii. 255–86, 341–7.

[25] *The Designs Of France Against England and Holland Discovered* (1686), repr. in *Harleian Miscellany* (1808–11 edn.), ix. 164–75.

Spanish Netherlands.[26] While the Princess of Orange remained King James's heir the hope of English support was not altogether lost either to the depleted forces of Continental Protestantism or to the growing anti-French coalition. All depended on Mary succeeding her father and her husband taking charge of English foreign policy. Her absolute determination to defer to Prince William in everything guaranteed that he would rule as well as reign in Britain.[27] Writing in Holland in 1687, the exiled Scot Gilbert Burnet did not doubt that William's 'martial inclination' would 'naturally carry him, when he comes to the crown of England, to bear down the greatness of France'. As the protector of the United Provinces and 'a hearty enemy to popery' he could do no other.[28] The large and increasing presence at The Hague and in other Dutch towns of British exiles—English, Scottish, and Irish Whigs and Protestant malcontents—symbolized an important and, as it eventually transpired, momentous commitment to the Protestant reversionary interest in British politics,[29] over and against that found in Anglican Tory England.[30]

It was at this point that dynastic events inside the Stuart royal family upset English and European expectations. The announcement of Queen Mary Beatrice's pregnancy, in December 1687, alerted William and Mary to the possible loss of their British inheritance, and stimulated a more intense interest on their part in the concealed development of an English paramilitary opposition to James's policies: an opposition which, within three weeks of the birth of the Prince of Wales on 10 June 1688, sent the

[26] G. H. Kurtz, *Willem III en Amsterdam 1683–1685* (Utrecht 1928), 140–80; [Benoît], *Histoire de l'Édit de Nantes*, iv. 492–3; André, *Louis XIV et l'Europe*, 242, cf. ibid. 225–6; G. Symcox, 'Louis XIV and the Outbreak of the Nine Years War', in Hatton, *Louis XIV and Europe*, 202–3; A. C. Carter, *Neutrality or Commitment: The Evolution of Dutch Foreign Policy, 1667–1795* (1975), 24–5.

[27] L. Pinkham, *William III and the Respectable Revolution* (Cambridge, Mass. 1954), 20–1; Baxter, *William III*, 223–4.

[28] H. C. Foxcroft (ed.), *A Supplement to Burnet's History Of My Own Time* (Oxford 1902), 193.

[29] J. Walker, 'The English Exiles in Holland during the Reigns of Charles II and James II', *Transactions of the Royal Historical Society*, 4th ser., 30 (1948), 111–25; D. J. Milne, 'The Results of the Rye House Plot and Their Influence upon the Revolution of 1688', ibid., 5th ser., 1 (1951), 81–108; Oudendijk, *Willem III*, 180, 184–5, 194; R. Ashcraft, *Revolutionary Politics and Locke's Two Treatises of Government* (Princeton 1986), 336 ff.

[30] I hope shortly to publish a paper on the two versions of the Orangist reversionary interest. Meanwhile see Baxter, *William III*, 175, 192, 197–8, 200, 201, 211, 224; Beddard, *Kingdom*, 20–1.

famous invitation asking William to come to its aid. The birth of a Catholic male heir—Prince James Francis Edward—was a disaster for Orangist and Protestant hopes. It cut off the foreseeable return of Protestant Stuarts to the throne.[31] The frustration felt by less scrupulous members of the Church of England (chief of whom was James's mischief-making younger daughter, Anne, who stood to gain from excluding her stepbrother from the succession[32]) was so profoundly disturbing that they openly impugned the child's legitimacy, and continued to maintain the lie in the face of incontrovertible evidence to the contrary.[33] Although William's sponsors made much of the allegedly suspicious circumstances of the Prince of Wales's birth, exaggeratedly claiming in their invitation that 'not one in a thousand' of the King's subjects believed it 'to be the Queen's', they did not invite him to take James's throne.[34] Nor, it must be said, did William go about to depose his uncle and father-in-law on receiving their invitation. Quite the opposite. Knowing that his 'descent' on England would be misrepresented by his enemies, especially France, he took care to assure his friends in Catholic Europe, 'que mon intention n'est nullement d'aller detroner le Roy d'Angletere, n'y extirper les Chatoliques Romains qui sont dans ces Royaumes'.[35] To Protestant friends he similarly disavowed any desire for James's throne.[36]

William's purpose in mounting his expedition to Britain was

[31] PRO PC 2/72, pp. 560, 564; SP 31/4, fos. 1, 2; R. A. Beddard, 'A Relic of Stuart Popery: Prayers for Queen Mary Beatrice, *anno* 1688', *Bodleian Library Record*, 8 (1971), 273; BL: MS Add. 32095, fos. 261–2: Albeville to James II, The Hague, 2 Apr. 1688; Marquise Campana di Cavelli, *Les Derniers Stuarts à Saint Germain en Laye* (2 vols., Paris 1871), ii. 222–3, 228; Mechtild, Countess Bentinck (ed.), *Lettres et mémoires de Marie Reine d'Angleterre* (The Hague 1880), 31 ff.

[32] E. Gregg, *Queen Anne* (1980), 52–8. See below, pp. 88–90.

[33] For English and Scottish doubts, see PRO SP 31/4, fo. 224: 'A Memorial of the Protestants of the Church of England presented to Their Royal Highnesses'; SP 8/2, pt. 2, fos. 109–12. James attempted to allay doubts by holding a public enquiry before an extraordinary meeting of the Council on 22 Oct. 1688, the report of which he published. SP 31/4, fos. 160–78.

[34] PRO SP 8/1, pt. 2, fos. 224–7.

[35] *Lettre de Guillaume III*, dated 'A Helvoetsluys, ce 29 d'Oct. 1688', ed. H. d'Orleans, in *Biographical and Historical Miscellanies* (Philobiblon Soc. 1, 1848), 4–5. For similar assurances to the Emperor Leopold I, see Beddard, *Kingdom*, 12–13.

[36] 'Extract of the States General their Resoluti‹on›, Thursday, 28th October 1688', St John's College, Cambridge: MS K 35, item 9; cf. P. L. Müller, *Wilhelm III von Oranien und Georg Friedrich von Waldeck: Ein Beitrag zur Geschichte des Kampfes um das europäische Gleichgewicht* (2 vols., The Hague 1873–80), ii. 126.

to reinstate the despised Protestant interest in government, to investigate the disputed issue of the succession to the crown, and to enlist the major Protestant monarchy in Europe, with its considerable revenues and enviable fighting power, as an ally in the armed struggle against Louis XIV and French aggression. In obtaining these ends he looked for the support, not merely the acquiescence, of Protestant England in 'a free and legal parliament' of the king's calling, but not of the king's choosing.[37] It was not an unreasonable expectation. After all, his aristocratic sponsors had confidently predicted that 'nineteen parts of twenty of the people throughout the Kingdom' were 'desirous of a change' of policy, and 'would willingly contribute to it'.[38] To begin with their prediction rang true. Success seemed to be his—his, at least, until 11 December 1688, when, all of a sudden, the prospect of a negotiated, peaceful, parliamentary settlement of his quarrel with the king, such as had been envisaged in his Declaration from The Hague, was overtaken by events in and around London, over which neither he, nor James, had any control, and which unexpectedly caused him to change his immediate plans, discard his original intentions, combine with the Whigs, and embark on a violent revolutionary course of action that culminated in James's deposition and flight to France.[39] Thereafter it was only a matter of time before he ascended the throne as William III, the 'great and noble instrument' of England's delivery 'from slavery, both in body and soule', and the staunch upholder of Protestant and anti-French policies.[40] Thus, right from the start, there were two distinct, yet interlocking, dimensions to the Revolution of 1688 which deposed James II and enthroned William and Mary and their Protestant successors: the one internal and British, the other external and European. Both of these dimensions are explored in this collection of Andrew Browning commemorative lectures, which, under the auspices of Balliol College and the Faculty of Modern History, were delivered to the University of Oxford in Michaelmas Term 1988.

[37] For William's First Declaration, The Hague, 30 Sept./10 Oct. 1688, see Beddard, *Kingdom*, 12–13, 18, 21, 22, 25 ff. and pp. 124–8, 145–9 (text).

[38] PRO SP 8/1, pt. 2, fos. 224–7.

[39] Beddard, *Kingdom*, 32–65.

[40] The concluding words of the Christmas Day sermon preached in London by Dr Symon Patrick, Dean of Peterborough, a resolute Williamite, Dr Williams's Library: MS Morrice Q, p. 394. For Patrick's support for William, see R. A. Beddard, 'The Sussex General Election of 1695', *Sussex Archæological Soc.*, 106 (1968), 146–8.

1

The Unexpected Whig Revolution of 1688

ROBERT BEDDARD

I

ON 1 November 1688 William's expeditionary force of 15,000 men, carried in some 200 transports and protected by 49 fighting ships, finally sailed for England.[1] It landed, unopposed, in Tor Bay on 5 November—the day yearly set aside for Protestant thanksgiving for the nation's earlier deliverance from the machinations of Popery in 1605. From the coast of Devon William made his way overland to Exeter, where amid popular acclaim he established his camp on the 9th. More than a week elapsed before the local gentry (mostly Tories) overcame their loyal scruples and rallied to his cause, by which time a number of his partisans (mostly Whigs) from other parts of the kingdom had joined him; significantly, their ranks were soon swollen by deserters from the king's army, which had been penetrated by Williamite agents. The prince's peaceful and increasingly rapturous reception in the West Country boded well for the success of his mission.[2] Yet, it took time for his secret sponsors in the nobility to raise the northern and midland shires in support of his declared aims.[3] As it happened their delays scarcely mattered, for James was similarly slow to take the offensive.

[1] E. B. Powley, *The English Navy in the Revolution of 1688* (Cambridge 1928), 35–6; J. Carswell, *The Descent on England: A Study of the English Revolution of 1688 and its European Background* (1969), 168–70, 172, 176–7; A. van der Kuijl, *De glorieuze overtocht: De expeditie van Willem III naar Engeland in 1688* (Amsterdam 1988).

[2] R. A. Beddard, *A Kingdom without a King* (Oxford 1988), 19–20, 21–3. Cited below as *Kingdom*.

[3] A. C. Wood, 'The Revolution of 1688 in the North of England', *Transactions of the Thoroton Society of Nottinghamshire*, 44 (1940), 72–104; D. H. Hosforth, *Nottingham, Nobles and the North* (Hamden, Conn. 1976), 84–99.

Because of widespread Protestant unrest in London it was not until 19 November that he reached Salisbury, the rendezvous appointed for his assembling forces. His late appearance in the field had an unfortunate consequence. It allowed religious dissatisfaction to demoralize his army. Far more serious than the damage done to the command structure by the desertion of a few officers, which was rapidly repaired,[4] was the common soldiers' crippling conviction that, should the king triumph, 'he intended to destroy the Protestant Religion, and especially the Church of England'. The efforts of the commander-in-chief, Feversham, to reassure the rank and file that his master had 'as much kindness for them as they could desire, and that he would establish the Church of England as much as any Protestant Prince ever could', were of little avail.[5] Their anti-Catholic prejudice, recently heightened by the arrival in England of Catholic Irish regiments, was immovable. Uncertain of the loyalty of his Protestant troops and in poor health James retreated without a fight. It was a humiliation from which he never recovered.

Back at Whitehall on the 27th, the king first conceded a parliament, which he summoned to meet him at Westminster on 15 January, and then opened negotiations with the prince at the unanimous request of the Tory peers in town, who, like the rest of the nation, were anxious to avoid hostilities.[6] William's status as a Stuart prince reinforced the all but universal reluctance to enter upon what would inevitably have proved to be another bout of civil war. James's Commissioners—the Marquess of Halifax, the Earl of Nottingham, and Lord Godolphin—received William's terms for a treaty at Littlecote House, outside Hungerford, on 10 December. All Catholic officers, civil and military, were to be dismissed; the Tower and Tilbury Fort handed over to the City of London; Portsmouth secured against an expected French landing; and, to ensure the freedom of the approaching

[4] J. Childs, *The Army, James II and the Glorious Revolution* (Manchester 1980), 185–90; PRO SP 44/165, pp. 138, 140–3, 145–7, 149–51, 154 ff.; SP 44/166, pp. 11–17; SP 44/97, p. 25.

[5] C. T. Gatty (ed.), 'Mr Francis Gwyn's Journal', *The Fortnightly Review*, 46 (1886), 363.

[6] Beddard, *Kingdom*, 24–5. This corrects the date of the Council meeting in J. R. Jones, *The Revolution of 1688 in England* (1972), 305.

parliamentary session, troop deployments outlined.[7] That William was willing to enter into a treaty with the king, against the strenuous advice of his Whig supporters, and without making a prior issue of the Prince of Wales's legitimacy, which both he and they doubted, showed that at this late stage in his expedition he did not challenge James's right to remain king and was content to refer the controversy over the succession to a parliament of his calling. His response to James's Tory-inspired initiative demonstrated that he still adhered to his First Declaration. He sought a change of policy, not a change of monarch. In this his views differed strikingly from those of the more ambitious Whigs inside and outside his entourage, who wanted him to dethrone the king.[8]

However, events in London, over which neither William, nor James, had any control, were to frustrate princely, no less than royal, inclinations to reach an agreement in the deepening political crisis. James, ten years older than he had been when he had first faced the Whig challenge under Shaftesbury, did not prove to be the man of iron resolution that he had been throughout the Exclusion contest. Confronted with William's unstoppable advance (for diplomatic as well as military means had failed to halt him), and surrounded by violent and encroaching anti-Catholicism in the capital, which William appeared to condone and the Lord Mayor was powerless to resist, he panicked.[9] On 9 December he dispatched the queen and his infant son to France. Only after they had left the country, and plans had been set in motion for his own escape in the small hours of the 11th, did he receive William's terms—too late to alter his decision to withdraw.[10] Even as he read them the boat hired to ferry him across the

[7] All Souls College, Oxford: MS 273, item xx, Littlecote, 9 Dec. 1688. The official correspondence of the Hungerford Embassy has been prepared for publication.

[8] Beddard, *Kingdom*, 25–9.

[9] Ibid., 29–31, 173. The anti-Catholic menace, which panicked James II, owed much to the publication of William's spurious Third Declaration, which appeared in London on 4 Dec. I disagree with the dates assigned by Carswell, *Descent on England*, 201 (8 Dec.) and J. Miller, 'The Militia and the Army in the Reign of James II', *The Historical Journal*, 16 (1973), 676 ('about 7 December').

[10] James did receive William's terms, contrary to what is stated in E. S. de Beer, 'The English Revolution', in J. S. Bromley (ed.), *The Rise of Great Britain and Russia 1688–1725* (New Cambridge Modern History, v; Cambridge 1970), 205. Beddard, *Kingdom*, 31–4, 170; H. Jenkinson, 'What happened to the Great Seal of James II?', *Antiquaries Journal*, 23 (1943), 1–13; E. S. de Beer, 'The Great Seal of James II', ibid., 42 (1962), 81–90.

Thames waited at Westminster Stairs. Having destroyed the parliamentary writs in his possession, he jettisoned the Great Seal as he was rowed over the river to Vauxhall *en route* for the Kentish coast and, he hoped, the safety of France. He believed—correctly as it turned out—that there could be no lawful parliament held without his writs of summons under the Great Seal.[11] His going thus created a hiatus in government, or interregnum, which was to be exploited by his enemies, the Whig Exclusionists, and by the Prince of Orange, whose patience was finally exhausted by this last unexpected bid to remain independent of him and the Protestant, anti-French cause that he embodied.

On hearing that James had left London without appointing a regency, or arranging for the submission of his forces, William decided to take the throne for himself. This he did in order to secure his political objectives and counter the chaos caused by the king's flight. Presuming that James had fled the kingdom, he immediately changed his plans.[12] Instead of going north from Abingdon to Oxford on the 12th, as he had arranged, he struck south and recommenced his march on London, eager 'to settle matters there and to prevent the effusion of blood', which, for want of his presence, he feared 'might happen, considering the heate people are in'.[13] His expedition, as he had originally conceived it, was at an end. Henceforth dynastic ambition replaced the notion of political intervention in his thinking and acting. His aim was now to supplant James as king, take over his abandoned army and navy, restore law and order on the basis of a reinvigorated Protestant Ascendancy, meet parliament on 15 January (for as yet he was ignorant of James's evasive action), and prepare to oppose France, which had already declared war on the United Provinces on 16 November.

But, once again, events in London did not wait on William's convenience, any more than they had on James's earlier. With the king gone there was a real danger that the capital, seething with discontent and in the throes of spectacular anti-Catholic

[11] F. A. J. Mazure, *Histoire de la Révolution de 1688 en Angleterre* (3 vols., Paris 1825), iii. 264; J. S. Clarke (ed.), *The Life of James II . . . Collected out of Memoirs writ of his own hand* (2 vols., 1816), i. 251. Cited below as Clarke, *James II.*

[12] Beddard, *Kingdom*, 34–6.

[13] Bodl. Libr., Oxford: MS Carte 40, fos. 502, 503^{v}: William of Orange to [James, Duke of Ormonde, as Chancellor of the University of Oxford], Abingdon, 12 Dec. 1688, printed in Beddard, *Kingdom*, 174: app. 7.

rioting, might subside into mob rule.[14] Without reference to either Stuart, a provisional government was hastily formed by a group of Anglican Tory peers loyal to the king.[15] Under the direction of James's former brother-in-law, the Earl of Rochester, they assembled at the Guildhall, in the City, on 11 December, and on the following four days in the Council Chamber, at Whitehall, under the chairmanship of 'the Trimmer' Halifax. By their unsparing vigilance the loyalists were remarkably successful in obtaining one of their two objectives: the restoration of public order in the metropolis and suburbs. But this they achieved at the cost of the other: the safeguarding of King James's authority.[16] In order to retain the co-operation of all the peers who had answered their summons to act in the emergency—some of whom were undoubted, though as yet undeclared, Williamites—they were forced to sacrifice their call for the king's return 'with honor and safety'.[17] Not until the 13th, when news came from Kent that James had been arrested and imprisoned at Faversham by a rabble of Protestant seamen, were they able to reassert themselves and persuade the peers to authorize his rescue. The operation, which involved sending a detachment of guards to him, was entrusted to four loyalist peers, and, to the relief of his 'old friends', was entirely successful. On the 16th the king entered the capital in triumph.

Buoyed up by his release, by the applause of the Londoners at his return, and by the congratulations of the Protestant bishops, who rejoiced 'to see the Head of the Church of England come home again', James proceeded to pick up the reins of government. Confident that all was not lost, he attempted to resume negotiations with the prince and to stabilize his position by renewing his alliance with the hierarchy of the Church of England.[18] Having invited William to St James's to confer with him on the 18th concerning the settlement of 'the distracted Nation', he met

[14] Beddard, *Kingdom*, 41–5. W. L. Sachse, 'The Mob and the Revolution of 1688', *Journal of British Studies*, 4 (1964), 23–40.

[15] R. A. Beddard, 'The Loyalist Opposition in the Interregnum: A Letter of Dr Francis Turner, Bishop of Ely, on the Revolution of 1688', *Bulletin of the Institute of Historical Research*, 40 (1967), 101–9.

[16] Beddard, *Kingdom*, 37–41, 45–8.

[17] R. A. Beddard, 'The Guildhall Declaration of 11 December 1688 and the Counter-Revolution of the Loyalists', *Historical Journal*, 11 (1968), 403–20.

[18] Beddard, *Kingdom*, 48–51, 54–5.

the bishops in a preparatory audience on the 17th. As a result of that meeting he arrived at an amicable understanding with them, which he expected would pave the way towards an Anglican Tory settlement. He would abide by the laws of the land, respect the privileges of the Established Church, confirm the Protestant monopoly of office, and commit 'all the power of war and peace', as well as ecclesiastical and political patronage, 'to the Prince for his lifetime'. Furthermore, he agreed to 'consent to bills in parliament', such as were judged necessary 'for the security of religion and civil rights'.[19] It seemed to the Church of England bishops that these were a sufficient basis on which to reconcile both king and prince and king and nation.

But William, who had set up court at Windsor, was in no mood to back down. Amid reports that James had appointed him 'captain general of all his forces by sea and land', he ignored his repeated invitations to reopen negotiations. Ever since the king's flight he had taken steps to assert his personal authority over James's subjects, his officials, and his officers. He simply was not willing to contemplate his father-in-law's continuance on the throne. Backed by a small revolutionary clique of Williamite peers, who argued that James's withdrawal from the capital on 11 December constituted 'a cession of his right to the crowne', he decided on the 17th to risk military intervention, believing that a show of force would clear his path to the throne. He sent an abrupt order to Whitehall, supported by troops, telling James to leave London. Delivered in the middle of the night, without ceremony, and after the Dutch soldiers had replaced the royal sentries who guarded the palace, it gave the king no alternative but to comply. Having prevailed on William to be permitted to go towards the coast, not inland, he left London for Rochester on the 18th under armed Dutch guard—much to the mortification of the loyalists, whose endeavours to reach a settlement, based on the known laws of the land and within the bounds of Anglican political propriety, were savagely curtailed.[20] James's expulsion from Whitehall allowed him to claim, with justice, that he had left the capital against his will and under duress. After a brief stay at Rochester, long enough to convince himself that further

[19] PRO SP 8/2, pt. 2, fo. 91: Dr William Lloyd, Bishop of St Asaph, to Hans Willem Bentinck, 17 Dec. 1688; Clarke, *James II*, ii. 261; Dr Williams's Library: MS Morrice Q, pp. 378, 380, 381, 382.

[20] Beddard, *Kingdom*, 56–60, 63–4.

delay was not only futile, but dangerous, he sailed for France on the 23rd. He went openly protesting that he did so to ensure his physical safety, and 'to be within Call whensoever the Nations Eyes shall be opened'. He also offered what William could not give England—'a Legal Parliament' for the composing of outstanding differences.[21]

William dared not have acted so outrageously against King James had he not prepared the ground before him. The military resources for expelling James were, of course, at his command, and, given Feversham's disbandment of the king's army, the plan was relatively easy to carry out, yet he had to be sure that the City of London, always sensitive to encroachments on its independence and still largely in Tory hands, would countenance armed intervention on his part. He had already been at pains to cultivate the metropolis which, as 'the bulwark of the Protestant Religion',[22] had been sorely tried by the Court-sponsored drive to win converts to the Church of Rome and by James's illegal employment of Papists and Dissenters.[23] Before coming into England he had published in his Declaration a demand for the restoration of 'the charter of the antient and famous City of London', the confiscation of which by Charles II, in 1683, had heralded the eclipse of Whig power in the Corporation and consequently of the Whig party that depended on it.[24] Since his arrival he had also signified from Littlecote, on 10 December, his readiness to admit the City as a partner in his proposed resettlement of the country by calling on James to surrender the Tower and Tilbury Fort into its possession: the former for its internal 'security and safety', the latter for its external protection and the easing of trade.[25] William's well-publicized concern to do right

[21] *His Majesties Reasons For Withdrawing Himself from Rochester. Writ with His own Hand, and Ordered by Him to be Published.* Dated 22 Dec. 1688; *Memoirs of Thomas, Earl of Ailesbury, written by himself* (2 vols., Roxburghe Club 1890), ii. 224–6. Cited below as *Ailesbury Memoirs.*

[22] Grey, *Debates*, viii. 10. Sir Thomas Player had prophesied that 'the first assault of the Papists will be London'.

[23] J. Miller, *Popery and Politics in England 1660–1688* (Cambridge 1973), 245–7; Beddard, *Kingdom*, 14–16.

[24] Beddard, *Kingdom*, 148; J. Levin, *The Charter Controversy in the City of London, 1660–1688, and its Consequences* (1969), 50 ff.; D. Ogg, *England in the Reign of Charles II* (2 vols., Oxford 1934), ii. 636–9.

[25] All Souls College, Oxford: MS 273, item xx, Littlecote, 9 Dec. 1688; 'Journaal van Constantijn Huygens, den zoon, van 21 October 1688 tot 2 September 1696',

by the City of London naturally evoked a grateful response from its citizens, Whig and Tory. In contrast to the peers of the provisional government, whose conduct towards the prince was at best politically reticent, the City fathers and even more the Lieutenancy of London had, on 11 December, warmly invited him to come to them 'with what convenient speed' he could 'for the perfecting', as they informed him, of 'the greate worke which Your Highnesse has soe happily begun':[26] an innocent-sounding phrase which was capable of being variously understood, but one which an increasingly confident band of City Whigs, led by Sir George Treby and Sir Robert Clayton, wished to construe in the revolutionary sense of a change of monarch. In their estimate, dynastic change alone could ensure a permanent change of policy in Church and State of the radically Protestant, parliamentary, anti-French kind that they desired.

II

Modern historians, keen to distance themselves from the seemingly archaic prejudices of Whig historiography, are nowadays in grave danger of travelling too far in the opposite direction. They overlook the real revolutionaries, the Whigs, and the vital part which they played in overthrowing James II and making possible William's peaceful seizure of the crown. Instead, they prefer to emphasize Tory involvement in the invitation to William, the extent of Tory passivity in the face of his invasion, and the participation of leading Tories in the raising of rebellion in the provinces. More often than not attention is drawn to the undeniably massive survival of Toryism and its legitimist principles beyond the debilitating events of 1688.[27] Battered but not destroyed, and hastily refashioned to fit the awkward circumstances

in *Werken Uitgegeven door het Historische Genootschaap*, new ser., 23 (Utrecht 1876), 39–40. Cited below as 'Journaal'.

[26] For the proceedings of the Lord Mayor and Court of Aldermen and of the Common Council of the City, together with the addresses made by the City and the Lieutenancy of London, see Beddard, *Kingdom*, 170–3: apps. 2–5.

[27] G. M. Trevelyan, *The English Revolution 1688–1689* (Oxford rep. 1981), 73–4, 77, 78–9, 81; J. P. Kenyon, *The Nobility in the Revolution of 1688* (Hull 1963), 14–18; Jones, *Revolution in England*, 295–7, 321; L. Pinkham, *William III and the Respectable Revolution* (Cambridge, Mass. 1954), 42–3, 73, 236–7. Cited below as *Respectable Revolution*.

of revolution by stressing the overriding operation of Providence in human affairs, much of the Church of England's traditional teaching on the divine right of kings was salvaged, and used to defend the Protestant 'deliverance' from Popery, thus enabling Anglican Tory conviction, as well as individual Anglican Tory politicians, to surmount the dynastic crisis.[28] This is all well and good, just as long as the role of the Tories—whether identified as the 'reluctant revolutionaries' of Drs Riley and Speck, or as the even more questionably conceived 'proto-Jacobites' of Dr Miller[29] —is not allowed to obscure the extraordinary resurgence of the Whigs that lay at the heart of the revolutionary process, and which, perhaps more than any other single development, gave rise to the bitter animosities and partisan divisions that characterized English domestic politics in the post-revolutionary period. It is the rapid revival of the Whigs, as a major political force in London and the nation at large, that holds the key to William's astonishingly successful take-over of James's kingship, and it is this utterly unexpected Whig revival, and its role in the traditionally acclaimed 'Glorious Revolution', which I now wish to explore. My exploration inevitably highlights the place of the national capital in the events of 1688–9, which has for too long been neglected or denied.

As the defeated advocates of Catholic Exclusion and Protestant unity, who had endured almost a decade of political ostracism and proscription from office, the Whigs were better placed and better qualified than their Tory rivals to work with William in dethroning the king. They had never wanted James to be king in the first place, and saw in his reign a complete justification for their having opposed his succession to the throne. They were neither compromised by association with the discredited Stuart régime, nor inhibited by scruples over resisting the Lord's Anointed.[30] Indeed, long smouldering resentment at previous

[28] G. M. Straka, *Anglican Reaction to the Revolution of 1688* (Madison, Wisc. 1962); 'The Final Phase of Divine Right Theory in England 1688–1702', *English Historical Review*, 77 (1962), 638–58; J. P. Kenyon, *Revolution Principles* (Cambridge 1977), 20–34, 65–6.

[29] P. W. J. Riley, *King William and the Scottish Politicians* (Edinburgh 1979), 6; W. A. Speck, *Reluctant Revolutionaries* (Oxford 1988), ch. 8; J. Miller, 'Proto-Jacobitism? The Tories and the Revolution of 1688–9', in E. Cruickshanks and J. Black (eds.), *The Jacobite Challenge* (Edinburgh 1988), 7–19.

[30] For the earlier history of the Whigs, see J. R. Jones, *The First Whigs* (1961); K. H. D. Haley, *The First Earl of Shaftesbury* (Oxford 1968), 498 ff.; B. Behrens, 'The

royal disfavour (no way assuaged by James's recent recruitment of a few inconsiderable Whig collaborators[31]) encouraged them to press matters to the extreme of dynastic revolution well before the king's flight, just as anger at their dismissal from office and subsequent political neglect spurred some Tories, such as Admiral Herbert, Bishop Compton of London, Viscount Newport, and Lord Culpepper, all of whom were leading Tory revolutionaries, to forsake James for William when the opportunity arose to transfer their allegiance.[32] As in the early 1680s the Court-favoured High-Church Tories had been able to capture the Catholic reversionary interest centred on James by exploiting the rise of anti-Dissent, so in the later 1680s the disgraced Low-Church Whigs took advantage of growing anti-Popery to colonize the Protestant reversionary interest focused on William and Mary. Many of them had willingly accepted exile, and chose to live in the United Provinces, or took service with a friendly Protestant power. Having afforded an impressive number of Whig fugitives countenance and protection in Holland, where he listened surreptitiously but attentively to their grievances against James and his Tory ministers, Protestant and Catholic, William had no qualms in employing them in his intelligence or propaganda service, in his household and army, and, once he had landed in England, in his administration. He welcomed others who came in to him on his march on London—for instance, Richard Viscount Colchester, Edward Russell, Thomas Wharton, William Jephson, and Sir Henry Capel; and he was soon in touch with his Whig supporters in the capital, who, even as he advanced towards them, were busily scheming to attach the City to his interest.[33]

Whig Theory of the Constitution in the Reign of Charles II', *Cambridge Historical Journal*, 7 (1941), 42–71; O. W. Furley, 'The Whig Exclusionists: Pamphlet Literature in the Exclusion Campaign, 1679–81', ibid., 13 (1957), 19–36. For the radicals, see R. Ashcraft, *Revolutionary Politics and Locke's Two Treatises of Government* (Princeton 1986), 143 ff.

[31] J. R. Jones, 'James II's Whig Collaborators', *Historical Journal*, 3 (1960), 65–73.

[32] For Herbert, see Carswell, *Descent on England*, 88, 93, 130, 150, 155, 157–9, 165–84; for Compton, E. Carpenter, *The Protestant Bishop* (1956), pp. 78 ff. and D. H. Hosford, 'Bishop Compton and the Revolution of 1688', *Journal of Ecclesiastical History*, 23 (1972), 209–18; for Newport and Culpepper, R. A. Beddard, '"The Violent Party": The Guildhall Revolutionaries and the Growth of Opposition to James II', *Guildhall Miscellany*, 3 (1970), 121, 122–3, 124–5, 133–6.

[33] Beddard, *Kingdom*, 20–2, 51–2.

Shortly after 2 December William heard from the veteran MP Sir Robert Howard, acting as spokesman for the London Whigs and their parliamentary allies. He wrote on purpose to add weight to the gathering efforts of those Whig recruits and *émigrés* already ensconced inside the prince's camp, men such as Sir Henry Capel, Sir John Hotham, and William Harbord, who were striving to widen the breach between nephew and uncle in the certain knowledge that they and their party could only gain from making the quarrel desperate.[34] Like them, he warned William against 'the delays of a treaty and the mistaken notion of an accomodation', insisting 'that nothinge of that would be endured, for their was noe roome left for trust, and everythinge must be built upon new foundations'. To negotiate with the king would, he maintained, 'cast a dampe on the spirits of people', who were sufficiently 'far from havinge any thoughts of setlinge things by an accomodation', that their sole 'hopes of remedy' lay in 'the totall change of persons' on the throne. In a revealing remark that anticipated by two months the celebrated revolutionary resolution of the Convention of 1689, which helped to debar both James II and his son from the crown, Howard stated that it was 'the greatest folly to graft anythinge upon the old stocke', that is King James and Prince James Francis Edward, having been 'taught by too sad experience that the difference of religion makes it irreconcilable to trust though but the name of power' to a Catholic king. A deeply committed contractualist Whig, who valued Protestantism not least as a political safeguard of civil liberty, he took a decidedly confessional view of the trust that was expected between a monarch and his people. It was a view which most Londoners had held during the Exclusion controversy, and still held, and one which was implicit in the political assertiveness of Restoration churchmanship with its addiction to the rule of law. The City was, Howard assured William, 'very well inclin'd, and resolv'd, upon your approach, to appeare in your assistance', as was convincingly demonstrated by the promptitude with which it acted nine days later on 11 December.[35] So quick were the City magistrates to invite the Prince of Orange to repair to them that,

[34] *The Correspondence of Henry Hyde, Earl of Clarendon*, ed. S. W. Singer (2 vols., 1828), ii. 220–3. Cited below as *Clar. Corr.*

[35] PRO SP 8/2, pt. 2, fos. 95–6: [Sir Robert Howard] to William of Orange [2 Dec. 1688].

after presenting their addresses to him at Henley on the 13th, Count Nassau told them that the 'greatest fears' of William's commanders had been 'lest the City should have been too forward in declaring for the Prince, before their Army could have come to their assistance'.[36] The hitherto unknown measures which William and his London adherents took on the 16th to stop the City from 'recoiling' by adopting a Tory proposal to welcome James's return to Whitehall, and thereby formally recognize his resumption of government, have been traced in detail elsewhere. Suffice it to say that, in concert, they killed dead the king's attempt to re-establish his authority in the capital, and left the way open for William to remove him by force.[37]

By 18 December—the day on which James was evicted from Whitehall and William entered the capital—it was clear to one, out-of-town, Tory peer that 'the King will be deposed and the Prince's favourites', meaning the Whigs and renegade Tories who had joined them in the South, 'will push him on to a crown'.[38] By then there was little that the Tories could do to prevent it, short of taking to arms, which all along they had been reluctant to do and which now they would never do. No wonder that the professed Whig and ardent Williamite Sir George Treby observed with obvious satisfaction on the 20th, when, as Recorder of the City of London, he congratulated the prince on his arrival in town:

GREAT SIR,
When we look back to the last Month, and contemplate the Swiftness and Fullness of our present Deliverance, Astonish'd, we think it miraculous. Your Highness, led by the hand of Heaven, and called by the Voice of the People, has preserved our dearest Interests. The Protestant Religion; which is primitive Christianity Restor'd. Our Laws; which are our ancient Title to our Lives, Liberties, and Estates; and without which this World were a Wilderness.

[36] *London Courant*, no. 2 (12–15 Dec. 1688).

[37] The key figures were the Whigs, Sir George Treby and Sir Robert Clayton. Treby had resumed the Recordership on 15 Dec., 'which till then he refused to do, tho' he had had multiplyed sollicitations from the City, on purpose to serve the Church, the state, and the City in this great juncture' by aiding William's takeover. Dr Williams's Library, MS Morrice Q, pp. 364, 365, 388. Beddard, *Kingdom*, 52–4 and 179: app. 16.

[38] *HMC, 14th Report, Appendix, pt. ix: Earl of Lindsey* (1895), 452.

But, what Retribution can We make to your Highness? Our Thoughts are full charged with Gratitude. Your Highness has a lasting Monument in the Hearts, in the Prayers, in the Praises of all Good Men amongst us. And late Posterity will celebrate your ever-glorious Name, till Time shall be no more.[39]

Before the week was out Whig gratitude had found a more tangible form of expression than that afforded by panegyric: it had won public recognition for his status as the uncrowned ruler of England.

Inadequate attention has been given to the solid achievement of William's partisans in the meetings of peers and commoners which he summoned to advise him on how best to end the crisis in government in late December 1688. Although virtually the whole of the country had submitted to him, he was acutely aware of the awkwardness and incompleteness of his position. The falling away of Tory support following his removal of the king on the 18th, and the abiding need to guard against offending his allies in Catholic Europe, ruled out any further show of force as a means of encompassing what he and his backers regarded as a vacant throne.[40] Having rejected out of hand the demand, made by some of his most enthusiastic supporters in the army and in the legal profession in London, that he should 'declare himself King', and call a parliament in his own name, William decided to rely on renewed consultation.[41] He turned first to the peers in London, who now included many of his adherents. The earlier sessions of the Assembly of Peers, held on 21 and 22 December, were a deep disappointment to him. Instead of 'resolving', as he had hoped, 'the hard questions about the King, a parliament,

[39] *The Speech of Sir George Treby, Kt. Recorder of the Honourable City of London, To His Highness The Prince of Orange. December the 20th. 1688* (1688). Treby led the delegation because the Tory Lord Mayor was 'disabled by Sickness'. *Clar. Corr.* ii. 232. *London Gazette*, no. 2411 (17–20 Dec.); *English Currant*, no. 4 (19–21 Dec.); *Universal Intelligence*, no. 5 (22–6 Dec.); G. Burnet, *A History of His Own Time* (6 vols., Oxford 1833), iii. 341–2. Cited below as Burnet.

[40] O. Klopp, *Der Fall des Hauses Stuart und die Succession des Hauses Hannover* (7 vols., Vienna 1875–88), iv. 309 ff.; F. L. Müller, *Wilhelm III von Oranien und Georg Friedrich von Waldeck: Ein Beitrag zur Geschichte des Kampfes um das europäische Gleichgewicht* (2 vols., The Hague 1873–80), ii. 119. Cited below as Müller, *Wilhelm III und Waldeck*; Huygens, 'Journaal', 68; Beddard, *Kingdom*, 62–3.

[41] *Clar. Corr.* ii. 225: 15 Dec. Dr Williams's Library: MS Morrice Q, pp. 378 ff. Müller, *Wilhelm III und Waldeck*, ii. 126.

and the army',[42] all of which had to be settled before he could give his mind to prosecuting the war against Louis XIV, they revealed alarming disagreement over what to do next: disagreement which barely disguised the acknowledged, but as yet unaddressed, issue of James's kingship. Such was the baffling consequence of dissension that the Whig hothead Lord Delamer pointedly complained of the 'great alterations in men's opinions within these few days'.[43] The contrast between the unanimity of the welcome accorded to William's expedition and the sharply divided response evoked by William's driving the king from Whitehall was frighteningly apparent to the Whig revolutionaries.[44] Delamer rightly saw in the revulsion of Tory feeling a threat to himself and those like him who had drawn their swords against James. Though most of them had not been called on to fight for the prince, he deemed it far 'too late to mince matters', holding 'that, if the King was King, he and his were rebells', and their lives and estates liable to the pains and penalties of the law of treason.[45] Confronted with what looked like Tory backtracking, which endangered the dynastic revolution, the Williamites redoubled their efforts to escape from the lengthening shadow cast across their former achievements by the fallen monarch. In this they were greatly aided by James's decision to leave England.

Only after receiving the news of the king's flight to France on the 23rd—a move which the beleaguered loyalists had strongly advised against[46]—did the Assembly of Peers come to terms with the revolutionary situation created by William's intervention on the 18th. While the loyalists did everything they could to fend off the Williamite challenge, they failed to carry the meeting of the 24th with them. The 'not-contents' defeated a vigorous attempt, led by the Earls of Berkeley, Clarendon, Lindsey, Nottingham, Abingdon, and Rochester, to send for James's parting letter, giving his reasons for going out of the kingdom—the surest sign, to date, that a majority of the seventy-three peers

[42] BL: MS Add. 36707, fo. 52: 22 Dec.

[43] Beddard, *Kingdom*, 154.

[44] Ibid., 62–3, 155; Dr Williams's Library: MS Morrice Q, p. 385. Burnet, iii. 358; cf. p. 350.

[45] BL: MS Add. 36707, fo. 54: 27 Dec. Delamer was consistently most 'violent' for William's succession. *Clar. Corr.*, ii. 218–19, 229, 253, 257. Bodl. Libr., Oxford: MS Ballard 45, fo. 22; Beddard, *Kingdom*, 23, 27, 56–9, 81, 122, 124, 150 ff.

[46] Beddard, *Kingdom*, 63; Dr Williams's Library: MS Morrice Q, p. 391; Burnet, iii. 343.

present at the meeting wished to distance themselves from the hapless king.[47] After 'a great silence', indicative of the loyalists' ultimate reluctance to push their opposition to extremes, the revolutionaries seized the initiative. Led by the Earls of Devonshire, Stamford, and Shrewsbury, Viscounts Mordaunt and Lumley, Bishop Compton, and Lords Delamer, Montagu, Wharton, Cornwallis, Paget, and North, they argued that, whether or not their lordships relished the thought, they were inescapably caught in an interregnum for which historical and legal precedent did not exist. Their meeting as they did, without the king's licence, was proof enough that there was no vestige of legal government remaining in England. Emboldened by the refusal to read James's letter and confident of Halifax's support from the chair, they made no pretence at hiding their conviction, first formulated under the Marquess's aegis at Windsor on the 17th, that 'the King's withdrawing himself from the government' signified 'a demise in law'.[48] Careful as they still were, on their part, to put their revolutionary sentiments to the meeting in the form of a question, it is noteworthy, on the other, that not a single loyalist responded to their needling repetition of the point. The reason for such silence is not hard to discern. Whereas before the 23rd the king's lingering presence at Rochester had prevented the Williamites from speaking out, for fear of incurring charges of treason, after the 23rd it was the prince's dominating presence at nearby St James's Palace that inhibited the loyalists from saying exactly what they felt, for fear of forfeiting all possibility of favour in his eyes.

Though Lord Montagu's blatantly Whig proposal to pursue the methods laid down in the Bill of Exclusion was not taken up,[49] no voice was raised against Bishop Compton's observation that there was 'an absolute necessity of a government': a remark

[47] Mulgrave thought it 'the first proof of the Lords intention of excluding their King, tho' many divisions arose among them afterwards about the best way of doing it'. *The Works of John Sheffield, Earl of Mulgrave* (4th edn., 2 vols., 1753), ii. 82. Cited below as Mulgrave.

[48] BL: Althorp MSS, Halifax Papers, item f: Halifax's autograph notes on the meeting of peers at Windsor, 17 Dec. (endorsed: 'Concerning the message to the King'); BL: MS Add. 29594, fo. 139: Nottingham to Viscount Hatton, 16 Dec., reporting 'that the discourse at Windsor is that the King's going away is a cession of his right to the crowne'.

[49] Montagu was a leading revolutionary. See Beddard, 'The Violent Party', 121, 125–6, 133–5.

intended to daunt the conscience-stricken loyalists, who, having been the mainstay of the provisional government, were supremely aware that the London populace had greater cause than ever to dread armed French aggression with the king's flight abroad. The recent and massive eruption of mob violence on the streets of the capital had profoundly shaken the peerage, to the point that the advocates of dynastic change were not above playing on the fear of anarchy in order to loosen still further the ties of loyalty and isolate the leaders of counter-revolution. Anxiety for the peace of the nation and the difficulty of choosing between competing dynasts weighed heavily on the minds of the assembled peers. Most sat still and said nothing. They were reluctant to take an irrecoverable step. The stalemate which threatened to paralyse the meeting was only broken by outside pressure from William. With the Earl of Devonshire's shock disclosure that the prince had lost patience with them, and that he had summoned a rival Assembly of Commoners—mostly Exclusionist MPs—to advise him, since they had not, the Peers bowed to William's determination to call a halt to the period of governmental uncertainty.[50] The Earl's well-timed revelation had the desired effect. It propelled the Peers into taking decisive action. Following a firm lead from Halifax in the chair, and encouraged by a rumour 'that the City apprentices were coming down to Westminster in a violent rage against all who voted against the Prince of Orange's interest',[51] they resolved without more ado to make two addresses to the prince: one requesting him to summon a Convention of lords and commons to be held at Westminster on 22 January 1689; and another desiring him to undertake the government of the kingdom until the Convention met. The resolutions passed without a division.[52] By the end of a fatiguing and nerve-racking session, which occupied most of Christmas Eve, the revolutionaries had got the better of their adversaries, and had done so without provoking a loyalist walk-out—an achievement of the utmost significance for the establishment of the Revolution.[53]

[50] Beddard, *Kingdom*, 160.

[51] Mulgrave, ii. 85.

[52] The proposal to summon a Convention 'passed not so unanimously'. Burnet, iii. 341.

[53] For the Peers' debate and the text of their two addresses, see Beddard, *Kingdom*, 161–2, 165–7. Bodl. Libr., Oxford: MS Don. c. 39, fo. 79^{v}: 25 Dec.; MS Rawlinson D 836, fos. 103–4; BL: MS Egerton 2717, fo. 418: 27 Dec.

It has been said of William that 'between the Declarations he published at the beginning of the expedition, and his message to the Convention . . . on 22 January', he 'did not make a single personal public declaration of policy' with respect to the future government of England.[54] It is a claim which cannot be admitted. Though the diarist Evelyn characterized the prince's conduct in the interregnum as 'reserved', and William himself claimed to have remained 'passive', stating that it was his supporters who would make him king, not any ambition of his own,[55] it is evident that on a number of occasions he went out of his way to publicize his wish to be king. Once more, historians have insufficiently pondered his purpose in calling an Assembly of Commoners, which was convoked specifically to provide a countervalent, if not an antidote, to the divided Assembly of Peers. Having previously resisted Whig demands to proclaim himself king at the head of his army, he subsequently found, to his chagrin, that the Peers were slow to recognize his changed status in the wake of James's dismissal. Summoned on 20 December to 'meete about an Expedient to call a parliament',[56] the Peers had declined to acknowledge that they sat at his summons, lest it harm their 'birthright', as peers of the realm, to act in the absence of the king; they had spent the 21st and 22nd avoiding the business which he had recommended to them; and, having reached the weekend with no solution in view, they had put off meeting again until the 24th.[57] William despaired of obtaining a settlement by their means. He turned for advice to his confidants —most probably to such parliamentary figures as Halifax, Powle, Howard, Capel, and Treby, and to those Whigs 'that ⟨had⟩ come over with him', who now thronged the 'greate Court' which daily attended him at St James's.[58] On their advice he decided to call together an Assembly of Commoners: men whose political record and recent actions guaranteed that their united counsel would be favourable to himself and hostile to James's interest. On Sunday the 23rd, the day on which the Peers had refused to

[54] Carswell, *Descent on England*, 221.

[55] *The Diary of John Evelyn*, ed. E. S. de Beer (6 vols., Oxford 1955), iv. 612. Cited below as Evelyn; Müller, *Wilhelm III und Waldeck*, ii. 126; Mazure, *Histoire de la Révolution*, iii. 301.

[56] Evelyn, iv. 611.

[57] Beddard, *Kingdom*, 124–8, 145–57.

[58] Dr Williams's Library: MS Morrice Q, pp. 366, 367, 382; *English Currant*, no. 4 (19–21 Dec.); *Universal Intelligence*, no. 4 (18–22 Dec.); *Clar. Corr.* ii. 231–2.

sit to transact business, and the very day on which James left Rochester for France, he summoned a meeting of the surviving MPs of Charles II's reign, with the Lord Mayor and Court of Aldermen of the City of London, and fifty representatives of the Common Council of London. This he did by circulating printed letters of summons, which were hastily run off the press by the London stationer–bookseller Awnsham Churchill.[59]

Whatever precedents could be cited in confirmation of the peers' inherent right to assemble and act as *consiliarii nati* in a national emergency (and plenty of them were produced),[60] the assembling of a motley crew of ex-parliamentarians and London citizens had no standing in law. The composition of this extraordinary body had, and could have, only one rationale, which was that it should do William's work for him. It was called to underpin the dynastic revolution—a revolution which had already taken place, but which needed to be consolidated—by arranging the smooth transfer of authority from the powerless king to the powerful prince, and, if it were possible, in such a way as would cloak the unseemly events of James's deposition. The constituent categories from which the Assembly of Commoners was recruited ensured that, when it met, it would contain a preponderance of old Exclusionists, who had opposed James's becoming king, and new Williamites, who were opposed to James's remaining king. By late December the two groups were almost indistinguishable. Thus, by limiting his choice of parliament men to 'such Persons as have served as Knights, Citizens or Burgesses in any of the Parliaments, that were held during the Reign of the late King CHARLES the Second',[61] and ignoring those who in 1685 had sat in James's one and only Parliament, William maximized the appearance of the members of the old Whig party at the same time as he minimized the response of the Tories. The general election of 1679, following Charles II's dissolution of the eighteen-

[59] Bodl. Libr., Oxford: MS Rawlinson D 691, pp. 36–7; Dr Williams's Library: MS Morrice Q, p. 393; Müller, *Wilhelm III und Waldeck*, ii. 125; N. Luttrell, *A Brief Historical Relation of State Affairs* (6 vols., Oxford 1857), i. 491. Cited below as Luttrell.

[60] Beddard, *Kingdom*, 36, 66; Bodl. Libr., Oxford: MS Rawlinson D 1064, fo. 12; MS Rawlinson D 836, fo. 77; MS Don. c. 39, fo. 82; Dr Williams's Library: MS Morrice Q, p. 360; *Universal Intelligence*, no. 5 (22–6 Dec.).

[61] '"Whereas the Necessity of Affairs does require speedy Advice . . ." (Printed for Awnsham Churchill, at the Black Swan in Ave-Mary-Lane MDCLXXXVIII.)'. Bodl. Libr., Oxford: Ashmole H 23/3, item ccccciii b.

year-old Cavalier Parliament, had witnessed the retirement of many superannuated MPs and the arrival at Westminster of many newcomers, mostly future Whigs,[62] who in ever-increasing numbers had gone on to dominate the last three parliaments of Charles's reign. This simple fact meant that William could be certain of an automatic Whig majority at St James's on 26 December, as indeed proved to be the case.

Nor did so large a presence of Londoners detract from the Williamite character of the Assembly of Commoners. The civic authorities in London were, as we have seen, well disposed to the prince, whom they had urged forward and whom they had hailed as their deliverer. Their inclusion in the Assembly was consonant with William's esteem of their political worth and a mark of his gratitude for their timely help. It was also a deliberate move to bind them permanently to his interest by associating them more closely with the rank and file of his Whig supporters. In the United Provinces, after all, he was used to cultivating the burghers of towns, especially the patricians of Amsterdam, so it was natural that he should have solicited the co-operation of the rich and influential citizens of London in his scheme to establish his authority in England.[63] The make-up of the London contingent is revealing. Acting on inside information which must have come from such staunch Williamites as Treby and Clayton, William carefully offset the predominantly Tory Lord Mayor and Aldermen with fifty representatives chosen from the Common Council men, among whom his support was greater. On entering into residence at St James's he had made no secret of his sympathy for the reviving Whig cause in London. Besides publicly welcoming individual Whigs at Court, the warmth of whose reception stood in marked contrast to the frigidity with which certain far grander Tories were received,[64] he strongly backed their efforts to stage a political come-back in the capital. On 20 December, the eve of the elections to the Common Council, which by tradition

[62] R. A. Beddard, 'The Retreat on Toryism: Lionel Ducket, Member for Calne, and the Politics of Conservatism', *Wiltshire Archæological Magazine*, 72–3 (1980), 79–80, 86; B. D. Henning, *The House of Commons 1660–1690* (3 vols., 1983), i. 27. Cited below as Henning.

[63] G. H. Kurtz, *Willem III en Amsterdam 1683–1685* (Utrecht 1928), *passim*. See below, pp. 221 ff.

[64] For the treatment of the Duke of Beaufort, see *Clar. Corr.* ii. 227; *Memoirs of Sir John Reresby*, ed. A. Browning (Glasgow 1936), 541.

were held each year on St Thomas's Day, he sent word to the Tory Lord Mayor, Sir John Chapman, and the Aldermen of the City, not to administer the customary Oaths of Allegiance and Supremacy, nor to insist on the Anglican sacramental test, required by law, 'but order'd them to act without it'. King James, who was still at Rochester, was immediately informed of William's action. He correctly apprehended in 'this so early a dispensing with the Laws & the peoples allegience . . . a manifest declaration that nothing less than the Regal Power would content him', and made up his mind to be gone before worse overtook him.[65]

It furnishes an instructive commentary on the prince's by now undisguised dynastic ambition that he first chose to exercise his influence in the City of London on behalf of the king's known enemies: the ultra-Protestant Whigs and their electoral allies, the Protestant Dissenters from the Church of England, who together had formed the backbone of the Exclusionist movement against Catholic James in the late 1670s and early 1680s.[66] The Anglican Tory Earl of Danby—William's main sponsor and chief collaborator in the North of England, who, for all his engaging in rebellion, had 'never thought that things would have gone so far as to settle the Crown on the Prince of Orange'[67]—found a very different political world waiting for him from that which he had expected, when at length he reached London on 26 December. It was not just the clergy, but High-Church Tory politicians generally, who were 'startled' to discover that 'at this first comming the Prince seem'd to countenance Presbutery more then thos of the Church of England',[68] whose support had so greatly contributed to the success of William's expedition. Neither Danby from the North, nor Sir Edward Seymour from the South-West, had bargained for a world in which Whiggery and Dissent were visibly in the ascendant.[69]

[65] Clarke, *James II*, ii. 272–3. *Ailesbury Memoirs*, ii. 222–3. *Clar. Corr.* ii. 233. Dr Williams's Library: MS Morrice Q, p. 387; Luttrell, i. 490; BL: MS Sloane 3929, fo. 121^{v}.

[66] D. R. Lacey, *Dissent and Party Politics in England, 1661–1689* (New Brunswick 1969), 112–49.

[67] W. Cobbett, *A Parliamentary History of England* (36 vols., 1806–20), vi. 847. *Ailesbury Memoirs*, ii. 196.

[68] *Memoirs of Reresby*, 541.

[69] *Clar. Corr.* ii. 238; A. Browning, *Thomas Osborne, Earl of Danby* (3 vols., Glasgow 1944–51), ii. i. 447; Bodl. Libr., Oxford: MS Ballard 45, fo. 31.

There can be no doubt whatsoever that the Assembly of Commoners was, in conception and intention, a Whig contrivance to secure the dynastic revolution by bringing the entire body of the old Whig party into play. Although the precise identity of William's advisers remains elusive, the existing evidence points unmistakably to Whig involvement from start to finish. It is not just that William and his Whig supporters were the joint beneficiaries of their agreeing to reassemble the Exclusionist MPs, as a means of cutting the Gordian knot of aristocratic indecision, but the silent conspiracy to pass over the Tory Parliament of 1685 reeks of the triumph (no matter how temporary it was to prove) of doctrinaire Whiggism at St James's. The 1685 Parliament was the Whigs' *bête noire*, not William's. Yet, in omitting to summon those MPs who had sat in the 'Loyal Parliament' of 1685, it has to be admitted that William cast a deliberate 'aspersion on his Matys government, as if nothing had been regular in his days'[70]—a point of view which was in line with partisan Whig thinking, but one which was wholly absent from William's acclaimed Declaration from The Hague. It was a monstrous view with which he would not previously have sympathized, having preferred all along to indict James's 'evil counsellors', not the king, in his studied appeal for nation-wide support.[71] The shift of emphasis reveals, as does little else, the straits to which he was reduced to make good his claim to James's throne even after the king had been expelled from London, and the narrowing political base on which his title to have supplanted the king finally came to rest.

Of the legality and regularity of James's Parliament there can be no question. Its objectionableness was purely political, and party political at that. It lay solely and exclusively in the eye of the Whig beholder. Elected after the rupture of organized Whiggery, and with the aid of exceptional Tory (and therefore unacceptable) ministerial interference in the constituencies,[72] James's short-lived Parliament had, the Whigs thought, to bear much of the blame for what had ensued in his 'violent and superstitious reign'. In voting 'a Popish King' an unprecedentedly generous revenue 'for life' it had acted with criminal irresponsibility.

[70] Clarke, *James II*, ii. 285.

[71] Beddard, *Kingdom*, 13, 20, 22, 28.

[72] R. H. George, 'Parliamentary Elections and Electioneering in 1685', *Transactions of the Royal Historical Society*, 4th ser., 19 (1936), 167–95.

Without such a revenue the Whigs doubted (as did some Tories by 1688) whether James would have been able to set aside statute law, embark on a programme of catholicization, and, after breaking with his Tory allies in 1686, undertake the systematic packing of the House of Commons on a scale which threatened the 'freedom' of parliament as a representative institution.[73] In the light of repeated Whig accusations of Tory complicity in the irregularities of the reign, first voiced in Holland and later renewed in England, William's preference for former members of the Exclusion Parliaments was perhaps predictable, and all the more because of his public commitment to 'a free parliament' as the instrument with which to effect a lasting release from Popery and arbitrary government. Yet, his sponsorship of the Exclusionist MPs was more self-regarding than that. It was both a clever dynastic ruse to discriminate against the bulk of those parliament men (mostly Tories) who had sworn fidelity to James in 1685, and might be disposed to dispute the Revolution, and a conscious political ploy to enhance the standing of his adherents (mostly Whigs) in the search for a settlement. Membership of Charles II's parliaments was, after all, the only parliamentary qualification possessed by some of the prince's most ardent and most useful supporters. This was as true of those who belonged to the ranks of the returned *émigrés*, such as Henry Sidney, William Harbord, Sir John Hotham, John Wildman, Sir Rowland Gwynne, Sir John Guise, and Henry Herbert, as it was of those who had rallied to his cause after arriving in England, such as Lord Colchester, William Jephson, John Trenchard, Hugh Boscawen, Sir Edward Harley, Sir Henry Capel, Sir Robert Clayton, Sir Robert Howard, Henry Powle, Henry Pollexfen, and Sir George Treby, none of whom had sat in James's Parliament and all of whom were active in promoting his advancement to the crown.

That the Whigs did in fact advocate the reassembling of the Exclusionist MPs, and endeavoured to put pressure on other, non-Whig Williamites to back their partisan objective, is borne out by their protracted, if somewhat syncopated, courting of the

[73] For a corrective to this contemporary view, see C. D. Chandaman, 'The Financial Settlement in the Parliament of 1685', in H. Hearder and H. R. Loyn (eds.), *British Government and Administration: Studies Presented to S. B. Chrimes* (Cardiff 1974), 144–54; J. Miller, *James II* (1978), 136–7. For James's attempt to pack parliament, see Jones, *Revolution in England*, ch. 6.

Marquess of Halifax. A recent convert from the ranks of the legitimists, 'the Trimmer' rapidly established himself as a foremost proponent of dynastic revolution, despite his late accession to the Williamite camp. Dismissed from the post of Lord President of the Council in October 1685,[74] he had joined the opposition to King James's Popish measures, going as far as to write and publish the influential *Letter to a Dissenter* of 1687 in a bid to disrupt the royal policy of religious toleration.[75] Confident that James's 'irregular methods' of government would be self-defeating, he held firm to his opinion that England's problems could be solved without 'unseasonable stirrings, or anything that looketh like the Protestants being the aggressors'. Notwithstanding his being 'unalterably devoted' to the prince's person, he had quietly discouraged Henry Sidney's attempts to recruit him to the party which favoured Orangist intervention.[76] As an old Tory he distrusted the Whigs about William, and in April 1688 had cautioned the prince against heeding the dangerous counsels of 'unskilful agitators, warm men who would bee active at a wrong time, and want patience to keep their zele from running away with them'—a perfect description of how he thought the Whigs had prejudiced the Protestant cause in 1680–1.[77] As late as November 1688 Sir Robert Howard had failed to prevent Halifax from acting as James's Commissioner in the (to the Whigs) unwelcome Hungerford negotiations, even though he confessed at the time that he had 'receiv'd the employment with some trouble'. Though warned by Howard that accepting such a mission, after the military débâcle at Salisbury, 'wou⟨l⟩d give very unhappy suspitions that he was engaged in a designe to give a stop' to William's 'advancinge' on London, he still went ahead.[78] It was not until James had, as Halifax put it, 'dealt il with

[74] PRO SP 8/3, no. 159: James II to William of Orange, 20 Oct. 1685; SP 31/1, no. 134.

[75] H. C. Foxcroft, *The Life and Letters of Sir George Savile, Bart., First Marquis of Halifax* (2 vols., 1898), i. 450 ff. Cited below as *Halifax*. M. N. Brown (ed.), *The Works of George Savile Marquis of Halifax* (3 vols., Oxford 1989), i. 71 ff.; K. H. D. Haley, 'A List of the English Peers, *c.* May 1687', *English Historical Review*, 69 (1954), 304.

[76] Browning, *Danby*, ii. 159–61; Burnet, iii. 274–8; Foxcroft, *Halifax*, i. 494.

[77] PRO SP 8/1, pt. 2, fos. 203–6: Halifax to William of Orange, London, 12 Apr. 1688.

[78] PRO SP 8/2, pt. 2, fos. 95–6: [Sir Robert Howard] to William of Orange, [2 Dec. 1688].

Barry University Library
Miami, FL 33161

him in sending him . . . to the Prince, and going away before he returnd', that he took the fateful step of transferring his loyalty to William.[79] Having done so, he acted with a vengeance. His defiant espousal of the Williamite interest during his chairmanship of the provisional government led him to flee London on 16 December, fearing that he might be arrested for treason on the king's return to the capital. Arriving at Windsor, he found that the fame of his services had gone before him. He was instantly admitted to the inner circle of William's English advisers, who included Lords Mordaunt, Macclesfield, Shrewsbury, Delamer, Stamford, and Wiltshire. While the Whig peers could not forget his part in voting down the Bill of Exclusion in November 1680, nor his contribution to launching the near-fatal Tory Reaction,[80] they were content 'to make use of the marquis for the Prince his service', intending to call him 'to account . . . when the government was once setled'.[81] His unwavering support for deposing the king by force and the conspicuous role that he took in the deposition, in which he acted alongside the Whig Lords Shrewsbury and Delamer,[82] convinced them that, for the present, his assistance was essential to the improvement of their party prospects, pinned as they were on making good the dynastic revolution. His considerable parliamentary talents and new intimacy with the prince marked him out as a coming power, a politician to be reckoned with.

Whatever discussions the Whig lords and gentlemen may have had with Halifax at Windsor and St James's, on returning to London the Marquess encountered fresh pressures. He received an appeal from an unknown Whig, who took advantage of the anonymity afforded by the penny post to address a private handwritten 'Memoriall' to him on the subject of how best to come by 'a free parliament'—the matter which was uppermost in

[79] *Memoirs of Reresby*, 552. With James's first flight Halifax became a convinced Williamite revolutionary, more than Kenyon allows (*Revolution Principles*, 21). By 16 Dec. he was 'in the head of the party that asserted a demise', and was 'for the Prince's assuming the title' of king. Dr Williams's Library: MS Morrice Q, p. 382. Beddard, *Kingdom*, 49–50, 54, 56 ff.

[80] E. S. de Beer, 'The House of Lords in the Parliament of 1680', *Bulletin of the Institute of Historical Research*, 20 (1943–5), 30, 32–5. R. A. Beddard, 'The Commission for Ecclesiastical Promotions, 1681–84: An Instrument of Tory Reaction', *Historical Journal*, 10 (1967), pp. 17 ff.

[81] *Memoirs of Reresby*, 550; cf. p. 563.

[82] Beddard, *Kingdom*, 56–60.

everyone's mind.[83] Pithy in content and terse to the point of being almost telegrammatic in style, it urged the immediate re-summoning of the last of the three Exclusion Parliaments as a means of avoiding a constitutional impasse and of obtaining a speedy and satisfactory settlement. As an exceedingly rare item from Halifax's postbag in the dying days of December 1688—one which he valued enough to preserve among a handful of important documents generated by the crisis that still remain in the Halifax Papers from Althorp—it deserves attention. It reads as follows:

> The Prince of Orange comes to restore our lawes and secure our religion. By what can it be better done (at a time when legall formes cannot be had) then recalling the Oxford Parliament? None ever soe freely and fairely elected. Illegally dissolved. Since which time all the outrages have beene committed against law and liberty, in murthers, tearing away charters and franchises to make way for such things the nation has suffered under. What remedy more proper and practicable then that that Parlement should goe on as they begun? It is quickly convened, easily fill'd. Our affaires require dispa⟨t⟩ch. Time pretious. It will wholly satisfye the nation.[84]

Held in Oxford in March 1681, the third Exclusion Parliament had contained a bigger Whig majority than either of its two predecessors, following a general election in which many constituencies had re-elected the sitting Members and returned them to Westminster with an express mandate to pass the Bill of Exclusion against James.[85]

The bold language and extreme sentiments of the 'Memoriall' distinguish it as the work of an unrepentant Whig militant, who regarded Charles II's dissolution of the Oxford Parliament, after sitting for less than a week, as not merely precipitate, but unlawful: a judgement which owed everything to party attachment and nothing to knowledge of the law. References to so-called 'murthers', by which were meant the suicide of the Whig Earl of Essex in the Tower and the execution of the Whig

[83] Bodl. Libr., Oxford: MS Don. c. 39, fo. 78: Sir John Lowther to Sir Daniel Fleming, London, 22 Dec.

[84] BL: Althorp MSS, Halifax Papers, item i: 'A Memoriall for calling the Members of ⟨the⟩ Oxford Parliament' (Halifax's autograph endorsement). It is stamped: 'Peny post paid'.

[85] Jones, *First Whigs*, 167 ff.; Haley, *Shaftesbury*, 627 ff.

'martyrs', Lord William Russell and Algernon Sidney, for engaging in the treasonable Rye House Conspiracy of 1683,[86] and resentment at the alleged 'outrages' of the *quo warranto* campaign, which had destroyed the Whigs' hold over municipal corporations, were similarly the effusions of violent Whiggery. Such views passed for articles of party faith among Exclusionist diehards, particularly 'those who had fled into Holland', who longed for an opportunity to settle old scores and, even before returning to England, 'gave out that all the Tory party . . . should at once be attainted and their estates taken away by parliament'.[87] Almost as if pausing to recollect Halifax's Royalist origins and Tory background, the Whig writer added a sort of mollifying postscript to the 'Memoriall', lest what he wrote struck too strident a partisan note with one who was so recent a convert to the Whigs' policy of Exclusion. Looking back to the Restoration of 1660—a revolution which had been gratefully embraced by Church of England politicians, though not initially a revolution of their making—he tried to present his suggestion to reconvene Charles II's Oxford Parliament in a more attractive light by likening it to the resummoning of Charles I's Long Parliament. He noted that 'no way' had then been 'found soe ready and certaine as that of recalling the Long Parlement to restore the King and Church after a much longer interruption'.[88] The implication was that comparable blessings would flow from recalling the Oxford Parliament. What use the Marquess made of this unsolicited piece of Whig advice can only be surmised. All that can safely be said is that the method of proceeding advocated by this unidentified memorialist to one of William's most intimate advisers substantially anticipated the prince's decision to reassemble the Exclusionist MPs, not as a parliament, but as the next best thing, an advisory body to tell him how best to pursue the ends of his Declaration: the restoration of the laws and the securing of the Protestant religion. 'Being lately chosen the representatives of the people' in a free election, they were, William concluded, 'likely to be best acquainted with their

[86] Robert Ferguson re-published his tract of 1684, *An Enquiry Into, And Detection Of The Barbarous Murther Of the late Earl of Essex* (1689), and Delamer published *The Late Lord Russel's Case, With Observations Upon it* (1689).

[87] A. Jessop (ed.), *The Lives of the Right Hon. Francis North* [and his brothers], (3 vols., 1890), i. 223.

[88] BL: Althorp MSS, Halifax Papers, item i.

concernes', and most fit to advise him 'in this extraordinary conjuncture' in his and the nation's affairs.[89]

In the two days before Christmas William's supporters prepared for the Assembly of Commoners called for the 26th. To begin with they took their cue from the 'greatest' Whig lawyers, Serjeant Maynard, Recorder Treby, and Henry Pollexfen, whose professional stature as legal counsel, already high in popular estimation, had been increased still further by the all but total disgrace which had enveloped the Tory bench of judges following James's dismissal. In response to 'the necessity of affaires' pleaded by the prince,[90] they replied that 'the law knows no name, nor title, but that of a king'. They therefore recommended that William and Mary should be advised to assume the throne forthwith by ordering themselves to be proclaimed king and queen. Their recommendation was, needless to say, eagerly endorsed by 'those that came in with the Prince', who had been urging William to do precisely that ever since 11 December. It was a course of action which offered distinct legal and political advantages, for the lawyers maintained that by virtue of Henry VII's statute of 1495 'whoever assumeth the title hath absolute authority to do all things that our lawes impower a King to doe'. The advantages would be immediate, in that they did not depend upon William and Mary's first being crowned. The new monarchs, acting on their titular sovereignty, would be able to summon a parliament without delay, and appoint new officers of the Crown, so that 'all persons might legally' give them 'their assistance'. New subjects as well as old partisans would be able to shelter under the protection of an act of parliament 'that indemnifies all persons in their obedience to him that is King *de facto*, and justifies them to fight for the King *de facto* against the King *de jure*, for that was the very case when that act was made'.[91] At St James's, where most of the nobility were 'inclined to waive his Majesty and to set up a new face of Government',[92] there had been clandestine hopes that the Peers would have called for an assumption of the crown, but, in the event, they had proved to be 'of another minde'. At their meetings on the 21st and 22nd the

[89] Dr Williams's Library: MS Morrice Q, p. 393.
[90] *Commons Journal*, x. 5.
[91] Dr Williams's Library: MS Morrice Q, pp. 378, 382, 393–4, 395.
[92] *HMC: Earl of Lindsey*, 455: C. Bertie to Danby, London, 20 Dec.

Peers had 'agreed of nothing about the assumption'.[93] Hence, William's summons to Charles II's MPs. However, before the Commoners could assemble on the 26th, the Williamites found by a disconcertingly ironic twist of fate that they had in a manner been forestalled by the laggardly Peers. Contrary to expectation, the Assembly of Peers had suddenly pulled to, late on the 24th, after almost eight hours of continuous debate, and voted an address to William calling on him to take charge of the government.[94] Once they had formally presented their address on Christmas Day, it was thought unlikely that they would be prepared to revoke their advice. To implement more ambitious plans for 'an assumption' was liable to set the Lords and Commoners at odds with each other. It was a liability which was best avoided.

Moreover, some of William's backers, among them the octogenarian Sir John Maynard, began to get cold feet just in case 'they could not carrey it' for the prince.[95] Clearly, a certain amount of political sounding and head-counting had been going on since the 23rd. According to the London Dissenter Roger Morrice, a close observer of the assembling Commoners, the opposition sprang from 'three parties', which, in spite of their differences, were united in one objective: 'to defeat the Prince's noble designe' to help himself to the crown. There were the loyalists, or strict 'hierarchists' of the Church of England, who were 'for recurring to the King'. They included 'some of the intreaguers' from Charles II's Cavalier Parliament, who, to remove the rebels' fears, undertook to obtain James's pardon for 'those that had taken up armes' against him—'as if', Morrice commented slightingly, 'that were all they must expect' for saving England from Popery. Then there were other Tories who were more 'concerned for their relations and friends', as being 'like to be punished for giving up charters and for destroying our fundamentall constitution', if the Whigs in general chose to act on the exiles' call for revenge and retribution. As a convinced Whig himself, and one that looked to William to break the 'rotten

[93] 'All deliberate experienced persons resolved to have advised the Prince or Princesse to have assumed and to have been proclaimed . . . and it was hoped the Lords would have done so.' Dr Williams's Library, MS Morrice Q, p. 395.

[94] Beddard, *Kingdom*, 65, 160–2.

[95] Yet 'few men in the House were more desierous' for 'the assumption' than Maynard. Dr Williams's Library: MS Morrice Q, p. 398.

narrow foundation that has ruined us' by opening up the Anglican Establishment to Dissenters, Morrice strongly suspected the Tories of scheming to hang on to their monopoly of office in Church and State. Finally, there was what he calls 'the least party', the republicans, who were 'for casting all into confusion, and seeing whether a commonwealth will not turn up trump'. When these were added together Maynard and his Williamite cronies were apprehensive that 'great numbers would oppose' any move towards an assumption of the throne, though Morrice firmly believed that both he and they were 'deceived in their thoughts'.[96]

Estimates of the number of MPs attending the Assembly vary in contemporary records from 'about 300' to 'near 400', a surprisingly high figure given the short notice that they received.[97] Morrice, who had excellent contacts at Westminster and in the City, and provides the only detailed account of the meeting, is probably nearer the mark in recording that of almost 400 persons crowding 'in⟨to⟩ the Commons' Howse and galleries' round about '220 were judged to have been Members' of Charles II's parliaments.[98] The Exclusionists were so thick on the floor of the House that Evelyn simply described the meeting as being composed of 'such Commons as were members of the Parliament at Oxford'.[99] Certainly, if judged by the official minutes of the the session, Serjeant Maynard need not have worried, for the Williamites dominated every stage of the proceedings. The prince's confidant, Henry Powle, who with Sir Robert Howard had managed William's dealings with the City of London,[100] was voted into the chair unopposed. On a committee of thirteen appointed to draft an address to the prince, twelve were known Williamites, of whom ten were Whigs (most of the familiar names were there: Maynard, Clayton, Wildman, Sidney, Capel, Treby, Herbert, and Jephson, plus Richard Hampden and Sir Thomas Lee) and two were political converts, like Halifax, from Tory 'Expedients' to Whig Exclusion (Powle and William

[96] Ibid., 395–6.

[97] Bodl. Libr., Oxford: MS Don. c. 39, fo. 81; *Memoirs of Reresby*, 542; BL: MS Egerton 2717, fo. 418.

[98] Dr Williams's Library: MS Morrice Q, p. 397.

[99] Evelyn, iv. 612. Mulgrave, ii. 84–5. *HMC, 11th Report, Appendix, pt. v: Earl of Dartmouth* (1887), 241: Lady Dartmouth to Dartmouth, 26 Dec.

[100] Beddard, *Kingdom*, 51–2, 55–6, and 179–80: app. 17.

Garraway).[101] At the close of the session a Whig *émigré*, the Earl of Wiltshire, successfully moved the signing of the Exeter Association, which the ambitious Williamites constantly promoted as a test of affection to the prince and the Protestant cause he represented. Of the 220 MPs present, Morrice estimated that 'not above 20 then declined it', the rest either signing then, or having signed it already.[102] There is no gainsaying the Williamite sentiment of the majority of the MPs. Had the prince's adherents chosen to press for 'an assumption', they would have won. Nevertheless 'the wisest, ablest, and honestest men', as Morrice appreciatively styled his fellow Whigs, decided to play safe by dropping their plan, and astutely fell into line with the Assembly of Peers.[103]

Under Powle's capable guidance from the chair the Commoners made quick work of their business. In well under three hours (the Peers took treble the time) they 'agreed unanimously, without any opposition or division, to make the same address in the substance of it that the Lords had made'.[104] The Williamites made no mourn over the laying aside of their earlier plan, and their reasons for abandoning it displayed a calm, sensible, and even statesmanlike approach to the difficulties of the national and international situation, which was a far cry from the impetuous, irrational, and intransigent attitude of the Whig leadership in the Westminster and Oxford Parliaments of 1680 and 1681.[105] They judged that the interests of the Whig party, of the prince, and of the nation were better served by preserving a show of unanimity in taking so significant a step as recognizing William's position as *Custos Regni*, guardian of the realm. The Peers' advice 'being counter' to what they had intended to move in the Assembly of Commoners, they considered that 'that was reason

[101] *Commons Journal*, x. 6.

[102] Dr Williams's Library: MS Morrice Q, pp. 397–8. The last act of the Assembly of Commoners was to recommend the Association to the City of London, in contrast to what had happened at the Guildhall meeting of peers on 11 Dec., when a proposal to enter 'an association of adherence to the Prince' had 'found none to second it'. Bodl. Libr., Oxford: MSS Rawlinson D 691, pp. 46–7; D 836, f. 105.

[103] Dr Williams's Library: MS Morrice Q, pp. 369, 398.

[104] Ibid. 397. *Clar. Corr.* ii. 236. Bodl. Libr., Oxford: MS Rawlinson D 691, pp. 38–45. Müller, *Wilhelm III und Waldeck*, ii. 127.

[105] For earlier Whig intransigence and its near-fatal results, see Beddard, 'Retreat on Toryism', 84, 95–100, 102–4, 105–6.

enough to quitt it'. They wished to avoid making 'a fatall breach betwene the two Houses'. Had 'the two great bodyes' of the nation been divided, they would have ineffably complicated, not simplified, William's search for a settlement. The prince 'would have been distracted, and not have known whose advice to have followed'. Delay, not speed, would have resulted. More than that, and a harbinger of times to come when they would regularly have to weigh the wider implications of domestic acts, they realized that public disagreement would have 'sounded much to the common disadvantage abrode' in Scotland and Ireland, and 'beyond seas' in Europe, 'where they thinke the Lords to be far more considerable then they are'. To have signalled English disunity to the dependent kingdoms of Scotland and Ireland, which were already religiously divided and politically troubled, would have been an act of grave irresponsibility, especially as James II by his flight to France remained a free agent. In war-torn Europe neither friend, nor foe, would have known what to make of serious internal division at such a critical time when Louis XIV was at war with the Dutch and with the Empire. Consequently, William's supporters 'rather thought fit to wa⟨i⟩ve this point' of an assumption of sovereignty 'then divide from the Lords'.[106] So it fell out that the Assembly of Commoners, called to redress the political balance in the prince's favour by proposing a firm dynastic and Whig lead in the face of unchecked aristocratic and Tory procrastination, came in its resolutions and addresses to emulate the Assembly of Peers it had been summoned to supersede.[107]

As if to show that he was not wholly beholden to their lordships, William deliberately postponed answering their addresses, which were presented to him by Halifax on Christmas Day, 'till he had spoken with the gentlemen who had been formerly in the House of Commons'.[108] He received the addresses of the Assembly of Commoners from Powle on the 27th. That both Assemblies gave him the same advice made his response easier. On 28 December the prince accepted the responsibilities

[106] Dr Williams's Library: MS Morrice Q, pp. 396, 398, 397.

[107] Müller, *Wilhelm III und Waldeck*, ii. 125: William to Waldeck, St James's, 24 Dec.

[108] *Clar. Corr.* ii. 236. Bodl. Libr., Oxford: MS Rawlinson D 691, p. 55; MS Don. c. 39, fo. 81^{v}; Mulgrave, ii. 84; *Memoirs of Reresby*, 542; Müller, *Wilhelm III und Waldeck*, ii. 125–6; BL: MS Egerton 2717, fo. 418: London, 27 Dec.

of government in identical speeches delivered in separate ceremonies in the Queen's Presence Chamber at St James's—at 11 a.m. for the Peers, and at 4 p.m. for the Commoners.[109] He agreed to do all that they asked of him: to issue his letters for the election of a Convention; to take care of 'the publick revenue'; and to endeavour 'to put Ireland into such a condition as that the Protestant religion and the English interest may be maintained in that Kingdom'. Having come over 'for the preservation of the Protestant religion and the laws and liberties of these Kingdoms', he assured his audience that he would 'always be ready to expose' himself 'to any hazard for the defence of the same'.[110] By being publicly and formally seen to respond to the addresses of the Peers and Commoners, after deliberately pausing to consider the magnitude of what they asked of him, William was able to ignore the underlying differences of Whig and Tory by portraying his admittance to executive authority as a gracious act of acquiescence in the will of a united and grateful nation.[111] In the eyes of many his acceptance of the administration, civil, military, and fiscal, 'reduced' all things 'to their proper channel', a reassuring state of affairs that was immediately announced to the City by the firing of 'all the gunns' from the Tower Ordnance. That night at St James's 'most of the nobility paid him their congratulation for that favour', while in and about the capital 'some bonfires were made to express a more publick rejoicing'.[112] Although England was still a kingdom without a king, it no longer lacked a recognized ruler—a Protestant prince who was fully resolved to fight to keep the country from falling victim to Popery and France.

III

The political developments of the last week of 1688 guaranteed the peaceful acceptance of the dynastic revolution in England. By

[109] This corrects S. B. Baxter's date (*William III* (1966), 247). *Commons Journal*, x. 7; Beddard, *Kingdom*, 167–8; *Clar. Corr.* ii. 237; Dr Williams's Library: MS Morrice Q, pp. 393, 395, 398; Bodl. Libr., Oxford: MS Rawlinson D 691, p. 55; *Universal Intelligence*, no. 6 (26–9 Dec.).

[110] For William's speech to the Peers, see Beddard, *Kingdom*, 168.

[111] William's delaying his reply to both Peers and Commoners had more to it than simply enhancing 'the grandure of the ceremony'. BL: MS Egerton 2717, fo. 418: London, 27 Dec.

[112] Ibid., fo. 419: London, 29 Dec.; Bodl. Libr., Oxford: MS Don. c. 39, fo. 83^{v}.

a deft admixture of effrontery and patience the Williamites had succeeded in establishing 'a new face of Government',[113] without unnecessarily or unduly antagonizing James's partisans. There had been only discussions and votes, leading to disappointment, not desperation. Consequently, there was no loyalist secession and no appeal to arms. For this 'happy issue' to the protracted crisis of the past eight weeks England had to thank, not any mythical exercise of innate political wisdom on the part of the English nation, but the timely withdrawal of the king and 'the prudent conduct' of the prince,[114] backed, as he was at all times, by the steadily rising ambition of his Whig supporters, with their unflagging determination to better themselves by skilfully asserting his interests against those of the king. Like William himself, the Whigs refused to let slip the opportunity which chance, much more than intelligent forward planning, had bestowed on them.[115] Astounding as it may well seem, when viewed against the savage breakup of organized Whiggery and the impressive achievements of Toryism in the early 1680s,[116] the Tories had been completely outpaced, outmanœuvred, and outclassed by their Whig adversaries, particularly in London. Yet, James had contributed substantially to the downfall of his 'old friends'. The reversal of Tory party fortunes which occurred at the Revolution was very largely a retrospective measure of the damage that had been inflicted on their political confidence and political system by the king's successive body-blows: his turning against them in 1686, his ejection of them from office thereafter, his prosecution of the Seven Bishops, and, more recently, after two attempts at a shot-gun reconciliation with the Anglican hierarchy,[117] his double desertion of them on 11 and 23 December. The fatality of James's flight had horrified

[113] *HMC: Earl of Lindsey*, 455: C. Bertie to Danby, London, 20 Dec.

[114] BL: MS Egerton 3336, fo. 128: Danby to Mary of Orange, 4 Jan. 1688/9 (autograph copy).

[115] As early as 11 Dec. the loyalists harboured 'very misgiving thoughts . . . that His Highness would not be a slave to his word, nor bate the great advantage success had given him'. Bodl. Libr., Oxford: MS Rawlinson D 836, fo. 108.

[116] See K. Feiling, *A History of the Tory Party 1640–1714* (Oxford 1924; repr. 1965), 187 ff.; J. R. Western, *Monarchy and Revolution: The English State in the 1680s* (1972), 45 ff.; L. K. J. Glassey, *Politics and the Appointment of Justices of the Peace 1675–1720* (Oxford 1979), 44–70.

[117] R. A. Beddard, 'William Sancroft, as Archbishop of Canterbury, 1677–1691', D.Phil. thesis (Oxford, 1967), 57–69, 132–67.

the loyalists. 'O God,' exclaimed the loyal Lord Dartmouth, 'what could make our master decert his Kingdomes and his friends!' They were disconsolate, 'struck to the heart' at the news of his final going.[118]

Whatever the private misgivings felt by the Tories at large, the clergy and army especially, among whom compassion for the king prompted a sense of shame at their having betrayed him to his enemies, the loyalist peers, prelates, and politicians had on the 24th and 26th played straight into the hands of the revolutionaries by not challenging outright the legality of the proceedings of the twin Assemblies. Their public failure to do so meant that they forfeited their independent ability to resist the Williamites' growing demand to make the revolution permanent, and made ordinary Tories less likely to oppose William's claim to their respect. Without James's presence in England they found it impossible to make headway against the fast-flowing tide of Protestant militancy, which more often than not both heralded and facilitated the encroachment of treason. Nor were they helped by Archbishop Sancroft's 'strange obstinate passiveness', which stopped him from waiting on William, or declaring his mind in public.[119] He, for one, saw where events were leading, and drew back aghast. When it came to the ungodly deposition of kings he perceived 'no difference' between Lord Protector Cromwell and the Prince of Orange, 'but that the one's name was Oliver, and the other William'.[120] Demoralized, disorganized, and disunited, but above all dynastically leaderless, the loyalists collaborated in what they feared wholeheartedly to oppose; either because of their deference to William's status as a Prince of the Blood Royal (he was fourth in the line of succession to the throne after the Prince of Wales and his half-sisters, Mary and Anne); or because they were genuinely grateful to him for his intervention on behalf of their religion and laws (he had rescued them from the jaws of Popery); or because they did not wish to disoblige him and lose all thoughts of favour and preferment (he was known to resent loyalists who cast aspersions on his

[118] National Maritime Museum, Greenwich: Dar./17, p. 48: Dartmouth to the Earl of Feversham, HMS *Resolution*, Spithead, 14 Dec.; *Clar. Corr.* ii. 233.

[119] Beddard, 'The Loyalist Opposition in the Interregnum', 109; Dr Williams's Library: MS Morrice Q, pp. 382, 385.

[120] Beddard, *Kingdom*, 7.

motives).[121] Whether they realized it at the time, or only later, is uncertain, but, by relinquishing their demand for 'a parliament of the King's owne calling', and agreeing to the summoning of a Convention, which had first been suggested by the loyal Earl of Pembroke,[122] they became unwilling participants in a revolution they heartily detested. They were trapped inside an agreed political process which, having begun with their consent, could have only one outcome: the enthronization of William the Usurper.

Paradoxically, the king's denial of a legal parliament to his subjects—an action intended to embarrass and perplex his enemies, which for a while it did—helped to seal his fate. It effectively prevented his friends from keeping the last vestige of his tattered authority in place. When the substitute Convention met on 22 January 1689 it was not just an anomalous body, unknown to the laws of England, but a body which assembled on William's sole authority and without the normal safeguards provided by the customary Oaths of Allegiance and Supremacy, which the law required all peers of the realm and all regularly elected MPs to swear to the King's Majesty before taking their seats and entering on business.[123] The electoral advantage to the Williamites of not having to take the oaths was not lost on the ever-watchful Whig peers, who were always on the look-out to do themselves and their cause a good turn. Lords Mordaunt and Delamer openly contended that to have to swear such oaths 'would take off the freedom of a parliament'—'the chief thing' desired by the nation.[124] They were understandably opposed to handicapping its work with redundant and irrelevant oaths which they and 'the associated lords' had already broken and had not the least intention of observing further. More to the point, they did not wish to see their Whig companions discouraged

[121] When the Duke of Northumberland laid down his commission, probably like other loyalists 'aledging his alegiance to the King', he was 'denyed the Prince's presence'. Bodl. Libr., Oxford: MS Don. c. 39, fo. 91; Foxcroft, *Halifax*, ii. 204. Many officers went to Rochester on purpose to resign their commissions into James's hands. Clarke, *James II*, ii. 268.

[122] Bodl. Libr., Oxford: MS Rawlinson D 836, fo. 105^{v}. Beddard, *Kingdom*, 39, 160.

[123] I cannot accept Pinkham's view that the summoning of the Convention rested on the authorization of the Peers and Commoners alone, when William had previously brought them into being. It forms part of the unwarranted Whig 'parliamentarization' of William's actions. Pinkham, *Respectable Revolution*, 220.

[124] For their speeches on 24 Dec., see Beddard, *Kingdom*, 161.

from standing in the approaching general election. The exaction of such oaths and declarations, according to the letter of the law, had been a characteristic weapon of the High-Church Tories in their systematic drive to dislodge and discourage Whigs and Dissenters from holding and accepting municipal office. In London Morrice claimed that it had had the effect of deterring 'the best citizens' from appearing in the Common Council elections of 28 November and 21 December, 'for they trembled at the thoughts of takeing such oathes . . . just when they were resolved and goeing on in the actuall breach of them'.[125]

As the Peers on the 24th and the Commoners on the 26th had made a once and for all break with the political past, so on the 28th the prince's acceptance of the administration, followed the next day by the sending out of his circular letters for the Convention, marked the passing of the old order in the state. After 28 December political life was never to be the same again—either for the dynasts, James and William, or for their supporters, or for the nation. James's rule was finally extinguished.[126] However William's custodianship of the government related to James's titular sovereignty, which his adherents still struggled to keep alive, it cut off all realistic hopes of his restitution, as they were the first to admit. That Francis Gwyn, a client of the Earl of Rochester's who had faithfully served as secretary to the provisional government and to the Assembly of Peers, understood this was shown by his remark that, for the ill-starred king, it was 'now all over; neither he, nor his . . . are like ever to set foot here again'.[127] The loyalists—most notably the Earls of Middleton, Clarendon, and Ailesbury, and Bishops Turner and Mews—had, like the foreboding chorus in a Greek tragedy, repeatedly warned their royal master against leaving the country, telling him that it would be fatal to do so, for 'the door would immediately be shut

[125] Dr Williams's Library: MS Morrice Q, p. 387. Bodl. Libr., Oxford: MS Don. c. 39, fo. 76ᵛ; *English Currant*, no. 4 (19–21 Dec.); *Universal Intelligence*, no. 5 (22–6 Dec.).

[126] For the notion of a 'demiss' or 'demise', see Bodl. Libr., Oxford: MS Don. c. 39, fo. 79ᵛ. Sir Robert Howard later argued in the Convention that the giving of the administration to William in Dec. 1688 could only be justified on the grounds that the throne was already vacant. Clarke, *James II*, ii. 301.

[127] *HMC, 15th Report, Appendix, pt. i: Earl of Dartmouth* (3 vols., 1896), iii. 141: Francis Gwyn to Dartmouth, Christmas Day 1688.

upon him'.[128] Within five days of his going from Rochester on the 23rd the door was, indeed, shut tight behind him.[129] He was no sooner gone than the Whigs gave out that it was their solemn duty 'to bolt the door after him and so foreclose his return'.[130] For them, and for those Englishmen who had sided with William against the king, it was 'as if he had never been'.[131]

As for the dejected loyalists, they had perforce to adjust to these changed circumstances.[132] With stoic fortitude, born of their legitimist beliefs and constitutional convictions, they evolved a new strategy. They made the painful switch from their initial objective of securing James's restitution 'with honor and safety', as had been proposed and pursued by the Earl of Rochester ever since 11 December, to the lesser objective of obtaining a regency in his name, as currently urged by the Earl of Nottingham.[133] To the more scrupulous of the loyalists the change of plan represented an unsatisfactory retreat. Given their unshaken devotion to the King's person and their passionate belief in the divine right of kings to rule as well as reign, 'a Regency *pro tempore*' was a poor second-best. Although a majority of the bishops thought the revised policy 'as liable to as great objections as the deposing' of the king, they went along with it, holding 'that the King's affairs were in such extremity any bargaine' they could strike 'for the present was better for him, even for him, than setting his

[128] *Clar. Corr.* ii. 232–3, 234; J. G. A. Pocock, 'Dr Robert Brady', *Cambridge Historical Journal*, 2 (1948), 101–3; *Ailesbury Memoirs*, ii. 222–4; Clarke, *James II*, ii. 270–1.

[129] Beddard, *Kingdom*, 63.

[130] [R. Ferguson], *A Brief Justification Of The Prince of Orange's Descent Into England, And of the Kingdoms Late Recourse to Arms. With A Modest Disquisition of what may become the Wisdom and Justice Of the Ensuing Convention In Their Disposal of the Crown* (1689), 22.

[131] *HMC: Earl of Dartmouth*, 241: Barbara, Lady Dartmouth, to Dartmouth, 26 Dec. 'This day thare was called a convention of those comons that sat at Oxford, who concured (you may imagin) with the lords yesterday, of putting the government into the Prince of Orange's hand till the 22th, and all the revenu, and the poore King not considered or mentioned, the dore shutt upon him as if he had never bin.'

[132] *HMC, 15th Report, Appendix, pt. i: Earl of Dartmouth*, iii. 141: Rochester to Dartmouth, Whitehall, 25 Dec.

[133] The regency was, of course, for James II, not for the Prince of Wales, as stated in E. Gregg, *Queen Anne* (1980), 68. In the Convention Lord Rochester, seconded by Pembroke, amended the proposal to a regency 'for life'. Bodl. Libr., Oxford: MS Rawlinson D 836, fo. 105^{v}. *HMC, 12th Report, Appendix, pt. vii: House of Lords, 1689–1690* (1889), 14.

crowne on another head, which except by force is never to be reverst'.[134]

There is room to doubt whether Lord Nottingham seriously wanted James's recall.[135] His approach to the monarchy was that of a lawyer, not that of a divine. He acknowledged parliament's power to alter the succession, but wished to avoid disturbing the foundations of a hereditary monarchy by slighting an existing title. To him it was more important to defend the Crown against the menace of popular election than it was to restore King James.[136] While a restoration was under discussion he had favoured pitching 'the terms' to be offered to James so high as to make his acceptance of them improbable. That way Nottingham hoped to legitimize the Revolution by obviating the need to forswear allegiance to the king *de jure*, which could only be done by vesting the exercise of royal authority permanently in the prince as *de facto* regent. His scheme had an extra incentive for an avidly aspiring Tory politician: he hoped it would allow him to overtake the Hyde brothers, Clarendon and Rochester, in the affections of the 'moderate' and 'prudential' Anglican clergy of London,[137] who, unlike the bishops, were alarmed at what the ecclesiastical consequences might be of bringing the king back into government.[138] Not unreasonably, James began to suspect that such terms were contrived on purpose to put him in the wrong by making any refusal of them a pretext for denying him real power.[139] For a monarch of his outlook and temperament an empty title and perpetual banishment (perhaps in Italy as Burnet contemplated[140]) held no attrac-

[134] The loyalists favoured a 'Regency *pro tempore*', hoping to do away with it once James was back in England. Beddard, 'Loyalist Opposition in the Interregnum', 107.

[135] Nottingham later told Burnet 'he should not be sorry to see his side out voted'. Burnet, iii. 357. For William's regard for him, see Foxcroft, *Halifax*, ii. 202. On 18 Dec. William had 'dined at the Earle of Nottingham's neare Kensington'. Bodl. Libr., Oxford: MS Don. c. 39, fo. 73.

[136] H. Horwitz, *Revolution Politicks: The Career of Daniel Finch, Second Earl of Nottingham, 1647–1730* (Cambridge 1968), 72, 75–6.

[137] 'Many of the worthyest divines are most confident that not only Nottingham, but the Marquess of Halifax, are most sincere for the publick good'. Dr Williams's Library: MS Morrice Q, p. 415.

[138] This was the start of Nottingham's effort to turn the Hydes' eclipse to his own advantage. For his subsequent endeavours, see G. V. Bennett, 'King William III and the Episcopate', in G. V. Bennett and J. D. Walsh (eds.), *Essays in Modern English Church History* (1966), 109 ff.

[139] Clarke, *James II*, ii. 292–3.

[140] BL: MS Add. 32681, fos. 315–16^{v}.

tions. The practical difficulties in the way of establishing a regency were manifold, particularly if, as seemed certain, it had to be maintained by force against King James by a regent who, in law, was deemed to act for him.[141] Inherent contradictions apart (and these the Williamites were quick to fasten on and expose to ridicule),[142] the revival of the restoration project after 23 December was short-lived. It was barely broached before it foundered irrecoverably in the clamours which the Whigs raised against 'the recurrers' as the underhand 'friends to Popery, and arbitrary Power', who would yet betray the nation into French bondage.[143] Fearful of being branded unpatriotic, the loyalists, who shunned the malevolent influence of Catholic France as much as their adversaries, saw that a regency was the most that they could possibly angle for, and contented themselves with that as best they could. By 15 January 1689 all the bishops were 'for a Regency, thereby to salve their Oathes'.[144]

But the break with the past was scarcely less dramatic for the Whigs than it was for the Tories. The vehemently Williamite stance which they had adopted in the two Assemblies on 24 and 26 December—a stance which consolidated the dynastic revolution and opened the prospect to improved party fortunes—marked the first stage in their long and arduous transformation into a Court party: the party which was ultimately to be that of the Junto lords.[145] Once their patron, William, had succeeded in ousting James with their help, the Whigs automatically ceased to be a functioning opposition, ranged against the government of a Popish king, and became the chief support of the government of a Protestant prince—with all the unexpected challenges that that abrupt about-turn posed for a party which had been largely recruited from men of the 'country' tradition in politics, which had been reared on the fixed principle of opposition to 'the growth of Popery' at Court, and which had shot into parliamentary prominence after fighting three general elections in a row, campaigning on the issues of 'no courtiers' in parliament, Popish

141 The main objection was that, if regency had been carried, there would be 'two kings at the same time: one with the title, and another with the power of a king', a receipt for disaster with the approach of war. Burnet, iii. 360.

142 Dr Williams's Library: MS Morrice Q, pp. 378, 381, 393.

143 Clarke, *James II*, ii. 292–3.

144 Evelyn, iv. 614.

145 Mulgrave, ii. 83. Cf. J. H. Plumb, *The Growth of Political Stability in England 1675–1725* (1967), 133 ff.

Exclusion, and Protestant unity: the very opposite of what the Crown had stood for in the years from 1679 to 1681.

After the combined onslaught of the Stuart kings and their Tory partners in the early and mid-1680s, the Whigs appeared to be a spent force, their political cohesion and organization seemingly shattered beyond repair.[146] This had been confirmed at the outset of James's reign by the humiliating Tory victory in the general election of 1685. Out of a total of 525 MPs returned to Westminster only 57 were Whigs.[147] Discredited and defeated, ejected and exiled, prosecuted and imprisoned, ostracized or simply ignored, the Whig stalwarts had lost their hold over the political moderates in the constituencies and, with it, the electoral strength of their party.[148] What they had not lost in many cases was their individual resolve to fight back if fortune should again smile on them. For the most part, they bided their time in fretful retirement: at home, where they watched James's every move to succour Catholicism with a feeling of increasing frustration at their inability to impede him and a grim satisfaction that events had more than justified their earlier stand against 'a Popish successor'; or abroad, in the freer political climate of Amsterdam and the Dutch cities, where they gave themselves with relish to 'contriving mischief and setting some villanous designs on foot' against King James, and never ceased to lament the loss of 'the Bill of Exclusion'.[149] William's intervention in English affairs was for them a godsend, and came not a moment too soon. His widely applauded design 'to retrieve and promote the Reformed interest and religion here and abrode, and to repress the tirany of France', was exactly what they had been waiting for.[150] They instantly seized the opportunity to emerge from their enforced hibernation on the Continent and at home, re-entered the mainstream of national political life by attaching themselves to the prince's cause, and picked up precisely from where they had been forced to leave off by Charles II and the Tories. That they lost little time in demanding Exclusion was seen in the pressure which both groups of Whigs, the returned *émigrés* and the stay-at-home

[146] J. R. Jones, *Court and Country: England 1658–1714* (1978), 220 ff.

[147] Henning, i. 47.

[148] Beddard, 'Retreat on Toryism', 96–104.

[149] Bodl. Libr., Oxford: MS Rawlinson A 266, fo. 107: anon. to B. Skelton, Whitehall, 23 Apr. 1686; MS Rawlinson C 983, fo. 103: Dr William Stanley to Bishop Compton, The Hague, 21/31 Dec. 1686.

[150] Dr Williams's Library: MS Morrice Q, p. 378.

London Exclusionists, put on William to take James's throne from him, even before he panicked and fled the capital. Once William had independently made up his mind to supplant the king their political and personal animosity for James became for him their greatest asset; to the extent that he progressively threw in his lot with them, believing by the time that he reached Windsor that they, not the Tories, were his most dependable allies, and that, by working closely together, they could establish his rule over Protestant England.[151]

Arriving in London on the heels of the king, whom he had expelled by force, 'the Prince and his freinds' found 'a joyfull reception in all parts of the Citty'.[152] The inhabitants of the metropolis, alarmed at the unaccustomed militarization of their city, felt a genuine sense of relief that the threat of hostilities had finally blown over, and took comfort from the knowledge that the prince's presence at nearby St James's would calm the anti-Catholic and pro-Orangist mobs which for three days and three nights had terrorized Westminster and the suburbs. The London Whigs, who had risked everything in bringing about William's peaceful admission to the capital, were exceptionally exultant, for, whereas King Charles had stubbornly refused their demand for James's exclusion from the throne, the prince had graciously bestowed it on them. His setting up court at St James's signified a good deal more than the victorious reinstatement of the Protestant interest, intensely gratifying as that was. It provided them with a rallying-point: a veritable party headquarters, a venue to meet frequently and openly in, which they had not had for some considerable time, and a place to concert measures under the benign patronage of a prince with whom they were wholly at one in not wanting James to return. Although there was nothing politically exclusive about William's Court, which was crowded from morn to eve with all manner of well-wishers, suitors, and the idly curious, the novel presence of the Whig noblemen—Bedford, Devonshire, Wharton, Montagu, Delamer, Mordaunt, Colchester, Lumley, Shrewsbury, Stamford, Lovelace, Macclesfield, Wiltshire, and the sprigs of the Russell, Paulet, Howard, Sidney, Gerard, and Wharton families, not to mention the locust swarm of *émigré* Scottish peers and, after 26 December, the newly

[151] Beddard, *Kingdom*, 35–6, 51–2, 55, 56–8.

[152] Bodl. Libr., Oxford: MS Don. c. 39, fo. 73: London, 18 Dec.

arrived lords from the North—was much commented on. They and their jostling clients were lionized by the prince.[153]

With such congenial company to introduce them the London Whigs were not backward in coming forward to congratulate their 'Deliverer and Restorer', and to sign the Association which was offered to all who visited St James's.[154] The prominent Exclusionist and Presbyterian sympathizer Sir Samuel Barnardiston, foreman of the Middlesex Grand Jury that had dismissed the Earl of Shaftesbury's indictment for high treason in 1681,[155] was in the van of those who ventured to Court, where he was introduced to the prince by the Earls of Bedford and Devonshire. They gave 'such a Character' of him that he was received 'with a particular marke of esteeme'.[156] Something of the tremendous uplift of spirit felt by the Whigs and their associates at finding an open-handed patron in William, his servants, and courtiers, may be glimpsed in an episode taken from the astonishing rehabilitation of the defrocked Anglican cleric Titus Oates, the fabricator of the Popish Plot of 1678 which had paved the way for the rise of the Whig party. Having been but recently discharged from King's Bench prison, in response to popular and aristocratic demand,[157] he was taken to St James's in the New Year and

[153] Mulgrave, ii. 81; Dr Williams's Library: MS Morrice Q, pp. 366–7, 379, 406. *Clar. Corr.* ii. 231 ff.; Bodl. Libr., Oxford: MS Ballard 45, fo. 41; BL: MS Egerton 2717, fos. 419, 420, 422; *English Currant*, no. 4 (19–21 Dec.); *Universal Intelligence*, no. 4 (18–22 Dec.). The entertainment was not one-sided. William was entertained by the Earl of Bedford, Lord Lisle, Sir Robert Howard, the City, etc. Bodl. Libr., Oxford: MS Don. c. 39, fo. 91; BL: MS Egerton 2717, fo. 426.

[154] The subscribers wrote 'their names in the same originall parchment'. Dr Williams's Library: MS Morrice Q, p. 382. It was believed 'that no person will be continued in any employment that will not subscribe the Association'. *HMC, 15th Report, Appendix, pt. i: Earl of Dartmouth*, iii. 143: P. Musgrave to Dartmouth, London, 26 Dec.

[155] For Barnardiston, see Luttrell, i. 146, 297, 302, 305; Henning, i. 596–7; PRO, Adm. 77/2, no. 79. For his up and down relations with James II, see PRO SP 44/71, pp. 349, 367; SP 44/56, p. 437; Luttrell, i. 441–2.

[156] Dr Williams's Library: MS Morrice Q, p. 367; *English Currant*, no. 4 (19–21 Dec.). He quickly set about reversing the judgement given against him for 'seditious libel' in the Tory Reaction. Luttrell, i. 534, 551–2.

[157] Lord Montagu called unsuccessfully for his and 'Julian' Johnson's release on 12 Dec. On 28 Dec. it was reported that both were to have 'libertie to goe abroade and will suddenly be discharged from theire imprisonments'. Oates took 'a great house at Westminster' and busied himself preparing to petition the Convention against his 'Tory' sentence. Beddard, *Kingdom*, 75. Bodl. Libr., Oxford: MS Don. c. 39, fo. 74; BL: MS Egerton 2717, fo. 428: London, 26 Jan. 1688/9.

'introduced to His Highness, who received him very kindly'. Oates was so 'elevated' by his reception, that, when 'some gentleman tould him he lookt well' after his hard usage, he replied cheerfully: 'it was a time for all honest men to looke well'.[158] Only months before he had been the very spectacle of the fallen Whig, having been publicly scourged and stood in the pillory for his perjuries; and only days before, at the height of the anti-Catholic rioting in London, he had been confidently reported dead—inevitably poisoned by the wicked Papists![159] Hated by the Tories as a vile and convicted impostor who had brought disgrace on the cloth, he was idolized by the Whigs, who saw in him a confessor for the Protestant Whig cause. Now, in what Evelyn in 1685 had called one of those 'strange revolutions' which had periodically shaped his career, the bogus 'Doctor' was again set on his feet by the admiring Whigs—a prelude to their insisting that he become a pensioner of the state. Oates's reception at St James's was a sign that the times had radically changed,[160] and few Tories doubted that they had changed for the worse.

It was not the only sign. With an eye to electioneering, and eager to repeat their earlier electoral successes of 1679 and 1681, the Whig peers returned to cultivating their old allies, the Protestant Dissenters. At the start of William's expedition 'very many more of the Dissenters' would have 'openly appeared' for him, than there did, but that 'many . . . about the Prince assured them ⟨that⟩ their appearance would give great offence to the hierarchy ⟨of the Church of England⟩, and induce them to oppose, or not to go on to assist the Prince in his purposes'.[161] With James gone, and William in charge of the kingdom, the Whigs cast caution aside and did all they could to get the Dissenters to stand up and be counted. It was part of their campaign to convince William of the powerful resources of their party. Not content to leave the Dissenting ministers of London to the casual good offices of the 'more moderate' Anglican clergy, the Earl of Devonshire and Lords Wharton and Wiltshire encouraged them to act independently of

[158] For his 'sufferings' and his petition, see PRO, Adm. 77/3, nos. 1, 23, 24; PRO SP 44/54, p. 353; Luttrell, i. 307, 310–11, 320, 326, 328, 341–2, 343, 454, 459, 498, 509, 537, 540.

[159] Evelyn, iv. 445.

[160] J. Lang, *Titus Oates* (1949), 278–329; J. P. Kenyon, *The Popish Plot* (1972), 241–63.

[161] Dr Williams's Library: MS Morrice Q, p. 392.

the churchmen. Though Bishop Compton of London—one of the 'Immortal Seven'—had agreed to four Nonconformist representatives[162] accompanying a one hundred-strong delegation of his diocesan clergy to Court on 21 December, to thank William 'for his great and noble attempt to deliver them from Popery and slavery',[163] their presence gave a totally inadequate indication of the numerical strength and organizational capacity of metropolitan Dissent.[164] Pleased at the way in which the prince 'tooke particular notice of the four nonconformist ministers' on that occasion, it was arranged that Devonshire, Wharton, and Wiltshire should introduce a comparable delegation of ninety-nine 'Nonconformable clergy of the Presbyterian and Congregationall denominations' to William on 2 January.[165] The number of ministers was significant. It was intended to rival that of the Church of England. Their spokesman was the ejected Presbyterian divine John Howe, who had accompanied Compton to Court on 21 December. He was no stranger to William. In May 1687 the prince had discussed the problems of Church and State with him 'with great freedom' in Holland, when he had advised him to resist 'any terms to fall in with the measures of the Court', especially James's scheme to repeal the penal laws and the tests.[166] Howe's congratulatory delegation was followed by a similar one from the Anabaptists of London, led by the Baptist pastor and rich merchant William Kiffin, who had commercial ties with Holland. Both addresses were 'well received' by the prince.[167]

[162] They were John Howe, Samuel Fairclough, Samuel Stancliffe, and Richard Mayo, for whom see A. G. Matthews, *Calamy Revised* (Oxford 1934), 279–80, 188–9, 458, 347.

[163] Dr Williams's Library: MS Morrice Q, pp. 383–4. Bodl. Libr., Oxford: MS Rawlinson Letters 109, fo. 112; MS Don. c. 39, fo. 75: London, 22 Dec.; Luttrell, i. 493; Burnet, iii. 340.

[164] 'Some Account of the Humble Application of . . . Henry Lord Bishop of London with the Reverend Clergy of the City, and some of the Dissenting Ministers in it, To . . . the Prince of Orange, on Friday, September [*sic*] 21. 1688', in *A Compleat Collection of Papers, in Twelve Parts* (1689), vi. 17–18.

[165] *The Address Of The Nonconformist Ministers (In and about the City of London) To His Highness The Prince of Orange* (London: Printed for Thomas Cockerill at the Three Legs in the Poultry, over against the Stocks Market. MDCLXXXIX).

[166] Dr Williams's Library: MS Morrice Q, p. 411; H. Rogers, *The Life and Character of John Howe* (s.a.), 168, 169–75, 176–81.

[167] J. R. Woodhead, *The Rulers of London 1660–1689* (1965), 104; PRO SP 29/65, no. 9; C. E. Whiting, *Studies in English Puritanism from the Restoration to the Revolution, 1660–1688* (1931), 83, 89, 96, 100, 110, 119, 128, 181.

Small wonder that the Tories began to resent 'the countenance he gave the Dissenters', who were the Whigs' staunchest supporters, as giving 'too much cause of jealousy to the Church of England', the source of their own party strength.[168] The Tories, even more than the Whigs, were endowed with long memories when it came to reckoning up old scores. They had not forgotten that Howe, as a busy young 'presbyter', had served Oliver and Richard Cromwell as their domestic chaplain at Whitehall in the 'trouble-church' 1650s, had plagued the capital with his persistent conventicling throughout the 1670s and 1680s,[169] and had left off only to volunteer, in 1685, to go as chaplain–companion to the aged Lord Wharton on his highly suspicious travels in Holland and the Rhenish territories of the Protestant Elector of Brandenburg–Prussia.[170] Nor could they forget that Kiffin, once an apprentice to John Lilburne, had sat as MP for Middlesex in the Protectorate, and had conventicled at a violent rate ever since 1662.[171] More recently, he had fallen under suspicion of complicity in the Rye House Plot of 1683,[172] had had two grandsons executed as rebels in 1685,[173] and had collaborated with James II against the Church interest in London by accepting an aldermanic gown in August 1687.[174] Howe and Kiffin were the sort of men who gave the Tories political nightmares.

What made all of this ten times worse was William's blatant offhandedness with the Tories. The impression which they formed of him was that he was cold and distant, to the point of discourtesy.[175] Individual Tory grandees of the stature of the Earl

[168] *Clar. Corr.* ii. 278.

[169] *DNB*; Matthews, *Calamy Revised*, 279–80; Bodl. Libr., Oxford: MS Rawlinson Letters 51, fo. 126.

[170] For Howe's accompanying Wharton abroad, see Beddard, 'The Violent Party', 128–30, 133.

[171] W. Orme (ed.), *Remarkable Passages in the Life of William Kiffin* (1823), *passim*; W. L. Sachse (ed.), *The Diurnal of Thomas Rugg* (Camden Soc., 3rd ser., 91, 1961), 49, 50, 79; PRO SP 29/24, no. 44; SP 29/34, no. 76; SP 44/7, p. 233; SP 29/61, no. 112.

[172] His son-in-law Joseph Hayes, a banker, was tried for treason on a charge of remitting funds to the conspirator Sir Thomas Armstrong, in the United Provinces, but was acquitted by a jury of his fellow citizens. Luttrell, i. 318–19, 321; PRO SP 29/436, no. 54.

[173] His grandsons, William and Benjamin Hewling, were executed in Sept. 1685. PRO SP 31/2, p. 64; SP 44/336, p. 193.

[174] PRO SP 32/2, p. 44; SP 44/336, p. 194; Luttrell, i. 411.

[175] 'The Prince keeps in great grandeur at St. James's and so high that some Bishops and other gentry are waiting a whole day before he will admit

of Clarendon, King James's brother-in-law, uncle to the Princesses Mary and Anne, a former Lord Lieutenant of Ireland, and an exemplary Church of England man, found it 'very difficult to get access' to him. Even when wanting to consult him on pressing Irish business, he had often to make do with seeing him briefly or 'only in the crowd'.[176] To Clarendon's brother, Lord Rochester, William was very disobliging, reprimanding him most severely for not waiting on the Princess Mary when he had visited Spa in 1687, although he had been forbidden to do so by the king.[177] Disgusted at his wife's uncles' siding with the king in his quarrel, and having been given 'a very ill opinion' of Rochester's alleged compliance with Popery, William rashly dismissed the Hydes as 'Knaves'.[178] It was a grave mistake which did untold damage to his already precarious relations with the High-Church wing of the Tory party, and needlessly prejudiced early communication with the beleaguered Protestants of Ireland, who instinctively turned for help to Clarendon, the last Protestant Viceroy, to plead their cause at William's Court.[179] The Whig impression of the prince was the reverse of that formed by the Tories. Taciturn and cold as William undeniably was by nature, they noted that he was accessible and courteous, treating 'all persons with great affability and respect'.[180] The different impressions were, of course, two sides of the same coin. The Whigs and Tories spoke as they found. Convinced that the Whigs, unlike the Tories, would stick to him through thick and thin, and persuaded that they were in any case the more powerful of the two parties, the prince showed himself infinitely more obliging to his proven Whig supporters than he did to his potential Tory opponents.

It did not take much scrutinizing to read the signs. Clarendon was under no illusion as to why he and other Tory loyalists merited so ill a reception. It was because they were 'looked upon as not to be

them. They begin to create whispers and mutinies which I pray God to increase'. *HMC: Earl of Dartmouth*, 238: D. Sullivan to Dartmouth, [20 Dec.] 1688.

[176] *Clar. Corr.* ii. 236, 240, 243–4, 245; Evelyn, iv. 612.

[177] PRO SP 8/2, pt. 2, fos. 116–20; Dr Williams's Library: MS Morrice Q, p. 438; *Clar. Corr.* ii. 217, 227; *HMC, 15th Report, Appendix, pt. i: Earl of Dartmouth*, iii. 141, 142–3: Earl of Rochester to Dartmouth, Whitehall, 25 Dec. 1688; P. Musgrave to Dartmouth, London, 26 Dec.

[178] Foxcroft, *Halifax*, ii. 202; cf. p. 244.

[179] *Clar. Corr.* ii. 235 ff.

[180] Dr Williams's Library: MS Morrice Q, pp. 364, 368, 381.

heartily . . . in the Prince's interest'.[181] While it was true that he had gone in to the prince upon his Declaration, 'which all honest men heartily concurred in', he had not done so 'to be against the King'. Not for the first time in later seventeenth-century English politics there was a distinction drawn between 'men worthy' and 'worthy men', only this time round those whom the monarch—for such William already was in terms of the government—deemed worthy were the Whigs, not the Tories. Hearing how the prince and Whiggery prospered to the detriment of Toryism and King James, other notorious, but hitherto more cautious, London Whigs decided to leave the safety of Holland: among them the resilient Anglo-Puritan Sir Patience Ward, who as Lord Mayor had defied Charles II and his Court in 1680–1;[182] the republican-minded Congregationalist Slingsby Bethel, who as Sheriff had harried the High-Church Tory parsons of the City in 1680–1;[183] and ex-Alderman Thomas Papillon, a Huguenot deacon and a member of Shaftesbury's *ignoramus* jury, whose record of political opposition to the House of Stuart stretched back into the turbulent events of the 1640s.[184] Having booked their return passage to England on a Dutch man-of-war, they prepared to enter the vertiginous politics of the Revolution as ready-made Whig activists.[185] Before leaving the Continent Papillon took the sensible step of writing to the Mayor of Dover, his old constituency, which he had represented no fewer than three times in as many parliaments between 1679 and 1681, to solicit the votes of the freemen in the election for the forthcoming (as he thought) parliament. As an unrepentant Exclusionist, he clearly and correctly understood the message radiated from England by the welcome accorded to the prince's expedition and William's taking up with the Whigs, and responded accordingly.[186]

[181] *Clar. Corr.* ii. 242, 246; BL: MS Add. 32096, fo. 334; Bodl. Libr., Oxford: MS Rawlinson D 836, fo. 105.

[182] C. E. Whiting, 'Sir Patience Ward of Tanshelf, Lord Mayor of London', *Yorkshire Archaeological Journal*, 34 (1939), 245–72; R. R. Sharpe, *London and the Kingdom* (3 vols., 1895), ii. 419, 475, 493.

[183] Luttrell, i. 49–50, 52, 56, 96, 119, 120, 124, 129, 132, 144, 187, 209, 257; Sharpe, *London and the Kingdom*, ii. 472, 473, 475, 493.

[184] Woodhead, *Rulers of London*, 125; PRO SP 29/415, no. 144; Adm. 77/1, no. 94; Dr Williams's Library: MS Morrice Q, pp. 154, 420, 505, 654; Lacey, *Dissent and Party Politics*, 431–2; Henning, iii. 202–4.

[185] BL: MS Egerton 2717, fo. 422: 8 Jan. 1689; Luttrell, i. 503. It was at this time that John Locke also came over. This corrects Beddard, *Kingdom*, 21.

[186] A. F. W. Papillon, *Memoirs of Thomas Papillon, of London, Merchant 1623–*

If William's thoughts could be read so accurately across the Narrow Seas, and could have such a galvanizing effect on Whigs living abroad, they were even more telling in their impact on those Whigs who lived at home. William did not need to issue a new declaration of policy. Since 17 December his actions had spoken louder than any words could have done, and they lost nothing in the journalists' retelling. Described in varying amounts of detail, William's actions, along with the reactions of James II and Louis XIV, which seemed more and more belligerent, were relayed throughout the length and breadth of the kingdom by the popular press and circulating newsletters. The publication of a rash of new, cheap, weekly newspapers—the *Orange Gazette*, the *Harllum Currant*, the *London Intelligence*, the *London Mercury*, the *London Courant*, the *English Currant*, the *Universal Intelligence*—catered for the sudden upsurge in the nation's insatiable demand for political news. Most of them had a perceptible Williamite bias, and all of them were fiercely Protestant and patriotic. They temporarily augmented the official coverage of news provided by the long-established, government-controlled *London Gazette*, which continued to appear in weekly instalments during the entire revolutionary period, and quickly conformed to a Williamite stance with the prince's advent to power. Together these newspapers and a spate of ephemeral literature kept the rest of England abreast of what was happening in London and, on a more selective basis, with what was occurring in Ireland (which as a colony was of more immediate concern to the English than Scotland) and in Europe. It looked for all the world as though the old, familiar, Whig clique, which had played such a dominant role in the politics of 'No-Popery' and Exclusion, was reviving apace. In 1688–9 the county communities were constantly informed of the latest developments in the capital by a growing fraternity of journalists, pamphleteers, and press men, who made no apology for the fact that they favoured the prince's dynastic pretensions.[187]

1702 (Reading 1887), 348–9 and 349–50: 'Address to the Electors of Dover', Utrecht, 10/20 Dec. 1688; J. B. Jones, *Annals of Dover* (Dover 1916), 194, 246, 248, 384–6; BL: MS Egerton 2717, fo. 434: 19 Feb. 1689.

187 The newsmongers need to be reckoned in with the Williamite propagandists examined by L. G. Schwoerer, 'Propaganda in the Revolution of 1688–89', *American Historical Review*, 132 (1977), 843–74. The major Tory propagandist, Sir Roger L'Estrange, who had long defended James, had been committed to Newgate by the City authorities. Bodl. Libr., Oxford: MS Don. c. 39, fos. 71, 72^{v}.

For instance, wide coverage was given to William's summoning the Exclusionist MPs to advise him, including a full account in the *London Gazette*.[188] His preference for Charles II's Whigs, as against James II's Tories, as his chosen helpmates in resolving the crisis of the interregnum was, therefore, communicated to the electorate well in advance of the general election of January 1689. The proprietors of Protestant England knew full well what William expected of them when they went to the polls. To make doubly sure that his message reached the scattered constituencies there was a massive and early exodus of Whig MPs from London. By the time that the prince was ready to signify his formal acceptance of the government to the Commoners on 28 December, no more than 'about 80', out of the 220 MPs who had answered his summons on the 26th were present at St James's, 'for many were gone into the countrey to promote the choice of themselves or others for this Convention'.[189] Closer to hand, in London and Westminster, his partisans mixed freely with the citizens, advocating his cause. The *émigré* Exclusionist MP Sir William Waller was one such. The son of the Parliamentarian General and raised a Presbyterian, he had acquired a deserved notoriety as a 'priest-catcher' in the wake of the Popish Plot.[190] Recognizing that Whiggery was doomed without a sitting parliament, he had decamped to Holland in 1682, before moving further afield as a soldier of fortune in the Protestant states of Germany. Even so, he kept in touch with the Court at The Hague, and during James's reign became a discreet disseminator of Orangist views in England. In 1688 the Prince had 'expressly' sent for him from Kassel, in Hessen-Nassau, to attend him on his expedition to England, intending 'to make use of him in his free parliament'.[191] No sooner had Waller reached town, on 19 December, than he 'appeared publiquely amongst his former accquaintance'.[192] By dutifully going the rounds of his old haunts, frequenting 'coffee-house, church, and meeting', he managed to

[188] *London Gazette*, no. 2414 (27–31 Dec.); *Universal Intelligence*, nos. 5 and 6 (22–6 and 26–9 Dec.); *English Currant*, no. 6 (26–8 Dec.).

[189] Dr Williams's Library: MS Morrice Q, p. 406.

[190] PRO Adm. 77/1, nos. 85, 108; PRO SP 29/416, no. 36; Luttrell, i. 7, 29; cf. pp. 24, 39, 69, 74, 78, 84, 91, 96.

[191] PRO SP 29/415, no. 8; SP 44/64, p. 203; Devon Record Office, Exeter: Courtenay Papers: ⟨Sir⟩ W⟨illiam⟩ W⟨aller⟩ to his brother-in-law, Sir William Courtenay, Utrecht, 8 Jan. 1687/8. This has been prepared for publication; Beddard, *Kingdom*, 21; Henning, iii. 660.

[192] BL: MS Sloane 3929, fo. 120: London, 18 Dec. 1688.

combine his old vocation as Protestant sleuth extraordinary with arresting absconding ultra-Tory lawyers and acting as unofficial electoral agent for the local Whig candidates. His canvassing of votes in Westminster was so energetic that it was rumoured that he himself would again stand for Burgess there, as he had successfully done twice before in 1680 and 1681. His efforts were most effective among the Dissenters—among the Presbyterians of Vincent Alsop's Tothill Street congregation especially—as they had always been.[193]

IV

By the New Year William bestrode the capital like a colossus. His political influence was pervasive, encouraging friends to undertake fresh endeavours on his behalf, and reminding would-be opponents that he was not to be easily denied. His ambition was by now as clear as the noonday sun. 'The Prince declared that he had noe designe for the crown', observed Sir John Reresby wryly, 'and yet sought it all he could.'[194] His public avowal of Exclusion had quite revolutionized the franchisal politics of the metropolis. For the first time since February 1681 the Whigs functioned as an efficient electoral force. With the Dissenting vote solidly behind them, they worked wonders in the general election for the Convention. At the hustings for the City of London, held on 9 January 1689, the liverymen voted in four Whigs in place of the four Tories elected in 1685. More amazingly, they were returned unopposed. The City Tories, despite their preponderance in the Court of Aldermen, had neither the courage, nor in most cases the will, to challenge them in Common Hall. They were completely overawed by their rivals' superior standing in the prince's affection, and were handicapped by their own wish to safeguard the Protestant interest in government—an interest which, in London, they found impossible to distinguish, in electoral terms, from that of the prince and his adherents. Considering the infamy of the Whigs' candidates, the lack of

[193] BL: MS Add. 36707, fo. 57; Dr Williams's Library: MS Morrice Q, pp. 337, 392; PRO, Adm. 77/1, nos. 48, 81, 82; PRO SP 29/417, no. 38; Lacey, *Dissent and Party Politics*, 217, 221, 453–4; *Orange Gazette*, no. 5 (10–17 Jan. 1688/9). R. A. Beddard, 'Vincent Alsop and the Emancipation of Restoration Dissent', *Journal of Ecclesiastical History*, 24 (1973), 161–84.

[194] *Memoirs of Reresby*, 553.

Tory opposition was indeed noteworthy, for, to echo Clarendon's on-the-spot comment, 'remarkable men they were' that the City had chosen.[195] Sir Patience Ward, Sir Robert Clayton, William Love, and Thomas Pilkington, whose records put them among the top dozen of the City's most committed Whigs, could be relied on to denounce the fallen King.[196] With the exception of Ward, who had served as Burgess for his native Pontefract, they had represented the City in all three of the Exclusionist Parliaments and had commanded unprecedented civic support for the key Whig demands: James's removal from the succession as a Papist and a measure of ease for Protestant Dissenters. By 1689 all four of them were confirmed Williamites, intent on making the prince king in James's stead and on freeing Dissent from the operation of the penal laws.

The political antecedents of the new Members speak for themselves. Ward we have already encountered as the Whig Lord Mayor who in 1683 had taken refuge in Holland to escape the pillory as a convicted perjurer. Though King James had seen fit to pardon him in 1687, in an ill-considered bid to recruit his support for his revised policy of Indulgence, Ward had not reciprocated, preferring to remain detached in the safety of retirement.[197] The others, who had braved Tory displeasure by staying put, were also tarred with the same brush of opposition to the Stuarts. Sir Robert Clayton, dubbed by Evelyn the 'prince of citizens', was a millionaire financier who had broken with the Court over the economic grievances of the City as long ago as 1673. A critic of France and a Low-Churchman of tolerationist tendencies, he had gravitated towards the 'country party', where he took up with Shaftesbury and the London Dissenters.[198] In 1679 he became the first Whig Lord Mayor. On the miscarriage of Exclusion in parliament he went on to defend the City charter

[195] *Clar. Corr.* ii. 243. *Universal Intelligence*, nos. 10, 11 (5–8, 8–10 Jan. 1688/9); *London Gazette*, no. 2417 (7–10 Jan. 1688/9).

[196] City of London Records Office, Guildhall, London: Repertory 94, p. 80. Bodl. Libr., Oxford: MS Don. c. 39, fo. 85: 10 Jan. 1688/9; Woodhead, *Rulers of London*, 170–1, 48, 110, 130.

[197] Luttrell, i. 258–9, 431; PRO SP 29/434, no. 611; 29/436, no. 54; SP 44/54, p. 378; SP 44/337, p. 351. See above, p. 57.

[198] Evelyn, iv. 121, 147, 185–6; Woodhead, *Rulers of London*, 48; D. C. Coleman, 'London Scriveners and the Estate Market in the later Seventeenth Century', *Economic History Review*, 2nd ser., 4 (1951–2), 221–30. See above, pp. 5–6.

against Charles II's *quo warranto* proceedings in 1682–3.[199] He was removed from the Corporation in 1683, and prudently abstained from politics thereafter.[200] Reinstated as an alderman on the restitution of the charter in October 1688, he declined to act;[201] at any rate not until James's withdrawal on 11 December, when, as the leading Whig in the Lieutenancy of London, he threw the weight of his very considerable influence behind the move to speed William's entry into the capital.[202] Later, on James's return to Whitehall from Kent on 16 December, he prevailed with the Common Council to refuse the king the City's protection to remain in London, thereby crippling James's efforts to resume the government. By any yardstick his was a major contribution to the success of the dynastic revolution.

William Love's opposition to the Stuart family was of even longer duration than that of Clayton. A rich Levantine trader and a dogmatic Congregationalist, he had been a Cromwellian Councillor of State and had served the City as Sheriff in 1659–60.[203] Having opposed the restoration of the monarchy in 1660, he had been removed from the Corporation by Charles II in 1662,[204] though he continued to represent the City in the Cavalier Parliament in spite of his refusal to take the Anglican sacrament.[205] Thomas Pilkington, stigmatized by Clarendon as 'a disturber of mankind',[206] was a Turkey merchant and a known favourer of the Presbyterians. His shrievalty in 1681–2 had been marred by acts of violence and by an unrestrained personal animus directed against James as heir to the throne. Charles II had shown his resentment of his conduct by denying him the customary knight-

[199] Luttrell, i. 22, 25, 70, 76, 83, 84, 91, 106–7, 158, 194, 210 ff.

[200] PRO SP 29/417, no. 167.

[201] PRO SP 44/338, p. 104; Luttrell, i. 471; *Clar. Corr.* ii. 224.

[202] Beddard, *Kingdom*, 40, 52, 54 and 173: app. 5.

[203] Sachse (ed.), *Diurnal of Thomas Rugg*, 29; Whiting, *Studies in English Puritanism*, 177; Lacey, *Dissent and Party Politics*, 419–20; F. P. and M. M. Verney (eds.), *Memoirs of the Verney Family* (2 vols., 1907), ii. 100; Woodhead, *Rulers of London*, 110.

[204] PRO SP 44/3, pp. 42, 59; SP 44/4, pp. 110, 123: Charles II to the Lord Mayor and Commissioners for regulating the Corporation of London, Whitehall, 5 May, and Hampton Court, 16 June 1662.

[205] At the hustings for the Cavalier Parliament shouts of 'no bishop' had helped to carry his election. PRO SP 29/32, nos. 82–95, 97–121, 1221, 123 ff.

[206] *Clar. Corr.* ii. 481.

hood conferred on sheriffs of London.[207] Pilkington subsequently spent over three years in gaol, having been condemned in an action of *scandalum magnatum* for maligning James as the incendiary responsible for firing the City in 1666.[208] At his release from prison, following King James's remission of his £100,000 fine in June 1686, Clarendon thought that 'such a fellow . . . ought to be watched' rather than pardoned.[209] Yet, for all his instinctive distrust of him, the earl did not foresee that Pilkington's private and public recovery would be mounted, like that of the Whigs generally, on the broad back of anti-Popery. He had no inkling, any more than any Tory had, that before the decade was out he would once again be the elected representative of the Protestant City of London—a political tribute posthumously paid to a departed Popish monarch.[210]

The London election proved something of a trend-setter. On 12 December a local news-writer reported, with evident satisfaction, that 'the election⟨s⟩ for the ensueing Convention goe on with great eunanimity', adding that 'that for London was . . . a leading card to others', and 'soe it afords matter for many reflections'.[211] On 21 December the neighbouring City of Westminster followed suit. A Tory stronghold in 1685, it too reverted to the Whigs in 1689. There the inhabitants elected two resolute Exclusionists—Sir William Pulteney, a cherisher of Dissenters, and Captain Philip Howard, 'an Eminent Protestant Sufferer' and the brother of the arch-Williamite courtier Sir Robert Howard —in an unruly seven-sided contest, in which one of the former Tory Members from 1685 stood for re-election and was rejected.[212]

[207] Luttrell, i. 87, 102, 110, 129, 157, 172, 176, 181–3, 185, 198–200, 207 ff.; PRO SP 29/415, nos. 119, 181; SP 29/416, no. 25; SP 29/417, nos. 110, 166; PRO Adm. 77/1, nos. 105, 107, 137; SP 44/62, p. 317.

[208] Luttrell, i. 192, 195, 236, 240, 241, 258–9.

[209] PRO Adm. 77/3, no. 11: London, 26 June 1686; Luttrell, i. 382; *Clar. Corr.* ii. 481.

[210] On 20 Mar. 1689 Pilkington was also elected Lord Mayor of London. Luttrell, i. 513. For his subsequent career, see Sharpe, *London and the Kingdom*, ii. 547, 551, 553, 555; and G. S. de Krey, *A Fractured Society* (Oxford 1985), pp. 16, 35, 37, 52, 53, 58 ff.

[211] Again, the newspapers relayed the outcome of the election to the provinces. Bodl. Libr., Oxford: MS Don. c. 39, fo. 87.

[212] PRO Adm. 77/1, nos. 81, 82; BL: MS Egerton 2717, fo. 421; Dr Williams's Library: MS Morrice Q, pp. 419–20; Jones, *First Whigs*, 178; *Orange Gazette*, no. 3 (3–7 Jan. 1688/9); *Universal Intelligence*, no. 10 (5–8 Jan. 1688/9). Henning, iii. 302–4; ii. 594–5.

There was an abundance of advice from Whig pamphleteers on how to vote. Electors were urged to shun the 'betrayers' of municipal liberties and those who were guilty of compliance with an 'arbitrary' Court. Support was to be pledged to 'zealous' Protestants and uncorrupted 'patriots'. The language was loaded with partisan innuendo, highly reminiscent of the era of 'No-Popery' that had ushered in the politics of Exclusion. William's well-advertised preference for working with Whig MPs, coupled with the fact that many elections were held within sound and sight of anti-Catholic rioting and the stereotypical 'Irish Fear', which in the last weeks of December 1688 had swept the country from south to north,[213] had the reassuring effect of closing the ranks of the electors and discouraging contests at the polls, which were markedly fewer than usual: fewer than had occurred in 1679, 1681, and 1685, or were to occur in 1690.[214]

The general election of 1689 was deliberately uncontentious for it took place under the influence of fear—the obsessive, haunting fear of Popery, which continued to incite measures against Catholics in the metropolis and provinces well into the New Year.[215] Only occasionally and then fleetingly did the issue of the succession raise its head in the localities,[216] though it was widely, and at times hotly, debated in the press and in private. The unity which undeniably characterized the nation at the polls was fundamentally confessional rather than political, Protestant rather than partisan, and that alone was dynastically portentous.[217] Nevertheless, as in the earlier period of the Popish Plot, Protestant militancy stimulated the return of Whigs, Low-Churchmen, and Dissenters, as the self-proclaimed asserters of Protestantism and the readily identified enemies of Popery and France. This

[213] G. H. Jones, 'The Irish Fright of 1688', *Bulletin of the Institute of Historical Research*, 55 (1982), 48–57; Beddard, *Kingdom*, 45, 82–4, and 177–8: app. 13.

[214] J. H. Plumb, 'The Elections to the Convention Parliament of 1689', *Cambridge Historical Journal*, 5 (1937), 235–54; H. Horwitz, *Parliament, Policy and Politics in the Reign of William III* (Manchester 1977), 329–34: app. A.

[215] R. Steele, *Tudor and Stuart Proclamations 1485–1714* (2 vols., Oxford 1910), nos. 3949–50, 3953a. Cited below as Proclamations. Corporation of London Records Office, Guildhall, London: Repertory 94, p. 8; Luttrell, i. 493, 499.

[216] H. Horwitz, 'Parliament and the Glorious Revolution', *Bulletin of the Institute of Historical Research*, 47 (1974), 41–2.

[217] The Whig Morrice estimated the 'recurrers', i.e., those favourable to James's restoration, 'not to be above one hundred in the whole House'. Dr Williams's Library: MS Morrice Q, p. 445.

national upsurge of Protestant feeling accommodated many Tories, especially those who had openly withstood the Popish Court, but it actively encouraged the political recovery of the Whigs as 'persons ill-affected to the unhappy King',[218] and simultaneously confirmed that the dynastic initiative would be theirs in the Convention, as the Prince had hoped and intended that it should be.[219]

In accordance with his invasion Declaration, William was punctilious in respecting the freedom of the election. He declined to entrust the delivery of his circular letters to private hands; he ordered his troops into barracks for the duration of the poll; and he appears not to have repeated the injunction he gave on 12 December to Danby and his Yorkshire cohorts to keep 'their inclinations' for him in the coming contest.[220] According to the Whig Roger Morrice, the elections were conducted 'with great regularity and fairness, and with less violence and arbitrariness than has been known'—a sly partisan thrust at the 'irregular' general election of 1685, which had produced James's hated Tory Parliament.[221] As predicted, the Whigs' success in the capital announced their return in force to Westminster. Despite some disappointments in the constituencies, they commanded 'a comfortable majority' when the Convention met on 22 January. With the adherence of the revolted Williamite or Court Tories, they numbered 319 against their adversaries' 232.[222] It was a remarkable achievement. Yet, their greatest advantage over the Tories lay less in their numerical strength than in their fixity of purpose. They were united in pressing for James's permanent exclusion

218 Mulgrave, ii. 85–6.

219 The Williamite Earl of Bristol, fresh from Dorset, reported at Court that the newly returned Members 'will make him king'. Huygens, 'Journaal', 67. The Whigs were not universally successful, even in the London area: e.g., Middlesex, where the Tories (Sir Charles Gerard and Ralph Hawtrey) were re-elected on 11 Jan., and the Whigs (Sir Robert Peyton and Thomas Johnson) were defeated, contrary to expectation. *Orange Gazette*, no. 4 (7–10 Jan. 1688/9).

220 *Universal Intelligence*, no. 5 (5–8 Jan. 1688/9); Steele, *Proclamations*, no. 3945; Dr Williams's Library: MS Morrice Q, p. 348; BL: MS Egerton 2717, fos. 424, 426: 15 and 19 Jan. 1689; J. H. Plumb and A. Simpson, 'A Letter of William, Prince of Orange, to Danby on the Flight of James II', *Cambridge Historical Journal*, 5 (1937), 107–8. Cf. Browning, *Danby*, ii. 155.

221 Dr Williams's Library: MS Morrice Q, p. 436. Cf. Grey, *Debates*, ix. 4. Notwithstanding these partisan opinions, there were irregularities, see *The Autobiography of Sir John Bramston* (Camden Soc., 1845), 346.

222 Henning, i. 42, 47, 54, 82.

from the throne by law, and, to that end, they were ably and confidently led by a tireless band of the prince's closest confidants: Powle, Howard, Capel, Treby, Pollexfen, Maynard, Wharton, Wildman, Harbord, and Lord Wiltshire, the men who by their sheer determination had brought him within reach of James's crown. They were well supported by Boscawen, Garroway, Pulteney, Pilkington, Love, Ward, Clayton, and a host of old and new Exclusionists. In the House of Commons they presented a dramatic contrast to the Tories, who were deeply divided, diffident, and in disarray.

Sentiment in London had declared itself in favour of James's exclusion early on, as the Whigs and their allies, building on the temporary, but unanimously effected transfer of government to William, familiarized all and sundry with their revolutionary notion of 'a demise' or 'cession'. By late December 1688 'a demise was granted by all parties at their meetings and caballs' about the town—all, that is, save the loyalists, and even they were in the process of lowering their sights from a restoration to a regency on James's behalf, without any guarantee that the king would accept their planned compromise with the prince. Before the Old Year was spent the three main platforms on which the argument for 'a demise' came to rest had been worked out. They were 'forfeiture', 'abdication and desertion' (which were either lumped together or treated as alternatives), and 'incapacity'. It was not the desired end—James's exclusion—but the political reasoning leading to that end which occasioned differences of opinion, though at no time did any one line of reasoning necessarily exclude another. The more doctrinaire Whigs (not all of whom were fully fledged contractualists) favoured the concept of 'forfeiture', arguing that James 'had broken the fundamentall lawes of the constitution by his dispensing power and otherwise', and had therefore forfeited his right to be king. Most Whigs and some Tories preferred to think that James had ceased to be king 'by abdication and desertion of his government and his trust': a convenient fiction which they strove to sustain by dwelling on his earlier and allegedly voluntary flight from Whitehall on 11 December, in an effort to deflect domestic and European attention from William's controversial expulsion of the king from London on 18 December. Finally, Whigs and Tories (though not, of course, the die-hard loyalists) agreed that James had lost his right to rule 'by incapacity', for, they maintained, 'he has no capacity to govern Protestants, because his religion as a Papist obliges him in conscience, and under the paine of damnation, to burn all hereticks when he is able'.[223] To William it mattered not a whit which of these arguments prevailed with Englishmen, so long as they recognized that the throne was vacant and allowed his adherents to clinch his claim to occupy the empty throne.

In making good the prince's claim his London partisans felt that they could count on support from a wide and powerful spectrum of political life in all three of the British kingdoms: from 'the generality of the Scotch nation', who, as long-repressed Presbyterians, were credited with harbouring anti-episcopalian and anti-Tory as well as anti-Catholic feelings; from 'the greatest part of Ireland', by which was meant, not the mass of the Catholic population, but the wealthy Protestant planters and absentee proprietors of England and Scotland, who were on the point of losing their estates and everything that they owned in Ireland, if the Catholic Lord Deputy, the Earl of Tyrconnell, held out for King James; and from 'all the Dissenters and W⟨h⟩igs in England, and many of the best interested clergymen in London', who had declared themselves the implacable foes of the Church of Rome and had set their faces against James's return.[224] The common factor uniting these scattered and ostensibly discrepant elements was their common commitment to 'the Protestant Reformed interest'—the cause for which William had hazarded so much in making his 'great attempt for the redeeming of this Kingdome' and its dependencies from 'Popery and arbitrary government.'[225] For more than a century anti-Catholicism had been an indelible characteristic of British society, one that was shared by all classes. Its presence, whether overt or covert, had informed every stage of James II's undoing, just as it had underpinned every step of William of Orange's advancement to the throne. The king's actions and those of the prince had possessed everyone 'with a strong opinion of the Protestant religion's being endangered by

[223] Dr Williams's Library: MS Morrice Q, p. 393.

[224] Ibid., 407.

[225] For the London clergy's assault on Catholicism, see E. Carpenter, *The Protestant Bishop*, pp. 67 ff., and *Thomas Tenison* (1948), 36–78. N. Sykes, *William Wake, Archbishop of Canterbury* (2 vols., Cambridge 1957), i. 19 ff.

the one, and protected by the other'.[226] For most of Britain the dynastic issue had become inseparable from that of religion.

In calculating the dynastic stakes the Dissenters' support for the prince could be safely assumed. They had been 'universally fixed' in their regard for William and Mary since 1687, having promised around the time of Dijkvelt's embassy to England that they 'would inflexibly do all in their power to promote' their succession 'against all others', should King James die.[227] But the accession to the prince's cause of the Anglican clergy of London was an unexpected bonus in the Revolution, for, traditionally, they had been among the most fervent servants of the restored House of Stuart. The Williamites were naturally exultant to discover that 'many of the Tory clergy' had not 'gone over to the bishops' in their schemes for a regency, but were well-disposed to the prince.[228] The suspension of Bishop Compton in 1686 had not prevented the clergy of his diocese from labouring to do down Catholicism, which from their pulpits and from the printing-press they had systematically reviled as rank idolatry, 'the spawn of Anti-Christ'. For them the impact of James's catholicizing policies, spearheaded by the London Catholic Mission, had been a traumatic experience, causing them to re-examine and re-evaluate the Church of England's teaching on passive obedience and non-resistance.[229] Having launched and successfully sustained a savage Protestant counter-offensive, which had incidentally contributed to the king's downfall by undermining the nation's trust in the rule of a Catholic monarch, they quite deliberately and cold-bloodedly led the way in omitting the state

[226] Mulgrave, ii. 83; *Memoirs of Reresby*, 561.

[227] Dr Williams's Library: MS Morrice Q, pp. 124–5; University of Nottingham: Portland MSS, PwA 2127c. Cf. J. Muilenburg, 'The Embassy of Everaard van Weede, Lord of Dykvelt, to England in 1687', *University Studies of the University of Nebraska*, 20 (1920), 85–161.

[228] Dr Williams's Library: MS Morrice Q, pp. 390, 447, 450. Burnet, now 'in seeming power' at Court, was elected Lecturer at St Mary le Bow, and actively campaigned for William among his brethren. BL: MS Add. 29563, fos. 377, 376^{v}; BL: MS Egerton 2717, fo. 425. His highly influential tract, *An Enquiry Into The Present State of Affairs* (1689), was 'Published by Authority' of the prince. Bishop Barlow's copy carries his note on the title-page: 'This paper proves that we owe allegiance to the Prince of Orange, now beeinge in possession of the crowne.' Bodl. Libr., Oxford: B 16. 7. Linc., item 5.

[229] R. A. Beddard, 'Observations of a London Clergyman on the Revolution of 1688–9: Being an Excerpt from the Autobiography of Dr William Wake', *Guildhall Miscellany*, 2 (1967), 408–9, 411, 413.

prayers for the Catholic Prince of Wales in the days following James's withdrawal to France.[230] From then on there was to be no turning back. Advised by the *émigré* clergyman Gilbert Burnet, who during his exile in Holland had managed to keep his finger on the clerical pulse of the capital, William took his newly appointed chaplains 'out of the most considerable Deanes and divines in and about the City', thus ensuring their lasting attachment to his interest.[231] His selection of *coram principe* preachers was equally sage, and his regular attendance at their sermons in the Chapel at St James's helped to establish his Anglican credentials by contradicting ultra-Tory suggestions that he was scarcely better than a Calvinist fanatic.[232]

The political understanding that rapidly developed between the two great historic professions of the capital—the clergy and the lawyers—also redounded to William's long-term advantage, as the City incumbents first accepted for themselves and then went on to propagate in others the *de facto* arguments formulated by their near neighbours in the Inns of Court. Under the guidance of such Williamite luminaries as Recorder Treby, Serjeant Maynard, Henry Pollexfen, Sir John Holt, Serjeant William Rawlinson, Sir Robert Atkyns, Anthony Keck, William Petyt, and the up-and-coming barrister John Somers, the legal profession swung solidly behind the prince's claim to the throne.[233] The political disgrace which had finally overtaken James's judiciary made it but a pale shadow of its former overmighty self.[234] Sunk into

[230] Luttrell, i. 496; Dr Williams's Library: MS Morrice Q, pp. 406, 430. For Compton's lead in altering the other state prayers, see ibid. 415, 426. Those who continued the old prayers had to face 'a great clamour ‹raised› against us not only by the mob, but from all sorts of people'. Bodl. Libr., Oxford: MS Add. C 180, pp. 1–5: 'Reasons against leaving the Prince of Wales out of the Prayers'. Mazure, *Histoire de la Révolution*, iii. 288.

[231] They were Burnet, Horneck, Freeman, Wake, Kidder, Gee, Brograve, and Birch. Dr Williams's Library: MS Morrice Q, p. 425; Luttrell, i. 497.

[232] BL: MS Egerton 2717, fo. 418^{v}: London, 27 Dec. 1688; Luttrell, i. 490, 492. Mazure, *Histoire de la Révolution*, iii. 288.

[233] Burnet, iii. 361; Beddard, *Kingdom*, 40, 52, 53, 149, 151, 153, 154, 156, 171, 179, 180, 188, 190, 197, 198. See also M. Landon, *The Triumph of the Lawyers: Their Role in English Politics, 1678–1689* (Tuscaloosa, Alabama 1970), 221–40; L. G. Schwoerer, 'The Role of the Lawyers in the Revolution of 1688–9', in R. Schnur (ed.), *Die Rolle der Juristen bei der Entstehung des Modernen Staates* (Berlin 1986), 473–98.

[234] A. F. Havighurst, 'James II and the Twelve Men in Scarlet', *Law Quarterly Review*, 69 (1953), 522–46. For their eclipse, see BL: MS Add. 36707, fo. 49: 27 Nov. 1688; Dr Williams's Library: MS Morrice Q, pp. 437, 384–5, 388, 390. Browning,

disrepute and depleted by desertions, it was unable to resist the swing against the king. Consequently, the London lawyers came out strongly in favour of William as the possessor of power, who had been acknowledged by the Lords and Commoners in the exigency created by James's removal from government. They gave it as their considered professional opinion 'that the people were not bound to examine the titles of their princes, but were to submit to him that was in possession'.[235] For them possession, even usurping possession, was, it seems, nine-tenths of the law, and for warranty they cited obscure fifteenth-century precedents: Bagot's case of 1469 (9 *Edvardi* IV, *Pas.* pls. 2, 20; *Trin.* pl. 3) and the so-called *de facto* Act of 1495 (*Henrici* VII, *cap.* 1).[236] Their unqualified verdict had a potent influence on 'the eminent clergy of the City', and through them on the laity of the Church of England, who constituted 'the most considerable and most substantial body of the nation'.[237] Even had the loyalist bishops and peers succeeded in getting the regency project accepted in the Lords, it is seriously to be doubted whether they could have carried the bulk of the nation with them, for, without the London clergy to give them popular support, they were looked on in the City as no more than so many 'single persons'.[238]

Just how the City of London—which we have been recently told 'did nothing to bring about the revolution'[239]—continued to back the prince to the hilt in his bid for the crown was again demonstrated by its unhesitating response to his appeal for help in January 1689. In spite of the establishment of 'a public purse' among his English adherents, and the seizure of the king's customs and excise revenues as he marched through the southern counties from Exeter to London, William's funds were approaching exhaustion. Certain it was that the moneys raised through the Amsterdam bankers, or what little remained of them, could

Danby, ii. 153. Beddard, *Kingdom*, 22. For William's list of offending lawyers, see PRO SP 8/2, pt. 2, fos. 135–6.

[235] Beddard, 'Observations of a London clergyman on the Revolution', 411–12, 415–17.

[236] S. B. Chrimes, *English Constitutional Ideas in the Fifteenth Century* (Cambridge 1936), 4, 16, 31–2, 55–6, and 369–70: app. 53. G. R. Elton, *The Tudor Constitution* (Cambridge 1960), pp. 4–5.

[237] *Clar. Corr.* ii. 238.

[238] Dr Williams's Library: MS Morrice Q, pp. 431, 447, 450.

[239] E. Cruickshanks, in Henning, i. 310. Equally mistaken is the view that the capital saw 'little disorder' in the Revolution. Ibid., i. 314.

not meet the huge and recurrent bills for two armies and two fleets: his own and King James's, which had come over to him.[240] The state of the Exchequer was also parlous. It was said that when William met the Lords of the Treasury 'about setling the revenue' on 29 December, he found that there was less than £1,000 in the Court of Receipt—such had been the disruption caused by two months of military alarms and political uncertainty.[241] Charged with the costly responsibility of carrying on government, he stood in dire need of cash.[242] On 8 January he wrote to the Lord Mayor and Aldermen of London, asking the City to make him a loan of £200,000 for the payment of the forces and for defraying the expense of military preparations to go to 'the defence of the distressed Protestants in Ireland', as the Assembly of Peers had recommended him to do in their address of 25 December.[243] The response of the Lord Mayor and Court of Aldermen was as instantaneous as it was generous. They 'unanimousely resolved . . . to serve His Highness . . . to the utmost of their power', and immediately agreed to raise the loan in full. They accepted the proffered security, based on the anticipated yield of Crown finances, but did not wait to settle arrangements 'with the officers of the publicke revenue'.[244] Instead, in what was plainly intended to be seen as a gesture of trust and goodwill, they straight away closed on the prince's word of honour and got on with the business of raising the large capital sum required of them.

The City's enthusiastic reception of William's appeal for financial aid in early January 1689 stood in stark contrast to its outright rejection of James's plea for physical protection in late December 1688.[245] That, politically, speaks for itself. But more impressive in some ways was the alacrity with which the Protestant citizenry at large responded to the prince's needs, once they were made known to them by the civic authorities. The City Chamberlain,

[240] Luttrell, i. 494.

[241] Bodl. Libr., Oxford: MS Don. c. 39, fo. 83^{v}: London, 29 Dec. 1688. Another report put the sum at £4,000. BL: MS Egerton 2717, fo. 419.

[242] *The Declaration of His Highness the Prince of Orange, For the better Collecting the Publick Revenue*, St James's, 2 Jan. 1688/9; Steele, *Proclamations*, no. 3942.

[243] *Clar. Corr.* ii. 243; Luttrell, i. 495; Beddard, *Kingdom*, 166.

[244] Corporation of London Records Office, Guildhall, London: Journal 50, fo. 365: 8 Jan. 1688/9. Sir Patience Ward was the first named in the committee appointed 'to acquaint His Highnesse with the said vote'.

[245] For the City's refusal, see Beddard, *Kingdom*, 53–4, 63 and above, p. 62.

Sir Peter Rich, soon found that the course authorized for collecting the contributions from the inhabitants of each of the City wards was 'allmost rendered needless by people thronging in to make subscriptions'. It was reported that at Guildhall there were 'not hands enough to receive the summes of money that flowe in . . . soe that a few dayes will raise such a summe as will be more then suffic⟨i⟩ent to supply the Prince's occation'.[246] between 12 January and 22 March the Chamber of London, which in this as in other emergencies acted as the City's clearing house, paid £185,675 into the Exchequer for William's use.[247] The prompt raising of the loan, like the uncontested election of four Williamite Whigs to serve in the Convention, was a convincing vote of confidence from the City in William's Protestant government—a government which Whig and Tory aldermen, Dissenters and Anglicans, and ordinary well-to-do Londoners, male and female, were not only happy to support, but eager to perpetuate.[248] As yet James's final fate had not irretrievably soured Tory feeling.

Well before the Convention met on 22 January to deliberate 'the State of the Nation', the prince's position was politically impregnable, and he knew it. On 30 December 1688, two days after he had accepted the administration of government, he had bluntly told Halifax that 'hee was sure of one thing; hee would not stay in England, if King James came again', adding for good measure, and 'with the strongest asseverations, that hee would go, if they went about to make him Regent'.[249] He was not prepared to be the pawn of those mercurial, blow-hot, blow-cold, Tory politicians who, like Danby and Bishop Compton, had invited him in to sort out the intractable problems posed by James's Popery, only to promote his wife's succession to the throne, once he had got rid of the king; or who, like the Earl of Abingdon and Sir Edward Seymour, had rallied to his cause, only to draw back in horror when confronted with the unpalatable fact of usurpation. William had made the mistake of rashly assuming that 'the King's going away', as he and his Dutch favourites

[246] Bodl. Libr., Oxford: MS Don. c. 39, fo. 87 (MS has *flowes*); MS Ballard 45, fo. 23a; *Clar. Corr.* ii. 243; Luttrell, i. 495, 497; Huygens, 'Journaal', 64.

[247] Corporation of London Records Office, Guildhall, London: MSS 133/25: Ward subscription lists; ibid. 40/34, 35: Loan accounts.

[248] Preliminary findings based on current research into the City's loan, which I hope to publish.

[249] Foxcroft, *Halifax*, ii. 203–4.

tactfully called James's expulsion, 'had totally altered the state of affairs',[250] to the extent that the whole of Protestant England, Tory and Whig, would automatically agree that the crown should be his, and his alone. The views of Hans Willem Bentinck and Halifax, the closest of his confidants, suggest that he expected nothing less than sole unconditional sovereignty. But such cavalier disregard for the prior hereditary claim of his wife was resented by his more conservative followers, including William Herbert, who had drawn his sword 'on the Prince's side', and Gilbert Burnet, who had accompanied him from Holland, both of whom were, it should be remembered, ex-Tories, not Whigs.[251] It took time and effort on the part of William and his adherents to work out an acceptable dynastic formula that answered his determination to rule as king, while taking into account the position of James's daughters, Mary and Anne. Though these dynastic tensions inevitably found an outlet in the debates of the hereditary chamber of the Convention, they were not settled there, still less in the House of Commons, but in a little-known series of informal meetings between the prince and the leading revolutionary magnates in and about the Court.

V

It is one of the more persistent errors of the Whig interpretation of history that it insists on presenting the Revolution of 1688 as a parliamentary revolution, when it was not. Notwithstanding the publication in 1988 of a so-called *Parliamentary History of the Glorious Revolution*,[252] as part of the singularly ill-informed tercentenary 'celebrations' sanctioned by the two Houses of Parliament, the error cannot be allowed to go unchecked. Although the

[250] *Clar. Corr.* ii. 246. Burnet thought similarly: 'Now the scene was altered, and new counsels were to be taken.' Burnet, iii. 354.

[251] Before the New Year it was said that there were 'differences or warme debates between the Prince . . . and the nobility, as if His Highnesse already tooke upon him contrary to his First Declaration'. BL: MS Sloane 3929, fo. 212. William's demands landed him in difficulties of his own making. On 14/24 Jan. 1689 Dijkvelt reported that he 'aensicht soo wel niet en stondt als te voren. Dat hij soo veel muyse-nesten en affaires in sijn hooft hadde, dat het schrickelijck was, exaggerende dat tot een reys of twee toe'. Huygens, 'Journaal', 68; Mulgrave, ii. 86 (it was not Admiral Herbert as stated in Pinkham, *Respectable Revolution*, 222).

[252] D. L. Jones, *A Parliamentary History of the Glorious Revolution* (HMSO, 1988) is an otherwise useful reprint of contemporary accounts of the opening sessions of the Convention of 1689.

last months of 1688 had seen a strong and growing demand for a parliament on the part of the political nation,[253] and although King James had twice made up his mind to call a parliament, first for 27 November 1688, then for 15 January 1689,[254] only to change his mind later on, no parliament ever sat during the revolutionary period. To regard the Convention as the parliament that decided the issue of the succession is to mistake the legal status and political function of that irregular revolutionary body. As a result of dynastic revolution—that is, of William's calculated deposition of King James on 18 December—England was a monarchy without a monarch, and, far worse, a hereditary monarchy without any lawful means of remedying that deficiency. The Convention was, as its name informs us, very definitely not a parliament. It was defective in its origin, in that it was not summoned on the king's writs, for those which James had not destroyed had been set aside by the Assembly of Peers.[255] It was also defective in its composition, for by constitutional definition a parliament is a trinitarian body, consisting of king, lords, and commons, and by general consent there was no king in being when it met on 22 January 1689.[256] To lose sight of these basic facts is to ignore the revolutionary situation in which Englishmen found themselves in what was widely termed an interregnum.[257] That the Convention was, in Lord Nottingham's words, 'the nearest to a free parliament' that could be devised in the circumstances did not make it one; any more than similarities of form and procedure between it and a properly constituted parliament, lawfully summoned by a reigning monarch, could make it one.[258] Moreover, the Convention was not the parent, but the offspring, of dynastic revolution. William, already acting as the ruler of the country, but not yet as king, summoned the Convention in much

[253] Jones, *Revolution in England*, 298 ff.; M. Ashley, *The Glorious Revolution of 1688* (1966), 166, 168 ff.; Carswell, *Descent on England*, 195, 204–5.

[254] Steele, *Proclamations*, nos. 3873, 3876, 3909.

[255] Beddard, *Kingdom*, 32, 34, 160, 161.

[256] The Whig revolutionaries argued against the necessity of royal writs, but William knew better. 'The Legality Of the Convention-Parliament, Though not called by Writ', in *The Works Of The Right Honourable Henry late L. Delamer, And Earl of Warrington* (1694), 510–11; *The Present Convention, A Parliament* (1689); Burnet, iii. 342. For William's view, see Müller, *Wilhelm III und Waldeck*, ii. 125.

[257] Burnet, iii. 346; cf. ibid., 342–6; [Burnet], *An Enquiry Into The Present State of Affairs*, 133; BL: MS Add. 36707, fo. 53: 25 Dec. 1688.

[258] Beddard, *Kingdom*, 161.

the same spirit as James had summoned 'the tool called Parliament'[259] on his accession to the throne in 1685—namely, to do his bidding. And that is just what it did in respect of the succession. The Convention of 1689 did not inaugurate the Revolution of 1688, but endorsed it.

From the beginning the Convention manifested a desire to oblige the prince by choosing for its Speakers two avid revolutionaries, Halifax and Powle, in preference to their noticeably less zealous Tory competitors, Danby and Seymour, of whom the former favoured Mary's claims and the latter a regency for the king.[260] On past showing Halifax and Powle could be relied on to prosecute William's cause, being at 'the head of the prevailing party'.[261] Besides much else, they had successfully chaired the Assemblies of Peers and Commoners that had turned the executive over to him. Almost the first act of the Convention was unanimously to renew the Assemblies' address, calling on William to continue his administration of the kingdom.[262] A spirited attempt by the outnumbered Tory Members to pass the initiative to the more conservative House of Lords, where the Tories were in a clear majority,[263] was frustrated on 25 January by the Peers' decision, at the insistence of Halifax, Devonshire, and the Marquess of Winchester, to postpone their debates until the 29th, in order 'to gather some lights from below'.[264] Like the prince, who, on the 22nd, had hailed the House of Commons with its comfortable Whig majority as 'a full and free Representative of the Nation',[265] his partisans in the Lords were determined to take their cue from the Whig Exclusionists in the Lower House. As if to steel his adherents to make one, last, supreme effort to press home the notion of 'a demise' or 'cession' in the

[259] *HMC: Earl of Lindsey*, 425: Lindsey to the Countess of Danby, 10 Dec. 1688: 'as great as the Prince is he can do little without that tool called Parliament'.

[260] *Lords Journal*, xiv. 101. The Williamite Lord Wiltshire proposed Powle as being 'very well experienced in Methods of Parliament, and every way qualified for that Place'. He was 'fully approved of, by a general Call', to the chair. *Commons Journal*, x. 9.

[261] *Clar. Corr.* ii. 260.

[262] *Commons Journal*, x. 9–11; *Orange Gazette*, no. 7 (21–6 Jan. 1688/9); *Lords Journal*, xiv. 103.

[263] Burnet, iii. 356.

[264] *Clar. Corr.* ii. 254, 252–3; A. Simpson, 'Notes of a Noble Lord, 22 January to 12 February 1688/9', *English Historical Review*, 52 (1937), 92; Burnet, iii. 356; BL: MS Add. 15949, fo. 10.

[265] *Commons Journal*, x. 9; Grey, *Debates*, ix. 3.

Commons, William again demonstrated his personal conviction that James's kingship was at an end by taking direct action against four of James's judges, who, after skulking in obscurity for several weeks, were reported to be on the point of challenging his authority through the courts of law.[266]

On hearing that Sir John Powell, Sir Thomas Stringer, Sir Thomas Street, and Sir John Rotherham had sufficiently plucked up their courage to let it be known 'everywhere' in town that they would hold the Law Term as usual in Westminster Hall, declaring 'that the commission they had from the King was legall', William stepped in to stop them from appearing in public in their official capacity as judges. Their announcement that they intended to sit in court 'by vertue of the King's commission' constituted an intolerable affront to him and to the position with which he had been entrusted by the Peers and Commoners. He could not ignore a point of view so diametrically opposed to his own. On the evening of 26 January—after a day spent hunting and dining in the company of his most dedicated Whig supporter and adviser, Sir Robert Howard, Auditor of the Receipt in the Exchequer and the newly elected representative for Castle Rising—he sent his private secretary William Jephson, the Whig Member for Chipping Wycombe, to the judges, telling them to 'consider well what they did' before the members of the Convention had 'signified theire sense to him or them'. This piece of intimidation, which threatened them with the expected hostility of the Williamite majority at Westminster, worked perfectly: 'upon this message the judges did acqiesse, and did forbeare to sitt'. The outcome was as Whig gossip had foretold. King James's forsaken judges, like his bereft Privy Councillors, did not have the 'courage to sit without the Prince or the Convention's privity' and allowance.[267] William's action was superbly timed. It took place thirty-six hours before the Commons were due to debate the postponed business of 'the Condition and State of the Nation', in good time

[266] Though it had been rumoured in late Dec. that 'new judges' would be 'speedily declared', William did nothing. Yet, when Powell and Stringer attempted to open the way for granting Jeffreys a *habeas corpus*, they were warned off by being told to 'take notice that he stood committed for misdemeanors of a high nature'. Bodl. Libr., Oxford: MS Don. c. 39, fo. 82; BL: MS Egerton 2717, fo. 418: London, 27 Dec. 1688.

[267] Dr Williams's Library: MS Morrice Q, pp. 437–8; Clarke, *James II*, ii. 286–90; Luttrell, i. 498; *Clar. Corr.* ii. 252.

for his action to become known and for its defiant message—of encouragement to his supporters, and of warning to his opponents—to sink in.

It took the Williamites less than a day to impose their will on the House of Commons. On 28 January in a Committee of the Whole, which met under the chairmanship of the Presbyterian Whig and ex-Cromwellian 'lord', Richard Hampden, the Commons voted by acclamation that King James II had broken 'the Original Contract between King and People', 'violated the fundamental Laws', 'withdrawn himself out of this Kingdom', 'abdicated the Government', and that the throne was 'thereby vacant'.[268] For the Tories, among whom the descendants of Charles I's Cavaliers were well represented, there was a disconcerting appropriateness in the fact that the committee which declared James's throne to be vacant should have been presided over by the son of John Hampden, 'the patriot', who, in 1643, at Chalgrove Field, had fallen as a rebel against the king's father in a charge led by the king's cousin, Rupert of the Rhine. It was as though the wheel of fortune had turned full circle, so that for them 1688–9 was a personal reversal as well as a dynastic revolution. Such was the overwhelming, often tumultuous, and sometimes savage performances of the Whig Members, who were no longer restrained by the Oath of Allegiance,[269] as they would have been in a parliament, that at the committee stage only three out of over two hundred Tories had the nerve to raise their voices against the thunderously deafening vote.[270] They were Edward, Lord Cornbury, Clarendon's heir and King James's nephew, whose desertion to William from the royal army at Salisbury in November 1688 had caused such a stir;[271] Charles, fourth Viscount Fanshawe of Dromore, an Irish peer and

[268] *Commons Journal*, x. 13. The Peers agreed with the first three resolutions on 30 Jan. *Lords Journal*, xiv. 111; House of Lords Record Office: Minutes, 30 Jan. 1688/9.

[269] BL: MS Egerton 2717, fo. 427: London, 22 Jan. 1689; *HMC: House of Lords, 1689–1690*, 1.

[270] L. G. Schwoerer (ed.), 'A Jornall of the Convention at Westminster Begun the 22 of January 1688/9', *Bulletin of the Institute of Historical Research*, 49 (1976), 261. Luttrell names Fanshawe, Seymour, Finch, and Sir Christopher Musgrave among the 'very few' opponents in the House who spoke out. Luttrell, i. 499.

[271] Bodl. Libr., Oxford: MS Don. c. 38, fo. 352; ibid., c. 39, fo. 5; Burnet, iii. 331–2; *Clar. Corr.* ii. 204–5; P. Rapin de Thoyras, *The History of England* (2 vols., 1732–3), ii. 778.

soldier-cum-diplomatist, who had inherited his father's brand of Cavalier Anglican churchmanship;[272] and Sir Edward Seymour, the redoubtable 'Prince Elector' of the South-West and the defeated candidate for the Speakership, who was mightily offended by William's taking up with Whigs and sectaries.[273] Between them they embodied the principal strands of Tory opposition to the dynastic revolution: family *pietas*, Anglican legitimist conviction, and political self-interest, the ingredients which had powerfully contributed to the physical make-up of the first Cavalier party in the Great Rebellion of the 1640s. On resuming, the House approved the Committee's composite resolution without a division —so helpless did the outnumbered Tories feel themselves to be before the irresistible advance of the Williamite juggernaut. Having adopted two of the three main platforms of 'a demise'—forfeiture and abdication—the Commons proceeded to affirm the third and final one, that of incapacity. The next day they resolved *nem. con.*, 'That it hath been found, by Experience, to be inconsistent with the Safety and Welfare of this Protestant Kingdom, to be governed by a Popish Prince'.[274] The principle of the Protestant Succession, taken for granted by English Protestants of all shades of opinion since the reign of Elizabeth I, was finally formulated as a fundamental requirement for inheriting or possessing the crown and government of England and Ireland; and, with the addition that no king or queen could marry a Catholic, was incorporated in the Bill of Rights, which was subsequently enacted by parliament in December 1689.[275]

So far the Williamites had carried all before them. But the hopes of 'unity and agreement' were dashed when, on 29 January, 'the grand affaire' of the succession was debated by the more conservative House of Lords, the composition of which, resting on birthright, was not only untouched by the Whigs' electoral victory, but was also predisposed to defend the claims of legitimacy.[276]

[272] Henning, ii. 297.

[273] Huygens, 'Journaal', 72; *Clar. Corr.* ii. 238; Horwitz, *Parliament, Policy, Politics*, 9.

[274] *Commons Journal*, x. 15; Grey, *Debates*, ix. 7–25. The titles of Charles I's Catholic descendants were discussed in the press, e.g., *The Necessity Of Setling The Crown of England* (1689). The Peers agreed with the resolution on 1 Feb. *Lords Journal*, xiv. 110, 113.

[275] E. N. Williams, *The Eighteenth-Century Constitution, 1688–1815* (1960), 32.

[276] BL: MS Loan 29/184, fo. 135; BL: MS Add. 40621, fo. 5; BL: MS Egerton 2717, fo. 428; Bodl. Libr., Oxford: MS Rawlinson D 1079, fo. 4.

Accustomed to seconding the Crown, the peerage was predictably and bitterly divided between the followers of the various members of the royal family who were deemed to have the best claim to the throne: between loyalists, who still wanted a regency for King James, and revolutionaries, who did not; and, in the case of the revolutionaries, between Maryites and Williamites. Expecting that there would be trouble from the peers, the prince's partisans in both Houses attempted to head it off by getting the Upper House 'to take aim from the gentlemen below', but as 'the violent party' in the Lords found, to its intense annoyance, it lacked the strength to carry through their joint initiative.[277] It was in anticipation of the failure of collusive action that one hardline Whig, Robert Ferguson, a Rye House conspirator and a survivor from Monmouth's Rebellion, had already pleaded in print that it would not diminish the 'grandeur' of the House of Lords 'to consider of what force and obligation the whole Commons of England' and 'the Declaration of their Representatives' would have in settling the kingdom, if it gave them a free hand and did not, as he put it, 'interfere in their Resolves about the Conveyance of the Crown'.[278] Given the 'domineering' temper of the Lords, Ferguson could well have spared his pains. His plea fell as snow in summer. It made not the slightest difference to their determination to steer an independent course. The conservative Tory peers, whether loyalists or Maryites (and together they made up a majority of the House), were wholly averse to truckling to a Whig-dominated Commons or taking the unsolicited advice of a Whig fanatic who palpably valued the vote of the hereditary peerage at a lower rate than that of the elected representatives of the commonalty.

The oft-told tale of the Lords' resistance to dynastic change, with its labyrinthine complexities, need not detain us.[279] It is enough to recall that on 29 January, 'after long Debate' and some 'very warme' disputes, involving 'severall sharpe speeches' critical of the Church of England bishops as the last-ditch defenders

[277] Simpson, 'Notes of a Noble Lord', 92; *Clar. Corr.* ii. 252 ff.

[278] [R. Ferguson], *A Brief Justification Of The Prince of Orange's Descent Into England*, p. 33.

[279] The best account is in Horwitz, *Parliament, Policy and Politics*, 9–13; and E. Cruickshanks, D. Hayton, and C. Jones, 'Divisions in the House of Lords on the Transfer of the Crown and other issues, 1689–94: ten new lists', *Bulletin of the Institute of Historical Research*, 53 (1980), 56–87.

of a Catholic king, the regency project was lost by a 'plurallity of 3 voyces'. The closeness of the vote, 51 to 48,[280] bore eloquent testimony to the Peers' reluctance to let go of King James despite everything he had done, and in spite of everything that had happened in England since 5 November 1688. In a sequence of well-documented votes—the most important of which occurred on 31 January, when a majority of 5 was cast against declaring William and Mary king and queen (52 to 47), and a majority of 14 against agreeing with the Commons' resolution that the throne was 'vacant' (55 to 41)—the conservatives demonstrated their unshakeable hold on the House of Lords and their unflinching opposition to the Commons.[281] Such daring independence, which flew in the face of William's iron determination to have the throne, and the equal determination of the Whigs to secure it for him, sent the political temperature, already at a high point, rocketing upwards. Having expressed themselves 'with the greatest passion and violence' imaginable, but to no effect other than to disorder themselves, the Williamites were at fever pitch.[282] The open breach between the Lords and Commons, the event that William and his supporters had feared all along and had consistently tried to avoid, had at last overtaken them, and they were powerless to disguise the fact from the general public. Its impact on opinion was instantaneous and deeply disturbing. Fearing the worst, people began to think that they might 'yet be in farr greater straites then hithertoo brought too', and started to draw in the 'money they lent for the publique Service of the nation' as fast as it became due.[283]

Amid the stridency of the Whig press, which continually demanded the crowning of William 'as the only way of securing religion and liberty',[284] and signs of growing Whig desperation,

[280] The Williamite Whig Earl of Macclesfield clashed with the Tory loyalist Earl of Abingdon, as well as 'others', which 'made the bishops a little uneasie'. Bodl. Libr., Oxford: MS Rawlinson D 1079, fo. 4; BL: MS Loan 29/184, fo. 135; Browning, *Danby*, i. 426–7; *Lords Journal*, xiv. 110; *HMC: House of Lords, 1689–1690*, 14–15; Dr Williams's Library: MS Morrice Q, p. 447.

[281] *Lords Journal*, xiv. 112; *HMC: House of Lords, 1689–1690*, 15–17; BL: MS Egerton 2717, fo. 429; Cruickshanks *et al.*, 'Divisions in the House of Lords', 60–1.

[282] *Clar. Corr.* ii. 253–4.

[283] BL: MS Egerton 2717, fo. 429; G. F. Nuttall (ed.), *Letters of John Pinney 1679–1699* (1939), 64–5.

[284] BL: MS Egerton 2717, fo. 426; *Reasons Humbly Offer'd, for Placing His Highness The Prince of Orange, Singly, in the Throne during Life* [1688/9]; Luttrell, i. 497.

which revealed itself in a revival of the Exclusionist practice of popular petitioning, on this occasion to pressurize the Convention into declaring for William and Mary, there was even unguarded talk of a resort to arms by the more militant Williamites in both Houses. On 31 January in the Lords Delamer had solemnly averred that, 'if King James came again, he was resolved to fight against him, and would die single, with his sword in his hand, rather than pay him any obedience'.[285] The trouble was, Delamer was not alone in voicing defiance against the Tory majority in the Lords. The animosity and rancour with which the Exclusionists conducted the debate can be gauged from Lord Wharton's motion that Clarendon 'might be called to the Barr for calling the Civil War a rebellion', though it was well known that he and his family had endured the privations of exile along with Charles II in the 1650s and that it had been officially designated a rebellion by the authorities of Church and State for the past thirty years.[286] His desire to set a mark of disapprobation on Lord Clarendon, the leading loyalist and King James's brother-in-law, can have left none in doubt that he and the rest of 'the violent party' were in deadly earnest, and would brook no denial of their dynastic objective, even if it meant that they had to resort to arms to achieve it. As a lifelong puritan, a veteran Parliamentarian who had fought against Charles I at Edgehill in 1642, and a long-standing advocate of Exclusion, Wharton's hostility to the Popish House of Stuart had not been lessened either by age or by adversity. Indeed, he had succeeded in transmitting it to his sons.[287] Five days later, on 5 February in the Commons, just before a division in which 151 Tories, emboldened by the Tory peers' audacious stand on 31 January, voted to agree with the House of Lords that the throne was not 'vacant' after all,[288] an exasperated Tom Wharton, heir to the Wharton barony and fortune warned: 'I own driving King James out, and I would do it

[285] *Clar. Corr.* ii. 257–8.

[286] Bodl. Libr., Oxford: MS Ballard 45, fo. 25: R. Sare to [A. Charlett], 31 Jan. 1688/9.

[287] G. F. Trevallyan Jones, *Sawpit Wharton* (Sydney 1967), 29 ff.; Beddard, 'The Violent Party', 121, 127–35.

[288] Bodl. Libr., Oxford: MS Rawlinson D 1079, fos. 11–12; Feiling, *History of the Tory Party*, 496–8: app. ii; E. Cruickshanks, J. Ferris, D. Hayton, 'The House of Commons Vote on the Transfer of the Crown, 5 February 1689', *Bulletin of the Institute of Historical Research*, 52 (1979), 35–47.

again. Let every one make his best of it.'[289] Such ferocious and uncompromisingly Whig sentiments scared the peace-loving members of both Houses and alarmed the most impassive of onlookers. After the welcome cessation of hostilities between the forces of king and prince on 11 December and the eventual subsiding of anti-Catholic rioting in late December, the nation had gradually returned to peace and calm, confident in the expectation that William and the Convention would reach an agreed and lasting settlement of its grievances. Now, four weeks into the New Year, disagreement between the two Houses shattered that expectation by suddenly threatening a return to the terrifying uncertainties of political discord and civil commotion.

Once again, developments in London began to look ominous. Stirred up by the petitioning activities of the Whig bravadoes, Lord Lovelace, an irascible Williamite with a penchant for rabble-rousing,[290] and Anthony Rowe of Whitehall, Monmouth's old adjutant whom William had commissioned to collect Crown revenues in the West of England,[291] the London 'rabble' flocked to Westminster in 'great numbers' to demonstrate their disgust with the Tory die-hards. There they virtually laid siege to the House of Lords. To defend its freedom against the menaces of the mob—which first assembled noisily at the doors of the House on 1 February, the day following its rejection of the claims of William and Mary, and continued unabated the next day with Sir William Killigrew, an ancient, disillusioned, and unemployed courtier of Charles II's, 'in the Head of them'[292]—the House was forced to take measures to control the encroaching crowds. Vehicular traffic, especially the plying of hackney coaches, was

[289] Wharton had been the first to move, on 29 Jan., that William and Mary be declared king and queen, knowing that it was 'not for mine, nor the interest of most here', meaning the Whigs, that James 'should come again'. Grey, *Debates*, ix. 64; 11, 29.

[290] For Lovelace, see Luttrell, i. 95, 171, 266, 341, 432, 461, 464, 475, 481, 484; Beddard, *Kingdom*, 122, 145, 158, 165, 168, 197 n., 202.

[291] For Rowe, see ibid. 22; BL: MS Egerton 2717, fo. 42; Bodl. Libr., Oxford: MS Don. c. 38, fo. 353; N. Japikse (ed.), *Correspondentie van Willem III en van Hans Willem Bentinck, eersten Graaf van Portland* (5 vols. in 2 pts., Rijks Geschiedkundige Publicatiën, The Hague 1927–37), II. iii. 70, 73, 79; PRO SP 44/336, p. 140; Luttrell, i. 477.

[292] 'The Lords were threatened yesterday by the Mob, and they are not yet dispersed.' Grey, *Debates*, ix. 45: Sir Edward Seymour's speech, 2 Feb.; Dr Williams's Library: MS Morrice Q, pp. 453–4; Bodl. Libr., Oxford: MS Rawlinson D 1079, fo. 7; *Clar. Corr.* ii. 258; Luttrell, i. 499.

also hindering the peers from getting to the House, for by no means all of those who rushed to Westminster belonged to the lower classes.[293] The Whig Dissenter Roger Morrice, for one, tells us how he 'was never at Westminster Hall, nor at the Parliament House since *anno* 1679', when the Whigs were in power, 'until Monday, February 4 ⟨1689⟩, nor have scarce ever walked one turn in that Hall without fear since *anno* 1662', when the Act of Uniformity had outlawed Dissent, 'until the day aforesaid, when I walked with true liberty and freedom, and saw very many persons that I knew well, of great worth and integrity, whom I was very glad to see there, and many others who were like to be instruments of much mischief'.[294] There was brisk lobbying of the peers and commoners by both sides, as they came and went, and much jeering and jostling by the crowds. With the recent scenes of metropolitan anarchy still fresh in their minds, the Lords realized that the potentially dangerous build-up of the rabble could not be allowed to continue; and all the more because the combined circumstances of a swelling mass of agitated riff-raff from the town and a complaisant citizenry recalled those which had brought on the dreadful disturbances of 11–13 December.[295] They therefore took the precaution of ordering the Steward of Westminster, together with the local JPs and, 'by their Care and Directions', the constables, to keep open the passages to and from Old Palace Yard and the surrounding streets.[296] Belatedly, on 4 February, William, feigning concern for the independence of the Convention's proceedings, ordered the Lord Mayor of London to suppress the petitioning campaign in the City[297]—but only after copies of an unsigned petition 'from great numbers of persons' for the crowning of himself and the Princess Mary had been presented on the 2nd by Lovelace in the Lords and by Rowe in the Commons. Although, when challenged by Clarendon and Lord Ferrers in the Lords, Lovelace had hastily withdrawn the petition, because it was unsigned, he did so with an ill grace, insolently protesting to the House that he did not question but in

[293] *Lords Journal*, xiv. 114.
[294] Dr Williams's Library: MS Morrice Q, p. 458.
[295] For the earlier disturbances, see Beddard, *Kingdom*, 41–2.
[296] *Lords Journal*, xiv. 115.
[297] Sharpe, *London and the Kingdom*, ii. 539; Luttrell, i. 499–500.

time 'there should be hands enough to it'.[298] Balked at Westminster, the backers of the petition promptly had it printed.[299] Disowned by cooler-headed Whigs, who in common with outraged Tories regarded the efforts of Lovelace and Rowe as unwarranted and misplaced, the episode none the less pointed to the rising crescendo of popular fury within the capital against those who opposed the Orangist solution.

But the Whig-led London populace was neither the unique, nor the most potent, source of political pressure to which the Convention was subjected from 'without doors'.[300] Only 'parliamentary' historians of a narrowly institutional kind can believe that an independent Convention, hermetically sealed from outside pressures, determined the succession. The deadlock between the two Houses was resolved not by further deliberation, which resulted in greater intransigence, but by decisive intervention by the dynasts themselves. One by one all four adult members of the Stuart dynasty intervened in a bid to end the crisis, which, irrespective of its national and international ramifications, remained essentially what it had been throughout: a family quarrel, in which the junior Protestant and senior Catholic branches of the royal family were ranged against each other.[301] In reality it was the personal decisions made by William at St James's, by Mary at The Hague, by Anne at the Cockpit, and by James II at Saint Germain-en-Laye, outside Paris, that dictated the political outcome of the proceedings at Westminster, as, sooner or later, their respective followers found out.

With his Continental commitments William could not afford to take an exclusively British, still less an English, view of things. As the absent *Stadhouder* and Captain-General of the United Provinces he was painfully aware of the dangers of tarrying in England while the Dutch and his allies, the Habsburg powers of Spain and the Empire, were exposed to the might of Louis XIV's France.[302] Such was his consuming desire to return to Europe, and to fight France with the aid of Englishmen and English resources, that Halifax came to the conclusion that 'hee tooke

298 Dr Williams's Library: MS Morrice Q, pp. 453–4. BL: MS Egerton 2717, fo. 431; *Clar. Corr.* ii. 258.

299 *London Intelligencer*, no. 7 (2–5 Feb. 1688/9).

300 Grey, *Debates*, ix. 45.

301 Beddard, *Kingdom*, 11–13.

302 Müller, *Wilhelm III und Waldeck*, ii. 124–9. See above, pp. 6–7.

England onely in his way' towards staging a final confrontation with France.[303] Even before James's withdrawal to France had played into his hands William had taken measures that were likely to force a rupture between the two countries. On 10 December, the day before James's first departure from London, he had ordered Admiral Herbert and the expeditionary fleet to fly the English flag in any encounter with French ships,[304] and on 22 December, four days after entering the capital, he had, without reference to James at Rochester, commanded the French Ambassador Barillon to leave the kingdom within twenty-four hours.[305] Between times he had on 13 December summoned William Blathwait, James's Secretary of War, to attend him with 'a perfect list' of the army, that he might 'know the exact number of troops now on foot', in order to deploy them as he judged 'best for the security and ease of the Kingdom'.[306] Despite the military difficulties inherent in his take-over from the king, he was most anxious to retain the services of as many of James's forces as he could, and, to that end, was as solicitous over their pay as he was over remodelling the officer corps in an effort to secure their loyalty. On James's navy he expended comparable pains.[307] His intention was, as he reassured Prince Waldeck back home, to commit English arms to the war against France at the earliest opportunity. In justification of his optimism that England would comply he cited the provisions of the existing Anglo-Dutch Treaty of 1678, by which she stood committed to supporting the Dutch in the event of aggression.[308]

303 Foxcroft, *Halifax*, ii. 219; cf. 210, 212, 235.

304 BL: MS Egerton 2621, fo. 71: William's instructions to Herbert, 10/20 Dec. Later he commanded Sir John Berry to send frigates to cruise off Southern England 'to prevent any effront that may be committed by the French or others'. Bodl. Libr., Oxford: MS Rawlinson A 170, fo. 210: William's orders to Admiral Dartmouth, Windsor, 16 Dec. 1688.

305 He was ordered to depart 'for he had entered into intreagues here prejudiciall to the Prince and this nation'. Dr Williams's Library: MS Morrice Q, p. 394. Bodl. Libr., Oxford: MS Don. c. 39, fo. 79; BL: MS Egerton 2717, fo. 418^v; Luttrell, i. 491; *London Mercury*, no. 5 (24–7 Dec.); Mazure, *Histoire de la Révolution*, iii. 287–8.

306 William to Blathwait, Wallingford, 13 Dec. 1688, printed in Beddard, *Kingdom*, 96.

307 William summoned the Earl of Ranelagh, Paymaster General of the Forces, to Windsor on 14 Dec. Ibid. 104; BL: MS Egerton 2717, fos. 420, 421; Bodl. Libr., Oxford: MS Don. c. 39, fo. 74; Luttrell, i. 494, 496, 497; Steele, *Proclamations*, no. 3945.

308 Müller, *Wilhelm III und Waldeck*, ii. 125, 127; Grey, *Debates*, ix. 3: William's letter to the Convention, 22 Jan. 1689.

Everything waited on the Convention's declaring him king. William was no democrat, as his treatment of his Dutch opponents showed, and what knowledge he had of fickle English parliaments made him wary of them. When drawing up his invasion Declaration, which had referred disagreements between the nation and James to the arbitration of a free parliament, he had secretly expressed his dislike of being 'placed entirely at the mercy of Parliament'. It was because of his abiding belief that 'handing one's fate over to them' was 'not without hazard' that he had, in concert with his Whig allies, contrived to obtain a House of Commons in the Convention elections that was more or less to his liking.[309] Having warned both Houses at the start of the session against the dangers of 'too great Delay' and 'unseasonable Divisions' in their consultations, he was annoyed by the Lords' protracted resistance to his claims. He felt he could not stand idly by when the Protestants of Ireland demanded 'speedy Succour' and his beloved Dutch needed 'early assistance against a powerful enemy'.[310] Indirect means having failed to settle the succession issue—as in the 'great meeting' held at the Earl of Devonshire's, when one of his Dutch entourage gave it as his opinion that 'the Prince would not like to be his wife's gentleman usher'—William intervened directly. He presented the House of Lords with an ultimatum.[311]

On or about 3 February he sent for six or seven of the leading revolutionary peers. They included the committed Williamites Halifax, Shrewsbury, Mordaunt, and Winchester, and, most importantly, the chief supporter of his wife's independent claim to the throne, the Earl of Danby. To them he spelled out his terms for staying in England. He would act neither as regent for King James, nor as consort to Mary, not wishing to hold 'any thing by apron strings'. His blank refusal to contemplate either solution cut the ground from under the Tories' proposals, and left only the Whig option standing: that of recognizing him as king. He did not 'think it reasonable to have any share' in government, 'unless

[309] Japikse, *Correspondentie*, I, i. 49.

[310] Grey, *Debates*, ix. 3.

[311] Lord Dartmouth's note on Burnet, quoted in Sir John Dalrymple, *Memoirs of Great Britain and Ireland* (3 vols., 1790), ii. 260. The anecdote names Fagel as Halifax's respondent, but it must have been Bentinck that was meant. Fagel remained in the United Provinces, where he died on 5 Dec. BL: MS Harleian 6584, fo. 287.

it was put in his person, and that for a term of life'. If that were unacceptable, he would bid England farewell and return with his army to Holland.[312] He was, however, prepared to make two meagre concessions to aristocratic concern for the hereditary principle: Mary was grudgingly to be admitted to share the title of sovereign with him, and Anne and her children were to be given precedence over any issue he might have by a subsequent marriage. The first meant little politically, for he insisted that the exercise of sovereignty should be vested solely in him and for life (so that in the eventuality of Mary dying before him, as she did in 1694, he did not cease to be king of England, as Philip II of Spain had done when Mary Tudor died in 1558).[313] The second barely entered the realm of practical politics, given William's disinclination to women and Anne's appalling gynaecological record (but it did help to rehabilitate the lineal succession among the Protestant Stuarts and their descendants on his death without issue in 1702). With these sops to conservative feeling and the threat of leaving his sponsors, including Danby and Bishop Compton, 'in the lurch', William convinced many peers of the error of their ways in opposing him.[314] They knew that the prince and his army constituted their solitary defence against James's return. In the Lords William's *éclaircissement* had a devastating effect on the Tories. Unhappy though most were to let slip any link in the chain of monarchical succession, they managed by only the merest of margins to sustain their opposition to the Commons in the two votes that were taken on 4 February. The motion reaffirming 'desertion', as against the Whigs' insistence on a wholly fictitious 'abdication', was carried by 3 votes (54 to 51), but the majority for rejecting a 'vacancy' in the throne fell dramatically

[312] Burnet, iii. 395; Huygens, 'Journaal', 81. Pollexfen's speech in the Convention on 5 Feb. echoed William's views: 'And', he asked, 'does any think the Prince of *Orange* will come in to be a subject to his own wife in *England*? This is not possible, nor ought to be in nature.' Grey, *Debates*, ix. 64.

[313] The Convention Commons was aware of the Tudor precedent. Clearly the Whigs feared a Jacobite restoration if William was not allowed to continue as king beyond his wife's death. Ibid. ix. 71, 75–6, 78.

[314] Mulgrave, ii. 86. In the Commons Sir Robert Howard warned against pressing Mary's claims on 5 Feb., telling the House: 'If you use the hand that delivered you thus, you invite him to be gone; and by his compliment to us, he may lose all here, and hazard the Protestant interest abroad.' William's declaration convinced Danby to the extent that his heir, Lord Dumblane, apologized to the House for having voted against the vacancy on 5 Feb. Grey, *Debates*, ix. 62, 73.

from a previous 14 votes to 1 vote (54 to 53).[315] As the opposition in the Lords visibly shrank as a result of his ultimatum, William intensified behind-the-scenes pressure on individual peers, bombarding them with alternating messages of pardon and favour in a frantic effort to get more of them to relent. His adherents—especially Shrewsbury, Mordaunt, Macclesfield, Montagu, and Fauconberg—were active in recruiting new supporters, regardless of their former affiliations, and in pressurizing the faint of heart, whether despairing loyalists or disappointed Maryites, to absent themselves, if not from the proceedings, then at least from the divisions of the House.[316] Attention was concentrated on those magnates who, like the Duke of Norfolk and the Earl of Chesterfield, had seemed initially to lend support to his expedition in their localities, and on those churchmen, mostly Nottingham's friends, like Viscounts Hatton and Weymouth, whose fears for the safety of the Church of England and for the peace of the nation appeared to outweigh their attachment to a Catholic king.[317]

In driving the unwilling peers remorselessly towards the desired goal William was seconded by his Protestant wife and sister-in-law, both of whom stood to gain from his accession: a point which is sometimes overlooked by too great an emphasis being put on *his* riding roughshod over *their* lineal rights. After all, had James returned, it is more than likely that they would have been relegated to the second branch of the succession to which they belonged by birth. Repugnant as many Tories found the prince's 'conjugal impositions on the most complying wife in the world',[318] Mary steadfastly refused to compromise his position by countenancing any attempt to separate her 'personall interest' from that of her husband. She rejected Danby's offer of support as factious and promptly dispatched copies of their exchange of correspondence to William in London, so that there could be no possibility of misunderstandings arising on that

[315] Cruickshanks *et al.*, 'Divisions in the House of Lords', 61–2.

[316] Montagu to William III, London, 18 May 1694, printed in Dalrymple, *Memoirs of Great Britain and Ireland*, ii, bk. vi, app. p. 257. This letter is wrongly ascribed to Mordaunt in Jones, *Parliamentary History*, 35 (Dalrymple's 'Lord Ashley' should also be corrected to Astley).

[317] *Clar. Corr.* ii. 261–2. Chesterfield's case is the best recorded. William sent Mordaunt, Fauconbridge, and Macclesfield to him. BL: MS Add. 19253, fo. 55.

[318] Mulgrave, ii. 69.

score.[319] Her reply to Danby, conveyed to him from The Hague before she came over, when coupled with the prince's forthright declaration, gave the Maryites little alternative but to throw their weight behind the Williamites. Having voted against the loyalists' project of a regency on 29 January, they had run out of options, for by now they were committed, not reluctant, revolutionaries. What none of Mary's supporters had at first realized (not even her old mentor Bishop Compton, nor Danby, the architect of her marriage) was that, well before the planning of the prince's expedition, she had sworn to prevent 'any disjointing between her interests and those of her consort'. It was a promise which the busybody Scot, Gilbert Burnet, had helped William to extract from her during his exile in Holland, and it was he who now, as one in seeming repute at Court, made her resolution widely known at Westminster.[320] That Mary remained firm in the face of dynastic temptation and the self-regarding blandishments of the High-Church Tories enormously strengthened William's hand in dealing with the rebarbative Tory peers.[321]

The attitude of Princess Anne, though of less significance, was also a matter of concern to William and the Tories. To begin with she showed a lack of 'complyance' with the prince's desire to postpone her rights to the succession, but seemed unwilling to air her views, perhaps because she saw how intent some of the Tories were to make use of her misgivings to deny her brother-in-law the crown, if they could. Her flagrant abandonment of her father ruled out reconciliation in that quarter, and the more so since she shared the Protestants' hatred of the 'pretended Brat beyond sea', her stepbrother the Prince of Wales. Governed by James's revolted general, Lord Churchill, whom even William found 'very assuming' in the crisis,[322] and completely under the emotional sway of his wife Sarah, her bosom friend, Anne was

[319] Browning, *Danby*, i. 421–3, 427–31; ii. 156–7.

[320] Burnet, iii. 311; H. C. Foxcroft (ed.), *A Supplement to Burnet's History of My Own Time* (Oxford 1902), 308–10; *HMC: Earl of Lindsey*, 456.

[321] For Mary's concern for William in his expedition, see R. Doebner (ed.), *Memoiren der Königen Maria von England, 1689–1693* (Leipzig 1886), 3, 6, 7; Mechtild, Countess Bentinck (ed.), *Lettres et Mémoires de Marie Reine d'Angleterre* (The Hague 1880), 81.

[322] Foxcroft, *Halifax*, ii. 202; *Clar. Corr.* ii. 255, 260; Churchill succeeded the Earl of Scarsdale as Groom of the Stole to Prince George of Denmark. BL: MS Egerton 2717, fo. 426: London, 19 Jan. 1689.

finally brought to drop her objection to William's becoming king for the term of his natural life—though not before the beguiling Sarah had turned for extra powers of persuasion to her Whig confidants: Dr John Tillotson, Dean of Canterbury, whom Burnet esteemed 'the most moderate and prudent clergyman of England',[323] and Lady Rachel Russell, that exemplar of Protestant piety and widow of the executed Exclusionist plotter Lord William Russell. In a private interview, arranged by Lady Churchill, Tillotson persuaded Anne 'to put an end to all the disturbance that her pretended friends', the High-Churchmen, 'had solicited her to give in that matter'.[324] As she was again pregnant, and knew how unlikely it was that William and Mary would ever have children, she contented herself with the hope that one day a child of hers would succeed to her father's throne, if she did not. Having been offered a number of *douceurs* by William, including 'a great pension by a settlement in parliament', suitable to her status as the new heiress presumptive, Anne sent Churchill with a message to the House of Lords on 6 February, 'wherein she earnestly desired their Lordships to concurr with the Commons, and that for the good of the nation and safety of the Protestant religion she was heartily willing to acquiesce therein'.[325]

This display of dynastic solidarity on the part of the Protestant Stuarts could not fail to impress. It ensured that William's terms would be accepted in full by the Lords. James's ill-managed attempt to disrupt the growing Protestant dynastic accord at Westminster, by addressing a letter to the Speaker of the House of Lords, totally miscarried and served but to alienate the Convention still further from his cause. His employment of the detested Scottish Secretary of State, the Earl of Melfort, who had joined him in exile, to countersign the letter sent to them from Saint Germain-en-Laye was seen as the last straw.[326] That Melfort, a Catholic convert, who was generally credited with having been 'a principall man in laying down and promoting the

[323] BL: MS Add. 32681, fo. 313. Tillotson was soon introduced at Court and was appointed to preach before William. Bodl. Libr., Oxford: MS Don. c. 39, fo. 88.

[324] Gregg, *Queen Anne*, 70.

[325] Bodl. Libr., Oxford: MS Rawlinson D 1079, fo. 13; BL: MS Egerton 2717, fo. 428: London, 26 Jan. 1689.

[326] Clarke, *James II*, ii. 286–90; *Lords Journal*, xiv. 14; *HMC: House of Lords, 1689–1690*, 18–22; *Clar. Corr.* ii. 258. Grey, *Debates*, ix. 45–6.

late methods' of government 'both in Scotland and England',[327] remained in office was seen as proof that the king was utterly incapable of learning the lesson of his ordeal, and that there was absolutely no point in listening to him, whatever guarantees he might propose for the preservation of Protestantism and property. In the Upper Chamber even 'the King's friends seemed cold after they heard my Lord Melfort named', and some were prompted to think again about the wisdom of their sticking to so perverse a master.[328] Following the example set by the Assembly of Peers on Christmas Eve, the Lords refused to read his letter. On 4 February, at Lord Newport's insistence, it was rejected out of hand 'as the letter of a private man; for he was no more King'.[329] James's credibility, for all that it had previously sunk so low, had touched rock-bottom.

By 6 February—the day on which a Free Conference between the deadlocked Houses yet again foundered in disagreement, but on which Anne's dynastic disclaimer reached the Lords—Clarendon frankly admitted defeat. The stream of Williamite sentiment 'was grown so strong since yesterday; and the confusion, or rather consternation, was so great, that nothing could be heard' in the House but a 'general cry' for a vote to agree with the Commons. With new recruits and loyalist defectors swelling the number of the revolutionaries, and some notable absences depleting the ranks of the conservatives, the House of Lords voted to accept both the 'abdication' and the 'vacancy' of the throne. The majority for the latter was a resounding 20 (65 to 45).[330] At last the way was open for the Whigs to establish the dynastic revolution on a permanent footing. Seconded by Devonshire and Delamer, the Marquess of Winchester moved that the Prince and Princess of Orange be declared king and queen. It was the fourth anniversary, to the day, of James's accession to the throne. Observing the irony of the occasion, Winchester told their lordships that 'they would make it a day to be remembered with all gratitude by all ages to come, if they would go on to set upon the throne that person that was likely to be an instrument to do as much for the

327 Dr Williams's Library: MS Morrice Q, p. 339.

328 *Clar. Corr.* ii. 259; Simpson, 'Notes of a Noble Lord', 93; BL: MS Egerton 2717, fos. 427, 429; Clarke, *James II*, ii. 290–1.

329 *Clar. Corr.* ii. 259. Cf. Beddard, *Kingdom*, 159–60.

330 *Lords Journal*, xiv. 118–19; *HMC: House of Lords, 1689–1690*, 17–18; Bodl. Libr., Oxford: MS Rawlinson D 1079, fo. 12.

securing our religion, liberty, and property, as the late King had done to destroy them'.[331] Though the motion was stiffly 'opposed, and strongly contested' by those who still maintained that such a revolutionary course could not be justified either by reason or law, and could only be defended by the sword, it was carried without a division, for none was so unmannerly or foolhardy as to offend against newly arrived majesty. Though leave was granted to enter dissents 'against the vote', none did; any more than any of the defeated peers responded to Clarendon's call that they should 'by consent' quit the House: a proposal which was intended, not as a preliminary to engaging in armed struggle, but as a means, as he himself stated, to 'have discomposed our undertakers', the Williamite Whigs, and to 'have putt the Prince of Orange upon new councels'.

Loyal to the end, Clarendon had seriously misjudged the mood of his allies. Whereas he did not hesitate to stricture the 'argument of necessity', which an overbearing Halifax had inexorably pursued from the chair, as one 'which will always be esteemed a weak one by sober men', none of his fellow loyalists agreed with him. After the prospect of renewed popular disturbance and the bellicose talk of the Whig militants, which they had seen and heard for themselves over the past few days, they preferred caution to valour. Like the Earl of Thanet, they believed that 'there was an absolute necessity of having a Government' and that it could not be got 'any other way than this'. When cross-questioned by Clarendon, Thanet was adamant: 'We must not leave ourselves to the rabble.' There was to be no loyalist exodus from the Convention. As men of title, estates, and fortunes, they had too much to lose to risk the dangers inherent in such a move. They had no wish to invite 'great severitys from the new government'.[332] They therefore knuckled under as best they could in the hope that they would be able to mitigate the more extreme demands of the Whig radicals with regard to the running of Church and State. Some of them had already demonstrated a capacity to acquiesce in what they despised, but could not by peaceful means prevent, by absenting themselves altogether from the crucial vote on 6 February 'from an apprehension that if they had insisted' on continuing their opposition to the William-

[331] Dr Williams's Library: MS Morrice Q, p. 460.

[332] *Clar. Corr.* ii. 260–1; Simpson, 'Notes of a Noble Lord', 94–6.

ites 'it must have ended in a civil war'.[333] In consequence, dynastic dissent went rapidly underground. Unlike in Scotland and Ireland, where opposition to the Revolution did lead to civil war, resulting in terrible slaughter and the draconian punishment of the defeated Jacobites, in England dynastic discontent survived intact. The Lords' deliberate removal of the words, 'rightful and lawful', from the revised Oath of Allegiance helped to calm troubled Tory consciences by allowing temporizing conservatives to accept William and Mary as *de facto*, not *de jure*, monarchs, if they chose.[334] The opportunity for dynastic equivocation was thus built into the very foundations of the revolutionary régime; for, whether by fair means or foul—and we have seen that force, intimidation, and cajolery were used by William and the Whigs every whit as much as were the gentler arts of courtship and persuasion—the prince cannot be said to have obtained the crown of England with anything approaching the 'free' and 'unanimous' consent of the nation, such as has been claimed either by the classical Whig apologists of the 'Glorious Revolution', or by those more recent historians who write misleadingly in modern terms of 'a bipartisan approach' and of 'a rare consensus' in the proceedings of the Convention.[335]

Protestant unity, which received its mandate against Popery in the general election, fell apart once the dynastic issue *was* raised at Westminster. Protestants were unanimous in opposing and prosecuting Catholicism, but were not unanimous in ousting James or in naming a successor. The issue of the succession, which was not new in 1688, and around which the Whig and Tory parties had originally formed on opposite sides, was by its very nature contentious, and was to remain contentious for a long time to come. As William's ambition for 'the false glitterings'[336] of a usurped crown had, in December 1688, turned his expedition from a welcomed intervention into unwelcome revolution for the

[333] Dartmouth's note in Burnet, iii. 404–5.

[334] 'Lord Nottingham moved that new oaths might be made instead of the old ones . . . which, he believed, few would take to a new King.' *Clar. Corr.* ii. 261.

[335] Burnet, iii. 359. See Sir Joseph Jekyll in *State Trials*, xv. 98. *An Apology for the Life of Colley Cibber . . . Written by Himself* (2 vols., 1925), i. 35; J. Miller, 'The Glorious Revolution: "Contract" and "Abdication" Reconsidered', *Historical Journal*, 25 (1982), 554; Speck, *Reluctant Revolutionaries*, 240.

[336] *A Speech To His Highness the Prince of Orange, By a True Protestant of the Church of England as Established by Law* (London, Printed for E.J. 1689).

Tories, so, in February 1689, it dictated the controversial outcome of the Convention. Indeed, the behaviour of the Convention bore an uncanny resemblance to that of the Second Exclusion Parliament in 1680. In both bodies there was an overriding Whig majority in the Commons which demanded James's exclusion, while in the Lords the balance favoured the conservative Tories. The vital difference was that in 1680 the Tory peers were not divided, because the ruler, Charles II, supported by his brother and heir, James Duke of York, was also against Exclusion; whereas in 1689 they were divided, because the new ruler, William of Orange, supported by his wife Mary and sister-in-law, Anne of Denmark, demanded James's exclusion. In both instances the attitude of the ruling dynast was decisive. Thus Exclusion, which had failed in 1680, succeeded in 1689. The slow and infinitely painful surrender of the House of Lords to dynastic extortion by the Protestant Stuarts and their henchmen scarcely justifies Dr Worden's description of the Revolution as a 'swift aristocratic coup'.[337]

VI

In politics there are always winners and losers, and to this rule the dynasts, politicians, and churchmen of the Revolution of 1688 were no exception. The Revolution not only marked the triumph of William III over James II, and of Protestantism over Catholicism, it overthrew the principle of primogeniture by which the crown had passed from one monarch to another since 1509. The establishment of the Protestant Succession set aside not only James II, but also his son and grandsons—James III, Charles III, and Henry IX, the last of whom did not die until 1807, as well as the senior Catholic branches of the royal family—Orléanist, Savoyard, and Palatine; so that when on the death of Queen Anne, the last of the Protestant Stuarts, in 1714, the little-known Lutheran Elector of Hanover ascended the throne as King George I, there were no fewer than fifty-seven members of the same family who had a better hereditary title to the Stuart inheritance than he: all of them Catholics debarred by the 1689 Bill of Rights and the 1701 Act of Settlement. One consequence of

[337] B. Worden (ed.), *Stuart England* (Oxford 1986), 15.

the Revolution was a narrowing of the dynastic marriage market. Whereas the English Stuarts, Charles I, Charles II, and James II, had looked to Catholic Europe—to France, Portugal, and Italy—for wives, the Hanoverians were forced to look to Protestant Europe—to the petty princelings of Germany and the diminutive monarchies of Scandinavia, or more recently, failing that, to the Protestant aristocracy of Britain. But the impact of dynastic revolution was by no means confined to Princes of the Blood. It was felt even more acutely and more immediately by the politicians and prelates at home.

William's deposition of King James revolutionized England's domestic politics. If, as we have seen, his long and laborious progress to the crown had stimulated an unexpected and large-scale Whig revival, which brought the Whigs, as a political force, from the brink of destruction into the promised land of preferment, it had also inflicted unforeseen and irreparable damage on the Tories—their leaders and their principles. Consensus politics, a concept of modern liberalism, found little place in the cut and thrust of William's struggle, first to take, and then to retain James's throne. In the state the Whigs won as assuredly as the Tories lost ground, just as in the church the Low-Churchmen won and the High-Churchmen lost royal favour. That there were some exceptions on both sides of the party divide ought not to disguise this revolutionary fact which continued to disorder the politics of Church and State well into the eighteenth century. The existing Tory leadership, which had been vested for a decade in the second generation of the Hyde family, the Earls of Clarendon and Rochester, and in their allies, the High-Church bishops and parsons, was a spectacular casualty of the Revolution. The total eclipse of the powerful coalition of the Hydes and Archbishop Sancroft in the running of the Church of England marked a definite turning away from the Cavalier legitimist ideals that had been the driving force behind so much of the achievement of Restoration Anglicanism—including the emergence of Tory loyalism, with its strong emphasis on the sacrosanct character of Stuart monarchy, in the late 1670s and early 1680s. Far from 'delivering' the Established Church from its time of troubles, William of Orange plunged it headlong into internecine strife and partial disintegration. His revolution occasioned the Non-juring Schism: the only High-Church schism in the four and a half centuries of the Church of England's brief existence, in which the Archbishop of Canterbury, five English bishops, the whole of the Scottish hierarchy, a handful of lay grandees (foremost of whom was the Earl of Clarendon), and several hundred clergymen, some of them of great learning and piety, were forced to leave the national establishment rather than perjure themselves by taking the new Oath of Allegiance to William and Mary.[338]

It has been stated that 'the key question about 1689 is whether it established a new king on the throne, or a new type of monarchy'.[339] But, with respect, the question introduces an unnecessary anachronism. It presupposes that a clear distinction existed between the monarch and the monarchy, to concede which would be precisely to obscure the contemporary significance of what happened in the Revolution of 1688. Seventeenth-century monarchy was from first to last personal monarchy. This was no less true of James II's England than it was of Louis XIV's France. After the shattering events of rebellion and regicide in the 1640s, and the creation of a republic in the 1650s, the Restoration legislators had as committed monarchists highlighted the personal nature of the restored Stuart régime. Charles II's reign was officially reckoned from the ignominious death of his father on the scaffold in 1649, not from his own glorious return in 1660. In 1661 Parliament decreed it high treason to distinguish between the person and the office of king, as the Parliamentarian rebels had done in 1642. That is why to contemporary Englishmen the events of 1688–9 were truly revolutionary. In pressing his claim to the throne during King James's lifetime William and his supporters drew the forbidden distinction, which was expressly revolutionary, between the institution of monarchy, which they were careful to preserve, and the person of the monarch, whom they unceremoniously discarded. The law of England did not countenance the forcible substitution of one dynast for another, such as had occurred. As William's overthrow of James's God-given right to the crown affronted loyalists, so too his refusal to

[338] For the Schism, see G. L. Cherry, 'The Legal and Philosophical Position of the Jacobites, 1688–1689', *Journal of Modern History*, 22 (1950), 309–21; C. F. Mullett, 'Religion, Politics, and Oaths in the Glorious Revolution', *Review of Politics*, 10 (1948), 462–74; T. Lathbury, *A History of the Nonjurors* (1845), 44 ff.; J. H. Overton, *The Nonjurors* (1902).

[339] J. Carter, 'The Revolution and the Constitution', in G. Holmes (ed.), *Britain after the Glorious Revolution, 1689–1714* (1969), 40.

allow James's crown (which, for convenience, he was deemed, albeit falsely, to have 'abdicated') to descend to the next Protestant heir, Mary, explains why the leading Tory revolutionary, Danby, sided with the loyalist Nottingham, against the Williamite Halifax, in insisting on a change in the wording of the new Oath of Allegiance to accommodate conservative scruples.[340] Willing as Danby and Nottingham both were to own William and Mary as *de facto* king and queen 'upon this crisis of affaires', they knew that they could not 'affirme they were rightfully so by the constitution'.[341] The revolutionary character of the dynastic change, as well as the dynastic character of the Revolution, has to be recognized. The substitution of William III for James II—of a foreign-born, Protestant, warrior-king with existing European commitments, for a native, Catholic, peace-loving king with domestic priorities—is alone sufficient to account for the revolution that took place in royal policies, and therefore in the direction eventually taken by the British kingdoms after 1688. The tragic fate of Catholic Ireland, the urgent need to subordinate Scottish interests to those of England, and Britain's entry as a principal in the bloody Nine Years War against France (once commonly referred to as 'King William's War') are standing proofs of this.

That the Revolution of 1688 was a dynastic revolution—one that came from above, from inside the royal family, not from below, as Restoration legislation, in response to the 1640s, had sought to guard against—meant that it would not be antimonarchical in its thrust. It was aimed against James personally, not against the kingly office. William had certainly 'not come over to establish a Commonwealth', and vowed to his followers that the crown should 'not be the worse' for his wearing it.[342] That he had obtained the throne with the unqualified backing of the Whigs, even of 'some hot-headed persons' whom he could hardly restrain, explains how from the point of view of the monarchy the Revolution came to be, in Macaulay's telling phrase, 'a preserving revolution'. The adverse circumstances of the Tory Reaction had taught the abler, saner, more ambitious

340 *Memoirs of Reresby*, 558; *Clar. Corr.* ii. 261; Browning, *Danby*, i. 432.

341 And this though Danby was reckoned 'in and in for the Prince and Princess'. Bodl. Libr., Oxford: MS Ballard 45, fo. 27a: 7 Feb. 1688/9.

342 Foxcroft, *Halifax*, ii. 203; A. Cunningham, *The History of Great Britain from the Revolution of 1688 to the Accession of George I* (2 vols., 1787), i. 115.

Whigs a salutary respect for the power of the monarch *to exclude them from office* to the detriment (as they saw it) of the nation's welfare. Having endured 'the frowns of the Court' under Charles and James II,[343] and seen their Tory adversaries gain power through the Crown's good offices, they were careful to stay on the right side of their newfound patron. Indeed, they did considerably better than that. They strove by frequent and tangible service to endear themselves to him. Realizing that it was essential to secure the throne for the prince, if they and the people they claimed to represent were to profit more fully from James's downfall, they worked hard to promote William's personal interests in the irregular Assemblies of 1688 and in the Convention of 1689, which they did by turning themselves into a 'new Court party'. The effect of so remarkable a transformation of their previous political role was, as the Tory Earl of Mulgrave noted, far-reaching: 'For some of the old Whigs, who had so long despair'd of Court Favour, were now so transported with it, not only out of their old principles, but even out of their very senses also, that such a good opportunity was lost, of re-settling our old Constitution, as perhaps England is never like to have again.' The power-hungry Whig aristocrats in the Lords and the aspiring Whig lawyers in the Commons, being 'assured of good employments under the Prince',[344] did their utmost to prevent the tender of the throne from being clogged by unnecessary and unpalatable conditions. The original 'confederacy' having 'brought the Prince in without any conditions',[345] they thought that it behoved them to ensure that he and his title should remain unencumbered.

Since the only potentially serious threat to the traditional prerogatives of the Crown came, not from the soundings-off of individual disgruntled Tories, but from the more radical and doctrinaire wing of the Whig party, which had long fostered genuinely contractualist and popularist notions of government, the Court Whigs acted as an automatic brake on the radicals' less acceptable demands. This was shown to advantage in the Convention's debates on the Declaration of Rights, in which they repeatedly showed their impatience with innovation, over-

343 The phrase was Treby's. Grey, *Debates*, ix. 68.

344 Mulgrave, ii. 84–5.

345 *HMC: Earl of Lindsey*, 452. Cf. *Memoirs of Reresby*, 546.

elaboration, and delay. Henry Pollexfen, the Whig lawyer who was known to enjoy the prince's confidence (and whom he was soon to serve as Attorney-General), stressed the need to perfect the dynastic revolution, and warned his colleagues in the Commons that 'to stand talking, and making Laws, and in the mean time have no Government at all' was to expose themselves and the nation to disaster.[346] In like fashion Maynard, another leading Williamite, besought them not to spend their time particularizing the causes of arbitrary government, in which they might 'sit five years and never come to an end', but simply to declare 'things obvious and apparent'.[347] It was this discreet kind of courtly advice which persuaded the House to confine itself to stating what were, for the most part, the existing rights of the subject. Most Members would have agreed with Sacheverell when he said: 'I do not suppose this Instrument of Government to be a new Limitation of the Crown, but what of right is ours by Law.'[348] Only when subsequently extracted from its proper political context, and treated in isolation as a 'constitutional document' can the Declaration of Rights be wrested into anything approaching a precocious call for 'limited parliamentary monarchy' of the kind that is familiar to twentieth-century Englishmen. Before it was given its grander sounding title (itself taken from William's Additional Declaration of 14/24 October 1688),[349] the Declaration of Rights started life as a schedule of 'heads of grievance' harboured against the deposed Catholic king, not directed against the incoming Protestant monarchs. In its final and much truncated form, shorn of its more innovatory and therefore controversial heads, it was informative rather than contractual in purpose, and horatory, not mandatory, in tone. Consequently, it set up no machinery for implementing its findings, and carried no penalties for non-observance of them.[350]

At the hastily improvised ceremony in the Banqueting House in Whitehall on 13 February 1689, William made it abundantly clear by his words and actions that he did not regard the tender of the throne to himself and Mary as being in any way conditional

[346] Grey, *Debates*, ix. 34. [347] Ibid. ix. 32. [348] Ibid. ix. 74.

[349] William had in his First Declaration from The Hague himself suggested the 'redress' of grievances in parliament 'by a declaration of the rights of the subject that have been invaded'. Beddard, *Kingdom*, 150.

[350] For the legislative version in the Bill of Rights, see Williams, *Eighteenth-Century Constitution*, 26–33.

upon his acceptance of the Declaration of Rights. He first accepted the crown for both of them, and only afterwards acknowledged the Declaration, which had been read to him.[351] Study of the text certainly confirms the impression formed of it at the time by one of John Locke's correspondents in Rotterdam, who, finding its contents disappointing, correctly concluded that William's new subjects had 'shewed themselves a most gratefull confiding people to a wise Prince, to whom they leave all'.[352] The Revolution monarchy, in common with its Restoration predecessor, depended upon trust, not upon contract. With the eradication of Popery from the throne the way was clear for a return to lawful Protestant kingship. Believing, as William did, that the maintenance of religion and the assertion of the 'civil rights' of the subject were 'the greatness and security both of kings, royal families, and of all such as are in authority, as well as the happiness of the⟨ir⟩ subjects and people',[353] the new king's respect for the rule of law allowed him to honour his Coronation Oath to govern 'according to the statutes in parliament agreed on, and the laws and customs of the same'.[354] It was evident from early on, even from December 1688, that the Revolution would have to be defended against James II and Louis XIV, who did not hesitate to comfort and aid his dethroned cousin. With the prospect of war plainly before them William's closest supporters —Whigs and Exclusionist converts to a man—knew that they required 'a King to go before us & to fight our battells'.[355] In the contest that lay ahead most realized that a strong king was their 'best weapon' against James's return. Indeed, Halifax had revealingly opposed a regency on the grounds that it was 'more like ⟨a⟩ change' in the constitution of the monarchy than setting up a new monarch. For him a king was 'more then a name': 'the word', he argued, 'comprehendes a government'.[356] Even the

[351] H. Nenner, 'Constitutional Uncertainty and the Declaration of Rights', in B. Malament (ed.), *After the Reformation: Essays in Honour of J. H. Hexter* (1980), 291–308.

[352] Bodl. Libr., Oxford: MS Locke c. 9, fo. 34: Benjamin Furly to John Locke, Rotterdam, 1 Mar. 1689.

[353] Beddard, *Kingdom*, 125.

[354] For the new Coronation Oath (1689) and its predecessor (1685), see Williams, *Eighteenth-Century Constitution*, 37–9.

[355] Schwoerer, 'A Jornall of the Convention', 255.

[356] BL: MS Egerton 3345, bundle 3: Danby's autograph notes on the Lords' debate, 29 Jan. 1689.

out-and-out Whig Tom Wharton favoured sticking 'as near the antient Government as can be'.[357] As for the House of Lords, it demonstrated its concern to vindicate the traditional concept of monarchy by substituting the words 'sole and full exercise of the regal power', for the weaker expression 'administration of the Government', in the section of the Declaration of Rights that related to William's kingship.[358]

There can be no doubt that what the Whigs wanted in William III was what the Tories had initially had in James II—a powerful king of their own making, who would, above all, defend them, uphold their principles, and reward them. If in time they, no less than the Tories before them, found that no monarch cared to be the creature of a single party,[359] their subsequent disillusionment cannot detract from the central and indispensable part which they had played in bringing about the unexpected Revolution of 1688.

[357] Grey, *Debates*, ix. 29.

[358] *Lords Journal*, xiv. 122.

[359] For William's defiant statement, 'I will be a King of my people and not a party', see J. Oldmixon, *The History of England during the Reigns of King William and Queen Mary, Queen Anne, and King George I* (1735), 105; Foxcroft, *Halifax*, ii. 206–7: 'Note hee ever told mee hee was a Trimmer.' Cf. Burnet, iv. 5–6.

2

The Political Thought of the Anglican Revolution

MARK GOLDIE

I

Almost from the beginning of James II's reign, Anglican churchmen and their lay followers engaged in extensive and concerted civil disobedience, and did so with the manifest aim of bringing his régime to a standstill. When the king sought the gentry's acquiescence in opening public office to Catholics, two-thirds of them baulked. When he ordered the clergy to desist from preaching against his religion, they responded with volleys of sermons and pamphlets on the evils of Popery. When he imposed upon the universities, the dons withstood him. When he sought addresses of thanks for his Declaration of Indulgence, he met with massive refusals. And when he demanded that the Declaration be read from every pulpit, 95 per cent of the clergy disobeyed and the Seven Bishops who published their reasons stood trial for seditious libel. By the winter of 1688 James had been deserted, in spirit or in fact, by nearly all of the natural allies of Stuart monarchy. And by the following summer nearly all the Tories, lay and clerical, had come to terms with a dynastic change that earlier they would have pronounced abhorrent.

How a clerical and gentry élite, who, in the shadow of civil war and Whig rebellion, had become so deeply committed to 'divine right' principles, came now to engage in systematic resistance has long been a central conundrum of the Revolution. This apparent apostasy from the vaunted doctrine of 'passive obedience and non-resistance' has forcefully struck almost everybody: the king and his apologists, contemporary Whigs, and generations of historians. James exploded with rage when he interviewed the Seven Bishops and, earlier, the disobedient Fellows of Magdalen

College: 'this is the standard of rebellion'; 'is this your Church of England loyalty?'[1] John Dryden, in his poetical allegory in defence of James, *The Hind and the Panther*, has the lines: 'The Master of the Farm [was] displeas'd to find | So much of Rancour in so mild a kind, | . . . The Passive Church had struck the foremost blow.' The Whigs' contemptuous judgement is well captured in John Asgill's remark, years later: 'I remember the latter end of the reign of King Charles II, when the pulpits blowed out their anathemas against all that doubted their *jus divinum*, or scrupled their passive obedience. After that, I don't forget the reign of the late King James, when this breath was sucked in again.'[2] And in the same vein modern historians have said that 'no logical process could reconcile' Tory political theory with constitutional and Protestant common sense, and that 1688 offers the classic example 'of the triumph of political pressure over ideological commitment'.[3] The Revolution has seemed, in short, a wholesale abandonment of the avowed principles of a generation—it is of course the volte-face immortalized in the lines of 'The Vicar of Bray', the song about the turncoat clergyman.[4]

It has rightly become customary to mitigate Tory guilt by stressing that the settlement was sufficiently ambiguous to allow substantial room for ideological manœuvre, so that few Tories turned Whig in resolving their consciences. By arguing that James had abdicated and that the Prince of Wales was an imposture, by deferring to a foreign prince's right of conquest, by alleging God's special providence, and by allowing limited allegiance to a *de facto* king, it was plausible to maintain that James had not been forcibly deposed by his subjects.[5] The

[1] *The Correspondence of Henry Hyde, Earl of Clarendon*, ed. S. W. Singer (2 vols., 1828), ii. 479. Cited below as *Clar. Corr.* T. B. Howell, *A Complete Collection of State Trials* (1811), xii. 454–5. Cited below as *ST.*; Henry Fairfax, *An Impartial Relation of the Whole Proceedings against Magdalen College* (1688), 15.

[2] *The Poems of John Dryden*, ed. J. Kingsley (Oxford 1958), ii. 531; Asgill, *The Assertion is, That the Title of the House of Hanover . . .* (1710), 5.

[3] K. Feiling, *A History of the Tory Party, 1660–1714* (Oxford 1924), 203; J. Carswell, *The Descent on England* (New York 1969), 69.

[4] The third verse has the lines: 'Old principles I did revoke, | Set conscience at a distance, | And prov'd religion was a joke, | And a jest was non-resistance.'

[5] For a list of the extensive literature on the allegiance controversy see M. Goldie, 'The Revolution of 1689 and the Structure of Political Argument', *Bulletin of Research in the Humanities*, 83 (1980), 527. Especially important are G. M. Straka, *Anglican Reaction to the Revolution of 1688* (Madison, Wisc. 1962); and J. P. Kenyon, *Revolution Principles: The Politics of Party, 1689–1720*, chs. 2–4.

remarkably energetic efforts of post-Revolution Tories to salvage what they could of the Restoration polity produced the amphibious régimes of William and Anne, and preserved a remodelled Tory ideology for future generations to cherish.[6] For, as the speeches at the Sacheverell trial testified, and as the pronouncements of Edmund Burke against the French Revolution amplified, the Glorious Revolution was astonishingly conservative in its ruling illusions. In the welter of vindicatory words, talk of popular revolution was marginal. A successful invasion by an authoritarian prince, whose career was built upon the wreckage of Dutch republicanism, offered only the roughest approximation to the model of a corporate people vindicating their natural rights against a tyrant.[7] And there is something of bathos in the publication of Locke's *Two Treatises*, a plangent and heroic argument forged in the desperate early 1680s, which now stooped to conquer in order 'to establish the Throne of our Great Restorer, our present King William'.[8]

But all this notwithstanding, the Oath of Allegiance to the new régime undoubtedly embroiled Tory consciences in an agonizing dilemma, and their pamphlets were unquestionably a hurried and circumstantial, if monumental, exercise in casuistry. The Jacobites and Nonjurors, their erstwhile brethren whose consciences would not bend, denounced the conforming Tories with terrible anathemas. They published anew the doctrine of non-resistance, declaring that nothing could justify the breach of

[6] For Tory ideology after 1688 see, J. A. W. Gunn, *Beyond Liberty and Property* (Kingston and Montreal 1983), ch. 4; M. Goldie, 'Tory Political Thought, 1689–1714', Ph.D. thesis (Cambridge University, 1978); J. C. D. Clark, *English Society, 1688–1832* (Cambridge 1985).

[7] See J. Scott, *Algernon Sidney and the English Republic, 1623–1677* (Cambridge 1988) and *Algernon Sidney and the Restoration Crisis, 1677–1688* (Cambridge 1991).

[8] J. Locke, *Two Treatises*, ed. P. Laslett (Cambridge 1963), 171. The fullest account of the circumstances of the composition of Locke's work is R. Ashcraft, *Revolutionary Politics and Locke's Two Treatises of Government* (Princeton 1986). The presumption that Locke's *Two Treatises* was marginal in the period after 1688 has been modified by R. Ashcraft and M. M. Goldsmith, 'Locke, Revolution Principles, and the Formation of Whig Ideology', *Historical Journal*, 26 (1983), 773–800. A newly published document of Locke's, dating from 1690, shows his anxiety to combat the prevailing Anglican political orthodoxies described in the present essay: J. Farr and C. Roberts, 'John Locke on the Glorious Revolution: A Rediscovered Document', *Historical Journal*, 28 (1985), 385–98. See also M. Goldie, 'John Locke and Anglican Royalism', *Political Studies*, 31 (1983), 61–85; Charles D. Tarlton, '"The Rulers now on Earth": Locke's *Two Treatises* and the Revolution of 1688', *Historical Journal*, 28 (1985), 279–98.

sacred obligations to King James, for the Dutch usurper could no more be legitimized than the tyrant Oliver.[9] They were surely correct to believe that, however decorously Tory the Revolution might come to seem in Queen Anne's reign, it was, from the perspective of Restoration dogma, an irreducibly Whig event.[10] It *was* the occasion for a recapitulation of the grand tradition of the Calvinist theory of revolution, and it saw the republication of exactly those seditious books which had been consigned to the flames by Tory Oxford in 1683.[11] Not only was William of Orange the beneficiary of the deposition of a monarch, but also, ironically, his coming confirmed what James had already so Whiggishly done in shattering for ever the dream of a purified Cavalier and Anglican régime which had so nearly been perfected in the early 1680s.

Moreover, the charge of apostasy may be pushed a stage further, for there is no doubt that, quite apart from the pragmatic need to reconcile consciences in 1689, the shock of James's régime dislodged a number of churchmen from principles they had previously held. Much the most prominent case is Gilbert Burnet, the one vocal clergyman in exile in Holland and a key propagandist in William's entourage. In 1683 he had, together with John Tillotson, pleaded with the Whig traitor Lord Russell, in his last hours before execution, to renounce the unchristian doctrine of armed resistance.[12] Burnet subsequently reconsidered, and in January 1689 he published an influential tract on behalf of the crowning of William.[13] A lay Tory who changed his mind was

[9] E.g., A. Seller, *This History of Passive Obedience since the Reformation* (1689).

[10] There has recently been something of a revival of a Whig slant on the Revolution: L. G. Schwoerer, *The Declaration of Rights* (Baltimore 1981); T. P. Slaughter, '"Abdicate" and "Contract" in the Glorious Revolution', *Historical Journal*, 24 (1981), 323–37; Ashcraft and Goldsmith, 'Locke, Revolution Principles'; H. T. Dickinson, 'The Precursors of Political Radicalism in Augustan Britain', in Clyve Jones (ed.), *Britain in the First Age of Party, 1680–1750* (1987), 63–84.

[11] G. Buchanan, *De Jure Regni apud Scotos* (1579); P. du Plessis Mornay [?], *Vindiciae contra tyrannos* (1579); and P. Hunton, *A Treatise of Monarchy* (1643); all reprinted in 1689.

[12] See L. G. Schwoerer, *Lady Rachel Russell* (Baltimore 1988), 130–1, 137, 193, 195; T. Birch, *The Life of John Tillotson, Archbishop of Canterbury* (1753), 102–15.

[13] [G. Burnet], *An Enquiry Into The Present State of Affairs* (Jan. 1689). His *Subjection for Conscience Sake* (1674) was reprinted by Jacobites in 1689 and 1710; the charge of apostasy was levelled by G. Hickes, *Some Discourses* (1695). For Burnet's tergiversations, see T. E. S. Clark and H. C. Foxcroft, *A Life of Gilbert Burnet* (Cambridge 1907), 109–11, 134, 174–6, 194–6, 198, 241–2, 244–5, 335.

Edmund Bohun. In the early 1680s he was Archbishop Sancroft's literary agent in publishing and defending Sir Robert Filmer's *Patriarcha*, the flagship of Tory absolutism.[14] But in 1687, amidst 'the popish fury', he set about translating into English John Sleidan's history of the Schmalkaldic League, the German Lutheran states which had resisted the Emperor Charles V. The most famous episode in Sleidan's story is the issuing in 1550 of the Admonition of Magdeburg, which declared that 'it is lawful for an inferior magistrate to resist a superior that would constrain their subjects to forsake the truth'.[15] In 1689 Bohun was one of the first Tories in the field in publishing persuasives to accept the Revolution.[16] A third influential case is that of White Kennett, who as an undergraduate in 1681 and a young priest in 1686, published high-flown paeons to Stuart monarchy.[17] In 1706 his *Complete History* appeared, which became a standard Whig account of Restoration history, a threnody on the tyrannies of Charles and James and the virtues of William. His enemies taunted him with his past, several times reprinting his Tory juvenilia.[18] More generally, it is a striking fact that the genre of defences of monarchical absolutism, so prominent in the early 1680s, in the expectation of a Papist but Tory-controlled monarchy, wholly lapsed after 1685. The only exception of any note was *The Excellency of Monarchy*, written by one of James's few Tory collaborators, Nathaniel Johnston, who reaped a reward of ostracism and penury.

[14] Bohun wrote *A Defence of Sir Robert Filmer* (1684) and published the 1685 edition of *Patriarcha*, from a manuscript supplied by Sancroft.

[15] J. Sleidan, *The General History of the Reformation* (1689), 496; *The Diary and Autobiography of Edmund Bohun*, ed. S. W. Rix (Beccles 1853), 79. Cited below as *Bohun Diary*. To Sleidan's *De statu religionis et reipublicae Carolo Quinto* (1555) Bohun added a continuation of Reformation history out of the admired French memorialist De Thou. On Sleidan see A. G. Dickens and J. Tonkin, *The Reformation in Historical Thought* (Oxford 1985), 10–19.

[16] By Jan. 1689 he was trying to dissuade the clergy from recalling James: *Bohun Diary*, 82–3; Bohun's *History of the Desertion* appeared in April 1689. See M. Goldie, 'Edmund Bohun and *Jus Gentium* in the Revolution Debate, 1689–1693', *Historical Journal*, 20 (1977), 569–86.

[17] [W. Kennett], *A Letter from a Student at Oxford* (1681); *An Address of Thanks to a Good Prince, Presented in a Panegyric of Pliny upon Trajan, the Best of Emperors* (1686).

[18] *White against Kennett* (1704); *The Conduct of the Reverend Dr White Kennett* (1717). See G. V. Bennett, *White Kennett, 1660–1728, Bishop of Peterborough* (London 1957), 10–12, 17 ff. For another apostate, see W. A. Speck, *Reluctant Revolutionaries: Englishmen and the Revolution of 1688* (Oxford 1988), 186–7.

II

Yet if the charge of apostasy carries some weight, there is none the less a crucial sense in which it is mistaken. The mistake lies in conflating the aspirations and utterances of the Tories during James's reign with their response to the unexpected circumstances of his deposition in 1689. Whatever the case for 'betrayal' after the fateful declaration of 6 February 1689, before that time their resistance to James took place within the boundaries of their existing political catechism. Throughout three years of stentorian remonstration against James nearly all churchmen remained unswervingly committed to his kingship, and to the view that coercive resistance, as opposed to civil disobedience, was never legitimate. What historians have generally taken to constitute the political thought of the Glorious Revolution is the 'allegiance debate' that took place in its aftermath. But that was the political thought of William's revolution, and in this essay I shall turn instead to examine the political theology of the Anglican revolution.

We need first briefly to dwell upon this distinction between the two revolutions of 1688. The second, the Williamite, superseded and overwhelmed the first, the Anglican, and led to a dynastic coup of unforseen magnitude. It is easy to see the trial of the Seven Bishops, which was the climacteric of the Anglican revolution, as a prelude to William's, but that is misleading. To the prelates and Tory magnates the Dutch invasion was little short of disastrous for the cause of their impending recapture of the king's administration. Between 1686 and 1688 they were embarked upon overturning not the monarchy but the monarch's ministers and policies. If unremarkable measured on the scale of revolutionary overthrow, it was still a momentous enterprise. Contemporaries called it a revolution, and it was what Lord Halifax intended when, in his famous tract *A Letter to a Dissenter*, he spoke of 'the next probable revolution'.[19] 'Revolution' meant not a violent overthrow, but a great change or cycle in affairs. It betokened a 'reformation' or 'restoration' of former proprieties wrongfully disrupted. It meant the recovery of a wayward sovereign to forsaken principles. The Church party aimed to force

[19] *Halifax: Complete Works*, ed. J. P. Kenyon (Harmondsworth, 1969), 116; cf. p. 338.

James back into the mould of the Tory régime of the early 1680s, which James had so brutally curtailed. The Church's campaign was scarcely a muted affair; still less was it an underground conspiracy for William's benefit. If successful, it would have returned to office the Hyde brothers, Rochester and Clarendon, the prelates Sancroft and Turner, and the rising Tory peer Nottingham. They remained sanguine that the king's precarious programme would collapse of its own accord, 'crippled with the difficulties it every day meeteth with'.[20] Their intention was to restore Stuart monarchy to its proper place in the Anglican firmament, to prolong and perfect their vision of what we have come to call 'Restoration England'. William would bring it to a close.

In the summer and autumn of 1688 the Anglican revolution very nearly succeeded. Had James capitulated in the aftermath of the trial he would certainly have kept his throne. In October he did capitulate, abjectly and totally,[21] throwing over everything he had so laboriously constructed, his remodelled magistracies, his electoral machine, his Ecclesiastical Commission, his Catholic college at Oxford. The bishops demanded that he 'restore all things to the state in which he found them when he came to the crown'.[22] The diarist Roger Morrice recorded that the ship of state, having been 'tossed up and down at sea and ready to sink', now sought a port: the bishops 'have now given the vessel a twig to take hold on whereby it may draw itself to land, but they seem yet to keep the hatchet in their own hand, by which they can cut off that twig at their pleasure'.[23] The king's now exhausted bureaucratic machine could scarcely have been rebuilt in the time he was likely to have left to his natural life. In substance if not in name, a long episcopal regency for his newborn son loomed. In a gamble to save himself from a worse fate, he resigned himself to being king of the Church party, and his experiment in Catholic and Dissenter absolutism was lost.

[20] Jones, 'James II's Whig Collaborators', 336; cf. pp. 335–43. See also Sir John Dalrymple, *Memoirs of Great Britain and Ireland* (1771–3), ii. 197, 207–8, 219–20, 235, 237; H. Horwitz, *Revolution Politicks: The Career of Daniel Finch, Second Earl of Nottingham, 1647–1730* (Cambridge 1968), ch. 4.

[21] The point is well made by J. R. Jones, *The Revolution of 1688 in England* (1972), 262–4.

[22] J. Gutch, *Collectanea Curiosa* (1781) i. 405, 411. Cited below as Gutch. *ST* xii. 489–90; G. D'Oyly, *The Life of William Sancroft, Archbishop of Canterbury* (1821), i. 340.

[23] Dr Williams's Library, London: MS Morrice Q, p. 303, 13 Oct.

William's entourage was taken aback by James's new stance. It spoiled the impact of his Declaration of his reasons for invading. He issued an Additional Declaration implying that the bishops' remedies were inadequate and repudiating suggestions that a conquest was intended. The Williamite Whig clergyman Samuel Johnson was beside himself with fury at the bishops' coup, for they 'intended to forestal our expected deliverance', and 'by a little priestcraft' have 'spoiled' and 'puzzled' the prince's design. Even more revealing of the tension between Anglican and Williamite objectives is Morrice's report of an encounter in December with a senior clergyman, who exploded at him 'with extraordinary passion', saying that before the prince landed 'they were in a sure way to deliverance', since 'all the papists' councils and endeavours were blasted'. James, this divine was convinced, could now be kept 'in constant bondage to the hierarchy', whereas he apprehended 'they can never keep the Prince in bondage'.[24] The invasion, in short, was unnecessary because the holy union of Crown and altar had been restored, and James rendered regal but impotent.

Even after William's landing it was by no means obvious that he would become king. He had been careful not to claim the crown, and most people believed that he had come as a regent or protector to restore his uncle's régime to its senses and to preserve his wife's inheritance. For as long as James remained in England at most some sort of regency was envisaged. If his flight drastically altered the balance of expectation, the idea of a regency remained strong until the early days of the Convention in January 1689.[25] Consequently, naïve though it seems to us, and seemed to them in retrospect, a great body of the political élite were shocked to discover William's dynastic ambitions. Even Danby, one of the seven noblemen who sent the letter to William inviting him to intervene, was to protest, at the Sacheverell trial, that 'he never

[24] *An Argument Proving . . .*, in *The Works of Samuel Johnson* (1710), 266–7; Dr Williams's Library: MS Morrice Q, p. 379, 22 Dec.

[25] For a fuller account of the Church party's position in 1688 and the salience of the regency proposal down to January 1689, see: G. Every, *The High Church Party, 1688–1718* (1956), ch. 1; R. A. Beddard, 'The Guildhall Declaration of 11 December 1688 and the Counter-Revolution of the Loyalists', *Historical Journal*, 2 (1968), 403–20; G. V. Bennett, 'The Seven Bishops: A Reconsideration', in D. Baker (ed.), *Religious Motivation* (Studies in Church History 25, Oxford 1978), 267–87; Schwoerer, *Declaration of Rights*, 143–9.

thought that things would have gone so far as to settle the crown on the Prince of Orange, whom he had often heard say, that he had no such thoughts himself'. His son swore: 'I take God to witness that I had not thought when I engaged in it . . . that the Prince of Orange's landing would end in deposing the king.'[26] In the midst of William's Revolution there remained, until the last possible moment, a remarkable ideological punctiliousness. In December Morrice was amazed to discover that at the elections for the London Common Council the Tory Lord Mayor was insisting upon the new councilmen swearing the statutory oath of non-resistance.[27] Only after January would Tories be forced to salvage what political and ideological baggage they could from the unlooked for catastrophe of James's deposition.

In the conduct of the Anglican revolution the senior divines of the Church of England bore the brunt. Contemporaries talked rather of the 'Church party' or 'the hierarchists' than of the Tories. To an unprecedented degree the clergy became the agents of the Tory cause. In part this was because after the autumn of 1685 no parliament sat until early in 1689, so that the ordinary secular channel for voicing grievances was absent. In large part it was because, under Sancroft's leadership, the hierarchy had achieved a high degree of political cohesion and moral self-confidence. The churchmen were prepared to take stands which the lay élite were reluctant to take, or even advised against. This was conspicuously so when the divines resolved to pick up the gauntlet deliberately thrown down by James in demanding that the Indulgence be proclaimed from the pulpits. Rochester and Nottingham urged compliance, Halifax was noncommital, and only Clarendon concurred with the divines' decision to refuse.

The clerical character of the enterprise had distinctive consequences for its ideological complexion. That James was embarked on an ambitious scheme of Popish proselytizing, that this was mingled paradoxically and frighteningly with an open

[26] *The Parliamentary History of England* (1810), vi. col. 847; E. Cruickshanks, 'Religion and Royal Succession—The Rage of Party', in Jones, *Britain in the First Age of Party*, 24. For other examples see *Memoirs of Sir John Reresby*, ed. A. Browning (Glasgow 1936), 522; *Clar. Corr.* 212, 214, 238; H. Hosford, *Nottingham, Nobles, and the North* (Hamden, Conn. 1976), 107–8, 119; E. Cruickshanks *et al.*, 'The House of Commons Vote on the Transfer of the Crown, 5 February 1689', *Bulletin of the Institute of Historical Research* 52 (1979), 41–7.

[27] Dr Williams's Library: MS Morrice Q, p. 328, 11 Dec.

encouragement of Dissent and of the old Cromwellian 'fanatics', and that he barracked the Established Church with his Ecclesiastical Commission, all unavoidably framed public debate in terms of the fortunes of the Church of England. Moreover, there was little incentive for the resurrection of older constitutionalist positions. It was not the absolutism of James that provoked Tory anger, but the uses to which it was put. Whatever the degree of his exploitation of his prerogative powers, he did not unequivocally step beyond them. And the character of his carefully nurtured intended parliament was too much in the balance to underwrite an appeal to parliamentary restraint upon him. The king's régime may have appalled the political élite, yet in its final months there was practically no revival of theories of mixed government and still less of Calvinist revolutionary theory. Tories eschewed them, and had devoted themselves to repudiating them; Williamites, seeking to placate English conservatives, were cautious about adopting them; and radical Whigs had either, like Locke, committed themselves secretly on paper in earlier circumstances, or had indeed gone over to James's side.[28]

Accordingly, nearly all the voluminous pamphleteering of James's reign concerned the theology of Popery, the advisability of religious toleration, and the rights of the Anglican Church. The ideological bulwarks against James were theological and ecclesiological rather than jurisprudential. With the almost complete eclipse in the early 1680s of the public acceptability of anti-absolutist political theory, which the clergy had done so much to secure, it was, ironically, only Anglican political theology which was capable of providing a legitimating ideology for resistance to the Crown. Continuing to hold that no temporal power had authority to overthrow even a Popish prince, they no less fervently believed in the duty of spiritual pastors to school their prince in true religion, because all Christians were subject to spiritual discipline. The Anglican revolution was an act of the Reformation, conducted by the clergy against their ungodly king.

[28] The level of Whig and radical Dissenter support for James is much underestimated. It is hinted at in J. R. Jones, 'James II's Whig Collaborators', *Historical Journal*, 3 (1960), 65–73.

III

In his classic account of divine right theory, J. N. Figgis showed that Anglican absolutism was essentially a Bodinian or Hobbesian doctrine of sovereignty expressed in the language of Protestant political theology.[29] With Bodin, with Hobbes and Filmer, churchmen had repeatedly insisted that in any state there must be a single, unimpeachable source of authority, and that to suppose that such an authority could legitimately be overturned by the Estates, by the Pope or by the people, was a contradiction of the nature of sovereignty, and was a solecism fraught with disastrous consequences. Yet, unlike Hobbes—the cases of Bodin and Filmer are less clear[30]—churchmen did not ally this view either with a strict legal positivism, by which 'law' can only be said to be the command of the sovereign, or with a philosophical nominalism, by which human judgement seemed to be made subject to the arbitrary choices of sovereigns. Neither law nor conscience were subsumed by the state, and so they might yet challenge the state. Churchmen did not offer an account of political or constitutional rights against the Crown, but they did invoke the moral law and constructed a case for the legitimacy of, so to speak, 'internal flight' from an ungodly Crown.

It thus would be misleading to suppose that in the absence of a theory of revolution or constitutional rights, churchmen were bereft of a considered case for resistance and that they must lamely acquiesce in despotism. Macaulay considered the divines to have been so besotted with Filmer that they gave the Crown a divine right to 'send mutes with bowstrings to Sancroft and Halifax', a reference to the supposed habit of Turkish sultans of having their political opponents strangled.[31] Like many other Whigs, Macaulay failed to distinguish between 'oriental despotism' and Christian absolutism, or rather between a conception of sovereignty as arbitrary, and the churchmen's presumption that there are discernible principles of right which, with the guidance of a sound conscience, may be invoked to overrule a wrongful

[29] J. N. Figgis, *The Divine Right of Kings* (Cambridge 1896).

[30] J. Daly has argued that Filmer's position sets him apart from other Royalists and was closer to Hobbes's, which I think is doubtful: *Sir Robert Filmer and English Political Thought* (Toronto 1979).

[31] Macaulay, *The History of England* (1889), i. 524. 'The most slavish theory that has ever been known among men' (p. 522).

sovereign. The Anglican position was distinct from that of Hobbes, with its unimpeachable sovereign will, and that of Locke, with its insistent right of armed rebellion. The twin preoccupation in modern commentary with Hobbes's nominalist absolutism and with Locke's revolutionary violence has tended to occlude the middle ground, a scholastic or 'church' absolutism, which made extensive room for a duty of passive resistance.

Restoration Anglicanism always contained within itself the seeds of a theory of passive resistance, and in opposing James churchmen did no other than what their doctrines had long allowed. As early as 29 May 1685, Restoration day, William Sherlock made this clear in his sermon before the House of Commons. This has often been seen as a characteristic panegyric to divine-right monarchy preached in the honeymoon months of the reign. So it was. But it was also a thinly veiled threat to the Crown. 'It is', he said, 'a Church of England loyalty I persuade you to', a qualification which carried a heavy penumbra of meaning. He told his audience that to be 'true to our Prince, we must be true to our Church and to our religion', and that it would not be an act of loyalty 'to accommodate or complement away our religion and its legal securities'.[32]

Two stories are recorded of unheeded warnings given to James. Burnet claimed to have told him in the 1670s of 'distinctions and reserves' in the doctrine of non-resistance, and Bishop Morley, on his death-bed in 1684, told him 'that if ever he depended upon the doctrine of non-resistance he would find himself deceived'.[33] These 'distinctions and reserves' resolved themselves into two strands of argument. On the one hand, it was contended that the king's godly subjects had a duty to disobey him if he exposed true religion to intolerable dangers, and if necessary they must do so on such a scale as amounted to a desertion of him. On the other, it was held that the bishops had a special obligation to defend the autonomy of the Church against the encroachments of the temporal sovereign, even to the point

[32] W. Sherlock, *A Sermon Preached at St Margaret's Westminster* (1685), 31–2. He extolled the virtues of the king's father and warned that 'persons nobly descended may degenerate from the virtues of their ancestors' (p. 16).

[33] G. Burnet, *A History of His Own Time* (1724), 359. Cited below as Burnet. Dalrymple, *Memoirs of Great Britain*, ii. 289.

of divesting him of his ecclesiastical authority. These two strands will be examined in turn.

In seeking to defend civil disobedience, the divines' first move was to recapitulate the position of the early Luther and the (somewhat more ambiguous) position of the early Calvin, in the period before Protestants were driven to more radical positions by Catholic counter-attacks upon them.[34] In his tracts of the 1520s, and particularly in *Temporal Authority*, Luther stressed the subject's duty to obey and never forcibly to resist God's ordained minister, the temporal prince. But he also urged upon princes their duties to preserve peace, prevent immorality, and defend true religion. Correspondingly, he called upon subjects to be on their guard against princes who neglect these duties, or, worse, who actually command ungodly acts. Whilst Luther on no account permitted armed resistance, even against tyrants, he no less insisted on the duty to disobey commands contrary to the word of God. If the penalty for such disobedience was punishment or even death, it must be endured, for temporal ease was not to be purchased at the cost of the eternal soul. Civil disobedience and public remonstration, together with 'prayers and tears', were the permitted bounds of resistance. Hence Luther's followers drew a clear distinction between 'active obedience' to godly commands, and 'passive obedience' to ungodly injunctions. The latter phrase was somewhat misleading, for obedience was not due to the ungodly command, but to the duty to suffer the tyrannical prince's wrath.

In defence of this position, Luther quoted St Peter: 'We must obey God rather than man'. This text, together with the rest of the Lutheran formula, was now remorselessly repeated by James's Anglican enemies, both during his reign and in self-exculpation afterwards. One pamphleteer put it thus: if the king commands that which is 'beyond that authority which the constitutions of the kingdom have assigned him' and yet 'which is not forbidden by the law of God', then 'for the sake of peace' a people ought to comply. But if, more 'extravagantly', the king sets about introducing 'a false religion', then, though he may not be repelled by arms, his people are obliged 'according to their stations, to resist

[34] See Q. Skinner, *The Foundations of Modern Political Thought* (Cambridge 1978), i. 12–19, 191–4; J. W. Allen, *A History of Political Thought in the Sixteenth Century* (1960), chs. 2, 4.

such proceedings, defending themselves and their own rights, not offending him, or retaliating injuries, but refusing to put in execution such illegal designs'. According to another, there was a 'vast difference' between 'the duty of passive obedience, and the false pleas for active assistance' made by those who would have us slavishly obey all his commands.[35] Bridget Croft wrote that she prayed that the nation will obey the king in all things lawful, but 'passively suffer when they cannot with a clear conscience actually obey, having no thought of other weapons than prayers and tears'. Another wrote that 'it is not a necessary consequence of the doctrine of non-resistance, that because we must never resist our prince, whatever he does, therefore he may *de jure* dispense with what laws he pleases'. In particular, the king's use of the dispensing power to propagate false religions could not be justified, and to oppose him in this was 'not merely a point of law, but a Gospel command', for there lay upon churchmen an absolute obligation to resist inundation 'by the popish and phanatick commonwealthmen'.[36]

These claims went along with a precise concern to distance Anglican resistance from the 'king-killing' doctrines of Whigs and Papists. John Williams defended Anglican resistance to a Catholic king in the same breadth as explaining that it was Popery which pulled down princes and Anglicanism which was the only religion of princely rights.[37] William Lloyd, one of the bishops charged with sedition, commenced his notes for the trial by urging that 'holy religion teaches us, under pain of damnation, not to rebel against our king, though he be of another religion'.[38] Such self-righteous fastidiousness in the midst of civil disobedience enraged the king's allies. The Attorney-General demanded to know why the bishops' 'passive obedience' could not at least have let them wait upon the next parliament, and Thomas Cartwright sneered at churchmen who 'passively rebel'.[39]

[35] *The Grand Problem Briefly Discussed* (1690), 5; *The Case of the People of England* (1689), 19.

[36] Henry E. Huntington Library, San Marino, California: MS HA 1785: to the Earl of Huntingdon, 21 August 1688; *Answer to the Late Pamphlet, Intituled, The Judgement and Doctrine . . .* (1687), 4–5.

[37] *An Apology for the Pulpits* (1688), 3–4, 29. Cf. W. Wake, *A Discourse Concerning the Nature of Idolatry* (1688), pp. vii–xvi.

[38] Gutch, i. 370.

[39] *ST*, xii. 401; T. Cartwright, *An Answer of a Minister of the Church of England* (1687), 52; cf. pp. 13, 32.

This allowance of civil disobedience led some Anglicans to note the inappositeness of the conventional terms 'non-resistance' and 'passive obedience'. It now became fashionable to prefer the term 'non-assistance', which indeed better conveys the true sense of the phrase 'passive obedience'. One author went on to claim that, far from being ineffectual, a strategy of passive resistance, 'if they [the people] would unanimously resolve on this', might 'be safe, since he [the prince] can never destroy them but by their own hands'. Thomas Bainbridge wrote that if 'a great part of the people should take up a resolution not to do, but to suffer, a prince would have a very ill bargain'.[40]

This train of thought was perfectly captured a generation later when Roger North, who pined for the golden days of Charles II's last years, wrote his *Examen*, an angry retort to Kennett's apostate *Complete History*, mentioned earlier. He wrote that although church doctrine required 'a negation of all active force', it was mistaken to see it thereby as an acceptance of 'exorbitant prerogative'. 'Non-resistance' ought rather to be styled 'non-assistance', since in 'disowning unlawful commands by patient suffering' a people had at its disposal 'one way, and an effectual one, of flying in the face . . . of an exorbitant power', so that, far from being a slavish doctrine, it was 'a principle of liberty and security'. That this was so was demonstrated by the 'heroic courage' of the 'passive obedience men' under James II. North's utilitarian gloss on Luther's doctrine was bound to find special favour in the aftermath of James's flight. Sherlock argued that for those 'who do not drive the king away, but only suffer him quietly to escape . . . this is no rebellion, no resistance, but only non-assistance, which may be very innocent, for there are some cases, where subjects are not bound to assist their prince; and if ever there was such a case, this was it'. This notion was not, however, only cultivated with hindsight, but even before William acquired the throne. An influential guide to Tory gentry on how to behave during the impending Popish reign, Bohun's *Third Address to the Freeholders*, of 1683, counselled that should James embark on a scheme to rout Protestantism 'the bare refusing to aid and assist him in such an enterprise would render it impossible'.[41]

[40] *Grand Problem*, 5; T. Bainbridge, *Seasonable Reflections on a Late Pamphlet, entituled, A History of Passive Obedience* (1690), 13.

[41] R. North, *Examen* (1740, but written *c.*1706), 331–2, 338; W. Sherlock, *The*

Here, Lutheran fatalism and readiness for martyrdom was modified by a secular appraisal of the political effectiveness of civil disobedience, and is suggestive of the view, widely purveyed in the eighteenth century, that all regimes ultimately rest on the opinion of their citizens. As Hume would insist, talk of contracts and revolutions were redundant and dangerous abstractions in the face of the simple fact that all government depended on the willingness of people to obey its commands.[42] A comparison with Hume does not, however, go far. The Anglican case, in its inflexible double imperative, to disobey unrighteous sovereigns but never to rebel, is more reminiscent of the rigid formalism of Kant's position. Like the Anglicans of 1688, Kant saw his doctrine as strictly entailed by the concept of sovereignty, but as mitigated by a duty of remonstration and civil disobedience, and as buttressed by a Lutheran political theology of suffering for righteousness' sake. Reflecting on St Peter, Kant wrote that the text ' "We ought to obey God rather than man" means that when men command what is evil-in-itself, that is, what runs directly counter to the moral law, we ought not to obey'. That Kant also equivocally approved of actual revolutions adds to the parallel. It is a position that has seemed insupportably paradoxical to later commentators, who have had as little patience with Kant as with Tory churchmen.[43]

IV

Those who resisted James regularly claimed to be standing upon conscience, upon the law of God rather than the law of the land,

Case of the Allegiance due to Sovereign Powers (1691), 50; cf. W. Payne, *An Answer to a Printed Letter* (1690), 29; E. Bohun, *Third Address* (1683), 66.

[42] For this point, in relation to Hume's judgement on 1688, see D. Forbes, *Hume's Philosophical Politics* (Cambridge 1975), ch. 3.

[43] Kant, *Religion within the Boundary of Pure Reason*, ed. J. W. Semple (Edinburgh 1838 [1792]), 125; H. S. Reiss, 'Kant and the Right of Rebellion', *Journal of the History of Ideas*, 17 (1956), 179–92; L. W. Beck, 'Kant and the Right of Revolution', ibid. 32 (1971), 411–22. Kant's most sustained comment on 1688 occurs in *On the Common Saying: 'This May be True in Theory, but it Does not Apply in Practice'* (1793), in Hans Reiss (ed.), *Kant's Political Writings* (Cambridge 1970), 83–4. Another important German commentator on 1688, this time contemporary, was Leibniz: P. Riley, 'An Unpublished MS of Leibniz on the Allegiance due to Sovereign Powers', *Journal of the History of Philosophy*, 11 (1973), 319–36; N. Jolley, 'Leibniz on Hobbes, Locke's *Two Treatises* and Sherlock's *Case of Allegiance*', *Historical Journal*, 18 (1975), 21–35.

and indeed had misgivings about standing solely upon temporal law. It is true that constitutional arguments were made by Tory lawyers, for instance by the defending counsel in the Seven Bishops' case; the bishops themselves pronounced the Indulgence illegal. Within the framework of Restoration absolutism, Anglican casuists could certainly appeal against the king to laws, customs, and precedents—especially as they conceived the rights of their religion as incorporated into English law—but they could not in the last resort baulk at obeying the command of the sovereign in any matter not touching moral or divine law. It is also true that divines were by training less apt than lawyers to construe politics within the framework of the 'common law mind', so to examine the political theology of divines is no doubt to distort the picture. But it is equally misleading to view the arguments of 1688 too narrowly in terms of a 'triumph of the lawyers' and of common law remedies against arbitrary rule.[44] It is easy to forget that the Church's refusal to read the Indulgence was grounded chiefly in abhorrence of its unlimited toleration. By it, said one, 'all religions would be let in, be they what they will, Ranter, Quaker, and the like, nay, even the Roman Catholic religion (as they call it)'.[45]

For the divines, therefore, the critical element at issue was not the distinction between legality and illegality in positive law, but that between lawful and unlawful in divine and natural law. Human positive laws were, they emphasized, of two types: those which were simply regulatory and useful, and those which gave definition and sanction to prior and transcendent principles of a moral or religious kind. In the former case the laws were said to forbid those things which were *malum prohibitum*, wrong because prohibited for some practical purpose. Here the sovereign was absolutely free to act according to his best judgement. In the latter case, the laws were said to forbid those things which were *malum in se*, wrong in themselves. Here the sovereign was merely the executive agent of prior laws. He was, in scholastic terminology, 'accidental' and not 'essential' to those laws, and could not dispense with them at will. In this area, the *absolute* prince had

[44] See M. Landon, *The Triumph of the Lawyers: Their Role in English Politics, 1678–1689* (Tuscaloosa, Alabama, 1970); H. Nenner, *By Colour of Law: Legal Culture and Constitutional Politics in England, 1660–1689* (Chicago 1977).

[45] *ST*, xii. 372; D'Oyly, *Sancroft*, i. 301; cf. p. 229.

no licence to be an *arbitrary* prince. A human command contrary to divine law was not properly a law at all, and to disregard it was not properly disobedience. This was Thomist legal doctrine and it was fundamental to the Anglican conception of law; it was utterly at odds with Hobbes's. For Hobbes, nothing can be 'essentially' wrong, independent of human laws and conventions, and thus we cannot legitimately do other than accept any authoritative command of the authorized sovereign.

The claim that the king was commanding things *malum in se* was at the heart of the debate over the dispensing and suspending powers. It could not plausibly be claimed that the king had no dispensing power, since a weight of legal precedent showed that he had—and since, for an Anglican absolutist, in the last resort the king's will in temporal matters was law. Nor could it be argued that the king could not instruct the reading of declarations from pulpits, since such a power had on earlier occasions been exercised without demur.[46] But it could be argued that the king must not dispense with the Test Acts and penal laws because they were a fundamental bulwark of true religion. And it could also be held that no churchman could countenance a royal licence of an 'infinite liberty' of worship, such that 'paganism itself might now be publicly professed'.[47]

When the Fellows of Magdalen College resisted the king, they stood partly but not ultimately upon their rights under positive law, emphasizing instead the sacred obligation of their oaths. They asserted that the king's *mandamus* in appointing a Catholic to the presidency overrode the College's statutes and that their subsequent ejection from their Fellowships violated their freehold properties. But they were careful from the outset to insist that the king commanded worse, a violation of something *malum in se*, namely their duty upon oath to preserve the seminary of the Church of England, together with their oath of allegiance to their hastily elected Anglican president. By their oath they were 'reduced to this unfortunate necessity, of either disobeying his [the king's] will, or violating their consciences by notorious perjuries'. The Vice-Chancellor told the king that no

[46] In 1681 the clergy had read the king's reasons for dissolving the Oxford Parliament and in 1683 a declaration against the Rye House plotters.

[47] Burnet, 737.

power under heaven could dispense with the obligation of their oaths.[48]

Another example is the argument of Bishop Compton's lawyers when he was arraigned for refusing to suspend John Sharpe for his anti-Popery sermons. They asserted that the bishop could not have suspended Sharpe without a citation and trial, for 'a citation is *jure gentium* and can never be taken away by any positive command or law whatsoever'; it is 'against the law of nature, which is above all positive law'. Consequently, the bishop 'has not been disobedient' to the king, for 'no man can be obliged to do an unlawful act, *id non sit, quod non legitime sit*: this rule obliges all men in the world, in all places, and at all times'.[49] Here the idea of 'lawfulness' was clearly not dependent upon the positive command of the temporal sovereign.

If we turn, by contrast, to the arguments of the king's defenders, we find them equally concerned to answer not just a case in positive law, but to meet doubts about the relationship between positive and divine law. Herbert Croft's tract in justification of reading the Indulgence dwelt not at all upon its legality under positive law, but upon whether the king had commanded anything contrary to God's law. He was satisfied the king had not.[50] Nathaniel Johnston, in the case of Magdalen College, extensively cited the discussion of oath-taking by the revered Anglican moralist Robert Sanderson, concluding that the king could release a person from an oath where that oath was required under the king's own laws, and thus that no higher principle was entailed.[51]

That the king's apologists shared the churchmen's premisses, but denied the corollaries, is best exemplified in the case which settled the king's right to dispense with the Test Act, *Godden v.*

[48] Fairfax, *Impartial Relation*, 5, 33; J. R. Bloxam, *Magdalen College and King James II* (Oxford Historical Society, 1886), 91. G. V. Bennett rightly calls the affair 'a textbook case of passive obedience': 'Loyalist Oxford and the Revolution', in *The History of the University of Oxford*, v: L. C. Sutherland and L. G. Mitchell (eds.), *The Eighteenth Century* (Oxford 1986), 18.

[49] 'That may not be so which is not legitimately so.' *An Exact Account of the Whole Proceedings Against Henry [Compton] Lord Bishop of London* (1688), 25–6; *ST*, xi. 1163.

[50] H. Croft, *A Short Discourse Concerning the Reading of his Majesties Late Declaration* (1688). Croft was Bishop of Hereford and had tolerationist leanings; he retracted his pamphlet when he felt the wrath of the Sancroftians, and so only in a qualified way was he one of James's collaborators.

[51] N. Johnston, *The King's Visitatorial Power Asserted* (1688).

Hales. Chief Justice Herbert began his judgement with a series of absolutist propositions: that the king of England was a sovereign prince, that the law-making power belonged to sovereignty, that the dispensing power was inseparable from the prerogative, and that these powers were not a trust granted by the people to the king. He went on to concede that only 'whatever is not prohibited by the laws of God' may be dispensed with. Next he produced an impeccably Anglican syllogism: God and not the prince is the sovereign of the moral law; only a sovereign can suspend a sovereign's laws; therefore only God can suspend that part of human laws which instantiate the moral law. Herbert then gave a classic instance: God could command Abraham to kill Isaac, but no earthly prince could command murder. Similarly, no prince could command an act of, say, usury or simony. But having conceded all this, Herbert turned to the case of the Test Act and concluded that it could not conceivably be construed as belonging to this category of fundamental moral laws.[52] And of course his conclusion seems transparently obvious to modern minds. Contemporaries, however, were so convinced that the Test Act embodied the moral law that they concluded that Herbert had gone over to Hobbes's 'Turkish' notion that there were no moral laws outside of sovereign command. Sir John Bramston said the judgement was 'like which the judges gave Cambises of old. He had a mind to marry his sister, and asked the judges if by the laws of Persia a king might not marry his sister. They answered they met with no such law, but they had a law that the king might do what he pleased'.[53] Anglican absolutism was not oriental despotism.

It is clear, then, that in the face of shared absolutist assumptions, the argument crucially turned upon establishing the matter of conscience. It was imperative for the Church party to be able to dramatize the issues of the Test and the Indulgence as the crisis of true religion in the face of 'pagano-Christian' forces. To read the Indulgence, Bishop Trelawny told Sancroft, would be to 'betray the church' and he would rather 'be hanged at the doors'

[52] *ST*, xi. 1192–3, 1195–9, 1253; Sir Edward Herbert, *A Short Account of the Authorities in Law . . . in Sir Edw. Hales his Case* (1688).

[53] *The Autobiography of Sir John Bramston* (Camden Soc., 1845), 232. Another of the king's judges, Allibone, would have confirmed Bramston's fears by his remark, 'If the king had been Turk or Jew, it had been all one; for the subject ought to obey.' Gutch, i. 397.

of his cathedral than do so. A priest at Chatham declared his refusal to read, saying 'I must choose suffering rather than sin.' The entire clergy, wrote Edward Gee, were ready to 'mark themselves out for destruction' for they 'valued their religion and their church more than their own safety'.[54] The divines did not construe themselves as patriots struggling for the constitution, but as martyrs suffering for the church. They knew that the final resort in Luther's position was the willingness to die in witness for the faith. The archetype of course was Christ's own suffering at the hands of misguided civil authorities: passive obedience was ultimately 'a doctrine of the cross'.[55] 'Christianity', Hickes had written in 1681, 'is a suffering religion . . . because when the supreme power happens to be infidel, idolator, or heretic, and so sets itself against the Gospel in general . . . it becomes the duty of all Christian subjects to suffer.' It was not only to theology they turned. Bainbridge invoked Stoic ethics: all the great moralists affirm that no one must flinch from duty for fear of suffering, 'to do so . . . is slavish'. Citing Cicero's *Offices* and 'the Pythagoreans', he concluded that 'in the exercise of virtue a man must have nothing of the slave in him'.[56]

Consequently, one of the most striking aspects of the Anglican resistance was its noisy self-dramatization as martyrdom under persecution. The mask of Christ-like humility and of abnegatory readiness to die was a potent and muscular weapon of defiance. In readiness for physical suffering they fortified themselves by engendering a mystical vision of re-enacting Christ's ordeal. Throughout the seventeenth century when men suffered brutality, for Christ as they thought, this ecstatic vision anaesthetized them: it is documented for Alexander Leighton, when he was ear-lopped and tongue-bored in 1630, and for Samuel Johnson, when he was flogged nearly to death in 1686 for inciting James's troops to mutiny.[57] Now, particularly as the bishops lay in the Tower, the divines readied themselves for similar fates. A print

[54] Bodl. Libr., Oxford: MS Tanner 28, fo. 158, 16 Aug. 1688; *Life of Pepys*, ii. 126–7: J. Loton to Pepys, 4 June; E. Gee, *Catalogue of all the Discourses* (1689), 4.

[55] Note, for instance, Robert Kettlewell's title: *Christianity, A Doctrine of the Cross: Or, Passive Obedience . . .* (1691).

[56] Hickes, *The True Notion of Persecution Stated* (1681), 2; Bainbridge, *Seasonable Reflections*, 15.

[57] S. Foster, *Notes from the Caroline Underground* (Hamden, Conn. 1978), 34; S. Johnson, *Works* (1710), p. ix.

was published showing 'the bishops who suffered martyrdom for the Protestant faith under the persecution of Queen Mary'—Cranmer, Ridley, Hooper, Latimer, and Farrar. In a dramatic sermon on 4 November 1688 Sherlock spoke of the Church as on the verge of destruction and mass martyrdom, recalling that 'the jail and the stake' brought glory to Ridley and Hooper, and praying 'Lord, let this cup pass from me.'[58]

Some months earlier, Sancroft, who cherished the memory of the 'martyrdom of . . . the pious and the glorious' Charles I, wrote a morbid letter to Princess Mary in Holland. 'It hath seemed good to the Infinite Wisdom to exercise this poor church with trials of all sorts and of all degrees.' The church has a 'steadfast loyalty' to her prince, but his Catholicism 'imbitters us' and 'makes us sit down with sorrow in dust and ashes'. Reflecting on the two royal brothers, Charles and James, he judged that the 'greatest calamity' of the century was that God permitted those who barbarously murdered their father to have driven the sons into exile in Popish lands, 'as if they had said to them, go and serve other Gods'. It was the awful destiny of these wayward Stuart sons to go astray 'from the inheritance of the Lord', and the consequent fate of the church to enter upon 'so dark and dismal a night'.[59]

If, as Protestants, the divines stood squarely in the tradition of the early Luther and of Foxe's martyrology, as Anglicans with a predisposition toward affirming their continuity with the apostolic and universal church, their own sense of their intellectual and spiritual resources lay rather in the teachings of the Fathers of the patristic age, the first four centuries after Christ.[60] They turned especially to the days of the Roman persecution of Christianity. We engage, wrote William Wake, in the spirit of the 'primitive church', when the Fathers accused the emperors of idolatry. 'The church', wrote Samuel Freeman, 'has sometimes been forced to hide . . . sometimes you find it privately in an upper room, sometimes skulking in caves . . . now be-smeared

[58] F. O'Donoghue and H. M. Hake, *Catalogue of Engraved British Portraits in the British Museum* (1922), v. 74; W. Sherlock, *Sermon Preached . . . November 4, 1688* (1689), 24–5, 27.

[59] D'Oyly, *Sancroft*, i. 43, 243–6; *ST*, vii. 434–5; Gutch, i. 300–2 (3 Nov. 1687).

[60] See G. V. Bennett, 'Patristic Tradition in Anglican Thought, 1660–1900', in *Tradition im Luthertum und Anglikanismus, Oecumemica* (1971–2), 63–87.

with blood.'[61] They turned to their copies of Lactantius and Tertullian, the primordial theologians of martyrdom. They endlessly repeated the ancient slogan *sanguis martyrum est semen ecclesiae*—the blood of the martyrs is the seed of the church.[62] Mentally detaching themselves from the Constantinian world of Christian kingship, they imagined themselves confronting a Diocletian. Or, rather, like the subjects of Julian the Apostate, they hallucinated an emperor who was merely pagan into a brutal tyrant.[63] By the perversity of their witness on behalf of the exclusive claims of their own church, the Anglicans, like the early Christians, vexed and antagonized an empire otherwise generally predisposed to tolerance.[64]

V

These claims of conscience against the state begged the unavoidable question: who is judge? The rhetoric of martyrdom was also to be found in the literature of the Anglicans' enemies, the Dissenters, who suffered persecution at the hands of the prelatical Antichrist.[65] The Anglican divines had constantly attacked Dissent, warning against the 'anarchy of private judgement'. They had no patience with the diseased consciences of Quakers and Baptists, those flouters of authority who were the spawn of 'enthusiasm' and spiritual pride. In hostility against them, they had occasionally been tempted towards the Hobbesian view that the civil sovereign alone must be judge on earth, even of the dispositions of worship and church government.[66] The essence of Hobbesism

[61] Wake, *Discourse Concerning Idolatry*, 9–11; S. Freeman, *A Plain and Familiar Discourse* (1687), 9.

[62] A paraphrase of Tertullian, *Apology*, ch. 50 (AD 197). Other key texts were Tertullian, *To the Martyrs* (c.200); Tertullian, *On Flight in Persecution* (212); Origen, *Exhortation to Martyrdom* (235); Lactantius, *On the Death of the Persecutors* (c.320).

[63] The motif of Julian the Apostate runs all through the debates. In 1683 Samuel Johnson had published *Julian the Apostate*, which urged a right of revolution against such an emperor; George Hickes had answered for the Tories with *Jovian* (1684); but both agreed on Julian's heinousness and only in the 18th c. was Julian rescued from centuries of Christian vilification.

[64] On the cult of martyrdom amongst the early Christians see R. Lane Fox, *Pagans and Christians* (London 1986), esp. ch. 9.

[65] See N. H. Keeble, *The Literary Culture of Nonconformity in Later Seventeenth Century England* (Leicester 1987), esp. ch. 2.

[66] Most notoriously, S. Parker, *Ecclesiastical Polity* (1670). It is not surprising that Parker became a supporter of James's ecclesiastical policies. For the diffi-

was that we must submit our *judgement* and not merely our *will* to the sovereign's determination of what is good and right, a doctrine which undermined 'conscience'. In attacking enthusiasm Hobbes had gone out of his way to subvert the pretensions of seekers after martyrdom: the age of martyrdom is past and a modern martyr is but a misguided and dangerous fanatic.[67]

But in fundamental ways the divines were neither modern nor secular in outlook. That they now pleaded the rights of *their* consciences against the king's indulgence of 'tender consciences' was of course a circumstance fraught with paradox. As Bishop White told the king, 'Sir, you allow liberty of conscience to all mankind: the reading this Declaration is against our conscience.'[68] Yet they saw no contradiction here; still less had they converted to a belief in the legitimate pluralism of consciences. For it was not to private conscience that they appealed, but to the rightly ordered conscience, which is the public conscience of the divine corporation of Christ's church. In their eyes, a martyr is not a sufferer for any passably elevated principle, but a sufferer for the authentic church of Christ; they deplored the modern heresy that mere sincerity or mere suffering earns the laurels of martyrdom.[69] Against the State they asserted not the right of the individual but of the Church, of *sacerdotium* against *regnum*. In particular, they began to reiterate more forcefully than hitherto the divinely appointed task of the episcopate as governors of consciences and guarantors of the true faith.

Seventeenth-century Anglicans had frequently resisted the Erastian tendency to incorporate spiritual power into the civil state.[70] The Church was asserted fundamentally to be an independent society, an autonomous corporation or *societas perfecta*,

culties churchmen got into on this score see J. Marshall, 'The Ecclesiology of the Latitude-Man 1660–1689: Stillingfleet, Tillotson, and "Hobbism"', *Journal of Ecclesiastical History*, 36 (1985), 407–27.

[67] T. Hobbes, *Leviathan* (Harmondsworth 1968), ch. 42, pp. 529–30.

[68] *Clar. Corr.* ii. 479.

[69] The traditional case was forcefully made in Hickes's *True Notion of Persecution* (1681). See M. Goldie, 'The Huguenot Experience and the Problem of Toleration in Restoration England', in C. E. J. Caldicott, H. Gough, and J.-P. Pittion (eds.), *The Huguenots and Ireland* (Dublin 1987), 185–8.

[70] See, for example, William Lamont, *Godly Rule* (1969), ch. 3. The extent to which the mainstream of Restoration churchmanship can be described as 'Laudian' or 'High-Church' remains controversial; what follows offers good evidence that it can be so described.

which had only historically come to be allied with the State. Hence a crucial distinction was to be drawn between the *potestas jurisdictionis*, the temporal authority and material trappings of ecclesiastics, which was the gift of the secular State, and the *potestas ordinis*, the spiritual and priestly authority which was the direct gift of Christ, which no prince could tamper with. If it was true that the State was divinely authorized through natural law, it was no less true that the Church was directly established in Christ's revealed law. And if the Pauline injunction to obey 'the powers that be' was foundational for the State, so the Petrine commission of the keys of spiritual authority was foundational for the Church. The temporal prince, even though the very hieroglyph of the divine economy upon earth, was never a priest: *rex* was not *sacerdos*. Christ had promised the keys of the Kingdom to his Apostles, to whom he gave an indefeasible authority in the defence of the church, an authority which the bishops in the apostolic succession inherited.

All this of course amounted to a catholic, albeit not Roman Catholic, ecclesiology. Anglican apologists readily used the term 'catholic' of themselves, even in the throes of defending their Protestantism against Popery. In the special circumstances of James's reign—a Papist king using the Elizabethan Royal Supremacy to attack the Anglican establishment—the divines had need of defining a position which was both defiantly anti-Erastian and anti-papal, and which also had an eye to the schismatic Dissenters. The outcome was a special emphasis on the character of the visible church as being constituted by an episcopal aristocracy ruling over a confederation of dioceses.

The fullest articulation of this hierocratic doctrine occurs in *The Catholic Balance* by Samuel Hill, a Somerset High-Churchman. His book was honed for a year in private circulation before appearing in print in May 1687. Its third chapter is a thoroughgoing critique of the royal ecclesiastical Supremacy, which aimed to 'fix bars' against the base principles of 'Erastian factors' who would encourage 'usurpations upon the state ecclesiastical'. He forthrightly contended that no temporal powers 'have any authority in themselves to usurp, extinguish, pervert, alter, or retard, but only to inspect, and assist with the regular operations of the powers hierarchical'. This was so because the Church was an independent society. The Christianizing of temporal states had been a contingency which was no necessary part of the providential plan. Consequently, the powers of the State impinge not intrinsically but only accidentally upon the functions of Christian pastorship. Christ has enjoined obligations to the State, but they are obligations which apply as much to heathen as to Christian states. Thus no new powers are invested in princes 'by their meer Christianity', and every prince 'that hopes to be saved by his Christianity' ought to be 'conducted in spirituals by the bishops that have the care of his soul'. In a signal ancient case, that of Theodosius and St Ambrose, a Roman emperor had submitted to his bishop for his sins. In citing this case Hill was invoking the most familiar of all hierocratic historical emblems, for if Constantine at the Council of Nicaea was the archetype of sacerdotal kingship, then the clericalist counterpoint lay in the famous humbling of Theodosius at the doors of the cathedral of Milan, forbidden sacramental grace until Ambrose was satisfied with his penance.[71]

Hill went on to insist that, in the last resort, under an ungodly prince, the Church had the right to sever its historic relationship with the State and re-establish its original autonomy. The essence of the Church's integrity lay in the episcopate, and it was the apostolic succession which preserved the continuity of doctrine. In order to preserve apostolicity and orthodoxy the church could, in particular, abrogate the king's acquired power of appointing bishops. Indeed, Hill contended, the princely nomination of bishops had dubious precedents, for the patristic canons had regarded the getting of a bishopric 'through the secular powers' as no less illicit than simony, and it was the heretic Arian emperors who were the first civil powers to force bishops to consecrate men of their own choosing. Hill was here repudiating that part of the 1534 Act of Annates which gave the Crown the right of episcopal appointment. Nor did Hill's critique of the Henrician settlement stop here. The church was furthermore 'not bound to advocate' the Henrician limitation upon the meeting of Convocation and the passing of canon laws, for the church as a corporation has an imprescriptable right of self-government. The absence of regular and free Convocations since the Reformation was an unwarranted 'cramping' of the church which gave

[71] S. Hill, *The Catholic Balance* (1687), sig. A2^r–A3^v; and pp. 107–10, 113–17, 121. The humbling of Theodosius occurred in AD 390.

the Romanists legitimate cause to deride the English church as no more than a department of state. The convening of convocations and synods was a 'primitive and fundamental power and duty' lying in bishops alone, and there was no case for the 'fetters' of the Reformation statutes.[72]

An even more forthright dissolution of the Reformation state-church was proclaimed in Ireland by William King, chancellor of St Patrick's Cathedral.[73] King provided the backbone of Anglican resistance to James in Dublin, vigorously preaching and publishing against Popery. At this stage he staunchly upheld two cardinal Tory principles, non-resistance and intolerance. On both scores, his later Williamite writing is misleading as to his pre-Revolution principles.[74] On the topic of civil obedience, King was, as late as 27 September 1688, still preaching that 'it is not lawful on any pretence whatsoever to take up arms against our lawful governors'. And in 1687 he indiscriminately assaulted 'all Dissenters', both 'Presbyterians and Papists'. He pronounced the Presbyterians guilty of schism and 'sinful separation', excommunicate, and thus deprived of grace, a judgement 'valid and ratified in heaven'.[75] The Anglican resistance to Popery did not license Dissenter resistance to Anglicanism.

King summarized his ecclesiology in an unpublished manuscript called 'Principles of Church Government', set out in thirty-five principles and forty-two corollaries.[76] His first principle was

[72] Hill, *The Catholic Balance*, 121–3. Hill, who later became Archdeacon of Wells, refurbished his High-Church views during the Convocation Controversy: *The Rights, Liberties, and Authorities of the Church* (1701).

[73] The following account draws upon A. Carpenter, 'William King and the Threats to the Church of Ireland during the Reign of James II', *Irish Historical Studies*, 18 (1973), 22–8; and his 'Archbishop King and Dean Swift', Ph.D. thesis (University College, Dublin 1970).

[74] King's *The State of the Protestants in Ireland* (1691) was the most important vindication of William in the wake of the Battle of the Boyne; King's apostasy was denounced by the Irish Nonjuror Charles Leslie: *An Answer to a Book Intituled The State of the Protestants in Ireland* (1692). King's autobiography of 1703 is a misremembrance of his earlier principles: C. S. King (ed.), *A Great Archbishop of Dublin: William King, DD, 1650–1729* (1906), 19–21.

[75] Carpenter, 'Archbishop King', 120, 127, 130–5, 151, 510; King, *An Answer to the Considerations which Obliged Peter Manby . . .* (1687), 34–5. See the pained response of the Presbyterian Joseph Boyce, *Some Impartial Reflections on D. Manby's Considerations* (1687; Wing wrongly gives 1697).

[76] Trinity College, Dublin: MS F. 1. 22, here cited from the transcript in Carpenter, 'Archbishop King', 477–512; which he discusses at pp. 167–79. See also Carpenter, 'William King', 23–5.

'that the church is a society instituted by Christ, that she has certain rights and privileges bestowed on her by her founder and that those are distinct from the rights and privileges of civil society'. Such a society cannot be at the mercy of civil powers, for it must have the 'power to do and require all those things that are necessary . . . to preserve it [as] a society'. It is an impossibility that Christ would leave his society under the 'imperfection' of a lack of means of governance, for no corporation is perfect without a right of self-subsistence. The magistrate may reward, encourage, and punish pastors in support of pastoral tasks, but ultimately, 'in matters that concern these acts the judgement of the church is always to be preferred to the judgement of the civil magistrate, because she is peculiarly entrusted with the execution of them, and they are properly and unappealably tried at her tribunal'. Thus the historical marriage of Church and State 'is only a union of these two societies, without confounding the acts, governments, offices or punishments, and as it began by the mutual agreement of the parties, so it may be broken again'.[77]

It was true that 'both these powers and societies being from God, they are obliged to help and assist one another'. Each awards the other privileges, to the State the privilege of nominating bishops, to the Church the attachment of civil punishments to spiritual censures. But this compact depends upon mutual benefit, and there are, tragically, circumstances when it is better dissolved, 'as where the civil magistrate turns apostate'. Commenting more directly upon Charles II and James II, King cautions that neither the 'personal debauchery' of a libertine prince, nor the mere 'private opinion' of an apostate prince, is sufficient to license the sundering of Church and State. But the church must resume her inherent power if the prince 'denies the church her priveleges in the state, and makes use of her condescensions to ruin her'. King here adopts the standard absolutist principle of *concessio*, 'condescension', long used by English conservatives to explain the existence of customary limitations upon intrinsically absolute authority. He asserts that the church has a recoverable reserve of prerogatives, which only by custom and gracious condescension have been lent to the civil magistrate. He does, however, seek equally to deny Romish claims, and goes on

[77] Carpenter, 'Archbishop King', 477, 478, 480, 481, 482, 486.

symmetrically to insist that it would be wicked for the church to deny princes their own 'just privileges, or make use of her spiritual weapons to dethrone him, or destroy the kingdom'. In this case the prince has the right to recover *his* own intrinsic rights, customarily lent to the church: that was the essence of the Reformation.[78] King had, with striking clarity, restated the 'Gelasian' doctrine of Church and State as coterminous but autonomous spheres, repudiating with equal firmness both papal and caesaro-papal pretensions, in the name of the Anglican idea of 'the catholic balance'.[79]

When King turned from 'principles' to 'corollaries' he addressed present circumstances more specifically. He posed and answered a series of questions. What if the prince refuses to nominate bishops (as was the case in Ireland)? 'The answer is that the nomination of bishops is absolutely necessary to the subsistence of the society', and so the church 'may resume the nomination to herself'. If he nominates somebody wholly unworthy, the church may refuse to consecrate; if he alleges *praemunire*, it would be an unjust law and hence no law.[80] May magistrates forbid clergy to preach the true religion (as James had endeavoured to do)? No, because preaching was an inviolable office of priesthood. May magistrates remove church governors (as James did in suspending bishops)? No, for only bishops may make and unmake bishops, although a prince may remove temporal privileges.[81]

Finally, King posed the most downright of questions: are magistrates liable to spiritual punishments? 'It seems no more unreasonable to subject the governors of commonwealths to spiritual punishments than the governors of the church to temporal.' How far could this go? 'So far as to deprive him of all those benefits that he can challenge [claim] as a member of the church

[78] Carpenter, 'Archbishop King', 485, 487, 488, 491–2.

[79] In the 5th c. Pope Gelasius formulated a doctrine of the complementary spheres of temporal and spiritual power, and of the rights of spiritual authority over all Christians including the emperor. Although he began the development of papalist theory, it could be said that he avoided what Anglicans took to be the exorbitant and unbalanced claims of later papalists and Erastians.

[80] Ibid. 488–90, 494–4. James left the Archbishopric of York vacant for two and a half years, and by 1688 one archbishopric and three bishoprics were vacant in Ireland.

[81] Ibid. 478, 479, 494. As well as suspending Compton of London, James deposed two Scottish bishops for non-compliance: Cairncross of Glasgow and Bruce of Dunkeld.

. . . thus when Constantius brought his gifts to the altar none would receive them.'[82] In the light of the enormous salience, in the long history of Roman–Protestant controversy, of the apparently arcane issue of whether princes may be excommunicated, this claim stands as the most shocking in the whole document. King is careful to say that such an excommunication can never extend to civil punishment: it was that false corollary that was at the very core of the Roman (and radical Calvinist) perversion of Christian politics. Anglicans rightly saw that the source of modern revolutionary doctrine lay in the pernicious claim that princes may be deposed for ungodliness. That notion was so shocking that many royalist Protestants, as well as Erastians, had denied that princes could be excommunicated at all; King recognized that to be an over-reaction and inconsistent with the duty of spiritual pastors. It was imperative to show that it was right to visit James II with every possible spiritual censure.

Hill's book and King's manifesto were astonishingly outspoken pieces of what must be called Anglo-Catholicism. Their sentiments were not isolated ones, and they recur in less systematic form in other writers. Sherlock denied that Protestant churches awarded spiritual authority to princes; on the contrary, 'in matters of faith the authority of the church is so sacred that all Christians are bound in consequence quietly to submit to her decisions'.[83] Freeman similarly argued that 'kings and princes are not properly officers and governors of Christ's church, as a church, it being not a civil or secular, but a distinct, spiritual society'. He allowed that princes have 'external management' of the church, and that Constantine was called a 'civil bishop', but his primary definition of the Catholic Church avoided all reference to civil magistracy, stressing instead the government of 'pastors and bishops'.[84] It was in this spirit that Bishop Compton repudiated the jurisdiction of the Ecclesiastical Commission. The Commission especially appalled churchmen since it had a power of excommunication and a quorum of laymen: the king had, perhaps inadvertently, made the most monstrous of Erastian claims, that the secular

[82] Ibid. 489–90.

[83] W. Sherlock, *A Discourse Concerning the Object of Religious Worship* (1685), 32; *A Short Summary of the Principal Controversies* (1687), 11–12; *A Vindication of Some Protestant Principles* (1688), 35–7, 23–30, 44, 50.

[84] Freeman, *Plain and Familiar Discourse*, 2–3, 6.

state could exercise one of the most fundamental of spiritual offices.[85] Compton asserted that the court had no jurisdiction to 'deny the right and privelege of a Christian bishop'. In a matter of the conduct of his spiritual authority, a bishop could only be tried by his fellow bishops, and this 'by all the laws in the Christian Church in all ages'.[86]

VI

The trial in 1688 by an apostate prince of seven bishops of Christ's church was an occasion that demanded a fulsome enunciation of these principles. In the event, the proceedings turned upon prosaic legal technicalities, and thereby gave some respite to James in not allowing a scene all too reminiscent of the humiliation of Theodosius. Had it been otherwise, this trial would have been as ideologically momentous as the Sacheverell trial a generation later. Whilst the bishops waited, John Nelson wrote that the case would be a 'most glorious confirmation of the truth, and the sacredness of our religion, which seems to be now brought on a public stage'—here was an opportunity to show the church's 'conformity to what the first confessors embraced'.[87]

Both Sancroft and Lloyd prepared notes for speeches which they did not have the opportunity to deliver. Sancroft explained that the Christian's duty was to defend the securities of true religion, and in this business Christ's bishops carried the heaviest burden. 'His duty, as a prelate' was 'to do his utmost endeavour to conserve the profession of the reformed religion' and 'to promote the honour and interest of the church'. An absolute liberty of conscience and the end of the Tests would be 'fatal . . . both [to] the church and religion established, and the laws of the land'. The Indulgence casts aside the discipline of the episcopal church and 'shook . . . the very foundation of the reformed Church of England'. He tactfully added that the Indulgence also demeaned the king's Supremacy 'which all good Christian kings have ever exercised', for it amounted to a renunciation of his

[85] Wood remarked, 'the Commission grants the temporal power a power of excommunication, which is a pure spiritual act': A. Clark (ed.), *The Life and Times of Anthony Wood*, iii (Oxford 1894), 193–4.

[86] *ST*, xi. 1160–1; Compton, *An Exact Account*, 9.

[87] Gutch, i. 360, 14 June. The proceedings of the trial are in *ST*, xi. 183 ff.

duty to support ecclesiastical unity and discipline with the civil sword. Sancroft's stance was echoed by another of the Seven: Bishop White remarked that although he longed to obey the king in all things, he was prevented by 'my dread of the indignation of the King of Kings', to whom he must give an account 'of my managing of the episcopal station'.[88]

Something of these arguments did surface in the trial, in the speeches of Sir Robert Sawyer and Sergeant Pemberton. Sawyer protested that by the Indulgence 'not only the laws of our Reformation, but all the laws for the preservation of the Christian religion in general are suspended'. Given this, the hierarchy's action was legitimate, because the bishops 'are entrusted with the care of souls' and are 'special guardians of the law of uniformity'. Pemberton asserted that the bishops 'have the care of the church, by their very function and offices; and are bound to take care to keep out all those false religions that are prohibited, and designed to be kept out by the law'.[89] Religious laws were not the arbitrary and random injunctions of kings, but the civil protection offered by Christian magistrates to support the spiritual officers of Christ's church.

The same ecclesiology is evident in the iconography of the remarkable number of images of the bishops produced in the aftermath of the trial. There are seven known prints and thirteen portrait engravings, many of them produced in multiple editions, together with eight different medals to be hung around pious necks.[90] Never have the images of English clerics been so widely dispersed. The most famous picture is of a pyramid of seven medallion portraits of the bishops, entwined with palm and laurel leaves, and surmounted by seven mitres, seven candles, and seven stars.[91] One version carries the title 'Primitive Christianity restored', and another '*Immobile saxum*', unyielding rock. All these icons carried biblical texts. Many of these signified the

[88] Gutch, i. 333, 363–9; *ST*, xii. 468; cf. pp. 470–3.

[89] *ST*, xii. 362–4, 372.

[90] *Catalogue of Prints and Drawings in the British Museum* (1870), i. nos. 1168–73, pp. 717–18; also no. 1155, pp. 709–10; O'Donoghue and Hake, *Catalogue of Engraved British Portraits*, v. 75–6; E. H. Plumptre, *The Life of Thomas Ken* (Isbister 1888), ii. 9–10, 292–3; J. R. S. Whiting, *Commemorative Medals* (Newton Abbot 1972), 74–7.

[91] Reproduced in J. Miller, *Religion in the Popular Prints, 1600–1832* (Cambridge 1986), 130–1; and in *History Today*, 38 (July 1988), 12. Another version is reproduced in Speck, *Reluctant Revolutionaries*, between pp. 116 and 117.

triumphs of the righteous. Especially prominent was the Petrine commission: one medal showed the church upon a rock, its steeple held steady by a heavenly hand, and carrying the motto 'the gates of hell shall not prevail against it'.[92] There were abundant emblems of the number seven, a Jewish holy number signifying perfection and completion, as, most familiarly, in the 'seven pillars of wisdom'. Most salient of all was a passage from the Book of Revelation: 'The seven stars are the angels of the seven churches: and the seven golden candlesticks which thou sawest are the seven churches.' The seven churches of Asia Minor—Ephesus, Smyrna, Philadelphia, and so on—were gloriously transposed to Peterborough, Chichester, Bath, and Wells. 'Fear none of those things which thou shalt suffer: behold, the devil shall cast some of you into prison, that ye may be tried; and ye shall have tribulation ten days: be thou faithful unto death, and I will give thee a crown of life.'[93] This apocalyptic last book of the Bible, the reverie of St John, a text born of passionate confrontation with Imperial Rome and once a favourite amongst millenarian Puritans, was here invoked by those who had been accustomed to magnifying the divinity of the Stuart *imperium*. It betokens the degree to which Restoration divines did indeed succeed in their dearest hope of emulating the Fathers, for, like 'the first confessors', they veered precipitately and circumstantially between St John's and Tertullian's alienation from earthly powers, and Eusebius's glorification of Constantine. St Augustine's middle way too often eluded them.[94]

Faced with such loudly hierocratic claims against the temporal power, it seems appropriate that the government should, after its defeat by the trial jury, have contemplated a new trial on a charge of *praemunire*, for 'they did conspire to diminish the royal authority, and royal prerogative, power, and government of the king'.[95] It had been a trial of *rex* versus *sacerdos*. The divines had brought into the fullest light the ambiguity at the heart of the Tory ideology. No earthly power could legitimately coerce God's anointed prince, but no anointed prince could violate a Christian's

[92] Whiting, *Medals*, 74; *British Museum Prints*, i. no. 1164, p. 717.

[93] Rev. 1: 20, 1: 11, 2: 10.

[94] See R. A. Markus, 'The Roman Empire in Early Christian Historiography', *Downside Review*, 81 (1963), 340–53; reprinted in *Saeculum: History and Society in the Theology of St Augustine* (Cambridge 1970).

[95] *ST*, xii. 358.

hope of salvation. Stuart kingship need not bow to secular constitutions, but to Christ's bishops it must, for, as Stillingfleet bluntly put it, 'truth is greater than the king' and, as Scripture taught him, 'the church is the pillar and ground of the truth'.[96] Of course what constituted truth in this case was the right of the Established episcopal Church to impose its doctrines and rituals uniformly upon all the people of England. Although at the time of the trial the hierarchy achieved some accommodation with the Presbyterians, it is arguable that this apparent conversion to a more tolerant position was only skin-deep.[97] Their priority remained the reconstruction of the politically and religiously intolerant polity they had nurtured in the early 1680s.

It is worth, finally, glancing again at the king's beleaguered defenders. Thomas Cartwright was the most forthright amongst the handful of bishops who collaborated with James. When Sancroft refused to serve on the Ecclesiastical Commission he took his place. His opinions amount to a straightforward Erastian absolutism verging on a definition of the civil sovereign as *sacerdos*. In judgement on the Fellows of Magdalen he pronounced that the king was God's 'vicegerant' and that he was thus the 'supreme ordinary' over the church, a phrase importing Constantine's office of civil bishop. To this authority Cartwright claimed that Anglican doctrine required 'an absolute and unconditional' loyalty. He defended the king's toleration policy, contrasting James's renunciation of 'unjust and cruel methods' with the church's 'unchristian heats'. The church's resistance to their Papist king upon a claim of preserving true religion was but a 'vain pretence'. The divines had gone over to the doctrine they professed to hate, the rebellious Puritan doctrine that 'dominion

[96] E. Stillingfleet, *A Vindication of the Answer* (1687), 1; 1 Tim. 3: 15. For the importance in general of placing ecclesiological alongside secular political ideas in this period see B. Tierney, *Religion, Law, and the Growth of Constitutional Thought, 1150–1650* (Cambridge 1982). There have been similar Figgisian efforts to trace 'the road from Constance to 1688': see F. Oakley, 'From Constance to 1688 Revisited', *Journal of the History of Ideas*, 27 (1966), 429–32. An implied point of the present essay is that there was not only a transference of medieval ecclesiological ideas into the secular constitutional sphere, but a direct continuation of them within Anglican ecclesiology.

[97] There is not space to argue the case here, but the point is made by Speck, *Reluctant Revolutionaries*, 186–7. Rather too optimistic a view of the Church's conversion to toleration is taken by R. Thomas, 'Comprehension and Indulgence', in G. F. Nuttall and O. Chadwick (eds.), *From Uniformity to Unity, 1662–1962* (1962).

is founded in grace'. Drawing the Erastian and tolerationist strands together, he urged that the church's continued attempt to reduce Dissenters 'to our way of serving God' in defiance of the Crown was 'to assume the prerogative of the civil power'. That was a 'revocation' of the king's Supremacy, a claim to a rival temporal jurisdiction, a *praemunire*, and tantamount to Popery.[98] Cartwright had earlier produced a more lapidary summation of his views in a sermon of 1686: 'the Keys of the Temple were not hung at the High Priest's girdle, but laid every night under Solomon's pillow, as belonging to his charge'. James, he pronounced, 'is not a Nero, but a Constantine the Great to us'.[99]

In his insistence on the prince's sacerdotal power, Cartwright and his colleagues, the 'Tory collaborators', were closer to Cranmerian Lutheranism, and to Hobbesian caesaro-papism, than were their orthodox fellow bishops, who were, in the proper sense, more 'catholic' than they. For Cartwright, godly duty and civil peace require submission to the prince's ordering of the Christian commonwealth in those things not manifestly hostile to God's word, construed in such a way as to amount to practically everything. This was, on some accounts, including Hobbes's, good Protestantism, but it was not good loyalty to the mainstream of Anglican political theology. James II managed to be both papal and caesaro-papal; his Anglican opponents took care to be neither.

[98] Cartwright, *Answer*, 9, 40–3, 49–50; Bloxam, *Magdalen College*, 114–17. Cartwright was made Bishop of Chester in 1686 against Sancroft's wishes.

[99] T. Cartwright, *A Sermon Preached upon the Anniversary Solemnity of the Happy Inauguration of our Dread Sovereign Lord King James II* (1686), 15. This sermon must have propelled Cartwright towards his bishopric.

3

The Scottish Nobility and the Revolution of 1688–1690

BRUCE P. LENMAN

To argue that the nobility was the most important single determinant of the timing, shape, and consequences of the Scottish response to the Glorious Revolution of 1688 in England is not to accept automatically a crassly over-simple view of the social structure of early-modern Scotland, one which sees in Scotland the simplest of two-tier societies with a mass of poverty-stricken peasants being ground down by an overbearing and tyrannical nobility. This is a seductive vision (for it spares commentators the burden of much thought about a complex reality resistant to generalization), and it has a long and distinguished pedigree. King James VI owed most of his considerable success as a ruler of Scotland to his capacity to co-operate with a Scots nobility most of whose members, not to mention their foibles, he knew intimately. Nevertheless, all his life he generated a continuous barrage of propaganda whose theme was that the Scots lords, left to their own devices, were a barbarous crew filled with what the king called in famous words their 'feckless arrogant conceit of their greatness and power'. In James's mode of discourse this in no way implied sympathy for the lower orders, whom the monarch regarded with undisguised distaste, insisting to Sir Robert Cecil that the histories of all ages and countries had taught him 'what a rotten reed *mobile vulgus* is to lean unto'.[1] It was, however, a logical step for those who wished to justify their assault on the decentralized Scottish polity to argue that in extending their own authority over the land they were really liberating the bulk of the people from the tyrannical abuses of their noble overlords. Oliver Cromwell is an interesting example of this. He was so

[1] G. P. V. Akrigg (ed.), *Letters of King James VI & I* (Berkeley 1984), 7 (Intro.) and 182: King James to Sir Robert Cecil, June (?) 1601.

conscious of the need for ideological justification that he took the pamphleteer John Hall along with him in his Scottish campaign, and after the final defeat of the Scots it was a platitude in Commonwealth governing circles that the new administrative and judicial arrangements being set up in Scotland would not only make English rule secure and effective but would also liberate the commons of Scotland from their long-standing 'absolute' dependence on their feudal superiors.[2] There was a genuine, if limited, radical commitment in the early Commonwealth government of Scotland, but it was fatally wounded by the trauma of Glencairn's Rising, and was replaced by an increasing tendency to appease rather than provoke the traditional rulers of early modern Scottish society.[3] In that sense an aristocratic reaction had set in long before the Restoration, but it must be stressed that the Scottish nobility, like other northern European nobilities in kingdoms with well-developed towns and internal and external trade, not to mention a university-educated intelligentsia, owed their pre-eminence to a general acceptance of their leadership of the complex regional and social hierarchies rather than to beastly assertiveness on what was otherwise a social *tabula rasa*.

As Professor Gordon Donaldson pointed out long ago, what the Restoration restored in Scotland above all else was public recognition of the right of the nobility to lead the country, and many noble houses which had at one time or another been active opponents of Charles I were beneficiaries of this situation.[4] Walter Makey may well be right that the Covenanting movement in its first flush did have embedded in it an important shift of social and economic power away from the high nobility, but even then it has to be said that there was no conscious assault on the traditional role of the nobles,[5] and David Stevenson is surely right when he argues that with the signing of the Engagement,

[2] W. C. Abbot (ed.), *The Writings and Speeches of Oliver Cromwell* (Cambridge, Mass. 1939), 585; L. M. Smith, 'Sackcloth for the Sinner or Punishment for the Crime? Church and Secular Courts in Cromwellian Scotland', in J. Dwyer, R. A. Mason, and A. Murdoch (eds.), *New Perspectives on the Politics and Culture of Early Modern Scotland* (Edinburgh n.d.), 118.

[3] F. D. Dow, *Cromwellian Scotland 1651–60* (Edinburgh 1979).

[4] G. Donaldson, *Scotland: James V to James VII* (Edinburgh 1965), 358–9.

[5] W. H. Makey, *The Church of the Covenant 1637–1651: Revolution and Social Change in Scotland* (Edinburgh 1979).

and the rallying of a large proportion of the Scots nobility to the cause of Charles I in 1647–8, Scotland saw a 'limited but dramatic counter-revolution', which in a sense went on to take over the governance of Scotland in 1660.[6]

As a polity, Restoration Scotland was extremely aristocratic, despite the ritual eulogies of virtually unbridled royal power uttered by conservative politicians who expected in practice to run the show themselves, and who must have had more than an inkling that they were unlikely to see Charles II again on the soil of the ancestral kingdom he had learned cordially to detest. Although Charles II even *in absentia* remained a potent figure in the politics of Scotland, it can be argued that Restoration Scotland saw the beginnings of a technique which is one of the distinguishing features of the political style of the British Establishment in the twentieth century: preposterous levels of public sycophancy towards a Crown whose extensive powers have been usurped by the politicians.

In the twentieth-century United Kingdom, all royal power has been concentrated in the hands of a single person through what Lord Hailsham has called the elective dictatorship of the prime minister, a formidable engine of personal rule, not least because of the coercive potential of the military, police, and bureaucratic machinery at its disposal. To understand the infinitely less powerful personal monarchy of Restoration Scotland it is essential to realize that it possessed virtually none of these resources. There was no police force as we understand the term, the paid servants of the Crown were few in number, and the restored Stuarts were quite unable to match the precocious military developments which on the Continent have been seen as amounting to a 'military revolution'. On the contrary, Scotland went just about as far as it was possible to go along the opposite path of evolving techniques which furnished the régime in power with adequate military security against current challenges without expanding, indeed whilst at several crucial points running down the professional army.

Nothing brings out more clearly the underlying realities of Restoration Scotland than the history of the Scottish militia. It is

[6] D. Stevenson, *Revolution and Counter-Revolution in Scotland, 1644–1651* (1977), 120 (where Stevenson is in fact confirming the view expressed by Professor Gerald Aylmer).

also a much underestimated and misunderstood subject. For example, if we take one of the Scots exiles who accompanied William of Orange when he landed in England in 1688, Andrew Fletcher of Saltoun, we will find that the importance of his writings on the militia question, of which the first was published in 1697, has been recognized and admirably demonstrated with particular reference to the sustained eighteenth-century debate in both England and Scotland on the desirable relationship between standing armies and militia in the light of contemporary ideas on civic virtue and limited government. This debate was particularly lively within the Scottish Enlightenment, a culture much given to talking about civic virtue in a country which was so deeply distrusted by English politicians that it was not allowed to have a militia.[7] What has been almost entirely ignored by historians is the massive reality of the militia in Restoration Scotland and in the early political life of Andrew Fletcher, for the simple fact is that the professional army which Charles II and his most prominent servant in Scotland immediately after 1660, the Earl of Middleton, managed to maintain went into relative eclipse within three years of the Restoration. Partly this was explicable in terms of the political clash between Middleton and his arch-rival, the Earl of Lauderdale, but the ability of Lauderdale and his able confidant Sir Robert Moray to undermine Middleton's attempt to use an expanded regular army, as a personal power base, was rooted in widespread noble support for their alternative proposals, which were carefully calculated to appeal to the economic and political interests of the aristocracy. Middleton, a jumped-up soldier of fortune, did not enjoy significant ties of blood or interest with the bulk of the older nobility.[8]

After the conclusion of the unpopular and unsuccessful Dutch wars, the Scotland of Charles II faced no threat of invasion from without. What the government needed was military capability against internal subversion of a regionalized and comparatively poorly-armed kind. For this an expanded militia was more than enough. It was commanded by politically trustworthy members of the nobility who earned credit with the Crown for their willingness to serve it in this capacity, but who also made secure

[7] J. Robertson, *The Scottish Enlightenment and the Militia Issue* (Edinburgh 1985).

[8] A. Robertson, *The Life of Sir Robert Moray* (1922), 119–21.

two objectives so basic to the aspirations of the nobility that it would have been the height of bad taste openly to articulate them. One was common to all rightist political groups rooted in conservative vested interests, then as now: to keep taxation low. Regulars had in theory to be paid for 365 days in the year. Militia, active service apart, could be paid for as little as ten days per annum. Secondly, the ultimate lever of power—physical force—was kept firmly in noble hands. Passive obedience was the official ideology of the Restoration social establishment in Scotland. Behind it lurked the possibility of passive disobedience by a nobility which knew full well that they could paralyse the Crown by folding their arms. Gilbert Burnet, another Scots exile who accompanied William's invasion in 1688 to act as part chaplain and part unofficial (and therefore repudiable) public relations officer, had been an intimate friend of Sir Robert Moray, the original architect of the Restoration 'militia option'.[9] Fletcher of Saltoun's earliest political activity of consequence took the form of attempts to obstruct the levying of his local county militia, because he disapproved of the uses to which it was being put. The Scots exile circle round William of Orange in 1688 was full of men who understood very well the realities of power in their native land.

Until the last years of the reign of James II and VII the militia system worked perfectly adequately. The so-called Highland Host which descended upon and intimidated recalcitrant Covenanting areas in the western Lowlands in 1678 did contain some irregular units raised in the Highlands, but the vast bulk of the force consisted of county militia regiments from the Stuart loyalist heartland north of the Forth, commanded by the Scots-speaking magnates who had originally raised them. There was still a small regular Scots army, but it was possible to reduce it to as little as a thousand men. This combination of militia and regulars proved adequate to crush Argyll's rebellion in 1685, after which the lands of the Clan Campbell were occupied by Perthshire militia units under the command of that county's leading magnate, a man later prominent in the politics of post-Revolution Scotland, John Murray, first Marquess of Atholl. In the year or two before the Revolution, however, James II undermined this whole security

[9] There is a convenient summary of Burnet's debt to Moray's sponsorship in the entry for Burnet in *DNB*.

system as he became increasingly obsessed with achieving his central objective of a government not dependent on the consent of the governed. That presupposed executive reliance on biddable professional soldiers, and rather implied that the more society in general could be disarmed, the better. The Scots militia system was allowed to fall into desuetude, on the specious pretext that James was worried about the burden it imposed on his subjects. As the militia decayed, the professional army was expanded to an efficient, but still small force of about 3,000 men.[10] It was the decision to move almost all the army into England during the tense period of confrontation which preceded the Dutch invasion that destroyed the entire Scottish security system, leaving the Scottish state defenceless. The situation was curiously similar to the one which Prince Charles Edward Stuart was to face late in 1745, when he argued passionately with faint-hearted supporters, pointing out that the Union government had so run down home-defence forces in Scotland that power could be seized by any resolute minority willing to risk its hand.

There is, of course, a controversy surrounding the decision to send the Scots troops across the border. It is largely the product of the fertile imagination of a man who succeeded in surviving in high office after 1688, despite having been Lord Melfort's under-secretary before the Revolution. This was the lawyer Sir James Stewart of Goodtrees (pronounced 'Gutters'), who alleged that he advised Melfort to reject an alternative proposed by his rival within the régime, Colin Earl of Balcarres, which alternative Goodtrees implied would have given King James a stronger overall military position. Balcarres, head of one of the two noble branches of the Lindsay family, put forward a joint proposal with his political ally the Earl of Cromarty. They suggested that the considerable reserves of money which had accumulated in the Scottish treasury should be used to raise ten battalions of foot, as well as 4,000 or 5,000 irregulars from the Highlands. In addition, Cromarty and Balcarres wanted to raise the 'Arrière Van' and select from it 1,200 horse which would be the final supplement to the regular army's 4,000 to 5,000 troops and would give a field army of some 15,000 men. This they contended would more than suffice to hold down the North of England. The plan was unhesi-

[10] B. P. Lenman, 'Militia Fencible Men and Home Defence 1660–1797', in N. A. Macdougall (ed.), *Scotland and War* (forthcoming).

tatingly and rightly rejected by Lord Melfort, a man who even Balcarres admitted was in the crisis of late 1688 trying to serve King James to the best of his not inconsiderable abilities. The reason for the rejection of the plan was its mixture of unrealism and political cynicism. The give-away, even to modern eyes, is the 'Arrière Ban' (to give it its more usual feudal title). This was technically an assembly of all tenants-in-chief of the Crown, supported by mounted men in proportion to the knight-service due for their estates. Regiments of foot of any use could not be raised at the drop of a hat, and the idea of trying to raise a feudal anachronism which had ceased to function centuries ago was lunacy. It was also a political ploy, for Balcarres belonged to the small group of Protestant Episcopalian magnates still prepared to work within a regime which had fatally alienated the bulk of their kind. Balcarres was confident that in the long run the ascendancy of a Roman Catholic convert clique, led by the Drummond brothers, was not viable. His unrealistic but super-loyal proposal was a paper position from which to move out after circumstances had forced James to compromise.[11]

Recent work has left us in little doubt that William of Orange always meant to try to make James run away, but even William could not be sure that the plan would work.[12] Most other observers of the mounting crisis assumed, reasonably, until very late in the day, that the outcome would be a bridled, but still reigning King James. The central problem facing James in Scotland was not treachery, of which there was very little within his administration, but self-imposed isolation. It was not that the Scottish nobility were violently biased against their Roman Catholic monarch. On the contrary, between 1679 and 1682, when James had been in Scotland a great deal, seeking refuge from the storms of agitation raging against him in England, the Scots nobles and learned classes had shown warm loyalty to his person and dignity, and the support which enabled the government to crush Argyll so easily in 1685 shows that those same groups still saw James as the keystone in the conservative Royalist political and cultural structure, which they hoped to build as the basis for a great renaissance

[11] The handiest version of this murky business is in Alexander Crawford, Lord Lindsay, *Lives of the Lindsays*, ii (2nd edn., 1858), 156–9, where the account in Balcarres's *Memoirs* is supplemented by additional correspondence.

[12] H. and B. Van Der Zee, *Revolution in the Family* (1988).

of Scottish achievement.[13] In the last two years before the Revolution James had by his violently Catholicizing policies, and the autocratic government which he saw as the only way to make those policies work, fatally alienated not only the nobility of Scotland, but also virtually every other influential group in the country. To make a bad situation worse, the Drummond brothers, Lords Perth and Melfort, had brilliantly manipulated the mind of an incompetent absentee monarch whose brain was a mass of violently held but often contradictory prejudices to monopolize power and position within the Scottish government. They broke with the Marquess of Queensberry, who had done so much to aid their own rise, and they drove him out of politics, patronizing only former associates of Queensberry who had quarrelled with him, like John Graham of Claverhouse, later Viscount Dundee. The second Viscount Middleton found it safer to abandon Scottish politics for English office, leaving his Scottish estates in the care of trustees.[14] An ultra-royalist political pedigree was therefore no protection against the predatory Drummonds, and though Perth's conversion, unlike Melfort's, was sincere, Perth joined his rascally brother in doing down all other interests, including the old Catholic interest.

Given his deep distrust of his heretic subjects, there was no way King James was going to modify his policy of concentrating all troops under his own immediate command. James therefore carries the responsibility for leaving the Scots nobles in a state of confusion and alienation at the same time as he left the Scottish state without any capacity to defend itself at a time of dramatic political change and turmoil. What James had done over a two-year period was to destroy the social compact on which his ability to govern rested.

It is important to stress the need for the exercise of imaginative sympathy, because the latest modern study of their activity at this time, Patrick Riley's monograph on *The Scottish Politicians and William III*, is written out of the camp of that 'Black Legend' of the Scottish nobility which we have seen can be traced back to at least the sixteenth century. Indeed, it is an extreme example

[13] H. Ouston, 'York in Edinburgh: James VII and the Patronage of Learning in Scotland, 1679–88', in Dwyer *et al.*, *New Perspectives*, 133–55.

[14] G. H. Jones, *Charles Middleton: The Life and Times of a Restoration Politician* (Chicago 1967), 70–1.

of this kind of writing. Even Riley describes his book as providing 'a bilious view of the seventeenth-century Scottish nobility and gentry'. Partly this is because his monograph takes an inexcusably teleological view of late seventeenth-century Scotland. It was clearly written as the opening chapters of a study of the incorporating Act of Union of 1707. Riley's central theme is that the instability of the combinations between Atholl, Argyll, Hamilton, and Queensberry—the four great magnate interests which flourished between 1688 and 1707 in the Scots Estates or parliament—and the fierce egotism with which the leading magnates sought their own personal advantage made the Scottish legislature something of which the kingdom was well rid. Since such a viewpoint requires that nothing but destructive factionalism ever influenced the evolution of Scottish politics after 1688, Riley has to argue that religion was of no importance whatever in the politics of late seventeenth-century Scotland. About most of the population of the realm he has nothing to say, and about deficiencies in kingship, which just possibly may have been of some consequence in an age of monarchy, he is almost equally coy. Despite the undoubted industry and learning so admirably displayed on successive pages of technical analysis in this book, it is more of a demonstration of misplaced and misguided Namierism than a piece of balanced historical writing.[15] Besides, it is written with no serious sense of the comparative dimension, even if that dimension be confined to England. Turberville, in his classic study of the English House of Lords in the reign of William III, concluded that the English nobility not only made the Glorious Revolution, but also contrived to extract from it a settlement in Church and State which broadly corresponded with their preferences and prejudices. Though as laudatory about parliamentary institutions in England as one might expect of a man publishing in 1913, Turberville did not contend that the peerage he studied was a band of haloed angels, rather a cross-section of humanity tending to the mediocre, albeit with some significant public spirit and some pockets of real ability.[16] In Scotland we must study something quite different: a nobility caught in a Revolution not of its own making, which produced circumstances that made it impossible to extract settlements in

[15] P. W. J. Riley, *King William and the Scottish Politicians* (Edinburgh 1979).
[16] A. S. Turberville, *The House of Lords in the Reign of William III* (Oxford 1913).

the Kirk by law established and in the political sphere which commanded the support of a broad aristocratic consensus.

The great achievement of the Restoration nobility of Scotland had been to keep the professional military establishment in the hands of the Crown to a bare minimum, thus ensuring that even James lacked the means to govern Scotland without consent once he lost control of his English power base. Once James fled to France, however, and then returned to Ireland with French troops to fight a civil war in the British Isles, the horrendous possibility existed that the lack of entrenched authority in Scotland would lead to a general relapse into the sort of bloody and destructive civil war which the Marquess of Montrose had unleashed on the nation in 1644–5. His kinsman John Graham of Claverhouse set out deliberately to do just that. With the gift of hindsight we know that the lucky bullet which killed him in his moment of victory at the battle of Killiecrankie in the summer of 1689 marked the beginning of the end of any serious Jacobite threat to the Lowlands, but this was less obvious at the time.

The establishment of effective Williamite government in Scotland owed a great deal to the Scottish nobility, not so much because of what they did, as because of what they chose not to do. A historian prepared to take seriously the power of political and religious ideas in early-modern society, especially when they intertwined, will realize how difficult it was for most Scots nobles to act against James. Ever since 1660 they, the Episcopal order in the Kirk by law established, which most nobles strongly supported, and the universities, which trained the clergy of that Kirk, had invested massive intellectual and moral capital in the linked ideologies of indefeasible hereditary succession, divine right, and passive obedience. For the bishops it was to prove impossible to jettison the Jacobite commitment implicit in that complex of ideas. Those ideas helped many nobles to make a transition to active Jacobitism in the sour years ahead.[17]

Yet, no noble of real consequence took the field for James during the crisis of the Revolution. Arguments *ex silentio* being always suspect, it is fortunate that we have an account of the mental processes of at least one major figure who had been an

[17] B. P. Lenman, 'The Scottish Episcopal Clergy and the Ideology of Jacobitism', in E. Cruickshanks (ed.), *Ideology and Conspiracy: Aspects of Jacobitism, 1689–1759* (Edinburgh 1982), 36–48.

active leader of militia forces during the counter-subversion operations of the Restoration governments. This is Patrick Lyon, third Earl of Kinghorne and first Earl of Strathmore. His father had held command under Montrose. He himself had been in charge of the commissariat for the forces which crushed Argyll's rising in 1685. He had married a daughter of the ultra-royalist first Earl of Middleton. From the point of view of the late Restoration régime in Scotland, here was a trusty of the trusties. He was of course a staunch upholder of an Episcopal order in matters ecclesiastical, having been married in Holyrood by Archbishop Sharp, the prelate subsequently martyred by Presbyterian extremists. Strathmore's first reaction to the threat of an invasion by the Prince of Orange had been the wholly loyal one of co-operating with the Earls of Southesk, Callendar, and Breadalbane in an attempt to reactivate the near-defunct militia. The earls found that the militia system had been allowed to decay beyond the point where this was a realistic option. Though they were trying to embody militia in the classic period for late military operations—after the harvest—they found that the few men they could get together just dwindled away. James II's militia policy had succeeded only too well. Thereafter, Strathmore looked on with awe as William's invasion achieved more at a lower cost than anyone could reasonably have expected. The earl recorded in his private record that 'all succeeded with the Prince to a miracle'. By the time James had fled England Strathmore was well aware that the bulk of the Scots nobility, plus a large section of the lairds, had flocked to London to lobby the Prince of Orange. Others told him, very fairly, that it was his duty to his family and dependants (in other words his duty as a conservative nobleman) not to be left behind. He himself recorded that it 'was obvious enow to myself a necessity for me to go', and go he did, bearing the address of the Scots Privy Council to William. He was accompanied by his son, Lord Glamis. Strathmore did decline to depute for the Marquess of Atholl as commander-in-chief in Scotland, but he took the oath of allegiance to William in April 1690 and lived quietly under his rule until death removed him from the Scottish scene in 1695.[18]

[18] A. H. Millar (ed.), *Glamis Book of Record by Patrick, First Earl of Strathmore 1684–1689* (Scottish History Soc. 9, Edinburgh 1890), see Intro. and p. 90.

This sort of record may not be the stuff of epics, but it showed surprising flexibility, great good sense, and public as well as private responsibility. There were many noblemen who followed a similar path, like the Earls of Southesk and Breadalbane, who joined Strathmore in September 1689 in the prudent but significant gesture of acceptance of the Williamite régime, at least *de facto*, involved in taking advantage of the indemnity which William had wisely offered to those who might fear persecution on account of real or alleged acts of support for the fallen King James. Of course, many noblemen would have much preferred to keep James as nominal sovereign. There was much to be said for this. The Earl of Arran, for example, had been so close to James that the Revolution strained even his capacity for changing horses. He had been a Gentleman of the Bedchamber, had acted as Ambassador to the Court of France, had commanded Household Troops, and was one of the four peers who accompanied James to Rochester when he was expelled from Whitehall. The Earl of Dumbarton, another of the four noblemen accompanying James to Rochester, could not bring himself to accept the Revolution. He had held overall command of the royal forces in Scotland during Argyll's rising. He was to die in exile at Saint Germain in 1692. His son never returned to Scotland, and after him the peerage became extinct.[19]

It is therefore wholly understandable that when the Scots nobility and gentry present in London convened in Whitehall in January 1689 to frame an address to the Prince of Orange, Arran stood up and stressed that, though he wished William well, deeming him the hero who had delivered them all from Popery, he had to distinguish between the Popery of his master, King James, and his person, to whom Arran, the unworthy heir to the Duchy of Hamilton, had sworn allegiance. Arran expressed a strong preference for a settlement by free parliaments under James.[20] Had he not said something like this, his stock in what was still a shame and honour society would have sunk even lower. Also, it was a safe thing to say, for James had already fled

[19] All otherwise unascribed material on members of the Scottish peerage is drawn from G.E.C., *The Complete Peerage* (13 vols. 1921–49).

[20] *A Speech made by the Right Honourable the Earl of Arran, to the Scotch Nobility and Gentry, met together at the Council Chamber in Whitehall, on the Eighth of January 1688* . . . (London: printed for T.J. 1689).

England and would clearly never swallow the idea of a dialogue with the English or Scottish ruling classes until he had exhausted every other way. In practice, Arran did actively work with the new Williamite régime in Scotland. So did Atholl, who like Arran had been one of the eight original knights of the Order of the Thistle, when James refounded it in 1687. In many ways it would have been preferable to keep James on his throne with suitable publicly registered safeguards enforced by statute. Not only would this have been tender of conservative consciences, but it would also have recognized the need for formal checks and balances within an extremely dangerous political system, a need which was in fact obscured during the crucial months of fluidity in 1688–9 by a tacit conspiracy between William and James.

Committed Williamites like Major-General Hugh Mackay of Scourie, the veteran from the Dutch service, who commanded the government forces during Claverhouse's rising, were forever complaining about the half-hearted and equivocal service rendered to the new régime even by its nominal supporters. Mackay moaned that Mackenzie of Tarbat was doing less than his all at the height of the civil war, and that Atholl should have been far more active than he was, given the prevalence of Jacobite elements in some of his territories.[21] Given the way both William and James had played their cards, passivity, equivocation, and tepid enthusiasm were the only likely responses from the bulk of the resident Scots nobility. This was neither entirely their fault, nor entirely to their discredit. Due to the nature of its cultural history in the recent past the Scots nobility as a body would have been quite incapable of subscribing to the sort of *apologia* produced by an activist minority of the English ruling classes assembled in Nottingham in the course of the Revolution, which said flatly that though resistance to a lawful king was always wrong, resistance to a monarch like James, who had violated the laws to introduce Popery and arbitrary tyranny, was a positive duty. Apart from a tiny minority, most Scots nobles found this sort of thing unthinkable.[22] What they could do was allow the Revolution to occur, mainly by doing nothing.

[21] Major-General Hugh Mackay, *Memoirs of the War Carried on in Scotland and Ireland 1689–91, with an Appendix of Original Papers* (Edinburgh 1833), 227–8.

[22] *The Declaration of the Nobility, Gentry and Commonality at the Rendezvous at Nottingham, November 22, 1688*. This is a broadside listed in Wing D717, and in

Yet, in a situation where, after Claverhouse had raised his standard, there was a small active Jacobite minority in Scotland, the passivity of the bulk of the nobility and lairds, though a massive discouragement to the Jacobites, would not by itself have ensured a change of régime. Some change in the balance of power would have occurred even if Claverhouse had been successful, for he was accompanied on his return to Scotland from the army in England by Balcarres, who carried a commission from James making him the head of the civil administration of the kingdom. Though never activated, that commission alone would have sealed the eclipse of his detested rivals, the Drummond brothers, and the convert interest. Arran's suggestion that James be asked to return from exile to face a free parliament would have made change more radical and secure, but it was never a realistic suggestion. What was needed in the regions of Scotland was a Williamite minority with sufficient local standing to neutralize the efforts of Jacobite agents to raise large numbers for King James. As Lord John Murray, heir to Atholl, explained to the Duke of Hamilton in June 1689, even in the Highlands, where arms and Jacobite sentiments were more abundant than in the Lowlands, it was difficult to raise a countryside in the absence of a broad political consensus:

> for here the weaker dare not take conterar courses to the stronger least they shoud destroy their goods and country; this is so true that I am certainly informed that our neighbours, the Badenoch men, tho they belong to the Duke of Gordon, would never rise with Dundee, tho he has been all this while in their country for fear of the Atholl men, who, if they should not joine too, would destroy their country when they were away, so that Dundee has been forced to burn their houses and take their goods.[23]

Murray's role in the campaign which culminated in the battle of Killiecrankie was notoriously unheroic, amounting to little more than an unenthusiastic siege of his own family's historic seat, Blair Castle, which was being held rather passively on behalf of King James by the family steward. The battle, like so many early-modern general actions, was precipitated by the

R. Steele, *Tudor and Stuart Proclamations, 1485–1714* (2 vols., Oxford 1910), no. 3906. It was most likely published in London in 1688.

[23] Lord Murray to the Duke of Hamilton, 4 June 1689, printed in the Appendix to Mackay, *Memoirs of the War*, 223–5.

siege nearby. However, Murray's real service to the Williamite cause lay in the hours of negotiation, in the course of which he persuaded his own people not to rise *en masse*, often at the cost of turning a blind eye to unmistakable signs of Jacobite sympathies. Murray even argued with the militantly Jacobite Robertson of Struan that it was cheating to poach Robertsons, who owed suit to Atholl and not to the Barony of Struan. Such Robertsons 'belonged' to Atholl and not to the Clan Donnachie over which Struan presided as chief. Atholl men did join Dundee, but there was a world of difference between this sort of seepage and what would have happened if the Atholl family had been unequivocally Jacobite.

The disproportionately effective dampening effect produced by the comparatively few supporters of the Revolution in the central area of the Highlands, which is where most of the active opposition to the Revolution was concentrated, can be demonstrated even more convincingly by the rage and fury which the Jacobites displayed towards these men. Two good examples are 'the laird of Balnagowen, the chief of the name of Rosse', and Grant of Grant. Next to Seaforth, chief of the Mackenzies, Ross of Balnagowan was the biggest landowner in the county of Ross, of which he was appointed Sheriff Principal by the Estates of Scotland in response to a request from General Mackay, who knew him to be an active Williamite, as well as a man with a large following. The 'laird of Grant', Ludovick Grant of Freuchie, was the most important man on Speyside. He had been a major in Claverhouse's cavalry regiment, and a most loyal supporter of James, aiding him with troops both in 1679 and 1685, but he had been fined by that monarch for supporting illegal Presbyterian preachers, and dismissed from the Privy Council for opposition to catholicizing policies. Earlier, he had co-operated with Andrew Fletcher of Saltoun in opposing royal policies in the Scottish parliament at a time when this required greater moral courage because of the presence of James Duke of Albany (always known as Albany, rather than York, in Scotland), the future King James. It is therefore less surprising that at the Revolution Grant emerged as a militant Williamite, rather than as an ambiguous pussyfooter. He became Sheriff of Inverness-shire, and raised a regiment of 700–800 men with which he rendered solid assistance to General Mackay. The laird of Grant never could effectively control the two outlying and separate parts of the clan territory on the other side of the Great Glen in Glenmoriston and Glen Urquhart, and in 1688–9 Grant of Glenmoriston was an active Jacobite. Nevertheless, the cause of the Revolution in the Highlands owed an enormous debt to the name of Grant.

It was scarcely less indebted to the name of Forbes. The Master of Forbes (i.e., the heir to the chief of the name or clan) was an active supporter of William of Orange.[24] The other Grant lairds included some of the most committed supporters of the Revolution in Scotland, most conspicuously perhaps in the shape of the Forbes of Culloden family. Duncan Forbes of Culloden, eldest son of John, Provost of Inverness, a burgh with which the family always had intimate links, had represented Nairnshire in Restoration parliaments or conventions and he went on to represent Inverness-shire in the Convention of 1689 which was to validate the Revolution in Scotland. More important by far was his activism in his native region, an activism for which the Jacobites made him pay heavily.

General Mackay, a Highlander himself, had a very realistic understanding of what the Jacobites were likely to do to the estates of such men. He told Lord Melville in June 1689 that 'som perticullar men may cum to suffer, perticullarly the Laird of Grant, at whom they have a great prejudice, as well as the rest of our friends, but he lyes the most exposed of all, but if the whole be saved the perticular breaches may be easily made up'.[25] It was a shrewd assessment, though biased towards the laird's lost rents rather than the tenant's burnt house, destroyed crops, and houghed cattle. In the end most of these Williamites were compensated for their losses, though not usually in straight cash, which with men like Forbes of Culloden claiming for damages of 54,000 pounds Scots (4,500 pounds sterling) would have cost the Scots taxpayer a great deal of money. Grant of Freuchie was rewarded in 1694 with a Crown charter which converted his barony of Freuchie into the Regality of Grant, one of the many mini-kingdoms which existed in early-modern Scotland. Apart from high treason the Crown writ did not normally run in the great regalities, though of course the co-operation of their lords enhanced rather than weakened royal power, which in such

[24] Mackay, *Memoirs of the War*, 242.

[25] Ibid. 230.

regions existed more by courtesy of local power than in its own right. Grant's principal seat, Ballachachastell ('the castle-holding') was renamed Castle Grant, and his own designation changed from Grant of Freuchie to Grant of Grant. The family debts, further enhanced by unrequited services for the House of Hanover in 1715, continued to mount until they go far to explain the undynamic performance of Grant of Grant during the '45, but that is another story.[26]

The compensation eventually granted to the Forbes of Culloden family was both ingenious and memorable. The Scots Estates bestowed upon them the perpetual right to distil into spirits the grain of their barony of Ferintosh, subject to the payment of a small specific composition in lieu of excise duty. Inevitably, the barony of Ferintosh became the site of a remarkable concentration of distilling activity, and the word 'ferintosh' became a synonym in Scots for 'whisky'. Burns so uses it in his poetry in the latter part of the eighteenth century. The effect of all of this on the Culloden family was mixed. Their finances were wonderfully braced, which is one reason why they retained their anti-Jacobite zeal right through to the '45. On their constitutions the effects were less desirable, for they developed a prodigious taste for the whisky which was available to them so cheaply and in literally unlimited quantities. Duncan Forbes, who was laird at the time of the Revolution was succeeded by his eldest son John, known significantly as 'Bumper John' (who died prematurely), and then by the younger son Duncan, a lawyer of distinction and man of business to the Argyll interest. Duncan was Lord President of the Court of Session at the time of the '45. His first biographer, who preserves intimate family material omitted from later, and more guarded, biographies, records that the two brothers were acknowledged to be 'the greatest boozers in the North'.[27]

To the Williamite activism of a minority and the apathy of the great bulk of the ruling groups, there must be added as an explanation of the course of events in Scotland in 1688–90 the quite extraordinary ambiguity and inactivism of some who at first sight might be thought to have been irreversibly committed

[26] *DNB* gives a useful account of the Laird of Grant of Revolution vintage. The subsequent fortunes of his house are traced as far as the '45 and its aftermath in B. P. Lenman, *The Jacobite Clans of the Great Glen 1650–1784* (1984).

[27] *DNB*.

supporters of King James. The history of the behaviour of the Duke of Gordon and of the potentially formidable Gordon interest in the North-East (Aberdeenshire and Banffshire) here provides the most instructive case-study. The Duke of Gordon was in a sense the head of the old Catholic interest in Scotland, though historically the males of his house had been more remarkable for general conservatism in religion than for great enthusiasm for its Counter-Reformation variety. At the time of the Revolution the Duke of Gordon was Governor of Edinburgh Castle, which he held for his master against the not too formidable siege of the forces supporting the Prince of Orange. As the latter lacked a siege train, and could do little more than lob the odd mortar bomb into the castle, the fray offered few opportunities for distinction to either side. The more interesting situation was that in the North-East, where the Gordon lands seemed to offer a reservoir of resources to any Jacobite army. After all, those lands included regions like the Enzie which were almost one hundred per cent Roman Catholic, and the Gordons were historically unique among the Highland clans because of their ability to put significant cavalry forces into the field.

In the county of Banff, where Sir James Baird of Auchmedden and Sir George Gordon of Edinglassie were joint Sheriffs-Principal, there had been no signs of spontaneous disaffection towards King James. The birth of the Prince of Wales, which helped precipitate the Revolution in England, merely provoked loyal sermons in Banffshire kirks. When a desperate James tried to reverse his militia policy in Scotland, and ordered the embodiment of the force he had tried to consign to oblivion, the Banff authorities did their best to raise the county militia with a view to its joining a concentration of northern militia forces at Brechin in Angus. Nothing very much seems to have come of this exercise, partly because the machinery of the militia was so rusty, and partly because the commander of these militia units was the Earl of Erroll. His wife was a sister of James's Scottish favourite Lord Chancellor Perth, but relations between brother and sister had been strained by Perth's heavy-handed attempts to pressure her into following him into the Roman communion, and in any case Erroll chose to maintain a cordially correct relationship with the Williamite régime which seized control in Edinburgh.

Thus, there was no way that the mechanism of county government could be used to create armed support for James in Banff. The possibility still remained that something could be done by mobilizing the interest of Alexander, first Duke of Gordon, a magnate with extensive interests in the counties of Aberdeen, Banff, Moray and Inverness, interests which made him the greatest man north of the Grampians. Banffshire provides an elegant illustration of the way in which key local men within the structure of Gordon power were able to ensure that it was never thrown into the scales on the Jacobite side. In the ducal stronghold of the Regality of Achindoun, his local administrator, the Baron Bailie Alexander Duff (Wadsetter of Keithmore by virtue of lending money to the duke on the security of those lands), along with his rising lawyer son, Alexander Duff of Bracco and Balvenie, proved to be more than willing to support the new régime, and thereby to lay the foundation of a new territorial power. By 1700, for example, they had brought out the Banffshire estates of the great Angus nobleman the Earl of Airlie, who was vaguely Jacobite in 1688, but who after a period of preventive detention by the government of the Williamite Estates displayed the distinct lack of enthusiasm for martyrdom characteristic of so many of the nominal supporters of James, and came to terms with the new dispensation by 1690. For a nobleman preventive detention was more like a restrictive hotel than a prison, as Mackay pointed out when Seafield prevaricated about subjecting himself to it as part of the process of sidling into a *modus vivendi* with the new rulers in a way that was compatible with the mandarinical Highland concept of saving face whilst facing reality.[28] Apart from anything else, a spell in Edinburgh Castle once it fell to William's partisans was a very convenient way of avoiding difficult decisions for families which prided themselves on their 'loyalty'.

Sir George Gordon of Edinglassie proved to be one of the most dedicated supporters of the Revolution in Scotland, for he raised men and fought beside General Mackay, who thought very highly of him indeed. The general reckoned that during the crucial early stages of the civil war launched by Claverhouse it was Edinglassie more than any person who ensured that Aberdeenshire and Banffshire produced only a slight reinforcement for the

[28] Mackay, *Memoirs of the War*, 349–50.

Jacobite army. As usual in such cases, the Jacobites expressed their assessment of the importance of Edinglassie's actions by extensive and destructive attacks on his estates, in the course of which they burnt his main residence. Appointed to a regular cavalry command by way of some compensation, he spent himself in the service of the Revolution, dying in the course of his duties of natural causes. He was accorded a military funeral, as befitted one who had done much to win a war which had not yet drawn to a close, though after Killiecrankie and Dunkeld in the summer of 1689 it was clear the Jacobites would be unable to turn it into a major challenge to the stability of Scottish society. Mackay may not have been a great general, but he was competent and tenacious, and though he had relatively little support in the Highlands, he was enough of a realist to see how that support could be used to isolate active Jacobites by persuading waverers to stay at home. Seaforth was no Jacobite militant, but his leanings in that direction were much checked by the knowledge that to the north of him ranged committed Williamites such as Lords Reay and Strathnaver, and to the south lay Edinglassie. Mackay was rather perturbed by the inactivity of Argyll, whose restoration to wealth and power undoubtedly helped to confirm the Jacobitism of some Central Highland clans, and the general worried about the lack of an Argyll counterweight to the ambiguities of the Breadalbane Campbells. Yet the Earl of Breadalbane proved no real supporter of King James.[29] For that matter, the Duke of Gordon surrendered Edinburgh Castle suspiciously fast before buckling down to the task of living with the new government. The North-East was merely an extreme example of a common fact of Scottish life at the time of the Revolution: Jacobitism had more bark than bite.

It had been deprived of any chance of extensive support by King James himself when he wrote that famous letter to the Convention of Estates in Edinburgh, in which he made it only too clear that he was back on his highest absolutist horse. The Convention had been opened with prayer by Bishop Alexander Rose of Edinburgh, who had prayed that God show compassion to and restore King James. Members of the Convention quite rightly saw no necessary contradiction between this and their

[29] Mackay, *Memoirs of the War*, 306.

iron resolve to 'settle and secure the Protestant Religion, the Government, Laws and Liberties of the Kingdom'. It was James who made the two concepts incompatible, which goes far to explain why only a half dozen members of the Convention left it with Dundee. Thereafter, as Justice-General the Earl of Lothian said in January 1690, political theory ceased to be of much help: the main thing was to exclude from power those mere 'Tools for Tyrannical and Arbitrary Men' who had already done so much to assist in the subversion of the liberties of the kingdom. With the accession of William and Mary, unavoidable as it had become, more and more of the Scottish nobility found it psychologically impossible actively to support the Williamite cause, but it did not make them support James, and even the Duke of Gordon found it possible to appear before the Privy Council in January 1690 and give his word of honour 'not to act any thing against the Government'.[30]

Given their divisions and dilemmas, the Scottish nobility handled the Revolution crisis rather well. They made necessary changes even when they did not much like them. They choked the dreadful threat of widespread civil war. Once James lost his grip on England, they made it clear that there was no way he was to return to arbitrary absolutism in Scotland. One reason why they achieved what they did was that they had few illusions about themselves, or the dangers which surrounded them. As the Countess of Erroll said in a letter to Dr James Fraser, a Scottish savant who had become Secretary of Chelsea Hospital in London by grant of Charles II, the problem in the spring of 1689 was to produce a quiet, stable government in a Scotland where the nobles were deeply divided and the common people expected so much from the Revolution that 'they want but a little of a disapointment to be on fire'.[31]

[30] The analysis of events in the North-East is largely based on the valuable collection of information about individuals, and contemporary letters and records to be found in J. Grant (ed.), *Records of the County of Banff 1660–1760* (New Spalding Club, Aberdeen 1922), chs. 1 and 2. The Duke of Gordon's submission to the régime is recorded in E. W. M. Balfour Melville (ed.), *An Account of the Proceedings of the Estates in Scotland 1689–1690* (Scottish History Society, 3rd ser., 47, Edinburgh 1955), i. 93.

[31] Anne, Countess of Erroll to Dr James Fraser, 22 Mar. 1689, printed in 'Letters to Dr James Fraser, 1679–1689', in *The Miscellany of the Spalding Club*, 5 (Aberdeen 1852), 196–8.

Necessarily, the executive had to be taken over by committed Williamites who were not representative of the bulk of noble opinion, though they were dependent on often tacit tolerance by their fellow nobles. At one point the government of Scotland leaned heavily on a clique of former political refugees who had returned from exile in the Netherlands when William invaded England. The classic illustration of this is George, Lord Melville, who after participating in Monmouth's rebellion schemes fled to Holland in 1685. Returning with William, he advanced to an earldom and ran the Scottish government from a variety of posts like Secretary of State, High Commissioner, Privy Seal, and President of Council. His eldest son, Alexander Melville, Lord Raith, was a man of very considerable capacity for business. Between 1689 and his premature death in 1698 he was Treasurer Depute, an office which carried with it the control of the public revenues of Scotland. Scottish government was to some extent a Melville family activity, and the role of the second son, who adopted the title of Earl of Leven, as commander of a regiment and Governor of Edinburgh Castle did nothing to weaken this impression.

There were plenty of other returned exiles in key positions beneath Melville. Henry Erskine, Lord Cardross, had suffered much on account of his zealous Presbyterianism, not to mention his opposition to the once all-powerful Earl of Lauderdale. At one stage he emigrated to Carolina, but he drifted from North America to the Netherlands, whence he returned with William of Orange, for whom he raised a dragoon regiment, and whom he served as a Scots Privy Councillor and as Governor of the Mint, a job which he must have found all the more satisfying because it had once been held (and abused) by Lauderdale's brother. Below the level of the nobles, laird families furnished a significant section of the exile community. Sir Robert Pringle of Stitchel came back from studies at Leiden to become William's Under-Secretary of State for Scotland, often acting as the linkman with Scottish government, when William was campaigning, by following the army around Flanders. Arthur Johnston, 'Secretary Johnston', was a younger son of the Covenanting leader Archibald Johnston of Wariston, who was executed in 1665. The family took refuge in Holland, where Arthur studied civil law. He was William's ambassador to Brandenburg in 1688–9, and in 1692 was appointed joint Secretary of State for Scotland with Sir John Dalrymple, a colleague whom Johnston, to his eternal credit, deeply disliked.[32]

This sort of narrow-based executive was perfectly normal in Scottish history after one of the periodic convulsions which the Scots usually refused to admit constituted a direct challenge to the Crown. After a year or two, when the new régime had become irreversible and accepted, the more conservative part of the nobility would begin to associate itself with government once again. To some extent, this process was at work in Scotland after the Revolution. If Anne, Duchess of Hamilton in her own right, and her husband, Duke William, were known before the Revolution to be unsympathetic to the political and religious policies of King James, their son James, Earl of Arran and future fourth Duke of Hamilton, was not, so his early association with the new Williamite government was as significant as the readiness of several Jacobite magnates to make their peace with it. Unfortunately, two developments occurred, one of which made it very difficult (though probably not impossible, given time) for the time-honoured process of healing and reintegration within the traditional ruling class to take place, and the other completely destroyed any chance whatever of political stability.

The first development was the Presbyterian settlement in the Kirk by law established in 1690. An exclusively Presbyterian settlement, as distinct from a change in the balance within the compromise between Episcopal and Presbyterian forms characteristic of the Restoration, had been urged on William by Presbyterian hardliners like the Earl of Crawford, a man whose activism after the Revolution compensated for his virtual seclusion as a political malcontent before it. His view was that 'our king has no steady friends in this nation but such as are of the Presbyterian persuasion'.[33] Even he had to admit that not all Episcopalian nobles were disaffected towards the new government, but he proved regrettably accurate in his insistence on the unqualified Jacobitism of the Scottish bishops and of the large proportion of the clergy who, like the bishops, had been only too successfully brainwashed in the doctrines of passive obedience and divine

[32] *DNB*.

[33] Lord Crawford to Lord Melville, 1 Aug. 1689, excerpt printed in Crawford, *Lives of the Lindsays*, ii. 431.

right in the Restoration universities. The unavoidable purges of the university faculties by the Williamite authorities bred a deal of bad feeling, but far worse was the endless bad feeling and trouble bred by the long-term necessity of replacing convinced Episcopalian and Jacobite ministers in the many parishes they occupied, especially north of the Forth. Worse still was the fact that they often enjoyed the personal regard and political support of the local aristocracy, who naturally thought of attempts to oust these clergy as assaults on their own dignity and local power. The whole problem became pressing after 1693 when the Scots legislature, on the grounds that further measures were required to safeguard the Protestant religion, passed measures demanding oaths of allegiance and assurance from all holders of civil, military, and ecclesiastical office. The Solicitor-General of the day wrote despairingly to a fellow law officer: 'I find this countrey verie peacable; bot almost the whole Episcopel clergie have refuised the oths, bot most of them continou to preatch in ther churches.' He was speaking of the North-East, but his words could have been applied to most of the rest of Scotland. He added that when Episcopal clergymen asked him if they could peacefully continue as before, he had to reply in the negative, because the penalty for preaching without taking the oaths was now deprivation. The power of the state to deprive was often minimal, but the harm was done with the threat.[34]

Infinitely more serious was the massive crisis of confidence in the new régime amongst almost all thinking members of the Scottish ruling class, whether Williamite, moderate (that is, non-active), Jacobite, or uncommitted, provoked by the style and personnel of William's government. That exiles like Melville returned to play an important role in the new dispensation was both inevitable and understandable. However, the survival in office beside them of some of the most soiled and disliked members of the pre-Revolution executive, men who many Jacobite sympathizers thought ought to go, shook confidence to the core. When Secretary of State Sir John Dalrymple wrote to the rising young Edinburgh advocate Sir James Ogilvie in March 1692, to tell him that the post of Sheriff of Banffshire which he had been

[34] Sir James Ogilvie to (probably) James Steuart Yngr. of Coltness, 19 July 1693, printed in J. Grant (ed.), *Seafield Correspondence 1685–1708* (Scottish History Soc., 2nd ser., 3, Edinburgh 1912), 109.

soliciting was his, he added unctuously that 'his Majesty hath retained many that did not deserv it at his hands, yett he hath givin us no example that he threw out any man that did not deliberately oppose him'.[35] Sir James Ogilvie was a sound Williamite who, though the second son of the Earl of Findlater, had been able to throw the weight of the family interest firmly behind the Revolution, helped by the fact that his elder brother, Lord Deskford, had 'verted' to Catholicism. Entering government as Solicitor-General in the Hamilton interest in 1693, Sir James went on to build a grand career as a reliable government supporter, finishing it as the Chancellor Earl of Seafield. His early patron Sir John Dalrymple, Master of Stair, was quite different in background, being one of the most disliked members of the pre-Revolution régime, and a man whose retention in office did William III much harm politically. Equally retention of Melfort in office in exile proved a dreadful political handicap to James after 1688. However, William was supposed to be some sort of new broom. As James Halliday pointed out in a classic article, in 1689 the Scots nobility had seen just how reluctant William was to surrender the most indefensible features of his predecessor's stranglehold over Estates and Kirk. The alliance of disillusioned Williamites and moderate Jacobites in 'the Club' to bring back a chastened James was not irrational. To break the plan William had reluctantly to give way on a series of points,[36] but he soon made it clear that he would not govern in the spirit of the limited sovereignty he had nominally endorsed. Rather he would abolish the Scots parliament by incorporation with that of England.

By 1693 similar ideas about restoring James with restricted powers were common coinage in England, and William needed the unsuccessful assassination attempt of 1696 to recover some popularity.[37] Absolute centralized sovereignty remained the core principle of English government, though it was only with the complete annexation of royal powers by the premier, and the evolution of Stalinist party structures that something like personal rule re-emerged and James VII and II, in his pre-1693 mode

[35] Sir John Dalrymple to Sir James Ogilvie, 8 Mar. 1692, ibid. 77.

[36] J. Halliday, 'The Club and the Revolution in Scotland 1689–90', *Scottish Historical Review*, 45 (1966), 143–59.

[37] J. Garrett, *The Triumphs of Providence: The Assassination Plot, 1696* (Cambridge 1980).

(before he was prepared to trade limited sovereignty for restoration), could be recognized for what he was, courtesy of William of Orange's stubborn rearguard action: the father of the modern British political tradition. That the Scots ruling classes spotted the central fact about the Revolution—that it did not change the spirit of government—was a tribute to their shrewdness. Had modern historians exhibited a fraction of that shrewdness, they would not have been as incapable as many have been of accounting for the turbulence of Scottish politics in the late seventeenth and early eighteenth centuries.

4

Ireland and the Glorious Revolution: From Kingdom to Colony

PATRICK KELLY

I

IN considering the question of Ireland and the Glorious Revolution, one is immediately struck by the fact that Ireland did not experience the Glorious Revolution in the sense in which the term is understood in the history of England and Scotland. The occupancy of the throne indeed changed as a result of the Glorious Revolution, as in the other kingdoms of the British monarchy, but this change and the settlement which followed was largely imposed from without as a result of more than two years of intermittent warfare. In Ireland the Revolution was not marked as in England and Scotland by constitutional debate, nor did it produce any central revolutionary document such as the Declaration of Rights or Claim of Right. By default, therefore, the central document of the Revolution in Ireland was the treaty which ended the Jacobite War, and for many reasons the Treaty of Limerick was ill-suited as the basis for a settlement, not least because the Irish Protestant colonists who emerged as dominant after the war had no voice in making the Treaty. The contrast with the circumstances of the Restoration in 1660 could not be more striking. Then an independent Irish Convention had taken upon itself to invite Charles II to resume the Irish throne, and the settler community was able in large measure to establish its own destiny rather than merely submit to the determination of the assembly at Westminster.[1] In the Glorious Revolution the

[1] For the Irish Restoration, see F. M. O'Donoghue, 'Parliament in Ireland under Charles II; unpublished MA thesis (University College, Dublin 1970), ch. 1; J. I. McGuire, 'The Dublin Convention, the Protestant Community, and the Emergence of an Ecclesiastical Settlement in 1660', in A. Cosgrove and J. I. McGuire (eds.), *Parliament & Community* (Belfast 1983), 121–46, *passim*.

settlement of the throne was imposed in London by an Act establishing that whoever should be recognized as sovereign by the English parliament was *ipso facto* ruler of Ireland, and the subsequent Act declaring the new oath of allegiance classed Ireland as a subordinate possession of the English Crown.[2]

Yet looked at in the broader conspectus of Irish history the years from 1688 to 1691 were of momentous significance, and these events still serve as a potent source of division in the twentieth century. The outcome of the Jacobite War was the completion of the tendency throughout the seventeenth century to dispossess the Catholic native landowners to the benefit of the Protestant settlers, and to judge from James's ungenerous warning to his son to be wary of the 'O and the Macs' he had little appreciation of what they had lost in his cause.[3] Yet ironically, though the Protestants were the local beneficiaries of the Williamite victory, the psychological scarring which they bore as a result of the Jacobite War and the Catholic resurgence which had preceded it was to leave them with a siege mentality that persisted for much of the eighteenth century. In the period following the Jacobite surrender at Limerick this siege mentality led the victorious Protestants to seek to prevent any similar threat to their domination in future through the repressive machinery of the penal laws, laws arguably intended more to underwrite the colonists' hegemony rather than to promote the conversion of the conquered. As the preface to the Jacobite Hugh Reily's *Case of Ireland Briefly Stated* (1695) put it, English Protestants were more anxious to convert Irish land than Irish people.[4]

In talking about Ireland and the Glorious Revolution I shall therefore begin by focusing attention on the Catholic resurgence

[2] Cf. An Act declaring the rights and liberties of the subject, and for settling the succession of the Crown (1 Wm. & M., sess. 2, c. 2); An Act for the better securing and relief of their Majesties Protestant subjects of Ireland (ibid., c. ix); An Act for abrogating the oath of supremacy in Ireland, and for appointing other oaths (3 Wm. & M., 1st pt., c. 2).

[3] The Catholics' share of the land fell from 59% in 1641 to 22% in 1665, to 14% in 1703. T. W. Moody (ed.), *A New History of Ireland*, iii. *Early Modern Ireland, 1534–1691* (Oxford 1976), pp. xxxviii–xl; Clarke, *James II*, ii. 636–8.

[4] Cf. M. Wall, *The Penal Laws, 1691–1760* (Dundalk 1961); P. J. Corish, *The Catholic Community in the Seventeenth and Eighteenth Centuries* (Dublin 1981), ch. 4; though S. J. Connolly, 'Religion and History', *Irish Economic and Social History*, 10 (1983), 73–9, asserts that the ecclesiastical authorities were more seriously intent on converting the Irish than has generally been realized.

of the early part of James II's reign, an event which (rather than James's replacement by William and Mary) constituted for some Protestants the revolution in Ireland.[5] Next I shall touch on the immediate impact of James's flight, going on to consider the aspirations of the various groups involved in the Irish war, namely the Irish Catholics, James and his English and Scots advisers, and his French backers, on the one side, and their opponents William of Orange, the English parliament, and the Irish Protestants on the other. The course of the war will be briefly touched on so as to illuminate the nature of the agreement embodied in the Treaty of Limerick, whether intended as a temporary cessation in a still-to-be-concluded war or as a 'Perpetual Edict' for the protection of the Irish Catholics. Finally I shall look at the kind of settlement that emerged in Ireland in the 1690s as the Irish Protestants sought to establish their twin goals of liberty and security, in the face of what they saw as English disregard for their interests. At the very end of the century various actions of the English parliament, such as the suppression of the Irish woollen industry, helped reinforce changes going back before the 1688 Revolution that tended to reduce Ireland's status from a theoretically independent kingdom to that of a colony. Such developments together with the debasement of the Catholics helped foster a distinctive identity on the part of the Irish landowning classes which laid the foundations of the Protestant Ascendancy of the later eighteenth century.

II

What ostensibly was at issue in the Revolution in Ireland, as in England and Scotland, was whether James II or William and Mary should rule. But in Ireland other issues lay more overtly at the basis of the conflict, notably religion. As a Catholic James had sympathized with the plight of his Irish subjects, but as an Englishman he shared the distrust of things Irish held by his English subjects.[6] Ironically one of the chief appeals which the

[5] Cf. *An Apology for the Protestants of Ireland. In a Brief Narrative of the late Revolutions in that Kingdom, And An Account of the Present State Thereof* (1689). This work, which deals only with Tyrconnell's administration and James's action in Ireland, is dated 27 May 1689.

[6] On religion as dividing factor, see R. Cox, *Hibernia Anglicana*, i (1689), Pref. to

Stuart dynasty had for the Irish was a sense of common origin with its Irish subjects.[7] But if religion was the major badge of difference in later seventeenth-century Ireland, the key issue was possession of land. From the accession of James in 1685 the real question for settler and native alike was whether James would modify or confirm the land settlement established at the Restoration. Reversal of the settlement was eagerly sought by the majority of Catholics, and as strongly resisted by the Protestants and by the section of prosperous Catholics who had bought up lands held under titles established by the Acts of Settlement and Explanation.[8]

The nature of the Catholic resurgence which took place under James II has been the subject of much discussion, though our understanding of what happened during the years 1685–8 is compromised by relative ignorance of what went before. Thanks to the work of Karl Bottigheimer and Larry Arnold the land settlement of 1660–5 is now fairly clear, but the subsequent history of Charles II's reign, particularly from the late 1670s, remains obscure.[9] The extent to which the Catholics made good their position in these years despite the Acts of Settlement is much disputed, but it is known that the latter part of Charles's reign was a period of considerable prosperity, characterized by the building of country houses by the richer gentry and the expansion of the towns, notably Dublin.[10] English control over the Irish administration had grown significantly, and Ormonde

Reader. For James's outlook, see J. G. Simms, *Jacobite Ireland, 1685–91* (1969), 19, 21–2; J. Miller, *King James II* (1977), 217.

[7] C. O'Kelly, *Macariae Excidium, or, the Destruction of Cyprus*, ed. J. C. O'Callaghan (Irish Archaeological Soc., Dublin 1853), 8, 172–3.

[8] J. G. Simms, *The Williamite Confiscation in Ireland, 1690–1703* (1956), 15–17; J. T. Gilbert (ed.), *A Jacobite Narrative of the War in Ireland, 1688–1691* (1971 repr.), 27. The *Narrative* is an extract dealing with the Irish war taken from the much longer manuscript history, entitled 'A Light to the Blind', written between 1702 and 1714 by (? Nicholas) Plunket. See further P. Kelly, '"A Light to the Blind": the Voice of the Dispossessed Elite in the Generation of the Defeat after Limerick', *Irish Historical Studies*, 24 (1985), 431–62.

[9] K. Bottigheimer, *English Money and Irish Land* (Oxford 1971), and 'The Restoration Land Settlement in Ireland: A Structural View', *Irish Historical Studies* 18 (1972), 1–21; L. J. Arnold, 'The Irish Court of Claims of 1663', ibid., 24 (1985), 417–30.

[10] Simms, *Jacobite Ireland*, 15–18; L. M. Cullen, 'Economic Trends, 1660–91' in Moody, *New History of Ireland*, iii. 403–7. Cf. *An Apology for the Protestants of Ireland*, 2–3; W. King, *The State of the Protestants in Ireland under the late King James's Government* (4th edn., Dublin 1730), 47.

was little more than a figure-head during his last viceroyalty in 1678–85. The Irish revenue was directly supervised by the English Treasury and the administration of the Irish army was also increasingly handled from London.[11] These developments, together with the fact that no Irish parliament had sat since 1666, were greatly to facilitate the programme of catholicization of army and civil administration that James wished to carry out.[12]

James's first move was to purge the Irish army of former Cromwellian officers and soldiers, and then of Protestants in general, a process already begun before Charles's death.[13] Protestant susceptibilities were somewhat reassured by the appointment of the second Earl of Clarendon as Lord-Lieutenant, though Catholics were alarmed by the arrival of the son of the man whom they saw as responsible for their betrayal in the Restoration settlement.[14] However, Clarendon's authority was rapidly undermined by the trust which James placed in the Old English Catholic soldier, Richard Talbot, whom he created Earl of Tyrconnell. Talbot was a long-time associate of James, who had acted as an agent for Irish Catholics in the 1670s, and had acquired an unenviable reputation as bully-boy and liar, having been censured and dismissed from Court by the English Commons in 1673.[15] Against this growing influence Clarendon was powerless, and Tyrconnell soon received independent command of the Irish army, hitherto controlled by the viceroy. Tyrconnell's victory owed much to the support of Sunderland, who saw him as an effective ally in his conflict with the Hydes. Once the latter had fallen, however, Sunderland was reluctant to give Tyrconnell an independent hand, and his reservations were shared by the

[11] S. Egan, 'Finance and the Government of Ireland, 1660–85', unpublished Ph.D. thesis (Trinity College, Dublin, 2 vols., 1983), ii. 144–94, *passim*; J. Childs, *The Army of Charles II* (Manchester 1976), 205–6.

[12] D. Szechi and D. Hayton, 'John Bull's Other Kingdoms: The English Government of Scotland and Ireland', in C. Jones (ed.), *Britain in the First Age of Party, 1680–1750: Essays Presented to Geoffrey Holmes* (1987), 262.

[13] J. Miller, 'The Earl of Tyrconnel and James II's Irish Policy, 1685–1688', *Historical Journal*, 20 (1977), 813; J. Childs, *The Army, James II, and the Glorious Revolution* (Manchester 1980), ch. 3.

[14] *An Apology for the Protestants of Ireland* (1689), 3–5; *A Full and Impartial Account of the Secret Consults . . . of the Romish Party in Ireland. From 1660 to this present Year 1689* (1689), 57. Cited below as *Secret Consults*; Miller, 'Tyrconnel and James's Irish Policy', 812.

[15] Simms, *Jacobite Ireland*, 6–7, 20–1; *Commons Journal*, ix. 270; Miller, 'Tyrconnel and James's Irish Policy', 805–7.

Catholic clique at Court.[16] In an excellent study of Tyrconnell's Irish policy prior to the Revolution, John Miller has shown how Tyrconnell commanded James's support by playing on his sympathy for the Irish as Catholics, and by exerting his forceful personality, particularly when recalled to Chester in August 1687 for what was expected to be the effective checking of his policy of reversing the Restoration land settlement, and perhaps even the prelude to his dismissal.[17] Parallel with the policy of catholicizing the army, Tyrconnell embarked on the introduction of Catholics to the judiciary and other forms of civil office. Even under Clarendon one of the three judges of the King's Bench, Common Pleas, and Exchequer were replaced, but from February a second Catholic appointment in each court gave them the majority.[18] The compliant Charles Porter was replaced as Lord Chancellor by a Catholic, Alexander Fitton, whose prior conviction for forgery was made much of by anti-Catholic propagandists.[19] Simultaneously Catholics were appointed to the Privy Council, and as sheriffs and JPs, while urban corporations—the jealously guarded monopoly of Protestants in Charles II's reign—were also opened to them.[20]

A key factor in Tyrconnell's policy was the promotion of old English Catholics as opposed to those of Gaelic extraction, which Miller argues enabled him to represent to the King that the English interest in Ireland was being safeguarded at the expense of the Irish. Miller's claim that James favoured Tyrconnell's plan for the establishment of a link between Ireland and France rather than England, when Mary should succeed James, does not altogether carry conviction.[21] However the news of the Queen's pregnancy changed Tyrconnell's options; on Sunderland's instructions preparations were made for calling a parliament in 1688 in which Catholics would have predominated, and the birth of James Francis Edward in June was welcomed as heralding the end of Protestant domination.[22]

[16] Miller, 'Tyrconnel and James's Irish Policy', 814–15; *Secret Consults*, 55, 88.

[17] Miller, 'Tyrconnel and James's Irish Policy', 806–16, *passim*; see also his 'Thomas Sheridan (1646–1712) and his "Narrative"', *Irish Historical Studies* 20 (1976), 105–26.

[18] Simms, *Jacobite Ireland*, 25–36, *passim*.

[19] King, *State of the Protestants*, 29, 66–7; *Secret Consults*, 74–5.

[20] Simms, *Jacobite Ireland*, 26–7, 35–6.

[21] *Secret Consults*, 121; Miller, 'Tyrconnel and James's Irish Policy', 821–2.

[22] *Secret Consults*, 125–6; Simms, *Jacobite Ireland*, 43–4.

The news of William's landing and James's subsequent flight confounded Irish expectations; the Irish attitude to Protestants became more conciliatory, and there were hopes that Tyrconnell would submit to the new government in England.[23] The Irish Protestants in many areas seized the initiative in forming armed associations, while the exiles in London even recommended concessions to Catholicism to persuade Tyrconnell to 'yield the sword'. A special Committee for Irish Affairs of the Privy Council was set up in February to organize the recovery of the colony, which retained overall responsibility for the 1689 campaign but was neither very efficient nor successful.[24] The course initially adopted of sending the Catholic Richard Hamilton to negotiate proved abortive; Tyrconnell asserted that his apparent hesitancy had merely been prudence in the face of Protestant strength in Dublin and uncertainty as to what James intended. By February Tyrconnell had disarmed the Protestants except in the north-west and was able to invite James to come to an Ireland loyal to his cause.[25]

Once James arrived, the major question was whether to concentrate on establishing full control of Ireland or to press on immediately to regain Scotland and then England.[26] James had to concern himself with the impact of his politics not merely in Ireland but on English opinion as well; while the Irish regarded the presence of the sovereign as a not to be missed opportunity to right ancient wrongs.[27] When James summoned a parliament on reaching Dublin, repeal of the Restoration land legislation became the chief priority of the Irish, together with the restoration of the Catholic Church. On the latter issue James was keener to temporize than his Irish supporters, and the two Irish Jacobite historians of the war saw his failure to reverse the religious settlement as resulting in a loss of divine favour which was the real reason for

[23] King, *State of the Protestants*, 110; Simms, *Jacobite Ireland*, 48–52.

[24] *HMC: House of Lords MSS, 1689–1690*, 137–43, 161–90; Simms, *Jacobite Ireland*, 120–1.

[25] Simms, *Jacobite Ireland*, 52–3; Clarke, *James II*, ii. 320.

[26] Gilbert, *Jacobite Narrative*, 50–1; O'Kelly, *Macariae Excidium*, 92–3; Miller, *James II*, 221.

[27] Clarke, *James II*, ii. 358–61; O'Kelly, *Macariae Excidium*, 34–5; Gilbert, *Jacobite Narrative*, 63. For Irish concern with land and religion, see R. H. Murray (ed.), *The Journal of John Stevens, containing a Brief Account of the War in Ireland, 1689–91* (Oxford 1912), intro., p. xxxvii. Cited below as Stevens, *Journal*.

James's defeat.[28] The desire to avoid alienating English opinion influenced James's determination to protect Irish Protestants from both their Catholic fellow countrymen and the French troops, but the effectiveness of such policies fell far short of what James hoped for, and was moreover gravely undermined by the Act of Attainder passed in the subsequent parliament.[29]

James's decision to hold a parliament rather than concentrate on winning the war has attracted the criticism of contemporaries and subsequent historians alike.[30] Apart from the way in which divisions over fundamental issues of policy served to open further the splits between his supporters, the actual meeting of the parliament and the hopes which the reversal of the Acts of Settlement awoke diverted energy from the war, as individuals turned to advancing their private concerns rather than the public cause.[31] Such risks cannot fail to have struck James and his immediate advisers, and one is left wondering what factors of overriding importance persuaded them to hold the parliament. The need to establish the façade of normality and legality must have weighed heavily; holding a parliament was a major demonstration of regal power and thus a direct challenge to the rebellious assembly sitting in Westminster. It also made clear that it was not James's intention to act in other than a legal and constitutional manner, even at a time of the greatest emergency. However, once the parliament met, it proved far from tractable. The Irish were determined to make good the losses which they had suffered at the Restoration, and in this they received the support of the French ambassador d'Avaux.[32] Despite his initial distaste for the

[28] O'Kelly, *Macariae Excidium*, 5–6; Gilbert, *Jacobite Narrative*, 69.

[29] On James's problem in convincing the Protestants, see Miller, 'Tyrconnel and James's Irish Policy', 811. Cf. *An Account of the Transactions of the late King James in Ireland* (1690), 10–25, *passim*.

[30] Stevens, *Journal*, 68–70; Clarke, *James II*, ii. 358–9. Criticism of holding the parliament came in Judge Daly's speech against repealing the Act of Settlement, which referred to the folly of 'dividing the Bear's skin before she is taken'. *A True Account of the Present State of Ireland* (1689), 16. For the most recent account of the 1689 parliament, see J. G. Simms, 'The Jacobite Parliament of 1689' reprinted in D. Hayton and G. O'Brien (eds.), *War and Politics in Ireland, 1648–1730* (1986), 65–90.

[31] Stevens, *Journal*, 69; R. H. Murray, *Revolutionary Ireland: Its Settlement* (1911), 126; Gilbert, *Jacobite Narrative*, 70, however, approved the repeal as just and timely.

[32] J. Hogan (ed.), *Négociations de M. le Comte d'Avaux en Irlande, 1689–1690* (Irish Manuscripts Commission, Dublin, 2 vols., 1934, 1958), i. 191; O'Kelly, *Macariae Excidium*, 34–5.

Irish, d'Avaux soon realized that their aspirations would serve the interests of Louis XIV better than the plans of Melfort and the proponents of immediate intervention in Britain.[33]

Holding this parliament in Ireland was highly offensive to English opinion; not only did it impugn claims to sovereignty over Ireland but the choice of Irish Catholics as Members of Parliament was regarded as an affront comparable only to the calling in of French help. The repeal of the Acts of Settlement and the passing an Act of Attainder against the leading Protestants helped stiffen Protestant resistance in Ireland. After the war the parliament's actions were frequently referred to as evidence of the long-term intentions of the Catholics in Ireland and, together with the barbarous treatment of the Protestants by Tyrconnell and the French, were held to justify the implementation of the penal laws.[34] English legislation in 1690 voided the acts of the Jacobite parliament, but the parliament that met in Dublin in 1692 refused to destroy its Jacobite predecessor's journals on the ground that they were a necessary warning for the future.[35] Ironically other legislation intended to reduce Ireland's dependence on England was to be copied by the Protestant parliaments of the 1690s and their eighteenth-century successors, as were the measures intended to end Ireland's economic subordination.[36] And when in 1697 an anonymous attack compared the Protestant

[33] Though d'Avaux's instructions bound him to conciliate the Protestants, he urged James to confiscate their estates and imprison them without legal process; see James to Melfort, 4 June 1689: J. MacPherson (ed.), *Original Papers* (2 vols., 1775), i. 304–5. Cf. *A True Account of the Present State of Ireland*, 7–8.

[34] See An Act for the better securing and relief of their Majesties Protestant subjects of Ireland (1 Wm. & M., sess. 2, c. ix) 1689; *Transactions of the late King James in Ireland*, 3–7.

[35] J. I. McGuire, 'The Irish Parliament of 1692', in T. Bartlett and D. Hayton (eds.), *Penal Era and Golden Age: Essays in Irish History, 1690–1800* (Belfast 1979), 16. The Acts and proceedings of the Jacobite parliament were voided in Ireland in 1695 (7 Wm. III, c. 3).

[36] The legislation included 'An Act Declaring that the Parliament of England cannot bind Ireland against Writs of Error and Appeals . . .', which denied in most express terms the English parliament's right to legislate for Ireland. James, however, refused to permit the repealing of Poynings's law. Later 18th-c. patriots frequently expressed admiration for this aspect of the Jacobite parliament, e.g. Grattan on Catholic relief in 1782: *Irish Parliamentary Debates, 1781–2* (Dublin 1782), 254. The economic legislation, which constituted about a quarter of the total, sought to free Ireland from the Navigation Laws and other English restrictions on Irish trade, as well as granting some minor concessions to the French. Simms, 'Jacobite Parliament', 69–71, 78–9.

Irish parliament directly with the Jacobite assembly, this analogy with 'King James's . . . Irish mob' was indignantly repudiated.[37]

As d'Avaux's intervention over the repeal of the Act of Settlement showed, French policy in Ireland was essentially opportunistic, despite Louis's genuine desire to aid his distressed kinsman.[38] Initially Ireland was seen as a diversion of questionable benefit; the backing for an Irish campaign came originally from Seignelay, the minister of marine, but even naval support was never adequate.[39] Despite Louis's commitment, the war minister, Louvois, feared the squandering of resources in Ireland, and from the beginning the benefits of aid from the French were offset by their secondary intention of securing Irish troops to fight in the French armies. A further French interest lay in obtaining economic concessions, particularly a monopoly over Irish wool exports, but despite great pressure James did not yield.[40] Several of the most prominent French officers who accompanied James were lost at the siege of Derry, and it was not till the second season's campaigning that Louvois was prepared to make a more substantial commitment. The 1689 campaign did, however, reveal the fighting qualities of the Irish levies and also make clear the advantages of tying down extensive English forces at relatively small cost. Only in the third year of the war did French commitment really become substantial in terms of money and materials, though in terms of men it always remained slight. Even at this point French help was extremely tardy; despite warnings from both the Irish leaders and the French officers in Ireland that the second siege of Limerick would be the decisive event of the war, the relief fleet reached the mouth of the Shannon three weeks too late. In the final analysis it would seem

[37] Sir F[rancis] B[rewster], *A Letter from a Gentleman in the Country, to a Member of the House of Commons in England; in Reference to the Votes of the 14th of December, 97. Together with An Answer to the said Letter* (Dublin, 1698), 24. The *Letter* was probably written by Toland, see P. Kelly, 'A Pamphlet Attributed to John Toland', *Topos*, 4 (1985), 81–3.

[38] On French policy in general see Hogan, *Négociations de M. d'Avaux* and S. Mulloy (ed.), *Franco-Irish Correspondence, December 1688–February 1692* (Irish Manuscripts Commission, 3 vols., 1983–4).

[39] Simms, *Jacobite Ireland*, 53–4, 59–61, 139–40; Mulloy, *Franco-Irish Correspondence*, i. xix, xxi. A notable opportunity was lost with the failure to attack William's expedition in 1690.

[40] The Irish on the whole were not enthusiastic for French service. Gilbert, *Jacobite Narrative*, 92; cf. the *Transactions of the late King James in Ireland*, 16. For refusal on wool, see Hogan, *Négociations de M. d'Avaux*, 255.

therefore that the desire to remove the Jacobite army intact from Ireland was the major French concern in the closing stage of the war.[41]

Williamite strategy was initially rather clearer: English attention had been focused on the Irish problem as far back as December 1688, when the assembly at Westminster invited Prince William to take on responsibility for the government following James's flight to France.[42] The hope that Tyrconnell would submit without a struggle had, as we have seen, proved abortive. Following that, despite the lobbying of the Irish exiles and the declaration of 22 February calling on James's supporters to submit, preparations for military intervention in Ireland in 1689 were extremely dilatory. The forces sent to the relief of Derry made a poor showing, and it was only thanks to the initiative of merchant seamen that the city was relieved at the end of July.[43] The major English expedition of 1689 under the aged Schomberg proved equally cautious, halting some way south of Dundalk in September, and disappointing the hopes that it would occupy Dublin by the end of the year. The exposed and unhealthy position of Schomberg's camp led to a high mortality amongst the ill-prepared English troops, who neglected the precautions of the more experienced Brandenburgers, Dutch, Danes, and Huguenots who constituted around 50 per cent of Schomberg's army.[44]

This lack of success persuaded William to intervene personally in Ireland in 1690, despite the disadvantages of losing a further year's campaigning in Flanders. The expedition which reached Carrickfergus in the middle of June was far better equipped than that of 1689 and, contrary to Schomberg's caution, William was anxious to engage in battle.[45] James was also eager for action, despite the misgivings of his own advisers and the French and despite having a substantially smaller army.[46] The encounter between the two forces took place at the Boyne on 1st July (OS), and though not the overwhelming victory that William had

[41] Tessé and d'Usson to Louis XIV, 17 Aug. 1691; [Jacobite] Lords Justices of Ireland, 12 Sept. 1691: Mulloy, *Franco-Irish Correspondence*, ii. 411–12, 492–3.

[42] *Commons Journal*, x. 6.

[43] Simms, *Jacobite Ireland*, 108–12.

[44] J. G. Simms, 'Schomberg at Dundalk' in Hayton and O'Brien, *War and Politics*, 91–104.

[45] Simms, *Jacobite Ireland*, 136–7, 143–4.

[46] MacPherson, *Original Papers*, i. 314; O'Kelly, *Macariae Excidium*, 48–9.

hoped for, since the Irish forces were able to re-form shortly afterwards, was decisive in its political and psychological effects.[47] James fled, barely pausing in Dublin, before taking ship for France, and much of Leinster passed rapidly into Williamite hands.

William's response was to offer peace terms to the rank and file of the Irish army in the Declaration of Finglas of 7 July 1690, but he held out no hope to what he termed 'the desperate Leaders of the present Rebellion'.[48] The Irish nobility and gentry were therefore forced to fight on, if they were to salvage anything from their predicament. Even the attempt to conciliate the rank and file, prompted partly by the need to preserve the countryside and crops, was thwarted by Williamite failure to make good protections given to those who submitted.[49] The motives which had prompted William to make the Declaration were a rather uncharacteristic lack of caution—corresponding to his eagerness to end the Irish conflict as quickly as possible—and a determination to maximize the amount of confiscated land available for regranting and paying the costs of the Irish war, as demanded by the English parliament. Competition between these two factors was to determine the progress of his future dealings with the Jacobites in Ireland.[50] After an initial hesitation provoked by the alarm generated in England by the French success at Beachy Head, William turned his attention to the reduction of the main Jacobite stronghold at Limerick. Though formidable in Irish eyes, the city was recognized by the French as lacking defences capable of resisting modern artillery. William's inability to take it in the late summer of 1690 was due to a combination of bad weather, the

[47] Simms, *Jacobite Ireland*, 144–52; Gilbert, *Jacobite Narrative*, 102–5 (which refers to the battle as a skirmish); Stevens, *Journal*, 126–7.

[48] Text of declaration in [C. Leslie], *An Answer to a Book, Intituled. The State of the Protestants in Ireland under the Late King James's Government* (1692), app. 22–4. George Story claimed in 1693 that the exclusion of the Irish gentry had been the result of the greed of the 'English Proprietors of that Countrey' for their estates, though he had made no such comment in the first part of his history. *An Impartial History of the Wars of Ireland, With a Continuation thereof* (2 pts., 1693), ii. 93–4.

[49] Gilbert, *Jacobite Narrative*, 105; Nicholas Plunket to Thomas Flower, 21 Mar., 14 Apr. 1691: National Library of Ireland MS 11474, asserts that the Jacobites were more efficient at making good their protections. Cf. [Leslie], *Answer*, 164: 'what sport [the Williamites] made to Hang up poor Irish People by dozens . . . they hardly thought them Humane Kind'.

[50] For details of negotiations see Simms, 'Williamite Peace Tactics, 1690–1', reprinted in Hayton and O'Brien, *War and Politics*, 181–202.

delay caused by Sarsfield's raid on the siege train, and the courage of the Irish and French defenders.[51] The successful resistance at Limerick in 1690 forced the Williamites to accept the need for a negotiated rather than an imposed peace settlement. However, a welcome development came in the autumn with Marlborough's capture of Cork and Kinsale, which together with the earlier submission of Waterford deprived the French of access to the southern ports. By the end of the 1690 campaign the Irish therefore had been deprived of control of Leinster and much of Munster (except Kerry and West Cork), while Ulster had passed out of their hands the previous year. This meant that the Irish had now effectively been driven west of the Shannon, but there was still a large swathe of disputed territory on the east bank of the river which suffered through the winter and spring of 1691 from the depredations of both sides.[52]

The element still to be considered is the Irish Protestants, though reference has already been made to their reaction to Catholic resurgence and their initial proposals for the reduction of Ireland. The Protestants had seen themselves despoiled of their property in numerous ways at the hands of James's government.[53] They had been deprived of army commissions without compensation, been dismissed from civil office, and had also suffered loss in a variety of less obvious ways: non-payment of rents, the cancellation of debts by partial judges, and the seizure of weapons, horses, livestock, grain, etc. by casual marauders or later by the Jacobite forces.[54] In some cases they had suffered physical attack, intimidation, and psychological strain as their privileged position together with the laws which seemingly safeguarded it had been progressively undermined.[55] Their church had been threatened; while benefices had not passed into Catholic

[51] Simms, *Jacobite Ireland*, 166–72.

[52] Ibid., 174–203, *passim*.

[53] See pp. 167–8 above. The classic account of their predicament is William King, *The State of the Protestants in Ireland, under the late King James's Government* (1691), which was reprinted at least ten times by 1768. King set out to justify the Irish Protestants' repudiation of James by showing that he countenanced a policy of genocide against them; his claims were challenged by the Nonjuror Charles Leslie in *An Answer to . . . The State of the Protestants* (1692).

[54] *Secret Consults*, 133–5; *Transactions of the late King James in Ireland*, 4–5; *An Apology for the Protestants of Ireland*, 5–8; King, *State of the Protestants*, 133–9.

[55] [Richard Cox], *Aphorisms relating to Ireland* (1689), 5–7; *A True Account of the Present State of Ireland*, 12–16. Both stressed how the Protestants' sufferings were increased by the fact that their persecutors were frequently their former servants.

hands to any significant extent, there had been isolated incidents such as the case of Peter Manby, Dean of Derry, the chapter of Christ Church Cathedral in Dublin, and the failure to fill vacant bishoprics.[56] Large numbers of Protestants had sought refuge in England, an exodus that had started with Tyrconnell's appointment as Deputy in 1687 and accelerated in 1688, continuing in isolated cases into the spring of 1689.[57]

For those who found refuge in England the two largest sources of temporary relief, apart from private and corporate charity, were the Church (including the universities) and the army. As John Childs has shown, the removal of suspect officers from James's demoralized forces came just at the right time for the exiles, offering the chance of commissions for the dismissed officers of the Irish army, while others with military experience served as reformadoes.[58] In the Church of England minor benefices were diverted to the relief of Irish clergy, and a special Act was passed dispensing them from the regulations against pluralism.[59] Even approximate figures of those who left Ireland are hard to come by: refugees tended to cluster together, and western port towns, such as Chester, attracted substantial communities.[60] Most important, however, was the group who gathered in London, which included peers and greater gentry, some of whom, such as the Duke of Ormonde and the Southwell family, also had substantial property in England.[61] As we have seen, an Irish lobby

[56] [E. Wetenhall], *The Case of the Irish Protestants: In Relation to Recognising, Or Swearing Allegiance to, And Praying for King William and Queen Mary* (1691), 4–5; King, *State of the Protestants*, 214–48. On Christ Church, see ibid. 235, and [Leslie], *Answer*, pref. Individual conversions to Catholicism were sufficient to require a special formulary for reconciling them after the Williamite victory. See 'A Form for Receiving Lapsed Protestants . . .' in *Book of Common Prayer* (Dublin 1700). It began, 'Whereas I, A.B. of the Parish of C., being . . . chiefly swayed by base fears of suffering Persecution and Losses . . . in the late Times . . .'.

[57] Simms, *Jacobite Ireland*, 36, 54; *A True Account of the Present State of Ireland*, 7–14; *Secret Consults*, 73.

[58] Childs, *The Army, James II, and the Glorious Revolution*, 72–5. Cf. Cox, *Aphorisms*, 5.

[59] An Act for the relief of the Protestant Irish clergy (1 Wm. & M., sess. 1, c. xxix); G[eorge] P[hilips], *The Interest of England in the Preservation of Ireland* (1689), Epistle Dedicatory.

[60] As shown in the experience of the Molyneux brothers, see J. G. Simms, *William Molyneux of Dublin, 1656–1698*, ed. P. H. Kelly (Blackrock, Co. Dublin 1982), 57–60.

[61] *HMC: House of Lords MSS 1689–1690*, 136–44, 160–89, *passim*; a delegation led by Ormonde met William at Windsor in Dec. 1688, and drew up a declaration

emerged even before William reached London in December 1688, though the prominent role assumed by the previous Lord-Lieutenant, the Earl of Clarendon, rather compromised them in William's eyes.[62] After the political passivity of Restoration Dublin the exiles were exposed to the ferment of political discussion and the explosion of political pamphleteering in the English capital, and judging by what happened in the Irish parliament of 1692 many were able to benefit from their forced political education.[63] Several of the exiles themselves resorted to print, if we may credit the titles and descriptions of authors in contemporary pieces such as *The Character of the Protestants of Ireland, Impartially set forth . . .* (1689); or *An Apology for the Protestants of Ireland. In a Brief Narrative of the Late Revolutions in that Kingdom . . .* (1689).[64] And in Richard Cox's *Hibernia Anglicana* (part I, 1689; part II, 1690) the urge to inform their English hosts of what was at stake in Ireland produced a valuable work of history.

Not all prominent Irish Protestants left the country, and the subsequent relations between those who went and those who stayed were not easy. Those who remained exposed themselves to charges of Jacobitism from exiles who believed that any recognition of James as king, following the settlement of the throne on William and Mary on 13 February 1689, was treason. Yet clearly this was not the case for those in Ireland, where the Stuart régime had remained intact and the sovereign was present in person for the fifteen months following March 1689. Protestant peers, bishops, and commoners recognized the validity of the summons to James's parliament, and some even served in his army.[65] Despite their later disclaimers, the point of no longer

at his request on 17 Feb. 1689. A 'Committee of Irish Lords and Commons' listing five peers and fourteen Commoners is given on p. 160.

[62] Simms, *Jacobite Ireland*, 52.

[63] The leaders of the two groups whom Sydney identified as responsible for the opposition in the 1692 Irish parliament, namely the 'lawyers' (Serjeant Osborne and Robert Rochfort), and the 'English troublemakers' (James Hamilton, James Sloane, and Francis Brewster), were all active in lobbying the English parliament in 1689. *HMC: House of Lords MSS, 1689–1690*, 136–44, 160–89, *passim*.

[64] Two publishers seem to have specialized in Irish material, namely Robert Clavell and Richard Chiswell; the former published King's *State of the Protestants* and Wetenhall's work cited in n. 56 above, as well as an edition of both parts of G. Story's *Impartial History*.

[65] King (*State of Protestants*, 262–8) was particularly concerned to justify those who had stayed, as was Bishop Wetenhall of Cork, who published *The Case of the*

recognizing James as legitimate sovereign must have been a moment of intense realization for individuals rather than a specific public event; for the future Archbishop King, for example, it came when he was sentenced to death for spying in December 1689.[66] None the less the mutual distrust between the returned exiles and those who had stayed behind, and had been threatened or actually suffered at the hands of the Jacobites, was long to remain, though we cannot equate one side or other with particular vindictiveness against the Catholics and Jacobites. Of the two leaders of the Protestant community in Dublin in 1689, one—Anthony Dopping—preached a notorious sermon against observing the terms of the Treaty of Limerick in October 1692, while the other—William King—formally protested in the Lords Journals against the Irish parliament's failure to ratify the treaty in its entirety six years later.[67]

Efforts to reach a settlement during the winter of 1690–1 foundered on the disapprobation of the Jacobite war party, but the discussions had revealed the importance of concessions for Catholicism in reaching terms that the Irish would find acceptable.[68] Though William did not consider it necessary to conduct the 1691 campaign in Ireland in person, the demands of what he and his closest associates called the 'common cause' called for a rapid ending to the war. The French, however, perceived the advantages which prolonging the Irish campaign offered and increased their provision of arms and money, sending as well a more experienced commander in the person of the Marquis de Saint Ruth.[69] Divisions had also opened up within the Irish camp; Tyrconnell returned from a winter mission to Paris strengthened by the renewed commitment of James II and his queen, as

Irish Protestants to justify their change of allegiance; see also Bishop Dopping's speech of 7 July 1690 in [Leslie], *Answer*, app. 29–30. Another interesting defence of those who stayed is found in James Bonnel to his cousin, the antiquary John Strype, 10 Nov. 1690, Cambridge University Library: Strype Correspondence, i. 65.

[66] William King, autobiography of 1702, in C. S. King (ed.), *A Great Archbishop of Dublin: William King DD, 1650–1729* (Dublin 1906), 21–7.

[67] Simms, *Jacobite Ireland*, 258; Wouter Troost, 'William III and the Treaty of Limerick (1691–1697): A Study of his Irish Policy', cyclostyle Ph.D. thesis (Leiden, 1983), 180–2.

[68] Concessions on the private practice of Catholicism had been offered in William's Declaration of 22 Feb. 1689. Simms, 'Williamite Peace Tactics', 190.

[69] Tyrconnell to Louvois, 10 June 1691, *Analecta Hibernica*, 21 (1959), 214–15.

well as the personal support of Louis XIV. However, to the Irish commanders Tyrconnell was suspect as one who had looked for a negotiated settlement after the Boyne, and these military leaders, including Sarsfield, showed themselves increasingly contemptuous of his authority.[70]

The loss of Athlone at the beginning of the 1691 campaigning season was a serious blow to the Irish, particularly as it seemed largely attributable to treachery, a factor which from the start had been a powerful solvent of Jacobite confidence.[71] Both Charles O'Kelly and the author of *A Light to the Blind* saw treachery as the explanation for a series of defeats from the relief of Derry, to the fall of Athlone, to the surrender of Galway and then of Limerick.[72] Yet though treachery there undoubtedly was, it cannot serve as a satisfactory explanation of eventual Irish defeat. Taking the broadest view, it is arguable that the Irish cause was doomed from the moment the prince of Orange successfully drove James from his English throne; even with a much more decisive French commitment to the Jacobite cause the chances of winning in the long run must have been slight against the resources of England.[73] When the Irish had been driven back across the Shannon in 1690, defeat in the medium term could scarcely have been avoided. Ginkel's declaration of 7 July, which held out the hope of preserving individual estates, was well timed to exploit that nascent feeling of *sauve qui peut* that had opened up amongst the Irish, and the horror with which they saw victory vanish from their grasp at Aughrim four days later eroded the will to continue.[74] Within a few days Galway had been surrendered by its citizens despite the determination of the governor and French garrison,[75] leaving Limerick as the only major stronghold in Irish hands. In Limerick the will to resist was also compromised, though Tyrconnell stiffened resolve by arresting the leading advocate of negotiation, Henry Luttrell, and imposing an oath of collective resistance shortly before he died.[76] As late as mid-September, however, the French officers remained confident of the city's

[70] Gilbert, *Jacobite Narrative*, 111–13, 126–9.

[71] Simms, *Jacobite Ireland*, 209–12.

[72] O'Kelly, *Macariae Excidium*, 152; Gilbert, *Jacobite Narrative*, 52, 84, 135, 146.

[73] *Pace* D. Dickson, *New Foundations: Ireland, 1660–1800* (Dublin 1987), 39.

[74] Gilbert, *Jacobite Narrative*, 146; O'Kelly, *Macariae Excidium*, 133–4.

[75] Simms, *Jacobite Ireland*, 232–6.

[76] Gilbert, *Jacobite Narrative*, 149–50, 152–3.

capacity to resist, though forage and other supplies were short. Should the promised fleet arrive, there seemed no reason why the Irish should not survive the winter and sustain a campaign in 1692.[77] The willingness of the Irish to agree to a truce on 23 September came as a surprise to both Ginkel and his subordinate commanders, as well as to the Jacobite historians. To O'Kelly, what was most astonishing was the complete volte-face of Sarsfield, while to the author of *The Light*, the surrender was due to a combination of self-interest and the lack of clear leadership, once Tyrconnell's guiding hand was removed.[78]

The terms of the Treaty of Limerick and the way in which they were subsequently observed have long been highly contentious.[79] It is clear that both Jacobites and Williamites viewed the terms of cessation as the terms for ending the war in Ireland; the military articles, in particular the concession of allowing the Irish to withdraw their forces to France, make it obvious that the larger theatre of the European war was seen as the ultimate arbiter of what the civil articles would mean.[80] Despite the indications which they received from their first talks with the Williamites, initially the Irish had hoped for very extensive concessions, including the public recognition of Catholicism, restoration of the estates of all who had taken arms against the Williamites (regardless of the terms on which they had already yielded), and a full indemnity for acts of war.[81] Though such concessions went far beyond what Ginkel was authorized to grant, the first article of the treaty relating to religion still had a nation-wide application.

[77] 'Nous osons asseurer Vostre Majeste que nous conserverons infalliblement Lymerick': d'Usson and Tessé to Louis XIV, 18 Sept. 1691; Fumeron to Barbezieux, 26 Sept. 1691 (NS). *Franco-Irish Correspondence*, ii. 498, 500.

[78] Ginkel to Lords Justices of Ireland, 23 Sept. 1691; Simms, *Jacobite Ireland* 249–50. Limerick surrendered on 27 Sept. O'Kelly, *Macariae Excidium*, 154–5; Gilbert, *Jacobite Narrative*, 168–75.

[79] The most recent consideration of the actual negotiations is J. G. Simms, *The Treaty of Limerick* (reprinted in Hayton and O'Brien, *War and Politics*, 203–25); while W. Troost, 'William III and the Treaty of Limerick' (cf. n. 67 above), deals with the fate of the treaty between its confirmation by William and Mary in Feb. 1692 and its truncated ratification by the Irish parliament in 1697.

[80] Withdrawal of the army was the chief point which the Jacobites sought in the preliminary discussions. Simms, *Jacobite Ireland*, 250. This choice, as opposed to fighting on, met with James's approval both immediately and in the longer term, see his Declaration of 27 Nov. 1691 (Story, *Impartial History: Continuation*, 289), and Clarke, *James II*, ii. 465.

[81] Ginkel to Lord Lucan [Sarsfield], 30 Sept. 1691: Trinity College, Dublin: MS 749 (Clarke Correspondence), no. 1205.

It promised that Catholics should 'enjoy such Privileges in the Exercise of their Religion as are consistent with the Laws of Ireland; or as they did enjoy in the Reign of King Charles II', and undertook that William and Mary would seek to improve their position by legislation in an Irish parliament. The ninth article limiting the oath to be demanded of Catholics who submitted to the Williamite government to the simple oath of allegiance (as specified in the second article) also had general rather than specific application, though it was promptly violated by the English parliament's requiring a declaration against transubstantiation from all members of the Irish parliament.[82] The other civil articles were specific to the forces in Limerick and those under their protection, as were the military articles with the exception of the seventeenth article, which provided for the general release of prisoners of war.

The main thrust of the articles was to conserve the rights and property of the members of the garrison and of those under their protection (the famous 'omitted clause' whose validity led to so much subsequent dispute).[83] The privileged group of articlesmen, together with those entitled to the benefit of other articles of surrender such as those of Galway, Sligo, Waterford, Drogheda, and Inisboffin, were permitted to retain their estates, once adjudged to be within the terms of the treaty, and to practise as barristers and attorneys, as well as to receive an indemnity for acts of war and protection from civil suits for debt.[84] To the Irish Protestants, who played no part in the drafting of the terms, this appeared to leave the defeated in a better position than themselves, and they together with Catholics who had submitted earlier without benefit of articles were left deeply dissatisfied with the way the war had ended.[85] In particular the returned Protestant

[82] An Act for abrogating the Oath of Supremacy in Ireland, and appointing other Oaths (3 Wm. & M., 1st pt. c. 2).

[83] Simms, *Williamite Confiscation*, 55–65; Troost, 'William and the Treaty of Limerick', 35–9, 169–73. Failure to include the 'omitted clause' in the 1697 ratification did not in practice result in articlesmen being deprived of their property.

[84] Of the 1,283 claims to the benefits of the articles of Limerick and Galway adjudicated, only 15 were rejected; a further 65 individuals were restored to their estates by royal pardon: Simms, *Williamite Confiscation*, 45–6, 174. The right to practise law was severely restricted by the 1704 oath of abjuration. Gilbert, *Jacobite Narrative*, 187.

[85] James Bonnel to Robert Harley, 3 Nov. 1691. *HMC: Portland MSS*, iii. 479–80.

colonists now regarded William and the English parliament in a very ambivalent fashion; they realized their dependence on England for security, but resented the way in which their interests had been, as they saw it, ignored in the settlement. These resentments were deeply to influence the course of Irish politics during the rest of William's reign, creating a legacy of misunderstanding that helped forge a new sense of independent colonial identity in the first three decades of the eighteenth century.

III

The search for a settlement that would provide the security which the restored Protestant landowners and officials were so anxious to achieve was responsible for the emergence during the 1690s of parliament as a regular part of the governmental machinery in Ireland. Of itself this was a major constitutional development, since the Irish parliament had notably failed to play such a role in the earlier part of the century.[86] Parliamentary sessions took place in 1692, 1695, 1697, and 1698–9, and with the coming of the eighteenth century soon took place on a regular biennial basis. Actual elections were far rarer; three in the 1690s, two in Anne's reign, while under the Hanoverians only a new accession to the throne prompted a fresh election till the passing of the Octennial Act in 1768. Apart from the initial need to establish a settlement following the Jacobite War, pressure for more regular sessions came from the fiscal demands of the Irish establishment, particularly the military side.[87] The burden of maintaining the Irish establishment (even leaving aside the costs of the war) was a net drain on English resources in the years to 1695, which given the developing crisis in public credit and government borrowing in England could no longer be sustained without help from the colony.[88] This burden on the

A cogent statement of the case for ending the war on non-punitive terms is found in Royal Irish Academy, Dublin: MS 24. G 7, item 83.

[86] McGuire, 'Parliament of 1692' (ref. n. 37 above), 1, comments 'Parliament had not been part of the normal governmental process in seventeenth-century Ireland'.

[87] D. Hayton, 'The beginnings of the Undertaker System', in *Penal Era and Golden Age*, 40–1.

[88] For Ireland and the English fiscal crisis, see P. Kelly, 'The Irish Woollen Export Prohibition Act of 1699: Kearney re-visited', *Irish Economic and Social History*, 7 (1980), 25–6.

English Exchequer was a very different pattern from the net contribution which Ireland had made to royal finances during the later Restoration period, though the placing of regiments on the Irish establishment could still to some extent alleviate English expenditure.[89]

As James Bonnel had predicted to Robert Harley less than six weeks after the surrender of Limerick, the very existence of parliaments in Ireland tended to awake English jealousy and suspicion that Ireland was pursuing her separate interest to the detriment of the mother country.[90] From the first of these post-Revolution parliaments, despite its very brief duration, there developed a sense of corporate identity and separateness, that if anything increased in its successors of 1695 and 1697. By 1698 the English parliament was condemning the spirit of 'independency' across St George's Channel and a major constitutional conflict developed with the row over Molyneux's *Case of Ireland, stated.* Anglo-Irish attitudes towards the relation with England evolved significantly in the later 1690s. The confession of Richard Cox in the dedication to *Hibernia Anglicana* that Ireland was a conquered country and that the English in Ireland rejoiced in this status, also echoed in Bishop Wetenhall's tract on the lawfulness of Irish Protestants submitting to William and Mary, yielded place to a very different sentiment.[91] In 1697 Bishop King of Derry could speak of the legislative subjection to England placing the English in Ireland in a state of slavery.[92] This claim of English men living outside the mother country to enjoy the liberties of freeborn English was also heard from the American colonies and was treated by the Westminster parliament with as little consideration as was accorded to that from Ireland.[93]

The subsequent fate of the Treaty of Limerick was dependent on ratification by the Irish parliament, and in neither the first parliament following the war, nor in that of 1695 did ratification

[89] Egan, 'Finance and the Government of Ireland, 1660–85' (cf. n. 11 above), ii. 190–2; Childs, *Army of William III*, 194–5.

[90] James Bonnel to Robert Harley, 3 Nov. 1691.

[91] Cox, *Hibernia Anglicana*, pt. i. Epistle Dedicatory to William and Mary; [Wetenhall], *Case of the Irish Protestants*, 6.

[92] William King to Bishop [Lindsay] of Killaloe, 13 May 1698; King letterbook 1696–8, Trinity College, Dublin: MS 750/1.

[93] D. S. Lovejoy, 'Two American Revolutions, 1689 and 1776', in J. G. A. Pocock (ed.), *Three British Revolutions: 1641, 1688, 1776* (Princeton 1980), 246.

prove possible in the face of the hostility of the Irish Protestants.[94] Ratification was one of the objects of summoning a parliament in 1692 but the parliament proved a disaster for the government, having to be dismissed within a month in the light of the intractable temper of the colonists. A novel sense of parliamentary independence was manifested—chiefly by members who had formed part of the Irish lobby in London in 1689–90—and an issue of constitutional importance emerged with claims to the 'sole right' to initiate the heads of money bills despite the provisions of Poynings's Act.[95] In the 1695 parliament, as David Hayton has demonstrated, the practice evolved of managing the parliament through handing over responsibility to a group of local politicians who would conduct the government's business in return for control of patronage, the practice known in the eighteenth century as the 'undertaker system'.[96] According to Burnet the Irish parliament adopted the English divisions of Whig and Tory in the 1695 session, though the meaning of these terms underwent change once across St George's Channel. By English standards all Irish politicians were Whigs, thanks to the potential for Jacobite invasion and the threat of the Irish Catholics. Irish Tories were divided from Irish Whigs by their attitude to the Church and their hostility to the Dissenters; they also differed in their views as to how the Catholics should be treated—not that they were particularly sympathetic to Catholics, but they accepted the obligations of public faith in regard to the treaty.[97]

Long before the ratification of the Treaty of Limerick in truncated form in 1697,[98] the issue of additional penal legislation brought up in Catholic eyes at least the question of the observance of the treaty. In general existing Irish legislation against Catholics at the time of the Revolution was less repressive than in England;[99]

[94] Troost, 'William and the Treaty of Limerick', 56, 60–4, 122–6, 151–3, 163–84 *passim*.

[95] McGuire, 'Parliament of 1692', 11–25.

[96] Hayton, 'Undertaker System', 32–45, *passim*.

[97] Ibid. 43–7. The actual terms Whig and Tory were not employed in Ireland till the beginning of Anne's reign.

[98] For the ratification and its background, see Troost, 'William and the Treaty of Limerick', 160–84, *passim*, esp. 174–82. Article I (relating to religion), and the 'omitted clause' in article II (referring to those under Jacobite protection) were omitted, while the date of the indemnity for acts of war in article VI was advanced from Nov. 1688 to Apr. 1689.

[99] Simms, *Jacobite Ireland*, 8–10.

but in the parliaments of 1695 and 1697 a considerable volume of legislation was introduced which (together with the additional acts of Anne's reign) constituted what has been seen as a systematic code aimed against Catholicism.[100] This legislation made nonsense of the undertaking in the first article of Limerick to provide Catholics with additional safeguards for the practice of their religion, though the English administration strenuously denied violation of the treaty.[101] Marriage with Protestants was prohibited; education abroad banned, and the number of religious holidays (against the excess of which Petty had inveighed) greatly restricted (2 Wm. III, cc. 3, 4, 14).[102] The most severe legislation of the reign came in the 1697 parliament with the Act banishing bishops and regulars, whose intention was effectively to end Catholicism in the country by preventing future ordinations and stopping clergy ordained outside Ireland entering the country (9 Wm. III, c. 1). An earlier proposal of this kind had been resisted thanks to the intervention of the ambassadors of William's Catholic allies in the war against Louis XIV, but in 1697 the war was nearly over and William was less than warm towards the emperor for his obstruction of the Ryswick negotiations and his demilitarization of Italy in 1696.[103] Further extensive legislation came in Anne's reign, particularly in 1704. The omnibus Act for Preventing the Further Growth of Popery (2 Anne, c. 6) affected the security of property by the inducement held out to sons to obtain sole possession of the family estate by conversion; forbade Catholics to acquire lands by purchase; and imposed an oath of abjuration against the Pretender. Separate acts required the registration of priests in the country (2 Anne c. 7), and forbade the entry of further priests from abroad (2 Anne c. 4). The Abjuration Oath was resisted more firmly than in England (though there were Irish priests prepared to take it), and in 1710 it was extended to all priests and, at the will of the magistrates, to any layman over sixteen (8 Anne, c. 24). Under this Act Catholics

[100] R. E. Burns, 'The Irish Popery Laws: A Study of Eighteenth-Century Legislation and Behaviour', *Review of Politics*, 24 (1962), 485.

[101] Shrewsbury to Galway, 9 July 1697: *HMC: Downshire MSS*, ii. 489.

[102] W. Petty, *Political Anatomy of Ireland* (1691), 118, 130.

[103] J. G. Simms, 'The Bishops' Banishment Act, 1697', reprinted in Hayton and O'Brien, *War and Politics*, 235–49; P. Kelly, 'Lord Galway and the Penal Laws', in C. E. J. Caldicott, H. Gough, J.-P. Pittion (eds.), *The Huguenots and Ireland: Anatomy of an Emigration* (Dun Laoghaire, Co. Dublin), 239–54.

could be required to testify on oath as to when they last attended mass, who celebrated it, and who was present, but it does not seem to have been strictly enforced.[104]

Behind this legislation, the motivation for which came mostly from the colonists rather than the English administration, lay the determination to put it beyond the capacity of Catholics ever again to challenge the colonists' hegemony in Ireland. Unfortunately for Irish Catholicism the loyalty of the Irish hierarchy to James II, manifested by the presence of several bishops at Saint Germain and James's continued exercise of the right of appointment to Irish sees, put the church's role in Ireland into question. It was arguably this relationship between the Stuarts and the Irish hierarchy outside Ireland rather than overt Jacobitism within the country that represented the perceived threat from Irish Catholicism. In fact few Irishmen were prominent at the exiled court, and Ireland played a distinctly minor role in Jacobite planning after 1691.[105]

The final tendency worth considering as a consequence of the impact of the Glorious Revolution in Ireland was the resistance to English legislative supremacy in Ireland that began in the late 1690s and received literary expression in William Molyneux's *The Case of Ireland's being bound by acts of parliament in England, stated* (1698). This influential work, widely read in the early stages of the American Revolution, owed its origin to the attempt to suppress the export of Irish woollen manufactures in 1697–8 and to the struggle between the Bishop of Derry and the Irish Society (of London) over lands and fishery rights in the Derry area.[106]

Molyneux's work (which was reprinted some nine times between 1698 and the granting of legislative independence in 1782), put forward a theory of the Irish constitution that notably failed to take account of the changed realities of post-1688 English politics—particularly the transfer of sovereignty to the Crown in Parliament.[107] Molyneux asserted that Ireland was by no means a

[104] Wall, *Penal Laws*, 15–19.

[105] Cathaldus Giblin, OFM, 'The Stuart Nomination of Irish Bishops, 1687–1765', *Irish Ecclesiastical Record*, 105 (1966), 36–8. By no means all Irish ecclesiastics favoured the link with the Stuarts, but the latter commanded the support of Rome. Ibid. 37–40.

[106] Molyneux, *Case of Ireland*, ed. J. G. Simms (Monkstown, Co. Dublin, 1977), intro.

[107] Simms, *Colonial Nationalism, 1698–1776* (Cork 1976), 59–68.

colony like the English possessions in America, but an independent kingdom with its own parliament, legislative system, civil administration, and courts which owed allegiance to the king of England in virtue of his subordinate title of King of Ireland.[108] However, in conceding the English parliament's right to determine in 1689 that whoever was king of England was *ipso facto* ruler of Ireland, Molyneux overlooked the crucial fact that the English parliament had exercised the supreme act of sovereignty over Ireland in determining who that ruler should be, and could well do so again. Molyneux's case was argued with learning and skill on the basis of legal precedent and history, and a minor part of the argument depended on natural-right theory, which he adduced from the writings 'of my excellent friend, John Locke, Esquire', particularly in his repudiation of the claim which the English parliament asserted over Ireland on the basis of conquest. Instead Molyneux showed that the existing Irish constitution derived from the voluntary submission of the Irish princes to Henry II in 1172, which established the original contract on which the present constitution rested.[109]

Molyneux's book and the supposed tendency to 'independency' which it was held to represent were condemned by the English House of Commons in an Address to the King in June 1698.[110] Although in the short run *The Case of Ireland, stated* evoked little sympathy amongst the colonists, the principle which it asserted as to the right to consent to government making it unjustifiable for one nation to direct the affairs of another was so applicable to the predicament of the Protestant official and landowning classes in Ireland that by the end of the second decade of the eighteenth century Molyneux's work came to be seen as the classic exposition of their rights.[111]

Moreover, within months of the condemnation of Molyneux's book the English parliament proceeded to two steps which both significantly increased its power over Ireland and seriously damaged the interests of the colonists. The English House of

[108] Molyneux, *Case of Ireland*, 40–2, 57, 88, 102–3, 115. In view of his failure to perceive the constitutional changes in England, it is ironical that Molyneux (p. 113) may have been the first person in Ireland to refer in print to the term 'Glorious Revolution'.

[109] Ibid. 26–30, 33–9; citation 39.

[110] *Commons Journal*, xii. 324–6.

[111] I. Victory, 'Colonial Nationalism in Ireland, 1692–1725: From Common Law to Natural Right', unpublished Ph.D. thesis (Trinity College, Dublin 1985), 144–6.

Lords allowed the appeal of the Irish Society against the bishop of Derry, finding that the Irish house had no appellate jurisdiction in equity matters, and the following May an English Act was passed prohibiting the exportation of woollen cloth from both Ireland and the American colonies except to the mother country.[112] A third step, also damaging to the colonists' interests, came with the English Act of Resumption in 1700 which overset the Williamite land settlement in Ireland by cancelling all grants made by the king. Those affected included not only the immediate grantees but bona fide purchasers to whom the lands had in many cases been subsequently sold, who were overwhelmingly members of the colonial landowning and official classes.[113] This bout of unprecedented direct intervention in Irish affairs by the English parliament was not, however, continued in Anne's reign, but the colonists acquired other grievances in relation to their administration from England. Most notable was the question of union with England; Irish interest in the possibility of union was particularly strong in the years from 1697 to 1706, and the sense of rebuff when Scotland was admitted to union but Ireland refused was effectively portrayed in Swift's *The Story of the Injured Lady, Being a true Picture of Scotch Perfidy, Irish Poverty, and English Partiality*.[114] Once Scotland had ceased to be an independent kingdom, the tendency to think of Ireland as merely the first of England's colonies was greatly reinforced. The colonists found themselves at a disadvantage in their own country with a growing tendency to appoint those of English birth rather than the colonists to civil and ecclesiastical office, which was much increased following the accession of the Hanoverians.[115]

Molyneux's theory received official sanction in 1719, when in the course of the conflict over jurisdiction with the British House of Lords in the final stages of the *Annesley versus Sherlock* case, the Irish Lords addressed a Representation to George I. This asserted Molyneux's 'dual monarchy' interpretation of the Irish constitution, in censuring the British Lords for attacking George's

[112] Kelly, 'Irish Woollen Export Prohibition Act of 1699' (cf. n. 88 above), 37, 41.

[113] Simms, *Williamite Confiscation*, 110–47, *passim*.

[114] *A New History of Ireland*, iv. T. W. Moody and W. E. Vaughan (eds.), *Eighteenth-Century Ireland, 1691–1800* (Oxford 1986), 7; J. Kelly, 'The Origins of the Act of Union: an Examination of Unionist Opinion in Britain and Ireland, 1650–1800', *Irish Historical Studies*, 25 (1986), 243–4.

[115] Victory, 'Colonial Nationalism', 127–32, *passim*.

prerogative as king of Ireland and in claiming the agreement between the Irish princes and Henry II as the 'Original Compact' of government.[116] Ironically this very success led in the following year to the British parliament's Declaratory Act of 1720,[117] which in defining in incontrovertible fashion the legislative and jurisdictional supremacy of the British over the Irish parliament can be said to have completed the transition from kingdom to colony that was arguably the most significant medium-term consequence of the Glorious Revolution in Ireland. For the Irish the immediate impact of this change was seen in the Bank Project of 1720–1, when it appeared that the prosperity of the Irish economy was to be subjected to the interests of English favourites and ministers, and similar dangers seemed to threaten in the Wood's Halfpence project of 1722–5. However, in both instances colonial resistance succeeded after considerable struggle in reversing the British ministers' decisions.[118] The full implications of the Declaratory Act were thus never made apparent, but Ireland's subordinate status continued periodically to irk the colonists till the early 1780s. Reversal of Ireland's reduction to the status of a colony came with the restoration of parliamentary independence to Ireland in 1782, when the second Rockingham ministry was forced to concede the demands of the patriot party in the Irish parliament, backed by the armed threat of the Volunteer movement.[119] The re-establishment of the traditional Irish constitution was both achieved and inspired therefore as a result of the demand for political liberty successfully asserted by the colonists in America. For the later eighteenth and early nineteenth centuries it was this recovery of legislative independence that constituted the Irish revolution rather than the events of 1688, which were referred to in the Irish parliament in 1795, as follows:

> The revolution of King William has been called by the gentlemen on the other side of the House, a glorious revolution—glorious it certainly was

[116] *Lords Journal [Ireland]*, ii. 655–60; p. 656 refers to 'the late happy Revolution', i.e. 1688.

[117] *New History of Ireland*, iv. 110–11, 138–9; Dickson, *New Foundations*, 65–6. For an illuminating discussion of the reasons behind the Declaratory Act, see Victory, 'Colonial Nationalism', 148–52.

[118] F. G. James, *Ireland in the Empire, 1688–1770* (Cambridge, Mass. 1973), 110–24.

[119] G. O'Brien, *Anglo-Irish Politics in the Age of Grattan and Pitt* (Blackrock, Co. Dublin 1987), 28–35.

for England—for Ireland it was disastrous in the extreme, and was attended with the most pernicious effects—the annihilation of her woollen manufacture—the extinction of her commerce, the total loss of her legislative independence. . . .[120]

[120] J. Gordon, *A History of Ireland, from the Earliest Accounts to . . . 1800* (2 vols., Dublin 1805), ii. 274–5. H. Grattan [jun.] (ed.), *The Speeches of the Right Honourable Henry Grattan, in the Irish, and in the Imperial Parliament* (4 vols., 1822), i. pref., p. xv; *Irish Parliamentary Debates, 1795* (Dublin 1795), 321.

5

Europe and the Revolution of 1688

JOHN STOYE

I

AMID much that is serious in these lectures let me begin convivially. A wonderful—even a stunning—musical party was given in Rome on 2 February 1687.[1] Many guests were there, above all the guest of honour Lord Castlemaine, English ambassador to the Pope. So was a large chorus of singers, with soloists who impersonated the city of London, the River Thames, and other muses. So were a hundred string players led by the great Corelli. So was the hostess, Queen Christina, the senior royal convert to Rome alive, offering her felicitations on this symbolic occasion to the junior, King James of England. The words said that day, as distinct from words sung or recited, were not recorded, but the event itself is a reminder that Christina, James, and a fair number of other princes or members of princely families, Protestant by upbringing, became Catholic during this period. The business of conversion, the strenuous efforts made to shift people from one confession to another, or to resist these efforts, was of course a characteristic element in both the popular and the intellectual culture of Europe after the Protestant Reformation; but changes of this kind in the dynastic network, in the cluster of sovereign families, were of particular importance. They were important because in practice it proved difficult to escape from the common contemporary assumption that rulers could or would impose their own religion on their subjects. I want first to consider this group of princely converts to which James II belongs, before leading you along highways and byways on the

[1] A. Guidi, *Accademia per Musica fatta nel Real Palazzo della Maesta della Regina Christina* . . . (Rome 1687); M. Wright, *An Account of his Excellencie Roger Earl of Castlemaine's Embassy* . . . (1688), 70–4.

mainland of Europe to within sight of the cliffs of Dover. It is the Revolution of 1688 in its European framework, rather than as an event in English history, which is our concern.

Having first confirmed the Protestant ascendancy in the Baltic region and north Germany by the Westphalian treaties, and then her regal ascendancy over the four Estates at Stockholm, the Swedish queen had decided—for various reasons—to abdicate, rather than announce her conversion and remain on the Vasa throne.[2] The next in succession duly succeeded in 1654, and maintained the existing Lutheran settlement in Church and State intact in the Swedish empire. Keeping only her royal title, with revenues from Mecklenburg and elsewhere, Christina departed. Rome therefore triumphed in a minor way, but gained from her less than it had hoped for, and far less than had been hoped for on the accession of the Catholic Sigismund Vasa in Sweden in 1592. Christina resided in Rome from the end of 1655 until her death in 1689, a number of lengthy excursions apart. The prestige of her presence, the royal convert who was the daughter of Gustavus Adolphus, attracted the attention of all those Protestants visiting the papal city in this period. She was a choice exhibit and exemplar, and counted for something in the continuing Roman propaganda to subdue or restrict the Protestant confessions.

Following her as a convert was young John Frederick of the ruling house of Brunswick, with its broad lands in Lower Saxony and many co-heirs. It was a good case of strong personal conviction following a period of residence in Italy, discussions with other converts, and despairing appeals from the people at home; but then he inherited the duchy of Hanover, in which from 1666 to 1679 he maintained the Lutheran establishment rock-solid.[3] If he placed the *Schlosskirche* in Capucin hands, collected Catholic relics, and welcomed Catholic craftsmen, his household and his officials remained exclusively Protestant. His Catholic wife failed to give him a son, he died in 1679, and a Protestant brother stepped into his shoes. In temperament John Frederick may have differed from a more notable princely convert; but their church settlements

[2] C. Weibull, *Christina of Sweden* (Göteborg 1966), 51–91, 179–80; G. Christ, 'Fürst, Dynastie, Territorium und Konfession', *Saeculum*, 24 (1973), 367–87.

[3] A. Kocher, *Geschichte von Hannover und Braunschweig*, i (Leipzig 1884), 351–77; G. Schnath, *Geschichte von Hannover im Zeitalter der neunten Kur und der englischen Sukzession 1674–1714*, i (Hildesheim 1938), 20–31.

were alike. Frederick Augustus, the Elector of Lutheran Saxony who presided over the Corpus Evangelicorum of the Holy Roman Empire, made his bid for the Polish crown in 1697. It was a political coup carried out with impeccable timing. Successive Diets at Warsaw having eliminated a large number of candidates domestic and foreign, the Elector made his offer, adding a guarded disclosure of his submission to the Roman obedience a short while previously. His envoy and his money won a startling success. A crown was surely worth a mass, even plus the heavy costs.[4] The Lutheran church and people of Saxony had to digest the change. Yet a Catholic regent or *Statthalter*, a Catholic chancellor, a small knot of more serious converts in the Elector's entourage were allowed to make very little difference to the régime. The Lutheran establishment remained intact. The Electress was and stayed a Protestant, and the Electoral Prince—everyone was assured—would be brought up as a Protestant. It is true on the other hand that an official edict in 1698 forbade Lutheran preachers to use insulting language in their sermons, while tiny groups of Jews and Calvinists, as well as Catholics in the Court, derived some benefit from the change; and that the equally small 'No Popery' mob in Dresden made little headway. A more important point may be noted. Rome had been surprised and shocked by the Elector's conversion, but in due course took a keen interest in the Electoral Prince's further education. A long spell in Italy would complete the process of bringing him into the Roman fold in 1711, and this was publicly announced several years later still. These matters, in Saxony but not in England, were taken at a slow pace.

To come nearer the Stuarts, the 'winter' Queen of Bohemia's son, Charles Lewis, became the ruling Elector Palatine in 1648. After thirty-five years of tolerant rule on both sides of the Rhine over his mainly Reformed, fewer Lutheran, and still fewer Catholic subjects, and some outright bullying of the neighbouring Catholic bishops of Worms and Speyer, he died in 1680; and his son Charles Philip died in 1685. There being no direct male heir, a Catholic cousin succeeded. Philip William of Neuburg, the Emperor's father-in-law, already ruling fairly tolerantly in other

[4] P. Haake, 'Die Wahl Augusts des Starken zum König von Polen', *Historische Vierteljahrschrift*, 9 (1906), 31–84; N. Davies, *God's Playground* (Oxford 1981), i. 492.

Rhenish lands, promised that in his new inheritance the position of the Reformed majority would remain unchanged.[5] It was added that Catholics were to have the right to public worship and some limited access to public office. This agreement of 1685 was on the whole honoured in the Palatinate in Philip William's lifetime (he died in 1690). Then, gradually, under his son and successor, the concessions enjoyed by an increasing number of Catholics—regarding feast-days, cemeteries, the possession or 'simultaneous' possession of churches, and the ringing of bells—were multiplied. The action of the French during the wars and the treaty of Ryswick, confirming the ecclesiastical changes which they had introduced in several Palatinate lands, were accepted with satisfaction by Elector John William. In due course the worsening of the Protestants' position would be such that the flow of emigration began; and other German states, England, then America, became familiar with the plight of the 'poor Palatines' during Queen Anne's reign.

These were the notable cases, in James II's lifetime, in which Protestant rulers went over to Rome or Catholic princes inherited Protestant countries. James must take a prominent place among them and such a survey makes it clearer than ever that his tempo, in trying to make major changes favouring the Catholic interest, was vertiginously fast. His declarations of February and March 1685, affirming the Anglican ascendancy in Church and State, exactly resemble those offered by Frederick Augustus to the Saxon Estates; and he appeared to be following in the footsteps of John Frederick of Hanover. He did not require, like Philip William in the Palatinate, some redress of Catholic grievances from the start. But then, late in 1685, James began to push much harder. He could reckon on a larger Catholic minority than would be found in the German Protestant states and on larger, more influential groups, of nonconforming Protestants than elsewhere. Continental comparisons still suggest that his tempo, his too rapid exclusion of the Establishment from influence with the Crown, was as risky as it showed itself to be. And the Saxon and Palatine examples, in particular, illustrate what advantages

[5] K. Jaitner, *Die Konfessionspolitik des Pfalzengrafen Philipp Wilhelm von Neuburg in Jülich-Berg von 1647–1679* (Münster 1973), 312–18; A. Hans, *Die Kurpfälzische Religionsdeklaration von 1705* (Mainz 1973), 15–22; L. Stamer, *Kirchengeschichte der Pfalz*, iii. 1 (Speyer 1955), 171–87.

the presence of a son and heir offered the specifically Catholic interest in the long run. In June and early July 1688, immediately following the birth of the Prince of Wales, it might be thought, James still had time on his side.[6]

In the absence of a corresponding movement from the Catholic side to Protestantism, or of Catholic princes away from Rome, the sequence of conversions looks like one element in a continuing and persistent movement of Counter-Reformation between 1650 and 1750.[7] Associated with this, but distinct, was the sweeping revocation of all Protestant rights in France and the eras of persecution in parts of the Habsburg empire, something much more extreme. James looked like belonging to the moderates before he too began, and then persisted in, trying to brush aside enacted laws.

II

Having begun with one entertainment, at Rome in 1687, let me now turn to another. This was a hunting-party held over a period of several weeks during the winter of 1681, in the region known as the Hümmling, heath and waste of Friesland in north Germany, equally distant from The Hague to the west and Celle and Hanover eastwards.[8] Among the guests were William of Orange and George William of Celle, old friends. Another was Count Waldeck, the German prince who was William's deputy military commander in the Netherlands and his political agent in Germany. George William's brother, of Hanover, declined to come and the Bishop of Münster, the host, was sick. A French envoy, anxious to discover whether anything hostile to France would be decided, quartered in a neighbouring village. That hunting party was one of several in the winters of this decade, in this part of Germany. They were social occasions when political decisions could be discussed: to switch alliances, recruit or disband troops, or lay plans for a joint assault on somebody else. The summers were not very different. The princes and their ladies went to spas like Pyrmont and Linsburg to meet each other; and they entertained at home. The routes between these places

[6] Cf. J. Kenyon, *Sunderland* (1958), 201.

[7] R. Krautheimer, *The Rome of Alexander VII, 1665–1667* (Princeton 1985), 131–47.

[8] Schnath, *Geschichte von Hannover*, i. 174–80.

carried a relatively heavy traffic of rulers and their agents on a continuous round of visits. Our concern is this political network of north Germany—including the lower Rhine, Westphalia, and Brandenburg—and its connection with William of Orange's successful invasion of Great Britain in 1688. It belonged to a part of the hinterland which was able, for reasons to be explored, to offer the Dutch sufficient minimum support at a critical time.

In such fragmented territory local rivalries were incessant. The Elector of Brandenburg, Frederick William, before he died in 1688, tried to parcel out his lands between the offspring of two marriages; Ernest Augustus of Hanover meanwhile insisted on the principle of primogeniture, and the union of the House of Brunswick. Succession was as dominant an issue as in contemporary England. Both rulers caused great bitterness within their respective families; and the rivalry of the two exemplified the competitive milieu of a whole region. Nearby the monarchies of Denmark and Sweden, after years of warfare, each retained possessions in Germany. Brandenburg and the Brunswick princes wanted to acquire them. Denmark in addition eyed the lands in Schleswig and Holstein held by the Duke of Gottorp, an ally of the Swedes, and eyed too the wealth and trade of the 'free' Imperial city of Hamburg. There were many lesser interests, by no means to be overlooked by the bigger antagonists, such as the bishops of Münster, and the duchy of Sachsen-Lauenburg, and Mecklenburg-Schwerin where the reigning duke was a Catholic convert resident in Paris.[9] In the distance were the superior powers, the Dutch and the courts of France and Vienna, each with a concern for their own interest in this area. They might offer bribes to the princes' ministers, or subsidies for the raising of troops, or subsidies for buying a state's neutrality. They might threaten one ally, in certain circumstances, with an attack by another. The question we must ask, therefore, concerns the changing priorities of the statesmen in that part of Germany, from the time of the hunting-party in the Hümmling in 1681 (which, according to his man on the spot, signalled nothing adverse to Louis XIV) up to 1688. In August of that year Bentinck,

[9] Christian Ludwig I (1658–1690) took the name 'Louis' on his conversion to Rome in 1663. Fighting a long battle with his Estates, he resembled James II in his warm defence of a ruling prince's authority. H.-J. Ballschmieter, *Andreas Gottlieb von Bernstorff und der Mecklenburgische Ständekampf 1680–1720* (Cologne 1962), 1–40.

acting for William of Orange and the States-General, reached agreements with four German governments for the hire of 4,000 cavalry and dragoons and 10,600 foot, replacing almost exactly the force shipped two months later for England.[10] More than three-quarters of those promised came from Brandenburg and Celle. How could this come about?

Perhaps the shortest answer, with a measure of truth in it, is that Hamburg was not Strasburg, nor was it Cologne. In August 1681 Louis XIV's troops had seized Strasburg, another of the 'free' Imperial cities. Waldeck, William, and many others looked for signs of a recoil in Germany which would produce a stiffer and more widely based resistance to French demands. But William's verdict, 'It is a terrible misfortune that *l'affaire de Strasbourg* alarms the Germans so little', if understating the alarm, describes accurately enough the negative result during the next few years.[11] A somewhat similar threat in the north was a different matter. The Danes first attacked Hamburg in 1679; they again attacked and then besieged it in 1686.[12] By February 1688 they also had 18,000 men on territory earlier held by the Duke of Gottorp, and began building a large new fortress half way between Hamburg and Lübeck—just as Louis XIV was doing on other princes' ground by the Moselle and Rhine at the same time. In each of the years 1686, 1687, 1688, and 1689 men's nerves in that quarter of Europe were much on edge, and war seemed likely if the Brunswick dukes, Brandenburg, and Sweden combined against the Danes. On each occasion King Christian V drew back just sufficiently and the hostile grouping hesitated. The empire-building age of Christian IV and Gustavus Adolphus was over; but while the neighbouring German states were now strong enough to stop the Danes moving any distance south, they—and the Swedes—on each occasion failed to agree on the terms for combining to force them back. The risk of a major armed conflict in the summer and

[10] F. I. G. Ten Raa, *Het Staatsche Leger*, vi (The Hague 1940), 269–73.

[11] P. L. Müller, *Wilhelm III von Oranien und Georg Friedrich von Waldeck. Ein Beitrag zur Geschichte des Kampfes um das europäische Gleichgewicht* (2 vols., The Hague 1873–80), i. 115. As another of their joint sorrows William and Waldeck repeatedly deplored the inactivity of the English Court in Europe after 1679.

[12] H. Kellenbenz, *Geschichte Schleswig-Holsteins*, ed. O. Klose, v (Neumünster 1960), 222–7; A. Zuschlag, *Die Rolle des Hauses Braunschweig-Lüneburg im Kampfe um Hamburgs Reichsfreiheit gegen Dänemark 1675–1692* (Hildesheim 1934), 48–94; P. Schramm, *Neun Generationen* (Göttingen 1963), i. 84–8; P. Tortoft, 'William III and Denmark–Norway, 1697–1702', *English Historical Review*, 81 (1966), 1–25.

autumn in 1688 over Hamburg, Schleswig, and Holstein looked real enough, but there was perceived to be at least some chance of a continuing deadlock, and of further negotiation. This was one reason why it appeared possible to take the calculated risk of sparing troops for the Dutch service.[13]

Another reason, of a more fundamental kind, was the routine of what had become established practice.[14] The stronger princes in the Empire were by now well accustomed to raising troops, quartering them on unarmed neighbours, or bargaining to send them off to distant places. In 1685 the three Brunswick courts contracted to supply a force of 10,000 for the war in Hungary. Others were sent to serve the Venetian Republic in 1685 and again in 1686; they fought in Greece. In that year, 1686, for the first time but not the last, Brandenburg sent 6,000 to fight in Hungary. If recruiting bounties and winter quarters and other charges were offered at the right time, and at the right price, the manpower could be found, coming either from freshly raised troops or from a state's existing force. The Dutch were of course one of the paymasters of the system. It helped them, both before and after 1688, to maintain an army large enough to confront France in the Spanish Netherlands. After 1688 the English government joined in, and began paying for foreign manpower of this kind. It did so throughout the War of the Spanish Succession, as also in Continental and overseas warfare later in the eighteenth century. Here was an important new link between Great Britain and the mainland of Europe after the Revolution, to be strengthened immensely in the course of time by an efficient constitutional mechanism for voting taxes and raising loans on a scale required to meet the new commitments. A distinctive military system was in this way extended across the Channel to Whitehall and Westminster. The novelty lay in raising foreign troops, not

[13] With the Danes in mind Ernest Augustus of Hanover reproached George William for taking this risk in 1688, and reproached him again in 1691. Zuschlag, *Die Rolle Braunschweig-Lüneburg*, 94, 96. On the other hand the 6,000 men promised in the Dutch–Swedish treaty of 13 Sept. did not leave Sweden in 1688. G. Landsberg, *Den svenska utrikespolitikens historia*, i. 3. 1648–1689 (Stockholm 1952), 238.

[14] Schnath, *Geschichte von Hannover*, i. 354; J. Stoye, *Europe Unfolding 1648–1688* (1969), 324–6; Ten Raa, *Het Staatsche Leger*, vii (1950), 337–54; J. Childs, *The British Army of William III, 1689–1702* (Manchester 1987), 268; P. G. M. Dickson, *Finance and Government under Maria Theresia* (Oxford 1987), ii. ch. 5: 'Subsidies in Wartime'.

for service in the British isles—that was a familiar practice in past emergencies—but for British operations in Europe.

Something else also brought together north Germany, the Netherlands, and England. In 1685 Frederick William of Brandenburg gave a reason for shelving his earlier designs against Sweden, asserting that this was a time for amity between Protestants. There seems no reason to doubt the evidence that he had already started to distance himself from France late in 1684 for ordinary reasons of state, but was then alarmed by the sequence of three events in the following year: first the death of Charles II of England and the accession of a Catholic ruler, second the death of the Elector Palatine and again the accession of a Catholic, and third Louis XIV's cancellation of the Edict of Nantes.[15] The Brandenburg embassy in Paris was told to give every assistance to the Huguenots; the welcoming Edict of Potsdam appeared soon after that of Fontainebleau. But the Elector had already approached the Dutch, and William quickly responded. Among several agents moving between The Hague and Berlin at the time, the most important was probably the Brandenburger Paul Fuchs. A committed Protestant statesman, he talked readily to the French Huguenots, who now began to play a bigger role in the Orange entourage, as they did in Berlin also. At length agreement was reached on the terms for renewing an earlier defensive alliance between the Dutch and the Elector, while the idea of a common Protestant interest gained more currency. Indeed Frederick William's idiom was changing. The defence of Protestantism played a bigger part in it, and this feature of the last phase in a long career illustrates a general change which occurred in the political atmosphere of western Europe. Soon after his death in May 1688 this change received enormous extra stimulus from the success of the Revolution in England.

Not only does that upheaval separate the era of Anglo-Dutch wars from the era of the Anglo-Dutch alliance, which with much effort survived decades of wear and tear; from it there also stretches ahead the long series of agreements joining Brandenburg-Prussia to these two states. Elector Frederick III, succeeding his father, did not hesitate in joining the Dutch. His troops

[15] G. Pagès, *Le Grand Electeur et Louis XIV* (Paris 1905), 555–66.

would fight for twenty-five years on behalf of the allies in various parts of Europe. Even more important, although obscure enough at first, was another new German connection. Early in 1689, while the Declaration of Rights painfully took shape in Westminster, an envoy from Hanover was in London.[16] He had instructions to persuade those concerned to give explicit recognition to the Duchess Sophia's claim through her mother in the English succession. The politicians listened but were reticent. In August the infant Duke of Gloucester was born and the issue was shelved. When he died the Duchess had become the Electress and in 1701 the Act of Settlement advanced the Hanoverian succession a long way further.

These political developments tend to fill up the stage. In the background there was a general Protestant movement of great complexity: Bayle opposing Jurieu in the world of Huguenot writers, the foundation of a new Lutheran university at Halle under Hohenzollern patronage, the spread from there of the Pietists under Francke's leadership, the visionary thinking of rebels in the Cévennes. These seem far enough removed from the English revolution with its subsequent settlement of the Anglican Church and State. But that busiest of men, Archbishop Wake, years after his youthful controversies as chaplain at the Paris embassy, was active in correspondence with Protestant church leaders, in Berlin as in Geneva,[17] while a generation later it would be John Wesley who crossed through Germany to seek out the Herrnhuters and Moravians, and learn from their example.[18] And there was George Frederick Handel. Born in Halle, a man of such talent and celebrity that he could have found work anywhere, he came from Hanover to England and some of his masterpieces would in due course be added to the spiritual fabric of the English Protestant churches.[19] Amid this diversity, and in spite of the sectarian rancour, there were certainly many who accepted that there was a common Protestant interest in which the new

[16] Schnath, *Geschichte von Hannover*, i. 491–7.

[17] N. Sykes, *William Wake, Archbishop of Canterbury* (2 vols., Cambridge 1957), ii. 1–10, 60–8.

[18] W. R. Ward, 'Power and Piety: The Origins of Religious Revival in the Early Eighteenth Century', *Bulletin of the John Rylands University Library of Manchester*, 63 (1980), 231–52, and *Studies in Church History*, 17 (1981), 275–305.

[19] For Handel's secular music, and George I's role in his career, R. Hatton, *George I Elector and King* (1978), 97, 264–7.

English monarchy after 1688—it was new as well as old—had a leading role to play.

III

Having brought into this account the hunting-parties of north Germany it seems fair to refer to the greatest princely hunter in Europe at this date, that Nimrod Sultan Mehmet IV.[20] He would leave Istanbul or Adrianople for months at a time to beat through a great tract of country. He was deposed in November 1687, little more than a year before the flight of James II from Whitehall. The link of their common fate deserves notice in this European context.

It was a widespread contemporary perception that Louis XIV's pressure on Germany relied to a certain extent on the Magyars and the Turks; the rebellions of the one or the warfare of the other, or on both combined. Therefore Dutch politicians in the 1680s, like William of Orange, would feel sceptical of the value of a Habsburg alliance; they wanted Leopold first of all to come to terms with the sultan. The Spanish ambassador in Vienna and his friends at Court felt the same. For converse reasons, from Versailles, Colbert de Croissy repeatedly warned the French ambassador at Adrianople to scotch any notion of the Turks that they should give up in Hungary, while insisting that Louis was doing his utmost to help the sultan by his actions in the west.[21] When Vienna was besieged in 1683, accordingly, William's colleague Waldeck had to defer his hopes for organizing German defences against French pressure. The French were able to invade the Spanish Netherlands and Luxemburg. The emperor, the Empire, and Spain in 1684 conceded that the French should continue to hold all their gains of recent years—which included 'reunions', Strasburg, Luxemburg and other territories—and the remaining signatories reserved only their theoretical rights of ownership. This, the so-called Twenty Years Truce, indicated that Leopold intended to honour the terms of his Holy Alliance with Poland and Venice and persist with the war in Hungary.[22]

20 J. v. Hammer, *Histoire de l'empire ottoman* xi (Paris 1838), 33, 193–5, 251–5.

21 Bib. Nat., Paris: MSS Fr. nos. 7162, fos. 1–17; 7163–6, *passim*.

22 The Holy League was ratified at Linz on 29 Mar. 1684, the 'Truce' at Regensburg on 15 Aug. O. Redlich, *Weltmacht des Barock* (Vienna 1961), 270, 272.

Louis, for his part, would simply pause. The uneasy settlement, while it lasted, enabled Charles II of England in the final months of his life and then James II to continue standing aside from Europe. It allowed that toughest of German statesmen, Ernest Augustus of Hanover, to spend nine months in 1685 and eight months in 1686 lolling in Italy. Amid many emergencies and alarms, in western Europe there was for four years a certain composure, a front of stability, and the use of what Louis XIV called 'voies de douceur'. There was stasis along the Rhine, but motion down the Danube.

Here, after a repulse before Buda in 1684, the Imperialists began an advance which proved irresistible. In 1685 they took the main Turkish strongholds on the old frontier. In 1686 they triumphally took Buda. In August 1687 they destroyed the Ottoman field army in a devastating battle, and the subsequent mutinies and uproar in Ottoman territory led to Sultan Mehmet's deposition. In September 1688 they took Belgrade. The Habsburgs occupied most of Hungary, Slavonia, and even Transylvania. The emperor's eldest son Joseph was crowned as the king of Hungary. These were changes on a grand scale, the greatest taking place in Europe during James II's reign, with significant repercussions. As the Turks weakened, so everyone thought, they were more likely to make peace; the emperor would then be able to shift his weight to Germany, with a stronger chance of collecting allies and checking Louis XIV. The question, easy enough to formulate but difficult to answer, was when—if the process of conquest in the east continued—this would actually take effect.

The ultimate answer is well known. It was in 1688 that the French advanced in force to the Rhine. The Revolution gave William his British partnership; he secured an agreement with the Emperor, and a general alliance fought the French for nine years before coming to terms. But the Turkish war still continued, and the western group of allies had been gravely weakened by the continuing Habsburg commitment in Hungary, which moderated the pressure on France. Peace treaties at Carlowitz in 1699—so much desired by William III of England—followed the treaties at Ryswick in 1697. In 1701 it was accordingly the emperor's government, feeling secure on its eastern front, that plunged first into the War of the Spanish Succession, with the English and Dutch following in his wake. But the Grand Alliance had its origins in the negotiations of an earlier period, at a time when James II was sending his engineers to study siege warfare in Hungary,[23] and French volunteers and agents accompanied the Imperial armies.

In 1686, before the fall of Buda, the Court of Vienna tried to persuade William of Orange and the Dutch, as well as Brandenburg, to join an association of states of the Empire concerned to resist further French demands. They prudently refrained. After Buda fell Leopold tried again, and also sent a mission to James II. That promising young statesman, the elder Kaunitz, spent several months in London in 1687; and his instructions and reports are both of interest.[24] While in general complimenting James, he was told to express the Habsburg Court's misgivings at the vigour of the king's measures favouring his Catholic subjects. These appeared to be diminishing his ability to unite with his people in defence against what was termed 'Gallic domination'. This view, said the instructions, was that of Pope Innocent XI; and Leopold, in adopting and maintaining it, unwittingly prepared the ground for his acceptance of an English alliance when it was offered by the new Protestant ruler in 1689. The road would be tortuous, his theologians would have to agree (as they did), but what we might today call the axis of Vienna–London was one of the substantial consequences of the Revolution in its European aspect. To return to Kaunitz: his account of James shows him unperturbed by evidence of new French military installations on the Rhine. They would not (the king thought) endanger the peace of Europe. On the other hand he applauded unreservedly the success of the Imperial forces in Hungary, and also referred to his own difficulties with the Dutch. But James did not anticipate, at least as Kaunitz reports him, that events in Hungary, Germany, and Holland might interact, and in doing so affect his own position. In July 1687 he courteously but firmly dismissed the proposal from Leopold. He felt safer in relative isolation. He had too little use for a dialogue

[23] J. Richards, *Journal of the siege and taking of Buda . . . 1686* (London 1687), and BL: Stowe MSS 447–8.

[24] O. Klopp, *Der Fall des Hauses Stuart und die Succession des Hauses Hannover* (7 vols., Vienna 1875–88), iii. 255–86, 341–7. Strictly speaking, Dominik Andreas Kaunitz was the grandfather of Maria Theresia's famous state chancellor.

with the Catholic emperor, and it was a significant error of judgement.

In the following year William of Orange and the United Provinces went to work very differently. After Admiral Herbert had seen William, and taken back to England the message soliciting an invitation to come over himself, a secret agent was sent to Vienna. By then the English queen's pregnancy was advancing, there were renewed French threats to the Empire, while the previous campaign in Hungary had apparently shattered the Ottoman armies and Ottoman morale. It would be the agent's task to offer the emperor a new defensive alliance with the Dutch while persuading him that James II's measures at home and abroad simply assisted Louis XIV and were opposed by his own Catholic subjects: the king did not deserve the emperor's support or that of other Catholic princes. The Dutch also offered to support Leopold in his claims on the Spanish succession.[25] After six months' diplomacy, in the first week of September 1688 Vienna agreed in principle to negotiate, and at this point the records show us a thread in the discourse of the negotiators which, after the Revolution, becomes more than a thread in modern English history. After the Ottoman collapse in Hungary in 1687 the Dutch were naturally among those who urged on Vienna the case for ending the Turkish war. It would strengthen the emperor's position in Germany and encourage general resistance to Bourbon aggression everywhere. But the Ottoman Court, after Suleiman's deposition, had determined to send formal notice to Leopold of the change of ruler. Their envoys, it was believed, were also authorized to listen to overtures for a truce or treaty; and these envoys had reached Austria by the late autumn of 1688. The Hague knew this.[26] At the moment when William of Orange was poised for his venture in England, therefore, he was also aiming for an alliance with the emperor, who—it seemed likely—would soon be free to use all his resources for the struggle in western Europe. Belgrade fell on 6 September.

We are at the start here of the discussions preceding the

[25] Müller, *Wilhelm III und Waldeck*, ii. 26–37; H. v. Srbik (ed.), *Österreichische Staatsverträge, Niederlande*, i (Vienna 1912), 251–2; H. Manners Sutton (ed.), *Lexington Papers* (1850), 329.

[26] Antal and Pater (eds.), *Weensche Gezantschapsberichten van 1670 tot 1720*, i (The Hague 1929), 327–60.

alliance between Leopold I and the States General, to which King William III subscribed on 9 September 1689.[27] The scope of the upheaval taking place in England could, and can, be measured by the irritations of statesmen in Vienna. They saw a marked discrepancy between the assurances given them by William and Fagel in September 1688 in respect of James, of the lawful succession in England, and the future status of English Catholics, and the reports they received of brutal 'No-Popery' mobbing in London, of the coronation, and above all of William's failure to have the Test Acts repealed.[28] On the other hand the Dutch, with William concurring, were displeased by the total failure of the Austrians to come to terms with the Ottoman envoys. It indeed weakened Leopold's position in western Europe, and in doing so may have made him readier to overlook the disastrous Catholic setback in England.[29] The axis of Vienna through The Hague to London, which would last long enough to be described in the eighteenth century as the 'old' alliance, was in the end firmly drawn in spite of the difficulties.

However there is something material to add: William III's extraordinary persistence in trying to bring Leopold's Ottoman war to an end. As the military effort against France extended to Ireland and Italy, Spain and America, while continuing in the Rhineland and the Netherlands, it seemed all the more urgent not to have troops, commanders, and supplies diverted to Hungary. There followed William's remarkable long-term diplomatic exercise, in which the Dutch and English representatives at Vienna and their colleagues at Istanbul were repeatedly instructed to try to reconcile the warring empires of south-east Europe. Of these men one was outstanding, William Lord Paget, a decided advocate of the Revolution in Church and State. He acted as ambassador first at Vienna and from 1693 in Istanbul.[30] In 1691 William had

[27] Srbik, *Österreichische Staatsverträge*, 255–77; Manners Sutton, *Lexington Papers*, 327–60; Klopp, *Fall des Hauses Stuart*, iv. 424–39, 512–22.

[28] K. Feiling, *A History of the Tory Party, 1660–1714* (Oxford 1924), 263–9.

[29] In the course of the propaganda battle fought in 1689 appeared an English version of a letter from Leopold to James II, in which the emperor expresses his wish that the king had listened to 'the friendly Remonstrance made you by our late Envoy the Count de Kanitz'. *The Emperor's Letter . . . dated the Ninth of April 1689*: BL: 816 m 3/63.

[30] For Paget, see BL: Add. MS 8880; PRO SP Turkey; and for discursive information about British diplomacy in south-east Europe in the 1690s, L. F. Marsili, *Autobiografia*, ed. E. Lovarini (Bologna 1930), 133–212.

sent an envoy down the Danube from the Habsburg to the Ottoman Court, to attempt a mediation; poor William Hussey died at Adrianople soon after getting there. He sent another next year to repeat the attempt; William Harbord died at Belgrade. Then it was Paget's turn; and finally, with circumstances at last in their favour, the king of England and the high mightinesses of the United Provinces were able to mediate a settlement. In considering the European aspects and consequences of the Revolution we should accordingly spare a thought for that improvised wooden pavilion at Carlowitz, on the shore of the great river above Belgrade, in which Paget sat with his Dutch colleague through an icy Christmas 1698, to preside over the peacemaking by representatives of the sultan, the emperor, the tsar and other powers. The new axis from London to Vienna appeared—if only momentarily—to be extending ever further. Paget's pavilion would one day become transformed into that monument of imperial influence in the nineteenth century, the old British embassy building still standing in Istanbul.[31]

IV

It is time to come to an entertainment which surpassed Christina's for Lord Castlemaine or the Westphalian hunts. This was the opening performance of *Esther*, by Racine, written for Mme de Maintenon's young ladies of Saint-Cyr and performed by them at Versailles on 7 January 1689. Louis XIV was present. He heard the recitation of lines resonant with echoes of the contemporary world: the good and strong king, the battle against heresy (in spite of a high priest's treachery), the destruction of the enemy's principal fortress.[32] We can be more precise, if less eloquent, about the conduct of the French government in the previous months.

The crisis of 1688 in western Europe culminated in two military operations. One was diffused and on the grand scale, the other on a smaller scale but just as intensively prepared. They were

[31] Built to designs approved by Sir Charles Barry, in 1844–7. H. Colvin (ed.), *History of the King's Works*, vi (1973), 634–8. For a contemporary drawing of the scene at Carlowitz, see *Österreich und die Osmanen* (catalogue, Nationalbibliothek and Staatsarchiv, Vienna 1983), plate no. 30.

[32] R. Picard, *La Carrière de Jean Racine* (Paris 1961), 393–414.

Louis XIV's advance on the Rhine, affecting the entire region between the Dutch and Swiss borders, and William of Orange's English enterprise. As to the first, the French government wanted to carry a stage further one of its greatest achievements during Louis XIV's reign: the piecemeal assimilation of a large territory which included most of Alsace, the Franche Comté of Burgundy, and Lorraine. There were other gains in prospect in the Palatinate and Trier lands, between the right bank of the Moselle and the left bank of the Rhine. A campaign was planned which included an initial parade of military strength on the further shore of the Rhine. Here outposts for France, the citadels of Breisach and Philippsburg, were previously secured by treaty in 1648 and again by treaty in 1679, when Philippsburg had been exchanged for the Habsburg town of Freiburg in the Black Forest. In 1688, it might be hoped, Philippsburg would be quickly recovered. By bargaining thereafter it was intended to compel the emperor and the German states to convert the truce of 1684 into a recognition of the French king's sovereign right *de jure* to all his gains *de facto*. These included that jewel of the crown, Strasburg. 'Louis miscalculates': one may read the caption at this point in the British Library catalogue of its fine 1989 exhibition on the Revolution.[33] One reads of Lord Sunderland's amazement at the news when it reached him near the end of September 1688, of the projected siege of Philippsburg, as if some mistake had been made. Yet the only real debate centres on the timing, not the object, of the move by Louis, Louvois, and Colbert de Croissy.

They too were responding to the events in Hungary. Since the year 1684 the French ministers feared that Leopold would seek a treaty with the Turks. From 1686 they feared that the Turks would sue for peace, that then the Habsburgs and their allies would turn and fight in the Empire. During the winters of 1686–7 and 1687–8, French diplomacy was intensely active at the Imperial Diet, many German courts, and also Rome, where the Pope appeared willing to mediate in the Empire. The Diet, if with hesitation, did not budge from the letter of the truce; and during the spring of 1688 it still seemed likely, in spite of manifold rubs

[33] BL, exhibition notes, 1989: 'All the King's Men: Personalities and Power in the Revolution of 1688'. This view of a 'miscalculation' was already forcibly expressed by Leibniz in a letter dated 12 September 1691. Klopp, *Fall des Hauses Stuart*, iv. 502.

and embarrassments in Vienna, that Leopold's advisers would manage to put together a combination of forces—with the elector of Bavaria as commander-in-chief—to move into the far distance of southern Hungary during the summer, with the intention of besieging Belgrade. It also looked as if the Danes would keep the north Germans hovering round Hamburg and Holstein. The Dutch and James II were increasingly at odds. If Louis XIV wanted to strike rather than to talk, to insist by a show of arms on a new settlement in Germany, the opportunity could be taken *now*—but perhaps not later.

This idea did as much as anything else to determine the course of events in 1688. It was tempting to draw the conclusion, for example, that if William of Orange and his government were embroiled with James, so much the better. However, the truly remarkable feature of the year was the linkage between Louis XIV's thoughts on Germany and his equal determination to persist, to go to the limit, in his long-standing disputes with Innocent XI.[34] The affair of the royal rights in vacant French bishoprics and other temporalities, the Pope's refusal to confirm the appointment of new bishops in France, and his condemnation of the Gallican articles of 1682, had been followed by Louis XIV's absolute refusal to sanction the abolition of his embassy's privileged status in Rome. By the end of 1687 Versailles threatened to occupy papal Avignon (nearby, William's principality of Orange had already been annexed) and Innocent took the extreme step of excommunicating Louis and his ministers. There was, in reply, in January 1688, an official hint given in Paris of an appeal to a general council of the Church against the Pope.[35]

This coincided with the celebrated storm which blew up on the lower Rhine. French influence in Cologne had been well maintained for thirty years by William Egon von Fürstenberg, acting as the Wittelsbach Archbishop-Elector's principal adviser.[36]

[34] For these disputes, see J. Orcibal, *Louis XIV contre Innocent XI. Les appels au futur concile de 1688 et l'opinion française* (Paris 1949); and B. Neveu, *Culture religieuse et aspirations réformistes à la cour d'Innocent XI* (Florence 1979).

[35] One of the victims of the deeply entrenched positions of both Innocent and Louis was James II, whose offers to mediate between them were ill received at Rome. B. Neveu, 'Jacques II médiateur entre Louis XIV et Innocent XI', *Mélanges d'archéologie et d'histoire*, 79 (1967), 694–764.

[36] M. Braubach, *Kurköln* (Münster 1949), 81–109; and his *Wilhelm von Fürstenberg 1629–1704* (Bonn 1972), 421–78.

Max Henry, that weird old alchemist in his laboratory, holding the sees of Liège, Münster and Hildesheim as well, duly had Fürstenberg nominated as his coadjutor in January 1688. The coadjutor could hope to succeed as Archbishop-Elector; but Fürstenberg, Louis XIV's man like the French bishops, did not receive the necessary confirmation of his appointment by Innocent before Max Henry died on 4 June. The canonical rules, requiring that the largely aristocratic and princely membership of the Cologne chapter should proceed to an election, put at a disadvantage any candidate who lacked papal approval. Here was an unlooked for challenge to French predominance at a sensitive point, and at a sensitive time; too much for comfort depended on the vote of the chapter and too much depended on the Pope. And Innocent was likewise involved over the Palatinate.[37] At the king's own invitation in 1685 he had been attempting to mediate in the dispute over the claims of the Duchess of Orleans (a Palatine princess) to goods and lands which the French wanted in that part of the country. In 1688 the Elector still stood his ground against these hostile demands, Louis moved towards a settlement by force, and the mediator now seemed to Versailles to be distinctly unhelpful. The Elector, moreover, with territories of his own adjoining the see of Cologne, had joined in the struggle there: two of his sons possessed valuable votes in the cathedral chapter, while his son-in-law the emperor sent an envoy to canvass support among the canons for a youth whom the Pope declared an eligible candidate, the elector of Bavaria's brother. Fürstenberg invoked French assistance to encourage his own party in Cologne and the other vacant sees, but without a decisive vote in his favour he would be at a disadvantage.[38]

It seems, then, that while the fateful trial of the Seven Bishops took place in Westminster in the summer of 1688, there were also controversies in matters of church law and regalian rights in France and Germany. In certain respects the Pope, the emperor, and the German princes were defending, and exploiting, rules

[37] M. Immich, *Zur Vorgeschichte des Orleansische Krieg* (Heidelberg 1898), 308–9, 318–28; B. Neveu (ed.), *Correspondance . . . Angelo Ranuzzi* (Rome 1973), ii, *passim*.

[38] For Innocent's disqualification of Fürstenberg's nephew as a voter, see K. Jaitner, 'Reichskirchenpolitik und Rombeziehungen Philipp Wilhelms von Pfalz-Neuburg von 1662 bis 1690', *Annalen des hist. Vereins für den Niederrhein*, 178 (1976), 124. For James II's unrewarding intervention at Rome in Fürstenberg's favour, Klopp, *Fall des Hauses Stuart*, iv. 87–96.

of law in the conduct of affairs. The French monarchy, also, was continuing to acquire new territory by appealing to rights of inheritance, rights under feudal law, and precedents of every kind; this was true of the 'reunions' or of the claims submitted by her French lawyers for the Duchess of Orleans against the Elector Palatine. In fact, on both sides of the Channel there were some similar arguments involved. They were being aired in law courts, in academic or ecclesiastical bodies, and among statesmen.[39] Then, between September and December 1688, all this would be transformed into more violent combat: warfare on one side of the sea, revolution on the other. Claims were now to be enforced. However, after 1688, in the part of Europe which was England, William of Orange reintroduced that element missing elsewhere, the voice and authority of parliament which James had appeared anxious to discard or subdue. And on the mainland, as in Ireland, there would be no lucky escape for the civil population, no settlement without recourse to war in wide areas. If troops had marched from Tor Bay by way of Exeter and Salisbury and then, before reaching Whitehall, had turned aside to Guildford and Winchester and burnt all these places down, and had tried to strip the country in between, this would hardly have equalled the events of January to August 1689 occurring on either side of the upper Rhine.[40] It was one aspect of the 'glorious' Revolution, hidden but important.

On 19 July the Cologne chapter chose Fürstenberg by a bare, but not by a sufficient, majority. Louis offered, in a highly secret negotiation at Rome, to give way on the immunities of his embassy there, even to consider a compromise in France, provided that Innocent supported Fürstenberg.[41] He was sharply rebuffed, and in due course the Pope confirmed the Wittelsbach candidate's election. Meanwhile from the end of July French officers prepared to occupy the territory of the Cologne archbishopric. A month later their troops were in Bonn and other strongholds further north, near Brandenburg's Rhineland territories and the Dutch; but on 21 September Louvois ordered his commanders in that

[39] See also L. G. Schwoerer, 'The Role of Lawyers in the Revolution of 1688–1689', in R. Schnur (ed.), *Die Rolle der Juristen bei der Entstehung des modernen Staates* (Berlin 1986), 473–98.

[40] K. v. Raumer, *Die Zerstörung der Pfalz* (Munich 1930), end map; A. Corvisier, *Louvois* (Paris 1983), pp. 460–4.

[41] Orcibal, *Louis XIV contre Innocent XI*, 23–5.

area to remain strictly on the defensive, and they did so.[42] In this fashion the French military enterprise of 1688 was extended down the Rhine in order to make good the ground lost by Fürstenberg's political defeat. Louis's manifesto to the Imperial Diet (of 24 September) demanded not only satisfaction in the Palatinate and recognition of his territorial gains since 1679. He wanted Fürstenberg duly installed as Archbishop-Elector of Cologne. By then his troops were in position along and—at certain points—across the Rhine. The siege of Philippsburg in the presence of the Dauphin began almost immediately. It surrendered on 30 October, just after the gales which had blown the first Dutch expedition back to Holland.

The significance of the new war in Germany for that venture has indeed been often noted. The priority which the French ministers gave to their campaign in the south, the extension of their military effort northwards, but its relative subordination, in fact gave William greater freedom to act; it took strong nerves, however, to see this. Perhaps as significant in the longer run was the deadlock reached in that part of Europe in 1688 and thereafter. The military resources of the Habsburg empire were partially redirected from Hungary westwards. Such commanders as the Elector of Bavaria, Prince Louis of Baden and the Duke of Lorraine, with their own hereditary lands under threat or already annexed by France, reappeared on the Rhine front. The states further north at last managed to collaborate, if still very erratically, and the French preferred to stand on the defensive. A more equal balance of forces had begun to appear in the Empire before William III could begin to contribute British resources to the struggle on any scale, either in the Netherlands or elsewhere. As a result the protagonists were locked into a struggle for supremacy which they could not resolve. A whole series of campaigns followed, indeed a whole series of wars into the eighteenth century. If we ask why Marlborough and his army found themselves near the village of Blenheim on the upper Danube in 1704, or why Dettingen was fought, part of the answer will be found by considering Louis XIV's advance into the Empire in 1688. And in the resistance to that advance. A limit, in fact, had been reached by both sides. The scenario here was being set for a long time

[42] Braubach, *Fürstenberg*, 452, 461.

ahead. Conversely, another part of the answer is that William of Orange's bold adventure in that year, 1688, fared as well as he could have hoped, even if he foresaw what would happen so astonishingly soon after his arrival in England.

There is a last entertainment to record here. On 5 February 1689 a further performance of Racine's *Esther* took place, at Saint-Cyr.[43] In front of a carefully selected audience of the good and the great were ranged three chairs of state. In the centre sat the queen of England, on her left Louis XIV, on her right James II and VII. One more Stuart exile on the mainland of Europe, against all the odds, had already begun.

[43] *Journal du Marquis de Dangeau* (Paris 1854), 323–4.

6

'J'equippe une flotte tres considerable': The Dutch Side of the Glorious Revolution

SIMON GROENVELD

Prologue

THE years between 1660 and 1715 form a distinct period in European history: the period of French expansion under Louis XIV. The decades before had seen the spectacular decline of the two Habsburg princes: the German Emperor and the King of Spain. By the Peace of Westphalia the Emperor had been forced to allow the German princes to create policies of their own; the Spanish king had had to recognize the independence of the Dutch Republic and to accept an unpleasant peace with France in 1659. Louis XIV, who on this very occasion had married a Spanish princess, thus became a potential heir to his father-in-law, Philip IV. In 1661 he decided to govern France on his own. From that time onwards he ruled over his 20 million subjects with the help of a strong, bureaucratic system of government, though one which was not as powerful as is often alleged. His country had enormous resources at its disposal, but, notwithstanding the efforts made by capable ministers such as Colbert, the overall character of its economy was old-fashioned and remained so for a long time.[1]

In 1660, however, France was not the only great power in Western Europe; England and the Dutch Republic were also considered great. Under the restored monarchy of Charles II

[1] Good analyses of French structures: P. Goubert, *L'Ancien Régime* (2 vols., Paris 1969–73); and *Louis XIV et vingt millions Français* (Paris 1966); A. Corvisier, *La France de Louis XIV 1643–1715. Ordre intérieur et place en Europe* (Paris 1979). For aspects of Louis's international activities, see R. Hatton (ed.), *Louis XIV and Europe* (1976).

5 million Englishmen entered upon a new era in their history. Their government was not so strongly centralized as that of France, so that local and regional authorities exerted more influence upon national politics, or at least felt that they could. As for the economy, fresh growth and modernization had started during the Interregnum, and were carried on after the Restoration, strengthening the country.[2]

Totally different was the picture presented by the small Dutch confederation with its 1.9 million inhabitants, of whom 872,000 lived in the province of Holland around 1680. The Republic—the core of its land bordered by the Meuse, Rhine, and IJssel—had between 1625 and 1648 conquered a series of territories beyond those rivers which were to serve as buffers against possible Habsburg aggression.[3] Its decentralized, aristocratic government was seen by some as a survival from the Middle Ages; others believed that it contained essentially modern traits.[4] Its own economic resources were so meagre that its people had to feed themselves mainly on imported cereals. They needed to import raw materials for their industries, and a great many of them had to earn their money chiefly by dealing in the products of other countries. Nevertheless an almost unprecedented prosperity had been created, at least in the western provinces: a prosperity that should not be explained solely in terms of the extraordinary qualities of certain Dutch merchants and industrialists, but in terms also of the internal weakness of other European nations, as competitors, in the first half of the century.[5] Political and economic

[2] J. R. Jones, *Country and Court: England 1658–1714* (1978), *passim*.

[3] S. Groenveld and H. L. Ph. Leeuwenberg, *De bruid in de schuit: De consolidatie van de Republiek 1609–1650* (Zutphen 1985).

[4] R. Fruin, 'De drie tijdvakken der Nederlandsche geschiedenis', in Fruin, *Verspreide Geschriften* (11 vols., The Hague 1900–5), i. 22–48; I. Schöffer, 'Ons tweede tijdvak', in Schöffer, *Veelvormig verleden: Zeventien studies in de vaderlandse geschiedenis* (Amsterdam 1987), 15–25.

[5] On Dutch economic history: J. G. van Dillen, *Van rijkdom en regenten, Handboek tot de economische en sociale geschiedenis van Nederland tijdens de Republiek* (The Hague 1970). P. W. Klein, 'De zeventiende eeuw (1585–1700)', in J. H. van Stuijvenberg (ed.), *De economische geschiedenis van Nederland* (2nd edn., Groningen 1979), 79–117. On Dutch trade: J. I. Israel, *Dutch Primacy in World Trade 1585–1740* (Oxford 1989). On the role of agriculture in Dutch economy: J. de Vries, *The Dutch Rural Economy in the Golden Age, 1500–1700* (New Haven and London 1974). For a recent study of the economy of the province of Holland, *c*.1650–*c*.1800, and a discussion of it, see J. L. van Zanden, 'De economie van Holland in de periode 1650–1805: groei of achteruitgang? Een overzicht van bronnen, problemen en

circumstances had driven the Republic to the centre of European power, notwithstanding problems of structure and the many financial deficits of its government.

During the 1660s all three great states—the United Provinces, England, and France—were seeking opportunities which they could seize within the new context. In these years all of them concluded a bilateral treaty with each of the others: the French and the Dutch in 1662, England and the Seven Provinces in 1668, France and England in 1670. In the last of these the basis was laid for the first of the three coalition wars of the period: the war of 1672, waged with the purpose of destroying the Dutch Republic. This struggle came to an end in 1678, with the Seven Provinces surviving intact despite their narrow escape; the subsequent Nine Years War (1688–97) and the War of the Spanish Succession (1702–13) brought new problems to large parts of Europe. Only at Louis's death, in 1715, was it seen that French expansion had been contained. At the same time it was clear that the Dutch Republic, as a state, had relapsed into the second rank, or rather, as is generally acknowledged today, into a rank more appropriate to its innate capacity.

Exactly in the middle of this period took place the invasion of England by William of Orange, an event which led to the Glorious Revolution of 1688. It was an operation in which the Republic was directly involved. A number of questions arise. How did this expedition relate to Dutch foreign policy? What part did the Seven Provinces play in it? Such questions can only be answered after considering the institutional and political history of the Republic. Further questions arise. Did the Glorious Revolution contribute to the decline of the Dutch Republic, and, if so, in what way? The first of these questions forms the focus of this essay.

The Institutions of Dutch Government

The Dutch Republic, which had grown in the late sixteenth century out of the Habsburg Netherlands, was a complex of seven autonomous States. The lordship of each of these was

resultaten', *Bijdragen en Mededelingen betreffende de Geschiedenis der Nederlanden (BMGN)*, 102 (1987), 562–609.

taken over by the provincial estates, which proclaimed themselves sovereign bodies.[6] Although the composition of the several provincial States differed greatly, because of institutional and social peculiarities, each was made up of delegations from the gentry and boroughs. In Holland, which was strongly urbanized, the gentry had only one vote, whereas each of its eighteen cities enjoyed a single vote. In Overijssel, one of the eastern provinces, the ratio between the gentry and boroughs was three votes each. The delegations, usually consisting of two or more persons, spoke according to a fixed order during the meeting of the assemblies, the gentry—the highest in status—first. Not only local or regional topics were discussed, but also federal and international issues. In many, if not in most cases, the opinions of the delegates sprang from local interests.

Everywhere the States had certain matters prepared by small committees—the so-called *besognes*. All of them possessed at least one standing committee: the executive committee, which remained in being when the States themselves were in recess. In Holland and Zealand this was called the *Gecommitteerde Raden*; elsewhere it was the *Gedeputeerde Staten*.[7] In the most influential province of Holland, the States set up additional committees. Originally these were intended to deal with a specific case, and to be of short duration. After the middle of the century some of them gradually became permanent in character.[8]

The States also had a few paid officials in their employ. The most important of these was a lawyer, who in Holland was called the Grand Pensionary or *raadpensionaris*, and the *Stadhouder*. The

[6] See for instance remarks by the States of Groningen. J. S. Theissen, 'Iets over de verhoudingen in de Republiek in 1684', *Bijdragen voor Vaderlandsche Geschiedenis en Oudheidkunde (BVGO)*, 5th ser., 7 (1920), 188–216, and 8 (1921), 81–97.

[7] R. Fruin and H. T. Colenbrander, *Geschiedenis van de staatsinstellingen in Nederland tot den val der Republiek* (2nd edn., The Hague 1922); S. J. Fockema Andreae, *De Nederlandse staat onder de Republiek* (3rd edn., Amsterdam 1969).

[8] On these *besognes*, those of the States of Holland as well as of the States-General, little research has been done, but see M. A. M. Franken, *Coenraad van Beuningen's politieke en diplomatieke activiteiten in de jaren 1667–1684* (Groningen 1966), 27–31. J. H. Grever, 'Committees and Deputations in the Assemblies of the Dutch Republic, 1660–1668', *Parliaments, Estates and Representations* (1981), 13–33. Both Franken and Grever are inclined to date the creation of standing committees too early; it took place at the time of Johan de Witt (1653–72). The members of these standing committees were appointed every year in January. See S. Groenveld, *Verlopend getij: De Nederlandse Republiek en de Engelse Burger oorlog 1640–1646* (Dieren 1984), 75–87.

Grand Pensionary of Holland was not only the advocate of the States, but also of the gentry. In the latter capacity he attended the meetings of the States, accompanying his superiors, for whom he acted as a spokesman. Because the gentry opened every discussion, the Grand Pensionary became in practice the chairman of the States. It was part of his task to formulate the conclusions after the various delegations had given their opinion, and to place them on record. Because he was a member of the *Gecommitteerde Raden* as well, a really capable Grand Pensionary could develop into the central figure of the provincial States.[9]

The *Stadhouder*'s office dated from the Habsburg period, when he functioned as the substitute for the permanently absent lord. In principle each province had its own *Stadhouder*, but in practice the same person was appointed in two or three adjacent territories. When during the Dutch Revolt the States usurped the provincial sovereignty and their *Gecommitteerde Raden* met daily, the office became superfluous. Nevertheless, it was retained, because the States wanted to employ a man of high rank: the princes of Orange were nominated in five provinces; Friesland appointed a member of the related family of Nassau-Dietz, as Groningen usually did. After the sudden death in 1650 of William II, father of the posthumously born William III, the States of Holland and those of the four other provinces decided to keep the office vacant. From 1667 to 1672 it was even abolished. So it was that in seventeenth-century practice the *Stadhouder* became the deputy of the new sovereign, the States. To him were delegated specific tasks of princely origin, such as the presidency of the provincial court of justice, the right to pardon, to appoint civil servants, and to choose every year the members of the magistracies of a great many cities from nominations offered to him. The last right proved the most important, for the appointment of well-affected persons in the cities could strengthen his position in the country. When the *Stadhouder*'s office was vacant, these rights reverted to the States, who then assigned the appointment of the magistrates to the city councils themselves.[10]

[9] H. E. Greve, 'Het ambt en de instructies van den raadpensionaris', *BVGO*, 4th ser., 2 (1902), 367–90.

[10] H. H. Rowen, 'Neither Fish nor Fowl: The stadholderate in the Dutch Republic', in H. H. Rowen and A. Lossky, *Political Ideas and Institutions in the Dutch Republic* (Los Angeles 1985), 1–31.

For the accomplishment of certain tasks the Republic needed federal institutions. The most important of these was the States-General. Here delegations from all the provinces met. Each delegation, numbering from one to around ten persons, had only one vote. Originally, they had primarily deliberated on the common defence of the Seven Provinces. In consequence decisions had to be made concerning the payment of troops and the financing of required military objectives. To this end the provinces were assessed under fixed quotas, though this did not in the least guarantee punctual payment. And because the winning of allies was an essential part of warfare, this task was also consigned to the States-General. In practice almost all foreign affairs fell eventually into the hands of 'Their High Mightinesses', as they called themselves. Almost all, but not all of them; for it continued to be the right of every province to keep up contacts with other nations or princes, provided those contacts did not harm the confederacy. Internal affairs were not delegated to the States-General, however. If they wanted to make a statement in this area, they could do so only in the form of an advice to the States of the provinces.

Like the provincial States, the States-General delegated many matters to small committees, of which a few developed into standing bodies. They were also supported by certain federal boards and officials, charged with particular tasks. The Council of State was one of these; it had to draw up the army estimates and, having received the money, purchase all war materials. Five Admiralties were created for the building and maintaining of the navy. From 1625 onwards, a Captain-General of the Union was appointed, who was charged with the execution of military policy, assisted by a small staff of high officers. Already by 1588 the same task in regard to the navy was assigned to the Admiral-General of the Union. A growing number of ambassadors, all of them drawn from the provincial States, represented the Republic in foreign countries. In all fields where these boards and officials were active it was the States-General which set out the lines of policy and checked that they were observed. Consequently, when the Captain-General, who was usually a Prince of the House of Orange, took the field with the armies, he was accompanied by a number of deputies, who in fact had the last word when decisions had to be made. They, not the prince, were formally the commanders-in-chief. In practice, many problems could be resolved harmoniously, but occasionally clashes were inevitable between the deputies and the princes of Orange, who, as we have seen, were both federal and provincial functionaries at the same time.[11]

Internal Institutional Practice

Tensions of this kind were also to be found at the local level, in the circles of the nobles and those of the regents. Everywhere members of the parochial gentry and urban patricians formed factions—small groups of persons of the same rank, often relatives, competing with each other mostly in order to get possession of, or hold on to, the local offices and to keep the ever-spying counter-factions out. When the brawls became acute, gentlemen and regents did not hesitate to draw their clients from the lower ranks of society into the conflict. D. J. Roorda, who was the first historian to call attention to this practice in the Republic, considered that the factions were above all driven by materialist considerations. More recent research, especially in Zealand, has shown that some of them were incited by ideological or, more precisely, religious motives.[12]

Whereas the first studies of factions were exclusively focused at the local level, recent investigations indicate that in the wider circles of provincial government related clusterings can be observed. Regents from various boroughs met repeatedly in the States. There some of them turned out to have corresponding interests or ideas, or merely the same opponent, and were

[11] S. J. Fockema Andreae and H. Hardenberg (eds.), *500 Jaren Staten-Generaal in de Nederlanden* (Assen 1964). *Raad van State 450 jaar* (2 vols., The Hague 1981–3).

[12] D. J. Roorda, *Partij en Factie, De oproeren van 1672 in de steden van Holland en Zeeland: Een krachtmeting tussen partijen en facties* (Groningen 1961). M. van der Bijl, *Idee en Interest: Voorgeschiedenis, verloop en achtergronden van de politieke twisten in Zeeland en vooral in Middelburg tussen 1702 en 1715* (Groningen 1981); and 'Familie en factie in de Alkmaarse stedelijke politiek', in *Van Spaanse beleg tot Bataafse tijd: Alkmaars stedelijk leven in de 17de en 18de eeuw* (Zutphen 1980), 12–32. S. Groenveld, 'Holland, das Haus Oranien und die anderen nordniederländischen Provinzen im 17. Jahrhundert: Neue Wege zur Faktionsforschung', *Rheinische Vierteljahrsblätter*, 53 (1989), 92–116. Studies in the formation of noble factions are very rare. See J. Aalbers, 'Factieuze tegenstellingen binnen het college van de ridderschap van Holland na de vrede van Utrecht', *BMGN* 93 (1978), 412–45. S. Groenveld, 'C'est le père, qui parle': Patronage bij Constantijn Huygens (1596–1687)', *Jaarboek Oranje-Nassau Museum 1988*, 53–107.

willing to concert their actions on those grounds. Sometimes their co-operation was of short duration; sometimes it lasted for years. Mostly they gathered round a powerful nucleus: for instance, the deputation of an influential city, or the faction of the Grand Pensionary, or the prince of Orange and his courtiers. Thus in the 1640s there existed in the States of Holland a faction comprising Amsterdam, Rotterdam, and Dordrecht, which continually clashed with a group led by Leiden (in size Holland's second city) and Haarlem, while the prince and his men alternatively sided in one case with the former and in another with the latter.[13] During the following decades the Grand Pensionary Johan de Witt—who was the leading politician from 1653 to 1672—relied on Amsterdam, Rotterdam, Dordrecht, and some smaller towns. At the end of the 1660s these political fronts changed yet again; Amsterdam turned away from De Witt, but the Grand Pensionary remained in touch with the combination Dordrecht, Delft, Leiden, and Rotterdam.[14] In the 1680s it appears that William III time and again encountered opposition in the field of foreign policy from a faction composed of Amsterdam, Leiden, Delft, Schiedam, Enkhuizen, and sometimes Dordrecht.[15] All this does not mean that each city delegate was a member of a faction. Some of them held an independent position, usually in the political centre, where, having decided to take a stand, they were capable of playing a decisive role.

It is clear that the formation of factions in the States could affect discussions in a positive and a negative sense. That is why leading politicians tried to dominate a majority of its members in order to manage the States. For Johan de Witt this was less easy

[13] Groenveld, *Verlopend getij*, 105–6; and 'The English Civil Wars as a cause of the First Anglo-Dutch war, 1640–1652', *Historical Journal* 30 (1987), 541–66, esp. 545, 549–50; 'Frederik Hendrik en de Stuarts, 1640–1647: Herziening van de opvattingen van Pieter Geyl', *Jaarboek Oranje-Nassau Museum 1987*, 7–28.

[14] Franken, *Van Beuningen*, 76. N. Japikse, *Johan de Witt* (2nd edn., Amsterdam 1928), 88–99. H. H. Rowen, *John de Witt, Grand Pensionary of Holland, 1625–1672* (Princeton 1978), 334–55.

[15] This is the result of analysis of documents, preserved in two municipal archives. Gemeentelijke Archiefdienst (GA) Amsterdam: Brieven van gedeputeerden ter dagvaart te's-Gravenhage aan burgemeesters en regeerders te Amsterdam (Letters from Amsterdam deputies in the States of Holland to the city government), 1682–1685. GA Leiden, nos. 9303–4: Particuliere notulen van de besprekingen in de Staten van Holland door de stadspensionaris Pieter Burgersdijck (Private minutes of the discussions in the States of Holland, written by the town's pensionary Pieter Burgersdijck), 1682–1686. These repeatedly show the opinions of individual city delegates, in contrast to the official resolutions of the Estates.

than for the princes of Orange, because he did not have the right to appoint local magistrates. He needed the help of relatives in some city governments, or of well-affected pensionaries, whose nominations he had brought about.[16] One group of noblemen he won over by granting them functions in the army or in polder-boards.[17] By recommending other confidants for high office in the provincial and federal bodies (the Court of Holland and the Council of State for instance) he also tried to gain greater influence in those colleges.[18]

William III, proclaimed *Stadhouder* of Holland and Zealand during the state of emergency in 1672, was immediately invested with the right to appoint the city magistrates annually. Independently of this he was given the further extraordinary power to dismiss regents in the interests of peace and order in the country while the emergency lasted. This power the prince put to good use: of the 460 active regents in Holland he replaced 130, most of them adherents of Johan de Witt.[19] In their places he appointed men of the same social status, members of factions that had earlier been forced out of office. Whether they were orthodox Calvinists, as William's teacher, the theologian Jacobus Trigland, had requested, is uncertain.[20] Nor must it be concluded that all surviving regents were convinced supporters of Orange. Above all things they were the zealous protectors of local interest. Thus

[16] R. Fruin, G. W. Kernkamp, and N. Japikse (eds.), *Brieven van Johan de Witt* (4 vols., Amsterdam 1906–13), i. 234–5 (11 Sep. 1654): De Witt to H. van Beverningh and W. Nieuwpoort as to the appointment of Adriaen van Stryen in Haarlem; ii. 209–11 (11 Aug. 1659), 212–13 (26 Jan. 1660), 214 (6 Feb. 1660): De Witt to C. de Graeff van Zuidpolsbroek concerning the appointment of Pieter de Groot in Amsterdam; ii. 517–18 (6 May 1664): De Witt to J. van Beveren van Zwijndrecht as to the appointment of Nicolaes Vivien in Dordrecht.

[17] Rowen, *John de Witt*, 154–69.

[18] Court of Holland: Groenveld, 'C'est le père', 77–80 (1655 and 1658); Fruin *et al.*, *Brieven van De Witt*, ii. 466–7 (22 Mar. 1663): De Witt to his brother Cornelis; Council of State: ibid. ii. 516, concerning the appointment of Godefried van Slingelandt of Dordrecht as a secretary to this board (1664).

[19] Roorda, *Partij en Factie*, 155–236. Van der Bijl, 'Familie', 15.

[20] M. van der Bijl, 'Willem III, stadhouder–koning: pro religione et libertate', in W. F. de Gaay Fortman *et al.* (eds.), *Achter den tijd: Opstellen aangeboden aan G. Puchinger* (Haarlem 1986), 155–82, esp. p. 164. For William's religious education and attitude: P. J. A. N. Rietbergen, 'William III of Orange (1650–1702) between European Politics and European Protestantism: The case of the Huguenots', in J. A. H. Bots and G. H. M. Posthumus Meyjes (eds.), *La Révocation de l'édit de Nantes et les Provinces-Unies, 1685* (Amsterdam Maarsen 1986), 35–50. See also M. van der Bijl, 'Prins Willem III, King William III: Een historiografische verkenning', *Groniek, Gronings Historisch Tijdschrift*, 101 (1988), 103–48.

quarrels in the cities continued. William, increasingly absorbed by international problems, felt inclined to look down haughtily upon it all and not interfere.[21]

This was, however, more easily attempted than done. For not only could the quarrels cause new unrest behind the prince's back and afford foreign ambassadors an opportunity to intrigue in the cities, but they might also have a disturbing influence upon the relations between factions in the States. William was compelled to occupy himself continuously with local affairs. Sometimes he made use of the services of confidants in the cities, or managed to get persons appointed on his private recommendation. Often he exceeded his powers. Towns in Holland repeatedly complained of his appointing persons born outside the city or of non-citizens in the magistracies. Occasionally he sent in troops to impose his will upon a city.[22] And in 1684–5 he even posed, supported by the Court of Holland, as the controller of the legality of the nominations offered by Dordrecht and Leiden, cities which opposed his foreign policy in the States of Holland. Only Amsterdam, their fellow opponent, came to their aid. Perhaps it was afraid that William intended to use the Court of Holland as a means of power in the future.[23]

Maybe many towns in Holland took no action against William's breaches of the law because of his growing political strength. Holland and Zealand in 1674 declared his office as *Stadhouder* hereditary. Utrecht, Gelderland, and Overijssel conferred the same dignity upon him in 1674 and 1675, after France and its ally, Münster, had evacuated those provinces. All three were, though not without hesitation, reincorporated in the Republic, being good buffers for Holland, Friesland, and Groningen against

[21] Roorda, *Partij en Factie*, 248.

[22] Ibid. 248–54; Van der Bijl, 'Familie', 16. J. E. Elias, *Geschiedenis van het Amsterdamsche regentenpatriciaat* (The Hague 1923), 173–92; J. J. de Jong, *Met goed fatsoen: Gouda 1700–1780* (Amsterdam 1985), 49–50; J. A. F. de Jongste, *Onrust aan het Spaarne: Haarlem in de jaren 1747–1751* (Amsterdam 1984), 89–93; L. Kooijmans, *Onder regenten: Hoorn 1700–1780* (Amsterdam 1985), 40–6; M. Prak, *Gezeten burgers: Leiden 1700–1780* (Amsterdam 1985), 59–63; H. F. de Wit, *Gorcums heren: Regentenpolitiek 1650–1750* (Gorinchem 1981), 20–31. For Zealand: Van der Bijl, *Idee en Interest*, 29–38.

[23] For the problems in Dordrecht and Leiden see: J. Wagenaar, *Vaderlandsche Historie* (21 vols., 3rd edn., Amsterdam 1790–6), xv. 259–82; also *Byvoegsels en Aanmerkingen*, 53–7; G. H. Kurtz, *Willem III en Amsterdam 1683–1685* (Utrecht 1928), 155–63.

aggression from the east. First of all the magistrates, having been in league with the enemy, had to be replaced, a task which William, assisted by the new Grand Pensionary Gaspar Fagel, performed thoroughly. In Utrecht twenty-nine of the new regents had not even been born in the province! Afterwards the prince high-handedly imposed upon Utrecht the so-called 'government regulation', drafted by himself and Fagel, according to which the *Stadhouder* was not only granted the right to appoint local magistrates upon nomination, but also without any previous recommendation provincial officers and officials. He was even given the power as well to approve of the choice of provincial delegates to the States-General. An *understadhouder* was charged with its execution, as was already the practice in Zealand.[24] The next year similar regulations were forced upon Gelderland and Overijssel.[25]

The Gelderland regulations were, moreover, William's second option. In the first instance the province—which, as the only duchy, was the highest in the hierarchy of the Seven Netherlands—offered him its ducal dignity, in other words its sovereignty. This was engineered by relatives of Fagel, so that the prince must have known of the plans beforehand. But then it was not merely by chance that Gelderland, the first of the provinces, not Utrecht, which was only the fourth, had made the offer a year before. For it was not to be expected that other provinces would lag behind once the prince had been created lord of the most distinguished of them. But when, in Holland as well as in Zealand, many objections were raised to the plan (though in the end by minorities in the States), he realized that it would be wise to reject the offer; and so he did, furiously. The prince did not dislike becoming a sovereign in the Low Countries; already in 1672 he had sought, in a secret letter to his uncle Charles II, the sovereignty of all Seven Provinces. This undoubtedly would have strengthened his position in Europe, though maybe not inside the Republic.[26]

[24] D. J. Roorda, 'Prins Willem III en het Utrechtse regeringsreglement: Een schets van gebeurtenissen, achtergronden en problemen', in H. L. Ph. Leeuwenberg and L. van Tongerloo (eds.), *Van Standen tot Staten: 600 Jaar Staten van Utrecht 1375–1975* (Utrecht 1975), 91–133, and an English summary in *The Low Countries History Yearbook*, 12 (1979), 85–109. The text of the regulation is summarized by Wagenaar, *Vaderlandsche Historie*, xv. 327–9.

[25] Wagenaar, *Vaderlandsche Historie*, xv. 358–61.

[26] Ibid. xv. 345–58, gives the opinions of all Holland and Zealand cities. In Holland members of the provincial faction, which opposed William's foreign policy in the 1680s, were now also among the dissentients: Amsterdam, Leiden,

Meanwhile, it has to be realized that all the attempts made to dominate the provincial factions—attempts made by De Witt as well as by William III—also aimed at achieving preponderance in the States-General. Although each province had only one vote in this body, it often sent a hydra-headed delegation to The Hague. Consequently, it was not easy for those delegations to give a balanced provincial view on contentious issues, which had already been vehemently discussed at home. Champions and opponents from all provinces met at the Binnenhof and consulted together, orally as well as by letter. Thus many factions were in touch with each other right across the provinces.

Previously such forms of co-operation were looked at through nineteenth-century spectacles and called 'parties'. As a result, the existence of a 'Holland States party' and an 'Orange party' were identified: the former, entirely filled with regents of the mightiest province and concerned only with trade; and the latter, under the command of the princes of Orange, made up of courtiers, nobles, burghers of lower rank and orthodox Calvinists, most of them living outside Holland and more monarchically and religiously minded. Current research, though not yet fully capable of analysing the relations inside the States-General, is already revealing another picture. Parties in the modern sense did not exist in the Republic. One can only perceive combinations of local and provincial factions, grouped around specific centres. For example, in Holland, the prince of Orange and his men might form one of these combinations, and Amsterdam with its friends might constitute another. In the alliances thus formed, only members of the same social strata are to be found—urban and noble patricians, and none of the lower rank; such people did not play a part in government. Moreover, members of oppositional clusters always came from the same provinces. In 1684, for instance, co-operation can be found between the Holland faction

Delft, and Enkhuizen. M. W. Hartog, 'Prins Willem III en de hertogshoed van Gelderland, 1673–1675: Een onderzoek naar voorbereidingen, motieven en re-acties', *Bijdragen en Mededelingen der Vereniging 'Gelre'*, 59 (1976–7), 125–55. For William's wishes regarding sovereignty in 1672, see N. Japikse, *Correspondentie van Willem III en van Hans Willem Bentinck, eersten Graaf van Portland 'Gelre'*, 59 (5 vols. in 2 pts., Rijks Geschiedkundige Publicatiën, The Hague 1927–37), iii. 80. Rumours that William, having accepted the dukedom of Gelderland, intended to get the sovereignty of the other provinces as well, caused a flight of capital from Amsterdam. V. Barbour, *Capitalism in Amsterdam in the Seventeenth Century* (2nd edn., Toronto 1966), 58.

of Amsterdam, Middelburg, and some Zealand cities, the borough of Utrecht, and the provinces of Friesland and Groningen; it was directed against William and his friends, who similarly came from all parts of the country.[27] It is obvious that the process of decision-making in the States-General might be wearisome, and that artifices were often needed to bring it to a conclusion.

The Making of Foreign Policy

These complexities were taken into account by De Witt, as well as by William III, in making foreign policy. Though the greater part of foreign affairs was delegated to the States-General, in the years before 1672 it was a majority in the States of Holland that was in control over the whole country. De Witt was the man who deliberated with foreign diplomats in The Hague and who, as much as possible, managed to have his friends appointed as ambassadors. He had, however, to accept the old restrictions: only members of provincial States were eligible, the ambassador in London ought to be a Zealander, and his colleague in Paris a Hollander. These ambassadors sent their official letters to the States-General, but secret ones were addressed to the secretary, the *griffier*. Even so, the *griffier* in charge having little personality, these documents were more and more often received by De Witt. In this many-headed government it was, however, almost impossible to keep the contents secret. Consequently the ambassadors, and certainly those born in Holland, kept up a private correspondence with De Witt on matters of top secrecy.[28]

De Witt, as a Holland official, initiated the decision-making in the governmental bodies of his own province. Sometimes he discussed letters privately with a few regents; on other occasions

[27] For early traces of this statement, see H. Wansink, 'Holland and Six Allies: The Republic of the Seven United Provinces', in J. S. Bromley and E. H. Kossmann (eds.), *Britain and the Netherlands*, iv: *Metropolis, Dominion and Province* (The Hague 1971), 133–55; Rowen, *John de Witt*, 139–40; S. Groenveld, 'Adriaen Pauw (1585–1653), een pragmatisch Hollands staatsman', *Spiegel Historiael*, 20 (1985), 432–9. The older version though with nuances: J. C. Boogman, 'Die holländische Tradition in der niederländischen Geschichte', in G. A. M. Beekelaar *et al.* (eds.), *Vaderlands Verleden in Veelvoud* (The Hague 1975), 89–104.

[28] Diplomatic uses are described by J. Heringa, *De eer en hoogheid van de staat. Over de plaats der Verenigde Nederlanden in het diplomatieke leven van de zeventiende eeuw* (Groningen 1961).

he sent those letters directly to a provincial *besogne*. There a resolution was prepared, which, having passed through the States of Holland, was transported by De Witt, now acting as a member of the States-General, to a committee of Their High Mightinesses. The final decision was intended to be taken in the plenary session, which discussed the case for a shorter or longer time according to the extent of the secrecy which was necessary. The concluding letters were, of course, drafted by De Witt.[29]

How unstable such an informal method could be became evident when, in 1670, a man of stronger personality was appointed *griffier* of the States-General: Gaspar Fagel. De Witt's power began to decline. He had to abandon parts of his foreign policy because of growing tension between himself and an Amsterdam–Haarlem faction, and because of the inescapable presence of William III. This period of transition, however, proved to be a short one. During the critical summer of 1672 De Witt retired, and was succeeded by Fagel. The new Grand Pensionary at once became the right hand of William III, who had just been invested with his offices. Even before his inauguration as *Stadhouder*, the States of Holland, not the States-General, had authorized Orange to negotiate personally with English ambassadors. William immediately did so, making use of the services of some of his own men. Quickness and secrecy would profit by it. Thus the prince was given a power, one he would never again trust out of his hands.[30] In 1685, Fagel even argued that it was 'the most important part of the office of *Stadhouder* to correspond with princes and potentates'.[31] Was the idea running through William's mind, perhaps, that he, a royal prince, whose attention was emphatically

[29] J. C. Boogman, 'De raison d'état-politicus Johan de Witt', *BMGN*, 90 (1975), 379–407, esp. 385–7. An English translation in *The Low Countries History Yearbook*, 11 (1978), 55–78; Franken, *Van Beuningen*, 22–33; Japikse, *De Witt*, 56–65; Rowen, *John de Witt*, 138–47, 160–1, 210, 238–50.

[30] Franken, *Van Beuningen*, 102–4. Japikse, *Prins Willem III, de stadhouder-koning*, i. 221–32. D. J. Roorda, 'Willem III, de Koning–Stadhouder', in Roorda, *Rond Prins en Patriciaat: Verspreide opstellen* (Weesp 1984), 118–42, esp. 126; and 'Le secret du Prince: Monarchale tendenties in de Republiek 1672–1702', ibid. 172–92, esp. 182. R. Fruin, 'Willem III en zijn geheime onderhandelingen met Karel II van Engeland in 1672', in Fruin, *Verspreide Geschriften*, iv. 338–56, esp. 349–50.

[31] GA Leiden, no. 9304: Particuliere notulen Burgersdijck, fo. 38^v (8 June 1685): It 'is 't voornaemste deel vant Stadhouderschap met princen ende potentaten te corresponderen'.

drawn to his high birth during his first visit to England in 1670,[32] *ought* to have the direction of foreign policy, because it was the most essential part of the royal prerogative everywhere in Europe?

Whatever may have been the case, William developed a method that deviated far more from the established rules than De Witt's did, and that was even more monarchical than his remarkable way of working in internal affairs. It is true that the old machinery was kept completely intact. But alongside it the prince created his own service, in which some twenty favourites were active during this entire reign. They included totally different types of people: relatives, such as Willem Adriaan van Nassau-Odijk; personal friends, like Hans Willem Bentinck; officers in the Dutch army, who, under the mask of military activities, had the opportunity to accomplish other tasks, Georg Friedrich von Waldeck first among them; dissenters, even Jews, for instance Franciscus Schoonenberg (alias Jacob de Abraham Belmonte); officials of the principality of Orange, such as Sebastien Chièze, or of his own household, like Johan Pesters—men of all ranks and stations who had one thing in common: they enjoyed Orange's entire confidence. Seventy short embassies are known to have been performed by one or other of them outside the official service, thirty of them before 1680. Sometimes they were also sent as members of a formal mission, with the States' ambassador. Mostly, these official ambassadors also stood in some special relation to the prince. For not only had William an important voice in their appointment, but he also required secret letters from them to be sent to him personally, or to Pesters, and not to the States-General.[33]

Meanwhile Orange's authority in military affairs was increasing. Whereas his instruction as a captain-general prescribed that he should obey the commands of the deputies-in-the-field, in practice the situation soon proved to be the reverse. It was William who nominated well-affected regents for the job of deputy, and it was he who gave the orders to be executed by them.[34] He also acquired much influence over the appointment

[32] Baxter, *William III*, 55–6. Japikse, *Correspondentie*, iii. 28–32 (1 July 1670): report by P. A. Rumpf.

[33] Roorda, 'Secret', *passim*; Franken, *Van Beuningen*, 33, 114, 124, 132, 153–4.

[34] See J. F. Gebhard, *Het leven van mr. Nicolaas Cornelisz. Witsen (1641–1717)* (2 vols., Utrecht 1881–2), i. 129–44; Japikse, *Willem III*, ii. 184–221.

of military officers, and instructed his appointees, in case of his absence, not to correspond with the States-General, but with the Grand Pensionary.[35]

Yet, notwithstanding the growth in his power, Orange, like De Witt before him, had to keep the formal conventions in mind, just as he had to take account of the diversity of opinions and interests in the Republic. In consequence, and as a pupil of De Witt, he sometimes consulted a few influential regents before a case was sent to the States and to the *besognes*. Further proceedings he left to the care of the Grand Pensionary. But especially in the field of foreign policy, even an adroit statesman like Fagel was unable to bridge the differences of opinion. Almost inevitably the clashes between the various factions caused problems, particularly when it came to controlling the instruments indispensable to international affairs: the army, navy, and money.

Foreign Policy under De Witt, 1660–1672

One cannot understand the background of ideas and the clashes in the foreign affairs of William's time without a knowledge of the period of De Witt. In these years two contrasting theories of common interest should, broadly speaking, be distinguished in western Europe. The first held that, when a king succeeded in strengthening his power, his state would flourish in consequence; the second, considering the state as a society, stressed that the nation was viable only when all citizens lived in prosperity. The former was primarily applicable to a land power, the latter to a maritime power. As a matter of course many people in the Dutch Republic, or more precisely in its western parts, held the second opinion. In Holland, especially, a host of writers tried to advance this view upon a strong theoretical basis. In many books and pamphlets prosperity was depicted as the product of trade, and the growth of trade as a consequence of international peace and order. On this point the friends of Johan de Witt and

[35] A. de Fouw, *Onbekende raadpensionarissen* (The Hague 1946), 91–163, see esp. 111. Müller, *Wilhelm III von Oranien und Georg Friedrich von Waldeck: Ein Beitrag zur Geschichte des Kampfes um das europäische Gleichgewicht* (2 vols., The Hague 1873–80), ii. 58, 162, 345; H. J. van der Heim, *Het archief van den raadpensionaris Antonie Heinsius* (3 vols., The Hague 1867–80).

staunch supporters of the House of Orange agreed.[36] More pragmatically disposed people declared in favour of this striving for profit, because the struggle for political power was too expensive,[37] and only brought misery to the inhabitants, particularly to farmers, as the experience of the eastern provinces, which were so often a theatre of war, showed.

According to many, wealth was only attainable by a policy of strict neutrality, without any alliance, except a treaty of commerce. This was De Witt's opinion at the outset too.[38] But, in daily practice, such a passive policy proved unrealistic: sometimes a nation was unintentionally involved by another state, or saw its interests damaged by struggles between third parties. Active neutralism seemed to be a better response to international questions: a policy of defensive alliances between all European states —a euphemism for non-aggression pacts in which parties promised each other to guarantee the status quo and to compel violators to climb down, if need be by force. De Witt tried to bring this policy of erecting one big security-system into practice in 1659–60, by co-operating with France and England to restore peace in the Baltic, although he trusted neither the French nor the English.

This system did not, however, allow for the unwillingness of England. Consequently in 1662 the Dutch and the French restricted themselves to a defensive alliance. The treaty was concluded because they both had an interest in the Spanish territories of the southern Netherlands. France would have liked to annex these lands without coming to war with the Dutch, whereas the Republic felt that they had to be maintained, in any form

[36] V.D.H. [Pieter de la Court], *Het Interest van Holland ofte Gronden van Hollands Welvaren* (Amsterdam 1662). Th. van Tijn, 'Pieter de la Court: zijn leven en zijn economische denkbeelden', *Tijdschrift voor Geschiedenis*, 69 (1956), 305–70. Also the Orangist author Pieter Valckenier, *'t Verwerd Europa* (2 vols., Amsterdam 1675).

[37] See below, pp. 233, 244 and the claim by the Holland nobility in 1673, that 'Nobles and inhabitants bring more prosperity to the country than merchants who quit the country in bad times' ('de Edelen en inwoonders meer oorsaak sijn van het welvaren van het landt, als de coopluyden, die het landt in quade tijden verlaaten'). Quoted by Franken, *Van Beuningen*, 120.

[38] On passive neutrality during the Eighty Years War: Groenveld, *Verlopend getij*, 105–6. In 1657 De Witt wrote in the same sense to Cornelis de Graeff van Zuidpolsbroek, the mightiest burgomaster of Amsterdam, see Fruin *et al.*, *Brieven van De Witt*, i. 515 (18 Oct. 1657); A. C. Carter, *Neutrality or Commitment: The Evolution of Dutch Foreign Policy 1667–1795*, 7–20.

whatsoever, as a buffer between France and the Seven Provinces. Negotiations on the status of the Spanish Netherlands, in which De Witt was supported by Amsterdam and its faction, nevertheless failed. Yet France met its obligations by combating Münster when, as an ally to England, it attacked the Republic from the east during the second Anglo-Dutch war (1665–7).

While the war between the English and Dutch dragged on, France seized the opportunity to invade the southern Netherlands. At the same time it took a series of mercantilist measures against Dutch trade. In these circumstances England and the Republic swiftly made peace, stepped up their contacts with Sweden, and in 1668 concluded a Triple Alliance. Once again the idea of a general guarantee of the status quo was central. The allies hoped to coerce France, to persuade it to climb down and accede to the alliance, and were even willing to cede Spanish territory to Louis in order to reach their aim. In a secret clause, however, they introduced a new element. In case of a French refusal the allies would, by means of their armies, force France back inside its old borders. They realized that, in this case, the re-establishment of the general security system would be impossible, and accepted the fact that there had to be a new agreement: that of a balance of power between two blocks of states.[39] De Witt, still supported by Amsterdam, was aware of the risks he was taking, but accepted them, although he preferred the old idea of collective security. This line of policy seemed to hold sway when France made peace with Spain, in which it won its first Netherlandish territory.

But reality proved otherwise in 1670. France and England concluded a secret offensive alliance, joined by Cologne and Münster, against the Republic. De Witt, however, did not expect England to participate in such a treaty. Giving prosperity a central place in his policy, he could only conclude that it would not benefit England if France acquired a stronger position on the opposite coast. He did not realize that politics, as practised by Charles II, knew other priorities: for instance, getting grants of French money in order to be more independent of parliament. The Grand Pensionary was left no other choice but to organize

[39] For the background of the Triple Alliance, see Boogman, 'Raison d'état-politicus', 396–8. W. Hahlweg, 'Barriere—Gleichgewicht—Sicherheit: Eine Studie über die Gleichgewichtspolitik und die Strukturwandlung des Staatensystems in Europa 1646–1715', *Historische Zeitschrift* 187 (1959), 54–89.

the defence of his country. During his last years circumstances had forced him to look for some *rapprochement* with England and to embrace in a measure the new principle of the balance of power, practices that would increasingly dominate the years ahead.[40]

Foreign Policy under William III, 1672–1685

The shock of 1672 not only caused a sudden change in Dutch government, but also influenced thought and action in the sphere of foreign affairs. Although a pupil of Johan de Witt, William III saw that the co-ordination of 'freedom, interest of the country, and well-being' could no longer be the starting-point of a realistic international policy.[41] A schedule of priorities had to be devised in which the survival of the Dutch state would take first place, and prosperity (trade being an essential part of it) only second place.[42] France, the greatest threat to Dutch existence, had to be combated by all available means. The army had to be strengthened, money had to be furnished, and citizens, when called upon, had to respond immediately. On the diplomatic front the French coalition had to be weakened, and allies had to be won from among the present friends of Louis as well as elsewhere in Europe. To this end William not only dispatched both private and official ambassadors throughout the Continent, but also put his propaganda machine to work, especially in order to influence the parliamentary opposition in England. From the outset French actions were depicted as striving after 'universal monarchy' and the dominance of the 'universal, that is Roman Catholic, church'.[43] All efforts were directed towards the

[40] See De Witt's memorandum of 1663, Fruin *et al.*, *Brieven van De Witt*, ii. 579–88; J. W. Smit, 'The Netherlands and Europe in the Seventeenth and Eighteenth Centuries', in J. S. Bromley and E. H. Kossmann (eds.), *Britain and the Netherlands*, iii: *in Europe and Asia* (1968), 13–36.

[41] Thus the Amsterdam burgomaster Nicholas Witsen saw the essence of Dutch policy in 1684 in co-operation ('de vrijhejt, het intrest vant lant, en welwesen'). Gebhardt, *Witsen*, ii. 91 (6 Sep. 1684): Witsen to the Amsterdam burgomasters.

[42] William's opinion on trade, in 1683, did not differ essentially from his views ten years before. Franken, *Van Beuningen*, 225.

[43] K. H. D. Haley, *William of Orange and the English Opposition, 1672–1674* (Oxford 1953), esp. 103–4; L. G. Schwoerer, 'Propaganda in the Revolution of 1688–89', *American Historical Review*, 132 (1977), 843–74; P. G. Hoftijzer, *Engelse boek verkopers bij de beurs. De geschiedenis van de Amsterdamse boekhandels Bruyning*

containment of France and the safeguarding of the Spanish Netherlands against possible French aggression. Thus William did not believe in a policy of collective guarantees. His purpose was to create a real balance of power. He was convinced that God had set him the task of becoming the leader of this new policy—a vision that sometimes caused him to run greater risks than, humanly speaking, could be considered acceptable.[44]

This policy was vindicated when the enemy was stopped short of the border of Holland. In 1673 an alliance was concluded with Spain (which stood to profit most by it), the Empire, and Lorraine, and afterwards with Brandenburg and Denmark. The threats and actions undertaken by William and his new allies caused France to evacuate the occupied provinces, while England, Cologne, and Münster chose to make peace. The war continued against France only, and was fought mainly in the southern Netherlands, but brought no successes at all to the Dutch and their allies.[45]

In the meantime William had gathered much support inside the Republic. First of all, the city of Amsterdam, where anti-French feelings were manifest before 1672, took a firm stand and provided him with the necessary money.[46] The city acted out of political and economic motives. It owed its wealth partly to its safe position in the centre of the Seven Provinces; all the world could deposit money and goods in Amsterdam without fear of danger. But how much longer could safety be guaranteed when hostile armies were able to come as close to the city as the French did? A flight of capital might be the consequence, as was the case in 1672.[47] During the next years William continued to obtain assistance from Amsterdam, though the nature of his foreign

en Swart, 1637–1724 (Amsterdam 1987), 133–57; also 'Een venster op Europa: Culturele betrekkingen tussen Groot-Brittannië en de Nederlandse Republiek', in A. G. H. Bachrach, J. P. Sigmond, and A. J. Veenendaal, jun. (eds.), *Willem III, de stadhouder–koning en zijn tijd* (Amsterdam 1988), 115–40.

[44] For William's religious ideas, see n. 20 above. Also Franken, *Van Beuningen*, 19–20, 115, 150, 188, 225, 235–6, 254–5; Kurtz, *Willem III*, 120–1, 132–3.

[45] P. Sonnino, 'Louis XIV and the Dutch War', in Hatton, *Louis XIV and Europe*, 153–78.

[46] Franken, *Van Beuningen*, 101–2. Quite rightly this author disputes the picture of listlessness in Amsterdam in those days, as painted by G. M. Trevelyan.

[47] Barbour, *Capitalism*, 57–8. See also S. Groenveld, *De prins voor Amsterdam: Reacties uit pamfletten op de aanslag van 1650* (Bussum 1967), 64–5, where fear on the same grounds is described in connection with the assault William II of Orange made on Amsterdam in 1650.

policy differed essentially from that of De Witt, which the city had supported earlier. However, for the time being, the new policy of balance and the old one of general security followed the same paths: a struggle against France and the winning of allies, especially England. In the long run differences appeared. Whereas William was ready to wage war along with the allies until France was bridled, even if it took many years, Amsterdam and Leiden, from 1675 onwards, wished to enter into negotiations with Louis, to make peace (even a peace bringing new losses to Spain), and involve France once again in a security system of defensive alliances. Not only did the lack of success during the war and the impotence of the allies inspire Amsterdam, but also the explicit unwillingness of England to join the anti-French coalition. Without Anglo-Dutch co-operation, a policy of guarantees might still have a certain chance, whereas a balance of power would be impossible. Leiden did not emphasize this point as strongly as Amsterdam did, but argued rather that the growing insolvency of the Republic could not bear war any longer.[48]

Thus, around 1678, two views opposed one another in regard to the war. This situation was not changed by the marriage of William III to the English princess, Mary Stuart, in 1677, and the first talks about an Anglo-Dutch defensive treaty, which was concluded in 1678. William maintained that he could not, and would not, promise that the end of the war was in sight. Meanwhile Amsterdam and Leiden were approached underhandedly by France with proposals for peace—the same method William had used in England some years before—and they considered giving Louis the benefit of the doubt. This did not mean that the prince might be labelled 'pro-English', or the Holland faction 'pro-French'. The latter, and thus the old policy of Johan de Witt, gained the day in the circumstances of 1678: peace was made in Nijmegen, separately from the allies.[49] In fury William saw the

[48] Franken, *Van Beuningen*, 123–63. For a clear picture of the discussions: GA Leiden, nos. 9299 and 9300: Particuliere notulen Burgersdijck 1675–Oct. 1679, esp. no. 9300, fos. 18–24: 30 Apr.–7 May 1678. Indeed trade stagnated during the last decades: see J. G. van Dillen, 'Honderd jaar economische ontwikkeling van het Noorden', in J. A. van Houtee *et al.* (eds.), *Algemene Geschiedenis der Nederlanden* (12 vols., Utrecht 1949–59), vii. 277–320, esp. 314–15.

[49] J. A. H. Bots (ed.), *The Peace of Nijmegen: La Paix de Nimègue, 1676–1678/79* (Amsterdam 1980). In older literature Amsterdam is too easily labelled 'pro-

alliance, of which the Republic had been the centre, crumbling away. But a Dutch majority did not possess the will to continue the war without great risks, and, if need be, almost alone.

However, peace had been made in an atmosphere of general distrust and egotism all over Europe. This atmosphere prevailed in the following years, when many international alliances were designed, but few were realized. One of the last of these suddenly received general approval in the Republic: the 'Association Alliance' of 1681 with Sweden, which William saw as the starting-point for a new anti-French coalition, and Amsterdam, though not blind to Orange's interpretation, envisaged as a security association in which France could also play a part.[50] Much depended, in the opinion of all, on England. But Charles II, having just received fresh French money and thus not being beholden to parliament, held aloof. English isolationism, 'l'insouffrable conduite de l'Angleterre', drove William to despair. In 1682 he complained, 'it is the principal cause of our present dangers because of which the situation at the end of this year will perhaps be even worse than in 1672!'[51]

William was also worried by Louis XIV's new activities. In 1681 the king sharpened his measures against the Huguenots. A year later he made a bid for more royal power in the Gallican Church. European Protestants reacted with anger and fright, as did the Pope. At the same time Louis attacked from his eastern border, taking Strasburg in 1681 and, in the next year, Orange, injuring William in his heart of hearts. When he afterwards fell upon Luxemburg it directly affected the Republic;[52] Brussels requested The Hague, on the score of the treaty of 1673, to send 8,000 soldiers as auxiliary troops. The same request was put to Charles II, but the English king was only ready to arbitrate, which Louis, later on, was willing to accept. In the Seven Provinces the Spanish request prompted a severe conflict in 1683–4.

French'; see for instance Kurtz, *Willem III*, *passim*. In the same way De Witt was wrongly called 'pro-French' during his lifetime.

50 W. J. M. van Eysinga, *Het Associatieverdrag van 10 October 1681* (Amsterdam 1947); Kurtz, *Willem III*, 28–32. Franken, *Van Beuningen*, 183–6. Franken considers the treaty as an anti-French alliance only, disputing the view of Van Eysinga, who interprets it as the starting-point of a general security alliance. In fact, both ideas had their adherents, as can be seen now.

51 Müller, *Willem III und Waldeck*, ii. 132 (23 Feb. 1682): William to Waldeck.

52 G. Symcox, 'Louis XIV and the Outbreak of the Nine Years War', in Hatton, *Louis XIV and Europe*, 179–212.

In order to assist his Spanish ally and at the same time slow down the aggressor, William proposed to send not only the 8,000 soldiers, but 16,000 more. He admitted the risk of war, but trusted in God's help.[53] His suggestion provoked new actions by the opposition faction in Holland, the members of which communicated with one another by word and letter, and were led by Amsterdam. It is true that the great city underwent a change in its thinking about foreign policy, and convinced itself that in the long run war against France was inevitable, as was the concept of the balance of power. But the Dutch did not have the means to wage that war without allies; co-operation at least with the English was needed, Spain and the Empire being too weak. Thus the views of Amsterdam and the prince on foreign policy drew nearer to each other, though not over the manner of executing it. According to Amsterdam, diplomatic, not military, means should be used as long as England held aloof. The city pleaded for two truces: the first between France and Spain, the second between France and the Empire.[54] The members of Amsterdam's provincial faction agreed, as did some patricians belonging to local factions not high in power. The Rotterdam regent, Adriaen Paets, for instance, whose city took William's side, argued that for a 'Republic of Commerce' a defensive war, 'without a host of many and mighty allies', could only be fatal.[55]

The problem being a fundamental one, the provincial faction made contact with like-minded groups in other provinces. In the city of Utrecht the strongest faction took the same stand, notwithstanding the government regulation;[56] in Zealand, Middelburg,

[53] Franken, *Van Beuningen*, 236; Kurtz, *Willem III*, 120–1.

[54] Ibid., 204–33; Kurtz, *Willem III*, 32–40, 53–140; Gebhard, *Witsen*, i. 206–56; ii. 46–77; Van der Heim, *Heinsius*, i. pp. xlix–lxi; GA Leiden, no. 9303: Particuliere notulen Burgersdijck, fos. 44–8 (Oct. 1683); unfoliated: 16–20 May 1684.

[55] Algemeen Rijksarchief, The Hague (ARA), Resolutiën der Staten van Holland 1684, 46: 24 Feb. Paets wrote: 'Dat, hoe-wel den Oorlogh in het algemeyn schadelijck is aen een Republijcq van Commercie, een defensieven Oorlogh echter van groote uytstreckinghe in societeyt van veele ende machtige Geallieerden, die veyligheydt misschien soude konnen uytwercken, doch dat een Oorlogh, buyten soodanige gemeynschap, fatael soude wesen voor de Republijcq.' On Paets, his congenial regents, and their mutual contacts, see Franken, *Van Beuningen*, 35 n. 4; C. W. Roldanus, 'Adriaen Paets, een republikein uit de nadagen', *Tijdschrift voor Geschiedenis* (1935), 134–66.

[56] M. van der Bijl, 'Utrechts weerstand tegen de oorlogspolitiek tijdens de Spaanse Successieoorlog: De rol van de heer van Welland van 1672 tot 1708', in

Goes, and Zierikzee acted similarly, arguing that the nation's lack of money prohibited William's policy.[57] Friesland and Groningen put forward quite different arguments. Remembering very clearly the disastrous events of 1672, they pointed out that, during the present tense situation, France might repeat its old strategy, Münster and Cologne being again pro-French. They argued that the Dutch army should be concentrated on the north-eastern borders, not in the southern Netherlands.[58] In Overijssel, many people also adopted the standpoint of Amsterdam.[59]

Both in the provincial States and in the States-General William and Fagel attempted the artifice of outvoting minorities to obtain their way, but they were too slow. Luxemburg was taken by France. At Ratisbon a Franco-German and a Franco-Spanish truce were concluded in August 1684. For the second time a strong opposition had obstructed Orange in the execution of his policy. The prince, for his part, combated the opposition by purging the magistracies in many cities,[60] and by coming to terms with Hendrik Casimir van Nassau, the *Stadhouder* of Friesland and Groningen.[61] On the other hand, the opposition factions apparently now adhered to William's balance-of-power policy, and with reason deemed only his methods of executing that policy to be risky. With the approaching demise of general security, and a permanent peace proving elusive, William was able, unlike in 1678, to use the contacts he had recently made.

Activities to win over England, 1685–1689

In spite of the truces Louis again caused unrest in the years which followed. The king expected some weakening of his position in western Germany, because of the succession of princes who might not automatically be his allies. He therefore fortified his eastern border. At the same time he dealt a last blow

Leeuwenberg and Van Tongerloo, *Van Standen tot Staten*, 135–99, esp. 143 and 181; Roorda, 'Utrechts regeringsreglement', 126.

[57] Van der Bijl, *Idee en Interest*, 29–44.

[58] Theissen, 'Verhoudingen 1684', *passim*; Franken, *Van Beuningen*, 173, 186.

[59] B. H. Slicher van Bath *et al.*, *Geschiedenis van Overijssel* (Deventer 1970), 130.

[60] See above pp. 221–3, and nn. 22–4.

[61] Kurtz, *Willem III*, 152–5, 160–1, 222–5; A. A. Kleyn, *De stadhouders van Friesland uit het Huis van Nassau* (Nijkerk 1904), 124–7.

to the Huguenots by revoking the Edict of Nantes in 1685. Hoping to strengthen the economy of his country by excluding aliens, in the autumn of 1687 he imposed a series of tariffs on imports, which could easily be interpreted as a violation of the peace of 1678 and the Truce of Ratisbon.

Louis's religious and economic measures sent a shock throughout the Dutch Republic. Until then, only local ministers, provincial synods, and city councillors had busied themselves providing financial aid to French Protestants, privileges for refugees, and advertising jobs for good Huguenot craftsmen in Dutch-printed French journals. Now the States-General took action, issuing placards and proclaiming days of prayer on behalf of the Huguenots.[62] Moreover, provincial and general States received complaints from Dutchmen living in France about seizures of their goods and restraints of their liberties, while manufacturers and fishermen from inside the Republic sent requests for measures against the new tariffs.[63]

Hostile feelings were spread among the population by means of propaganda in journals and pamphlets. Louis was depicted as an oppressive, duty-forsaking king; in contrast, William III was seen as a new Moses or a new David.[64] By 1684 the wave of anti-French pamphlets had already reached its peak, just before the Revocation; when it receded, it was followed by a new billow of

[62] F. J. R. Knetsch, 'Les Églises réformées des Pays-Bas et la Révocation', in *Tricentennaire de la Révocation de l'Édit de Nantes: La Révocation et l'extérieur du royaume* (Montpellier 1985), 173–92; E. Buning, P. Overbeek, and J. Verveer, 'De huisgenoten des geloofs: De immigratie van de Hugenoten 1680–1720', *Tijdschrift voor Geschiedenis*, 100 (1987), 356–73; J. A. H. Bots, G. H. M. Posthumus Meyjes, and F. Wieringa (eds.), *Vlucht naar de vrijheid: De Hugenoten en de Nederlanden* (Amsterdam 1985), 70–7. For the international situation in those years: J. Carswell, *The Descent on England: A Study of the English Revolution of 1688 and its European Background* (1969).

[63] ARA, Resolutiën Staten van Holland 1685, 422–4 (13 Sep.), 621–3 (11 Oct.). GA Leiden, Particuliere notulen Burgersdijck: no. 9304, fos. 49 (13–16 Sep. 1685), 56, 56^{v} (10–12 Oct.); no. 9305, fos. 48 (30 Nov. 1687), 51^{v} (Jan. 1688), 60^{v} (30 Mar.–2 Apr.), 69 (14–20 Sep.). The estimates of the number of Huguenots emigrating to the Dutch Republic vary from 35,000 to 80,000: H. P. H. Nusteling, 'The Netherlands and the Huguenot Émigrés', in Bots and Posthumus Meyjes, *Révocation*, 17–34.

[64] J. A. H. Bots, 'L'Echo de la Révocation dans les Provinces-Unies à travers les gazettes et les pamphlets', in *La Révocation de l'Édit de Nantes et le protestantisme français en 1685* (Paris 1986), 281–98. C. G. Gibbs, 'Some Intellectual and Political Influences of the Huguenot Emigrés in the United Provinces, *c.*1680–1730', *BMGN*, 90 (1975), 255–87. F. R. J. Knetsch, 'Pierre Jurieu: Theologian and Politician of the Dispersion', *Acta Historiae Neerlandica*, 5 (1971), 213–42.

anti-English propaganda. The Dutch were terrified not only because the new king of England, James II, was strengthening the position of Catholicism in his country, but also because he was reinforcing the English army: 'the king makes big preparation, equips, filles his storehouses, ambassador Skelton in Paris, pretensions Bantham, etc. *omnia suspecta'*, noted a member of the States of Holland, writing minutes for the use of his city.[65] Was a new Anglo-French coalition being formed, monarchical and Catholic by nature? Was 1672 to repeat itself? William himself was not totally convinced of the contrary. Thus, the States-General in January 1687 resolved, upon Orange's nomination, to send Everard van Weede van Dijkvelt as their ambassador to England. Dijkvelt was instructed to win James over to a defensive alliance against France.

A defensive alliance. After the Truce of Ratisbon William had worked more intensely at concluding treaties of that kind, and now the tide was turning. Princes of other countries were likewise alarmed by English and French events. Moreover the Emperor had gained a stronger position against his enemy, the Turks, on his eastern borders, and was able to pay more attention to the problems in western Europe. In 1686, in Augsburg, he concluded with Sweden, Spain, and the electors of Bavaria, Saxony, and the Palatinate, an alliance of mutual defence in the case of French aggression against one of their territories inside the Empire. Although this restriction to the Empire made it impossible for William to be admitted to the alliance, the prince could profit by it in the future. In the meantime discussions between himself and Brandenburg had resulted in a treaty which might be used as the starting-point of an anti-French coalition. England undoubtedly had to be the next member. But, in 1687, Dijkvelt did not succeed in winning over James, who paid attention only to internal English affairs. So it remained primarily Orange's task to concentrate on the co-operation of England, that incalculable factor in Europe.

William's second task undoubtedly was to win over the Dutch

[65] The quotation in GA Leiden, Particuliere notulen Burgersdijck: no. 9305, fo. 22 (9–19 Jan. 1687): 'alsoo de koning groote preparatie maect—equipeert, voorsiet magasynen, ambassadeur Skelton te Parijs, pretensien Bantham etc., *omnia suspecta . . .*'. On the pamphlets: Hoftijzer, *Boekverkopers*, 133–57; 'Venster', 127–30.

themselves. Inside the Republic the situation quickly improved for the prince, because of the change in the political views of the opposition,[66] the general anti-French and anti-Catholic feeling, and the stimulating influence exerted by the new international alliances. Only in Friesland and Groningen did other interests and sentiments sometimes prevail. William, for his part, repeatedly consulted the Amsterdam burgomasters beforehand on important matters. He used this method all the more, because of the private aspects of his English policy.

The intertwining of Dutch and personal interest concerning England, a part of William's policy ever since 1672, played a stronger role from 1685 onwards. Half an English prince, William was a potential heir to the English throne both by birth and by marriage. The intertwining also played a role in Dijkvelt's mission. Being one of William's twenty favourites, the ambassador was charged by the prince, alongside his official instructions, to discuss with members of the parliamentary opposition in what way his master could assist in solving the internal problems in England. The matter, as is well known, became urgent for the prince when, in the last month of 1687, the pregnancy of the English queen was announced. The birth of a son might weaken Orange's chances both in regard to the British succession and to his introducing Albion into the anti-French camp.

But in what capacity could he cross the North Sea? As a royal prince he undoubtedly enjoyed high status in England, but no means of power. As *Stadhouder* of five Dutch provinces he had gained much influence, which made it possible for him to negotiate with England on international affairs, but not on internal ones; neither did he possess in this capacity any command over the army and navy. This last power he did have as the captain and admiral-general of the Union, but these offices did not give him any political authority. Besides, through an action based only upon his Dutch offices, the Republic might easily be labelled an aggressor in an international conflict. No doubt the States would not consent to any action which might weaken their standing in their own country and in Europe. Nothing was left

[66] Kurtz, *Willem III*, 140–80, argues that Amsterdam underwent a total change, and was consequently reconciled to William. Instead of changing their minds suddenly, however, the city and its adherents altered their political views slowly, over three to five years.

William but his position as Prince of Orange. Though a prince without a country, he was generally accepted as a sovereign who, according to the standards of his time, was allowed to perform international actions, even military ones. In this capacity he could cross the sea with his train; in England he might combine it with his being a 'grandson of England', entitled to intervene in English affairs. A part of the required troops and ships he was able to recruit and equip himself; the other part he sought to get from the States-General in the shape of assistance for a friendly prince. According to the rules an aiding government might not be involved in a war.

In the first half of 1688 William started to build up the army without consulting the States, while the admiralties (save the Frisian) equipped the fleet at his command.[67] His favourites travelled through Germany in order to ensure safety behind him, once the Dutch army had left the country. The aim was kept top secret; it looked as if war preparations against France were being made. Not before June (well before the official request for assistance arrived from England) did William have two reliable Amsterdam burgomasters informed by Dijkvelt of his plans, and then under the utmost secrecy; the third was absent, while the fourth burgomaster, a merchant to Rouen, was regarded as pro-French. On this occasion the threat of an Anglo-French coalition, and thus the repetition of 1672, was again used as an argument.

Not until 20 September, when preparations were almost finished, did William discuss with the States of Holland and the States-General the acquisition of troops from German princes to secure the borders against France. Four days later he gave a *besogne* of the States of Holland confidential information as to his real purpose, and three days afterwards the French ambassador knew of it.

Final discussions in a *besogne* of the States-General were held on 8 October, when William not only put forward the international character of his plans, but the private side as well. It was, he said, not at all his intention to dethrone King James. But neither could he afford any longer that a realm where he himself had such high rights should ruin itself, and at the same time drag international society along with it. He and Princess Mary, taking into account

[67] For the equipment: A. van der Kuijl, *De glorieuze overtocht: De expeditie van Willem III naar Engeland in 1688* (Amsterdam 1988).

the private side of the problem, had resolved to take action themselves. The States-General, for their part, approved 'that His said Highness has decided to start the said matter upon His Highnesse's and Her Royal Highnesse's own names, and to make use of the States' power only as auxiliary'.[68]

By then the machinery was already running at full capacity. Only more money had to be found. The States-General placed at William's disposal 4 million guilders, originally earmarked for the strengthening of the borders on land, and the prince privately received some 2 million from Jewish confidants.[69] The expedition could only start, however, after the season had gone by, which increased the risks which, as usual, William had already calculated. On 11 November the fleet put to sea. From the top of the great mast of the frigate *Den Briel*, in which William sailed, the prince's and princess's banner flew. Upon it was emblazoned the text 'For Liberty and Protestant Religion', and beneath those words the device of the Oranges—'Je maintiendrai'.[70] This was more than propaganda. It also showed the real aim which the Dutch attached to the enterprise: the conclusion of the urgently needed Anglo-Dutch alliance against Louis XIV of France, who in September had invaded the Rhineland, thus initiating the Nine Years War. Would Louis again launch an attack on the Dutch eastern borders? It was not the coronation of William and Mary as king and

[68] Gebhardt, *Witsen*, i. 310–34. For the leaking out of the secret: Van der Bijl, 'Utrechts weerstand', 143–4, 184–6 nn. 47–61. The distrusted Amsterdam burgomaster Johan Appelman started his career by appointment of William in 1672; he had French connections. ARA, Secrete Resolutiën der Staten-Generaal 1688, nos. 4029, 4030, and 4592 (21 and 25 Sep. and 8 Oct.); Secrete Resolutiën der Staten van Holland 1688, 22, 24, 25, 27 Sep.; GA Leiden, Particuliere notulen Burgersdijck: no. 9305, fos. 69 (14–20 Sep. 1688), 69^v (22–5 Sep.), 70 (29 Sep.–2 Oct.). For the secret resolution, taken by the *besogne* of the States-General on 8 Oct. 1688, see *Kronijk van het Historisch Genootschap*, 3rd ser. iv (1858), 135–42. The quotation: 'dat hooghgem. Zijne Hoogheyt heeft geresolveerd de voors. zake aan te vangen op den naam van Zijne Hoogheyt en van Hare Kon. Hoogheyt, en zig van de magt van den Staat alleen als auxiliair te bedienen'.

[69] As to the supply of 2 million guilders by Francisco Lopes Suasso to William III there are some doubts. J. I. Israel, *European Jewry in the Age of Mercantilism 1559–1650* (Oxford 1985), 134. Recent research, however, confirms that a transaction like the one that has frequently been mentioned really took place. L. Schönduve, 'Antonio Lopes Suasso: Joodse baronnen in Holland. Op zoek naar merites van een mythe', *Holland. Regionaal-Historisch tijdschrift*, 20 (1988), 175–85; D. J. Roorda, 'De joodse entourage van de Koning–Stadhouder', in Roorda, *Rond Prins en Patriciaat*, 143–55.

[70] Japikse, *Willem III*, ii. 257–8.

queen of England, but the Anglo-Dutch maritime treaty of August 1689 and English accession to the Grand Alliance, and consequently to the Nine Years War, which were the desired results of the Dutch assistance to William III. The French invasion of 1672 had proved to be a lasting trauma for the Dutch.

Epilogue

The Glorious Revolution created a kind of personal union between England and the Republic. William, being the leading statesman of that union, usually spent the winter in England; in summer he campaigned with the army; and only during some weeks in the spring and autumn did he reside in the Seven Provinces. Consequently he was many times troubled by nostalgia. During the first half year of his kingship, he repeatedly said to his favourite Dijkvelt: 'I see that this [English] people is not created for me, neither am I for this people.'[71] This was one of the reasons why he surrounded himself with his old entourage, it being mostly Dutch. He also introduced as much as he could in the English administrative system his former political practices. Ruling in co-operation with favourites had to be continued. For this reason, he had firstly to appoint some of those men to important English positions, just as he had done in the Republic. Hans Willem Bentinck for instance, being Gelderland-born, had in 1676 been introduced by the prince into the nobility of Holland, and in that way became a member of the provincial States; now he was created Earl of Portland, and thus became a member of the House of Lords. Assisted by these confidants, and not by the two secretaries of state, William made his foreign policy, getting in addition administrative aid from his English secretary, William Blathwait, who outwitted his Dutch colleague, Constantijn Huygens. His tug-of-war with the provincial and general States in the Republic had prepared him, better than any of his predecessors, for establishing realistic relations with English parliaments. His personal experience, gained in dealing with local and

[71] 'Journaal van Constantijn Huygens, den zoon, van 21 October 1688 tot 2 September 1696' in *Werken Uitgegeven door het Historisch Genootschap*, new ser., 23 (2 vols., Utrecht 1876–7), i. 192 (23 Oct. 1689): 'Ick sie wel dat dit volck niet voor mij, noch ick voor dit volck gemaeckt zijn.'

provincial Dutch factions, facilitated intercourse with Whigs as well as Tories. With respect to local quarrels in the English counties, he showed the same disdain as he had shown in the factional clashes inside Dutch cities. Besides, having grown up in a society so pluriform in religion as that of the Netherlands, he felt himself able to break the deadlock into which England had fallen on account of James's policy of toleration. Many times, and with reason, the English complained of the great influence of William's Dutch confidants and William's Dutch methods.[72]

On the other hand, not a few Dutchmen were equally convinced that their private, as well as public, interests were often neglected in favour of English ones. Already in 1689, when the maritime treaty was in preparation, the Dutch ambassadors found the *Stadhouder*–king trying to keep both of his states independent of each other, and unwilling to favour the Dutch and have the hated Act of Navigation revoked or even altered; Hollanders amongst them were also angry that William did not give the Republic a dominant position in the war at sea. For some, this was a motive to make new contacts with France in following years; new clashes occurred between William and Amsterdam, and between William and the provinces of Hendrik Casimir, but they never assumed such proportions as in 1683–4.[73] From his point of view, William tried to keep in touch with all these matters, though usually at a distance. In winter-time the policy of both England and the Seven Provinces—the international and also, partly, the internal policy of the Dutch state—was made in Britain. Much of the work for which William was responsible in the Republic was delegated to the capable, and somehow tedious, Grand Pensionary Antonie Heinsius, the successor to Fagel, who had died in December 1688. Meanwhile, as the war continued, with the Dutch no longer capable of supplying larger sums of money, a growing part of the financial burden was, in the context of the personal union, laid upon England. William, a man of political courage and great projects, but with little insight into financial and economic matters, had no eye for the material pressure that the wars exerted on the Republic; on the contrary, the Amsterdam

[72] A. Lossky, 'Political Ideas of William III', in Rowen and Lossky, *Political Ideas*, 35–56. J. L. Price, 'William III, England and the Balance of Power in Europe', *Groniek*, 101 (1988), 67–78. K. H. D. Haley, 'William III', in Bachrach *et al.*, *Willem III*, 31–50.

[73] Gebhard, *Witsen*, i. 335–416; Kurtz, *Willem III*, 181–218.

faction and its allies who, no less courageous but more pragmatic than the prince, had long seen very clearly that the wars were exhausting the Dutch state, now tacitly carried their point.[74] Yet William was able to keep a firm grip on all policy, notwithstanding these many contrasts.

But after William's death in 1702, the allies drifted apart, slowly but surely. Queen Anne established an English-oriented, and Heinsius a Dutch-oriented, policy. Marlborough proved to be the brilliant commander of the coalition army in the War of the Spanish Succession, but with an English outlook; consequently he repeatedly clashed with the Dutch deputies-in-the-field. In the Seven Provinces the preference for neutrality, to the fore in De Witt's time, revived, usually in its passive form. Even so, the conviction of the late Grand Pensionary that *pacta sunt servanda*, a conviction kept alive by William III, proved to be stronger in times of war. Thus, though it was difficult to resist French enticements, the Dutch Republic did not make a separate peace with the enemy, whereas after 1711 secret bilateral negotiations between the English and the French laid the basis of the Peace of Utrecht in 1713. This development, as well as the peace clauses, proved that the centre of gravity in the anti-French coalition had shifted towards England. The Seven Provinces, after so many decades of war, went bankrupt in 1715.[75]

Thus before 1688 the Dutch Republic, though a house divided against itself, had in its actions against Louis XIV formed the nucleus of a group of largely impotent allies. In those years England had avoided almost all Continental warfare. This central position had, however, greatly overburdened Dutch vigour. Consequently, when William III, the leading statesman of the

[74] D. J. Roorda, 'De Republiek in de tijd van stadhouder Willem III 1672–1702', in D. P. Blok *et al.* (eds.), *Algemene Geschiedenis der Nederlanden* (15 vols., Bussum 1979–83), viii. 282–96; Van der Bijl, 'Willem III, stadhouder–koning', 172–82; J. R. Jones, *The Revolution of 1688 in England* (1972), 253.

[75] J. G. Stork-Penning, *Het grote werk: Vredesonderhandelingen gedurende de Spaanse Successieoorlog 1705–1710* (Groningen 1958). J. Aalbers, *De Republiek en de vrede van Europa*, i. *Achtergronden en algemene aspecten* (Groningen 1980), and 'Holland's Financial Problems (1713–1733) and the Wars against Louis XIV', *Britain and the Netherlands*, vi: *War and Society*, A. C. Duke and C. A. Tamse (eds.), (The Hague 1977), 79–93; R. Liesker, 'Tot zinkens toe bezwaard: De schuldenlast van het Zuiderkwartier van Holland 1672–1794', in S. Groenveld, M. E. H. N. Mout, and I. Schöffer (eds.), *Bestuurders en Geleerden. Opstellen aangeboden aan J. J. Woltjer* (Amsterdam 1985), 151–60.

anti-French policy, left for England and applied growing British power to the war-effort, the English acquired an increasingly dominant position. It is obvious that, in this development, the Glorious Revolution had a pivotal place. It is obvious, too, that the Revolution of 1688 played a quite different role in Dutch history to what it played in English history; for the Republic it was, in the short run, an essential stage in the continuing struggle against France and, in the long run, the starting-point of its decline to the status of a second-rank power.

7

The Revolutions in America

K. G. DAVIES

THE transmission of the English Revolution to the plantations was not expected to give rise to difficulties and in most places did not. The colonies were not invited to concur in what had happened, though one or two responded as if they had been; they were simply instructed to proclaim William and Mary.[1] No explanation of events in England was provided, let alone justification, and no special measures were taken to ensure that the colonies complied. In two particular instances the order to proclaim the new sovereigns was associated with what might be construed as an inducement. As early as 11 January 1689 the Prince of Orange wrote to Jamaica appointing a governor, restoring officers suspended or evicted by the late Duke of Albemarle, and cancelling acts of assembly passed since Albemarle's death. These orders were repeated on 22 February when William was able to write as king.[2] This singling out of Jamaica probably owed more to the efficiency of that colony's lobby in England than to anything else. In regard to New England, however, there was some recognition in London of the value of a conciliatory gesture. On 26 February an order in Council provided for the drafting of a new charter for Massachusetts to replace that which had been annulled in 1684 and 'a new establishment' for preserving the rights and properties of the people of New England.[3] These were special cases; no prospect was held out of alleviating general colonial grievances.

There was no reason to expect resistance except conceivably in Maryland, where a mainly Catholic government ruled over a mainly Protestant people; and this danger, such as it was, seemed

[1] In Barbados the governor called a meeting of the assembly to concur in the proclamation. See PRO, *Calendar of State Papers, Colonial Series, America and West Indies, 1689–1692* (1901), no. 103. The *Calendar* cited hereafter as *CSPC*.

[2] Ibid., nos. 6, 29.

[3] Ibid., no. 37.

to have been averted when Maryland's proprietor, Lord Baltimore, attended the Lords of Trade on 20 February 1689, accepted his copy of the proclamation of the new sovereigns, and dispatched it to his colony by special messenger.[4] Well before they knew the Prince of Orange was their new king the Council of Barbados wrote to assure him of their island's firm Protestantism.[5] Much the same could have been said of every colony, Maryland apart, in the English empire. Yet the Revolution in England engendered major upheavals in Massachusetts and New York as well as Maryland, took Virginia to the edge of revolution, and brought about the resignation of the governor of the strategically important Leeward Islands. One explanation of these disturbances was the fitful arrival of news in the colonies, especially of official communications. News from England could be expected to reach an accessible colony such as Barbados in five or six weeks, thence to be dispersed to the Leewards, Jamaica, and mainland America. New York and Boston were as likely to get their first advice of events in Europe from the West Indies as from England. But this dispersal of news depended on the chance of wind and weather and the incidence of commercial activity. Colonies off the main trade-routes could remain in ignorance for a long time. Hence the complaint of the governor of Bermuda on 10 May 1689: 'Wee are here in remote and private isles in the sea and are allmost destitute of news, not having any sometimes for several months.'[6]

Official communications travelled more slowly than news. Events in Europe separated by weeks might in the colonies be separated by months, or conversely telescoped into a shorter time. The Prince of Wales was born on 10 June 1688; Barbados celebrated the event on 19 August, but the Council of Virginia did not order a public thanksgiving until 13 December and was still thinking about it on 27 February 1689.[7] Two or three weeks later 'the joyful nuse' of happenings in England—or some version of them—was in the colony; and by 29 April the order to proclaim William and Mary had arrived from London and been duly executed.[8] Virginia, with its unpopular governor, Lord Howard of Effingham, away in England, might easily have

[4] Ibid., no. 25. [5] Ibid., no. 47. [6] PRO CO 37, 25, fo. 16.

[7] *CSPC 1685–8*, nos. 1876iii, 1950; *CSPC 1689–1692*, no. 40.

[8] D. S. Lovejoy, *The Glorious Revolution in America* (New York 1972), 238; *CSPC 1689–1692*, nos. 92, 93.

experienced another convulsion on the lines of Bacon's rebellion a dozen years earlier, but for the exceptionally rapid transmission of these official instructions. As it was, Virginia became the first colony in the empire to proclaim the new sovereigns.

The conveyance of the English Revolution to the colonies may be roughly plotted by three official circulars: King James's warning, of 16 October 1688, of an invasion preparing in Holland; the Prince of Orange's letter of 12 January 1689, announcing that he had taken the administration of the country upon himself and ordering all officers to remain in post; and the letter of 19 February, signed by Halifax, Winchester, Devonshire, and Shrewsbury, among others, ordering the proclamation of William and Mary.[9] Unfortunately it is not possible to establish the dates on which the first two were received in more than a few colonies. James's circular was in Jamaica in the first or second week of December, in the Leewards about the same time, and in Boston by early January. Bermuda did not get it until 31 January, the governor responding with a firm declaration of loyalty to a king whom parliament had already displaced.[10] Orange's letter reached Barbados in the first week of March, the colony's Council replying on 11 March with an expression of hope that the prince's name would be glorious through all ages.[11] The outcome of the third circular is much clearer: Virginia proclaimed William and Mary on or before 29 April; Barbados on 9 May; the Leewards in May; Massachusetts on 31 May; Plymouth and Connecticut in the first fortnight of June; New York on 22 June; and Albany, not wishing to be associated with New York, on 1 July.[12] Maryland, in circumstances to be explored later, did not proclaim the new sovereigns until September.

As these official circulars made their erratic way to the colonies every merchant ship brought news of some kind, a good deal of it garbled, some of it false. Rumours abounded: that King James had been put to death, that William Penn had been arrested (which he had been) and executed as a Jesuit (which he had not),

[9] *CSPC 1685–1688*, no. 1910; *CSPC 1689–1692*, nos. 6, 8, 20–2.

[10] *CSPC 1685–1688*, no. 1948; *CSPC 1689–1692*, nos. 1, 32, 88.

[11] *CSPC 1689–1692*, no. 47.

[12] Ibid., nos. 91–3 (Virginia); nos. 103, 155, 158 (Barbados); no. 143 (Leeward Is.); no. 158 (Mass.); no. 183 (Plymouth); no. 205 (New York); C. M. Andrews, *The Colonial Period in American History* (New Haven and London 1964), iii. 126 n. (Conn.); Lovejoy, *Glorious Revolution in America*, 257 (Albany).

and so on.[13] Tension was high, with colonial authorities uncertain or unwilling to act upon unofficial information. Mostly they waited for orders. Waiting for orders, however, and in some colonies trying to suppress unofficial news and rumour, proved fatal to the rulers of Massachusetts, New York, and Maryland; and, but for the unusual speed with which the orders were delivered, would in all probability have unhinged the rulers of Virginia.

The Reception of the English Revolution in the West Indies

The English West Indian colonies had no cause to be grateful to King James. Following the restoration of monarchy in 1660 the Crown had extended its authority and enhanced its revenues in the islands.[14] Proprietary governments were replaced by Crown-appointed governors. In Barbados and the Leeward Islands permanent revenues were secured for the king, diminishing the bargaining power of the elected assemblies. Jamaica was brought into line in 1683, when the assembly was induced to grant a revenue for twenty-one years. Meanwhile in 1660, 1663, and 1673 Acts of Trade and Navigation imposed on the colonies a commercial system confining them to English markets both for their staple products and for the purchase of manufactures. Notoriously these regulations were often evaded, but their intentions and their occasional effects were sharp enough to cause resentment and some hardship to planters and merchants. Worse came in 1685. New and heavy duties were placed on sugar and tobacco by James's only parliament, additional to those laid on sugar at the Restoration, and additional to the 4½ per cent duty payable in Barbados and the Leewards. At a time of declining profits these taxes bore hard on the producer. One complainant spoke for all: 'They would use us like Sponges: or like Sheep. They think us fit to be squeezed and fleeced.'[15] The price of sugar in London, the

[13] Lovejoy, *Glorious Revolution in America*, 258; Beddard, *A Kingdom Without a King* (Oxford 1988), 76–7.

[14] A. P. Thornton, *West-India Policy under the Restoration* (Oxford 1956) discusses in detail the establishment of imperial control.

York, Evanston, and London, 1970), 102. Edward Lyttelton's pamphlet, *Groans of the Plantations*, was published in London in 1689 to influence the new government. Short extracts from it are printed in Greene's selection of documents.

truest index of the state of the West Indian economy, sank in 1686 to its lowest level in the century.[16]

These were not the only grievances. Next to a good price for sugar, planters clamoured for a plentiful supply of cheap slaves and got, so they complained, an inadequate supply at prices they could not afford. For this they blamed the monopolies created by Charles II: the Company of Royal Adventurers chartered in 1660, and its successor in 1672, the Royal African Company. In both companies James, as Duke of York and later as king, was prominent as shareholder and governor.[17] Critics of monopoly got nowhere. Jamaica, with the potential for rapid expansion, suffered most. And it was Jamaica which in 1687–8 underwent a period of exceptional misgovernment at the hands of Christopher Monck, second Duke of Albemarle. The king had sent him to govern Jamaica to be rid of him; Albemarle accepted in order to repair his private fortune, his first interest being the salvage of a Spanish treasure-ship from which he had already collected £50,000 and wanted more. As governor he did little right. He dismissed leading planters from office, interfered with elections and packed the assembly, courted popularity among the buccaneers and poor Irish, and gave appointments to 'tapsters, barbers and the like'. Jamaica was in turmoil, so much so that the last act of King James recorded in the colonial state papers was the repudiation of most of what his own governor had done. Albemarle's political temper, such as it was, and his recklessness might have qualified him to be a Jacobite leader; happily for Jamaica he died in October 1688 from an illness brought on by drinking to excess when celebrating the birth of the Prince of Wales. Sir Francis Watson, president of the colony's Council, took on the administration, proclaimed martial law, and continued to act in an arbitrary fashion. For Jamaica, certainly for the island's greater planters, the Revolution in England was nevertheless a relief.[18]

There was never any likelihood of the West Indian colonies violently opposing the line laid down by England. Edward Lyttelton, a most trenchant critic of Stuart colonial policy, put it so:

[16] K. G. Davies, *The Royal African Company* (1957), 366.
[17] Ibid. 103–4, 156.
[18] R. S. Dunn, *Sugar and Slaves* (London 1973), 160–2; *CSPC 1685–1688*, nos. 1940, 1943; *CSPC 1689–1692*, no. 50.

It is Obedience as well as Observance, that we owe eternally to England; and though our dear Mother prove never so unkind, we cannot throw off our Affection and Duty to her. We had rather continue our Subjection to England, in the sad condition we are in; then be under any others in the World, with the greatest Ease and Plenty.[19]

Lyttelton made a virtue of necessity. Barbados was already a slave-society, Jamaica, Antigua, St Kitts and Nevis moving in that direction. They grumbled ceaselessly and schemed for redress of grievances, but they took care not to rock the boat. Even at the worst of times Jamaica contemplated nothing like Bacon's rebellion in Virginia. Vulnerable to slave-mutinies and the disorderliness of poor Whites, the islands were exposed, too, to foreign assault. Barbados and the Leewards lay close to French colonies: Jamaica too near for comfort to the Spanish Main. All looked to the Royal Navy for protection of their shipping and coasts. Time increased this dependence. As slavery advanced island-militias dwindled; troops from England came to be needed for land-defence. The colonies usually built and paid for their own fortifications, but for artillery, gunpowder, and all warlike stores they had to rely on England.

The West Indies are not the place to search for conscience-Jacobites: the few on record can be quickly enumerated. In Barbados, still probably the richest of the colonies, the proclamation of William and Mary was celebrated 'in the most solemne, splendid and glorious manner' on Ascension Day 1689. Following a military parade and salutes fired from the forts and ships in harbour, 1,200 sat down to dinner with the governor, while his sister entertained 400 more. Good wines and choice liquors were served, delicate young hogs, sweetmeats, and fruits. There was Madeira and a meal for the soldiers, a banquet and a ball for the quality. Proceedings closed with a bonfire and fireworks. Two things only marred this magnificent display of loyalty. The first was a boycott by the Anglican clergy, all but one, 'on a mistake or scruple of conscience in reference to the oath of allegiance they had formerly taken to the late king'. No lasting harm was done, the governor assured the Earl of Shrewsbury. For the next two or three Sundays the island did without services and sermons; then the clergy had second thoughts and resistance ended. The other

[19] Lyttelton in Greene, *Great Britain and the American Colonies*, 100.

flaw in the Ascension Day proceedings, if anyone remembered, was that nine months earlier the same governor had used the identical formula—dinner, bonfire, fireworks and all—to mark the birth of the Prince of Wales.[20]

The only Nonjuror in the ranks of the trusty and well-beloved was made of sterner stuff. Sir Nathaniel Johnson had been promised the government of the Leeward Islands by Charles II, received it from James II, and arrived at his post in the summer of 1687. When news came of William's landing in England Johnson through a friend offered his services to James, following up with a letter to the king in person, unwisely sent via the French governor of Martinique. This correspondence led to a spiteful charge of treason in Nevis, but Johnson's patriotism was never doubted in Antigua, where he resided, nor, it seems, in London. His position was clearly stated. 'I am noe Roman Catholique,' he wrote in April 1689, 'but I think the Church of England teaches me the doctrine of non-resistance.'[21] In two powerful and dignified letters to the Lords of Trade he reported that according to orders he had proclaimed William and Mary, but declined to take the new oath of allegiance, and would, therefore, resign as soon as a successor could be found. On 15 July he wrote:

> I did and ever shall wish and pray for as heartily and sincerely as any man the establishment of the Protestant religion and the prosperitie and flourishing of my native country . . . it is my duty with the last drop of blood and mite of fortune to defend and maintain the English interest under any forme of government and in whatever hands against the attempts of all foreigne enemies whatsoever.[22]

James's embroilment with France left Johnson no honourable option but retirement. On 25 August he handed over his government to Christopher Codrington and sailed for the obscurity of South Carolina. It is difficult to decide whether his closing words suggest more of irony than perplexity. It cannot, he wrote:

> seeme strange that doubts and scruples in this matter should occurr to me in these remote parts of the world, where I want the advantages which those in England have of discoursing with learned and knowing men who perhaps might unriddle and better explaine to me what I have

[20] PRO CO 28, 37, fo. 9. See also *CSPC 1689–1692*, nos. 88, 155, 158.
[21] CO 152, 37, fo. 35.
[22] Ibid., fo. 82d.

hithertó apprehended to have bin the generale voice of the English Church and State.[23]

Catholics and Nonjurors were not a major problem in the West Indies; the Irish were, though most were poor and without influence. In conjunction with the French they could be, perhaps not formidable, but certainly a nuisance. The small island of Anguilla furnishes an example. Frenchmen from St Martin and St Bartholomew attacked and took it in the summer of 1689, installed an Irishman as governor, and administered an oath of allegiance to King James: three English ships had to be diverted there to recover the island. Later three Irishmen from Anguilla were hanged at Barbados for treason and rebellion.[24] More important was the loss of St Kitts, an island jointly settled by French and English and now partitioned between them. Here the Irish, on hearing of events in England, declared for King James, marched over to the French sector, and began to mount raids upon the English plantations. The English were forced to ship off their women and children and retire into a small fort. A French fleet arrived, and on 5 August 1689 the fort surrendered. The Irish, perhaps mindful of Drogheda, wanted the garrison put to the sword, but were restrained by the French commander. This little Jacobite victory in the New World was of no lasting consequence. The Irish in Antigua, Montserrat, and Nevis were disarmed, and St Kitts was recovered the following year.[25]

The West Indies gained something from the English Revolution, but not all they hoped for. James's tax on sugar was not repealed, but was allowed to expire at the end of the eight years for which it had been voted. The monopoly of the Royal African Company was not formally broken until 1698, but in practice private slave-traders were unmolested after 1689 on the African coast and in the ports and courts of the Caribbean. The authority of the great planters in Jamaica was restored during the long governorship of one of them, Sir William Beeston. But the Acts of Trade remained firmly in place and the wartime enhancement of sugar prices in

[23] Ibid., fo. 92. See also *CSPC 1689–1692*, nos. 88, 143, 256. On 18 June 1702, three months after the death of William III, Johnson accepted appointment as governor of North and South Carolina from the hands of the Lords Proprietors. The appointment was confirmed by Queen Anne in Council. See *CSPC 1702*, nos. 614, 615, 699–71, 692.

[24] *CSPC 1689–1692*, nos. 444, 548.

[25] Ibid., nos. 333, 345, 361, 397, 444.

London was offset, perhaps more than offset, by high costs of freight and insurance. The Revolution in the West Indies was glorious, in the sense of being bloodless, only if the casualties of William's War are omitted from the butcher's bill. All colonies suffered from French privateering and from the revival of piracy. Jamaica's misfortunes were especially grievous. Disorganized by the earthquake of 1692, the island was attacked by a large French force in 1694, which ravaged the south coast for six weeks, carrying off 1,300 slaves and burning 200 houses and 50 sugar-works.[26]

Such good intentions as William may have had towards the West Indies proved difficult to carry out. He was aware of the utility of colonies and of the part they might play in his fight against Louis XIV, but was distracted by the claims on his time of the war in Europe and faction at home. He grew impatient of the complexity of administering and defending so many separate little communities. An instance of his frustration is supplied by the fate of Monmouth's followers, premature anti-Jacobites, transported to the West Indies by the hundred in 1685. There, at King James's instance, local laws had been passed condemning the rebels to servitude, not far short of slavery, for ten years. At the Revolution they felt they had a claim on William's indulgence: freedom and a passage home were the least to be looked for. So William thought, and in July 1689 he gave orders for the repeal of the local laws. Twice in 1690 petitions were presented on behalf of the convicts showing that the orders had not been obeyed. At last, in September 1690, an explanation came from the governor of Barbados. The planters had paid good money for the services of the rebels, had trained them in the skills of sugar-making, and were loath to give them up. Besides, with a war on, every able-bodied man was needed for defence. The governor advised a reduction of the period of servitude from ten years to seven. William compromised: the local laws must be repealed; the convicts must not remain in servitude; but the colonies were left free to impose restrictions on the freedmen departing from their islands.[27] This or something like it seems to have taken place in Barbados, and probably elsewhere.

[26] Dunn, *Sugar and Slaves*, 163.
[27] *CSPC 1689–1692*, nos. 229, 698–700, 871, 968, 1183, 1193.

The Revolutions in North America

North America offered fewer opportunities of profit than the West Indies to the restored monarchy and until about 1680 was the scene of fewer initiatives on the Crown's part. In 1660 the king had little to do with America beyond appointing the governor of Virginia, the only Crown Colony on the mainland. The second, New Hampshire, did not come into existence until 1680 (for the purpose of blocking the northward extension of Massachusetts). For most of the reign of Charles II the old formula of colonization by private interest, with a royal charter as incentive, continued to be favoured. Connecticut and Rhode Island were given charters in 1662 and 1663; the Lords Proprietors of Carolina received a charter for their new colony in 1663; New York, conquered from the Dutch, was bestowed upon the Duke of York in 1664, the land between the Hudson and Delaware Rivers being amputated to form the separate proprietary colony of New Jersey; and in 1681 William Penn was given a charter for the colony he meant to call New Wales, but which the king named Pennsylvania, though by then the Crown had perceived the need to write more guarantees of royal supervision into the grants it made.

The creation or confirmation of so many chartered governments in America does not denote complete inactivity by the Restoration monarchy. After 1673 Crown-appointed customs officers began to appear in the colonies to try to enforce the Acts of Trade, particularly the Plantation Duties Act, which seemed to hold out some hope of financial benefit to the king. But, without royal governors to back them up and without admiralty courts to legitimize their seizure of smuggling vessels, the customs men had small success. In 1684 the king's collector of customs in Maryland was murdered by George Talbot, Lord Baltimore's nephew and the acting governor of the colony.[28] Relations between king's officers and proprietary governments were not generally as bad as this, but the need for the Crown to have a stronger presence in America was everywhere apparent. To some extent the colonies drew upon themselves the misfortune of Whitehall's attention. Bacon's rebellion in 1676—against a governor who for

[28] Lovejoy, *Glorious Revolution in America*, 84.

many years had run the colony for the profit of himself and friends—spurred the king to action. A force of a thousand men was sent from England to restore order; the soldiers arrived too late to be of service in Virginia and did not stay long there, but their presence made the point, for the first time, that England was ready and able to enforce royal government in Virginia. A new governor arrived in 1680 to apply West Indian methods. The House of Burgesses was persuaded to turn the annual duty of two shillings per hogshead on tobacco exported into a permanent royal revenue and steps were taken to make Virginia's quitrents, hitherto seldom collected, into a regular source of income for the king.[29] It is possible to believe that none of these things would have happened, but for Bacon's rebellion.

The rulers of Massachusetts called attention to themselves even more forcefully than Governor Berkeley and the Virginia rebels. In 1660 they enjoyed little less than complete independence from England: they openly refused to acknowledge that statutes made in England had application to Massachusetts; forbade appeals from the colony to English courts; issued their own coinage; persecuted those who dissented from their own brand of Calvinism; and imposed a religious test upon electors.[30] The king's ambitions here were not boundless; Massachusetts could have made good terms in the 1660s. But the Puritans acted as if their charter of 1629 was a divine gift and could never be revoked. Unlucky in their principal opponent in America, Edward Randolph, an able investigator and reporter who worked tirelessly against them, the rulers of Massachusetts declined compromise, and, when *quo warranto* proceedings were begun against the charter, failed to plead. In 1684 the unthinkable happened: the charter was annulled by the English Court of Chancery. When James came to the throne, therefore, Massachusetts needed a new government and a new definition of its place within the empire.

New York, too, needed attention. Since the conquest the Duke of York had ruled it more like a private estate than an English colony. No representative assembly was provided for and none

[29] W. F. Craven, *The Colonies in Transition* (New York and Evanston 1968), chs. 4 and 5.

[30] Greene, *Great Britain and the American Colonies*, 68–70; M. G. Hall, *Edward Randolph and the American Colonies* (Chapel Hill, NC 1960), 13, 25.

met: the laws were the 'duke's laws', a code of standing orders drawn up in 1665. The want of an assembly may not at first have much worried the Dutch population, but settlers on Long Island, English and Puritan, resented the deprivation. New York as a proprietary colony was not, however, a going concern. Even James's distaste for representative institutions turned out to be negotiable: in time financial exigency enforced a change of mind. With the duke's approval an assembly met in 1683, passing among other laws a remarkable Charter of Liberties, the nearest approach to a seventeenth-century American declaration of rights. Derived from the Petition of Right and English constitutional practice, the charter asserted liberty of conscience and worship for all Christians and a guaranteed place for the assembly in the making of law. Taxation without consent was forbidden, as were the billeting of troops and the imposition of martial law on civilians. James's first reactions were favourable and he gave his consent in October 1684. But a more radical resolution of New York's problems, and indeed of New England's too, was already being canvassed in London. James's approval was never forwarded to America and in 1686 the charter was disallowed by the Privy Council.[31] Instead of New York being assimilated to the model of New England, New England was to be assimilated to the model of New York.

It was to restructure the government of Massachusetts, define New York's status as a royal colony, and provide for the defence of the northern colonies against French and Indian attack, that James and his advisers styled the Dominion of New England, the boldest initiative to come from an English government in the colonial period.[32] At first the Dominion comprised Massachusetts, Plymouth, New Hampshire, and Maine; Rhode Island and Connecticut were added in 1686 and 1687, New York and New Jersey in 1688, the whole to form a single unit of government with a single head. Given time other provinces might have been added or a second dominion created for the colonies to the south. As it was in 1688 the Dominion stretched from the Canadian border, wherever that might be, to the Delaware, the colonies

[31] D. S. Lovejoy, 'Equality and Empire: The New York Charter of Libertyes, 1683', in S. N. Katz (ed.), *Colonial America* (Boston 1971), pp. 160–81.

[32] V. F. Barnes, *The Dominion of New England* (New Haven 1923; repr. New York 1960).

within it reduced to little more than administrative districts. Military power was vested in Sir Edmund Andros, commissioned captain-general and governor-in-chief, with authority 'to levy, arm, muster, command, or employ, all persons whatsoever residing within our said territory and dominion of New England, and as occasion shall serve, them to transfer from one place to another'.[33] Andros could also execute martial law, build castles, and fortify towns. To advise him and to make laws he was given a nominated council, picked from the component territories, afforced by three commissioners from England, one of them Edward Randolph. Andros was empowered to suspend any member of this council. To the power to make law was added the power 'to continue such taxes and impositions as are now laid and imposed upon the inhabitants' until such time as other taxes should be devised.[34] All public moneys were at the governor-general's disposal, to be issued on his warrant. Andros and the council could create courts of judicature and appoint judges, justices, and sheriffs throughout the Dominion. They could also hear appeals in suits worth more than £100 sterling; and in suits worth more than £300 sterling an appeal lay to the king in England. With power to pardon non-capital offences and stay execution of death sentences, Andros was little short of a viceroy.

The Dominion of New England should be viewed more as a blueprint than as a fully working system of government; but the actuality was frightening enough. Colonial assemblies no longer met. The apparatus of elections, built up over many years, and the participation of representatives in legislation and the granting of taxes, ceased to function not in New York alone, but throughout the Dominion. The new régime began to operate. Taxes were collected. Town-meetings were restricted to once a year. Grants of land for the future were made subject to quitrents, a burden New England had not hitherto borne. Worse, existing land-titles were marked for scrutiny, with the possibility of confirmation after composition.[35] Enough was attempted in the Dominion's short life, especially in Massachusetts and Plymouth, to suggest that such threats were to be taken seriously.

[33] From Andros's commission of 7 April 1688 printed in M. Jensen (ed.), *American Colonial Documents to 1776* (1969), 242.

[34] Ibid., p. 242.

[35] Barnes, *Dominion*, chs. 4 and 8.

James and his advisers expected the Dominion to function without serious opposition and they were proved more right than wrong. There was some resistance in Essex County, Massachusetts, to the imposition of customs and excise duties in 1687, led by the Revd John Wise of Ipswich; it was promptly dealt with, Wise and others arrested and fined, and the taxes collected.[36] Andros was given a company of one hundred men from England, the first redcoats to take station in Boston; Francis Nicholson, the Dominion's lieutenant-governor at New York, had about the same number.[37] These handfuls of men were useful for quelling occasional local disturbances and for stiffening the militia against Indian raids, and they could serve as a governor's bodyguard; but they cannot be described as a standing army. The absence of concerted opposition to the Dominion is attributable, not to the superior force at Andros's disposal, but to a want of confidence among the colonists to engage in treason. The Dominion had few friends. There were those in Massachusetts who had had enough of Puritan rule and wanted closer relations with England and lawful participation in England's commercial empire; but even they did not want to lose their old institutions and be ruled by one man.[38] Most New Englanders were simply aghast at the movement beneath their feet of hitherto firm ground. Collective action was out of the question. Several colonies had long-standing disputes with their neighbours; communications almost everywhere were poor; the great engine of unification at the time of the American Revolution—the press—did not exist. The *Boston News-Letter*, America's first newspaper, did not begin publication until 1704. Any colony contemplating resistance to King James and his Dominion of New England would have had to go it alone; none did.

The Revolution in England changed everything; without it the uprising in Boston would not have taken place. On 18 April 1689, with seeming spontaneity, crowds appeared in the streets with weapons in their hands.[39] In the course of the day more came in

[36] Ibid. 81–9; Craven, *Colonies in Transition*, 219–21.

[37] J. Shy, *Toward Lexington* (Princeton 1965), 25.

[38] B. Bailyn, *The New England Merchants in the Seventeenth Century* (New York 1964), 189–92.

[39] Accounts of the revolution in Lovejoy, *Glorious Revolution in America*, 237–45; M. G. Hall, L. H. Leder, M. G. Kammen, *The Glorious Revolution in America* (Chapel Hill, NC 1964), 38–54.

from the countryside. Some of the king's troops were away on Indian duty; when the fort was attacked the remainder capitulated. Andros, Randolph, and twenty-three other leading lights of the Dominion were secured and imprisoned. A king's ship in the harbour declared for the Prince of Orange.[40] Within hours the town was in the hands of the insurgents and a council of safety, comprising substantial citizens, had taken charge. Clearly there had been some planning: in the afternoon of the uprising the council issued a declaration of grievances signed by fifteen leading men including Bradstreet and Stoughton, two Winthrops, and Elisha Cooke, a good cross-section of opinion in Massachusetts. Some signers would probably have preferred to wait longer before declaring themselves. It was known for certain that the Prince of Orange had landed in England and probably known that James had fled; but of the outcome of those events Boston was ignorant. To that extent the town put itself at risk; and the declaration was correspondingly guarded. Despite a reference to the Popish Plot—a major event in Puritan mythology—and the catalogue of suffering under King James, the declaration stressed the submissiveness of Massachusetts: 'We bore all these, and many more such Things without making any attempt for any Relief.' Only now 'that the Almighty God hath been pleased to prosper the noble Undertaking of the Prince of Orange to preserve the three Kingdoms from the horrible brinks of Popery and Slavery' had the colony risen to follow England's lead.[41] With the overthrow of the Dominion of New England in its nerve-centre, and a new provisional government in place, Boston's uprising meets the requirements of most ordinary definitions of a revolution. Yet it was revolution over a safety net, begun only when a signal had been received suggesting it might be acceptable in England. It was also a nicely timed piece of opportunism. The unsophisticated in Boston may have feared that Andros would hold out against the Revolution in England, even perhaps deliver his government to the French; but that was unlikely. The real danger was that Andros would declare for William and Mary and be retained in place with all or part of the Dominion intact. With the exertion of minimum force by Boston that threat receded.

[40] *CSPC 1689–1692*, nos. 196, 305.
[41] Declaration printed in Hall *et al.*, *Glorious Revolution*, 42–6.

New York's revolution was a more complicated story, partly because of the mixed Dutch and English population, partly because what New England had suffered for two or three years New York had known for more than two decades. Grievances ran deep and were intensified by the emergence of landowners and merchants—Livingstons, Van Cortlandts, Bayards, Phillipses—who had attached themselves to the proprietary régime and prospered accordingly. In 1689 they were evicted from power and influence, at least for a time, giving to the revolution in New York a greater appearance of bitterness than in Massachusetts.[42]

New York was influenced by the example of Boston as well as by uncertainty about events in England. Boston's coup was known there not later than 26 April; by 4 May disorder was stirring among the English inhabitants of Long Island, where magistrates and militia officers were thrust out and replaced by others of the people's choice. Queen's County and Westchester followed suit.[43] Nicholson, Andros's deputy, tried to conceal what he knew of events in England, only adding to the dangerous confusion. By 15 May many of the militia had defected and were threatening to attack the fort in New York City; on 31 May they did so and, as in Boston, the depleted regulars gave in. Nicholson, aware of the fate that had overtaken Andros, fled on 11 June and made for home. A militia officer, Jacob Leisler, German by birth but thirty years in the colony, emerged as leader of the revolution. On 22 June, a copy having been obtained from Connecticut, the proclamation of William and Mary was publicly read at New York.[44] A committee of safety, dubiously elected by the counties, met at the end of June, appointed an agent to wait upon the king, and made Leisler captain of the fort, in effect commander of the militia. A loyal address was dispatched to the king and queen asserting that what the militia had done was solely in response to William's declaration; but neither this, nor Leisler's subsequent letters to England, nor the mission of Joost Stoll to London, brought the recognition Leisler needed; nor indeed a response of any kind.[45] Leisler was not the Masaniello his enemies depicted.

[42] Lovejoy, *Glorious Revolution in America*, 295.

[43] *CSPC 1689–1692*, nos. 104, 121.

[44] Ibid., no. 241.

[45] Address, ibid., no. 221. Stoll was appointed on 15 August to go to London, ibid., no. 353. Leisler and the committee of safety wrote many letters to the king and persons in his government but received no answer. There was not the same

New York was not badly ruled in the two years the provisional government lasted. But without a favourable word from King William, Leisler was doomed. He tried to convince himself and others that a letter addressed to Nicholson, which he received and opened, implied royal recognition; but of course it did not. He began to correspond with the governors of other colonies, Bermuda and Barbados as well as Maryland and New England, as if this would in some way legitimize his position. Some replied; Bermuda even sent him twenty barrels of gunpowder.[46] But when he summoned a meeting of governors to New York to concert defence measures against the French, only Massachusetts, Connecticut, and Plymouth, sent representatives. William appointed his own governor of New York in September 1689, but Colonel Henry Sloughter did not reach his government until March 1691. Leisler foolishly tried to put off the hand-over of power: a scuffle took place in which the militia killed two of the king's troops and wounded others. Leisler and seven others were tried for treason and found guilty: Leisler and his closest associate were hanged, the remainder pardoned. Possibly justice miscarried: four years later the English parliament reversed the attainder and restored the estates of the dead men to their heirs. With these executions New York's revolution ended, but the colony continued for years to be divided between Leislerian and anti-Leislerian factions.[47]

Maryland's was the only revolution which might have taken place independently of events in England. The colony suffered from most of the troubles that had led, in Virginia, to Bacon's rebellion: low price of tobacco, restriction of office to the governor's favourites, the collection of excessive fees, pressure to pay taxes in cash instead of kind, want of confidence in the colony's handling of Indian problems; but in Maryland there were additional irritants.[48] Lord Baltimore, the proprietor, had a Stuart sense of his own prerogative, ruling his colony in person and

refusal to correspond with the self-appointed provisional governments in Massachusetts and Maryland.

[46] These letters are of interest. See, for example, ibid., no. 211, a letter of 26 June 1689 from two Connecticut deputies urging Leisler to proceed against Papists and offering help against 'intestine or foreign enemies'.

[47] Craven, *Colonies in Transition*, 240, 280.

[48] M. G. Kammen, 'The Causes of the Maryland Revolution of 1689', *Maryland Historical Magazine* (1960), pp. 295–305.

sometimes acting in arbitrary fashion. He did not, like the Duke of York, dispense with an elected assembly, but did what he could to lessen its representative character and reduce its powers. In 1670 he restricted the franchise, hitherto enjoyed by all free men, to freeholders of land and those with personal possessions worth £40. In 1676 he claimed the right to choose two members to serve in the assembly out of the four elected by each constituency. And in 1684 he stretched his veto on legislation to include the nullification of laws passed and consented to years earlier.[49] Such things were hard to bear from the proprietor in person; when he left the colony in 1684 it was harder still to accept them from his deputies. What made revolution in Maryland easier to contemplate was the awareness that James himself was losing patience with the charter. The murder of the royal customs officer in 1684 could not be passed over and on 30 April 1686 the king's orders were issued for *quo warranto* proceedings to begin. This did not mean that James had irrevocably decided to put an end to the rule of the Calverts, but it must have weakened proprietary government in the colony.

Much of what happened in Maryland can be explained without reference to religion: in 1689 a group of 'outs' displaced the 'ins'. Religion, nevertheless, came into it at last. The proprietor and most of his officers were Catholics; Protestants, perhaps a majority by ten to one, were not persecuted, but neither were they promoted. There were Catholic schools in the colony and a handful of Jesuits in residence: in America, where fear of Popery sometimes passed into paranoia, these things could not but be provocative.

The colony was certainly ripe for trouble at the beginning of 1689. News came of William's landing, though nothing official. The government's response was to call in all militia weapons for repair, in effect disarming the Protestants. Rumour as elsewhere played its part: here it was a canard that the Seneca Indians had been hired to perpetrate a massacre of the Protestants.[50] Had orders come from the proprietor to proclaim William and Mary, probably they would have been obeyed; but they did not come.

[49] Hall *et al.*, *Glorious Revolution*, 160–2, print 'The Grievances of the Lower House, 22 November 1688'; also, at pp. 179–86, 'Mariland's Grievances Wiy They Have Taken Up Arms'. See also Lovejoy, *Glorious Revolution in America*, 76–89.

[50] Lovejoy, *Glorious Revolution in America*, 258.

Baltimore in London duly ordered the proclamation, but his messenger died before leaving England. A second was dispatched but never arrived.[51] By May 1689 fear and uncertainty were mixed to the point of explosion. John Coode, a planter–lawyer of Rabelaisian speech, a known maker of trouble for the Calverts and a classic 'out', formed a Protestant association and in July marched on St Mary's, the capital. The government surrendered at once. Coode issued a declaration, somewhat exaggerated, to show 'how the *jus regale* is improved here and made the proroga-tive of his lordship', how Protestants had suffered, and how the rulers of the colony had conspired to deny the people the fruits of the Revolution in England.[52] An elected assembly met on 22 August and declared for William and Mary; the proclamation finally took place in September. Maryland's revolution succeeded to the extent that the proprietary rule of the Calverts was suspended and a royal governor appointed to the colony in 1691. The charter was not, however, annulled and in 1715, when the fourth Lord Baltimore had quit the Church of Rome and joined the Church of England, his colony was given back to him.

The Revolutionary Settlement in America

There was no 'revolutionary settlement' for the colonies in the sense of a general revision of the laws and practices for governing the empire established in the reign of Charles II. No new definition was proclaimed of the rights of colonists. There was not even, on England's part, a repudiation of King James's innovations in the colonies, let alone rejection of the officials who had imposed the Dominion upon New England. William Blathwait, secretary of the Lords of Trade since 1679, served King William as he had served King Charles and King James and lived to serve Queen Anne as a member of the new Board of Trade.[53] Francis Nicholson was made lieutenant-governor of Virginia in 1690, where he enforced the Acts of Trade and collected the quitrents, drummed up support for the College of William and Mary, and recreated

[51] Lovejoy, *Glorious Revolution in America*, 264.

[52] Hall *et al.*, *Glorious Revolution*, 171.

[53] G. A. Jacobsen, *William Blathwait, A Late Seventeenth Century Administrator* (New Haven 1932), pp. xi–xii.

the Olympic Games. From 1694 to 1698 he was royal governor of Maryland, then returned to Virginia for seven more years. Confidence in him was such that he was fetched out of retirement in 1720 to be the first royal governor of South Carolina. Plainly neither his reputation as Andros's auxiliary, nor the memory of his ignominious flight from New York in 1689, did the slightest harm to his career.[54] Andros himself, after ten months' close imprisonment by the provisional government of Massachusetts, was returned to England in 1690 and acquitted of all charges of misgovernment. In 1692 he took over from Nicholson as governor of Virginia, serving there until retirement in 1698. Joseph Dudley, assistant to Andros at Boston from 1686 to 1689, was back in office in the colony by 1691 and rose in time to be governor of Massachusetts. Randolph, the most industrious if not the most influential upholder of the Dominion, was made surveyor-general of customs in North America in 1690, a job which suited his talent for scheming, meddling, and disputing with other officials. He kept it until his death in 1703.[55]

William's colonial policies were flexible enough not only to employ notorious standard-bearers of the Dominion of New England, but to borrow some of its features. That experiment, one must remember, had its positive side: it was not just an elaborate means of punishing Massachusetts and hamstringing New York. One notion behind it was that the colonies of North America were unable or unwilling to concert measures for their own defence: some kind of supra-colonial authority seemed to be necessary to compel them to act together. Hence the power given to Andros over the colonial militias. William made no move to reconstitute the Dominion in its old form, but, as a soldier whose first interest was the war with France, he was unlikely to overlook any device for making America's war-effort more effective. Unity of military command was one such device. In 1692 Benjamin Fletcher, already governor of New York, was commissioned royal governor of Pennsylvania to try to bring the Quakers to do their duty, and was given at the same time command of Connecticut's militia and part of New Jersey's.[56] In

[54] S. S. Webb, 'The Strange Career of Francis Nicholson', *William and Mary Quarterly*, 3rd ser., 23 (1966), pp. 524 ff.

[55] Hall, *Edward Randolph*, 135 ff.

[56] Craven, *Colonies in Transition*, 243, 256.

1697, following some signal failures by the colonies in both attack and defence, the Earl of Bellomont was made governor of three colonies, Massachusetts (with which Plymouth had been incorporated in 1691), New Hampshire, and New York, and was appointed to command the militias of three more, Connecticut, Rhode Island, and New Jersey. He was also made vice-admiral of all six colonies.[57] The experiment was not a success and was dropped in 1701, perhaps an indication that in this respect the Dominion of New England would not have succeeded either. Queen Anne's war in America, like King William's, was fought chiefly by one colony, Massachusetts.

The 'Glorious Revolution' was a turning-point for the colonies in style more than substance, William and his advisers revealing a patience and discretion lacking in the 1680s. Then there had been the headlong assault on colonial charters, beginning with *quo warranto* proceedings against Bermuda in 1679 and culminating in the overthrow of the Massachusetts patent. Like actions were started or threatened against Connecticut, Rhode Island, Pennsylvania, and Maryland, deferred not from a change of heart, but because the attorney-general's office could not handle so much business at once.[58] After the Revolution the practice of trying colonial charters in the courts was given up. For a time there was uncertainty in which direction the new government would go. In 1690 Connecticut and Rhode Island were allowed to resume their old charters, which had never been invalidated in a court in England. To the end of the colonial period these two 'corporate' colonies elected their own governors and appointed their own judges and officers. Save for the irritating presence of customs men they remained astonishingly free of supervision by Whitehall. They did not submit their laws for royal approval; they seldom corresponded with either the Secretary of State or the Board of Trade. From time to time there was talk in London of turning them into royal colonies—for example, when Rhode Island in the 1730s flooded New England with paper currency—but no action was taken. They were, by a long way, the greatest gainers by the accession of William and Mary.

57 *CSPC 1696–1697*, nos. 909–11; *CSPC 1697–1698*, no. 709.

58 R. S. Dunn, 'The Downfall of the Bermuda Company: A Restoration Farce', *William and Mary Quarterly*, 3rd ser., 20 (1963), pp. 487–97; Philip S. Haffenden, 'The Crown and the Colonial Charters, 1675–1688', ibid., 15 (1958), 310.

Massachusetts fared less well, despite the best efforts of Increase Mather, sent to London in 1688 to try to negotiate Massachusetts out of the Dominion of New England, who nimbly turned himself into a negotiator with King William for a reissue of the charter of 1629. Early indications were favourable, but there was never the probability of William's advisers letting him go to such lengths. Mather, watching the passage of an Act for restoring the charter of the City of London, tried to interest parliament in his own application, but failed to make progress.[59] Perhaps Boston's violence in 1689 and the long imprisonment of Andros played some part in this failure, though there is no specific evidence to this effect; more likely the long-standing reputation of Massachusetts for independence with those who advised William moved him to insist on change. A new charter was granted in 1691, a compromise less generous than the old and displeasing to Puritan diehards, but proving in time too generous for the comfort of colonial administrators in the eighteenth century. In the same year Maryland's charter was suspended and the colony given a royal governor, as was Pennsylvania in 1692, though both proprietors eventually recovered their colonies. William's advisers did not, however, take long to arrive at the same conclusions as their predecessors. Whether the matter was the enforcement of the Acts of Trade, or the suppression of piracy, or the mobilization of America to fight the French, the chartered colonies were found to be an obstacle to efficiency. Yet there was no stampede to the lawcourts. In 1697 the Board of Trade hit on the idea of inviting parliament to take over the problem and at last in 1701 a bill was brought forward for reuniting all the proprietary and corporate colonies to the Crown.[60] On and off the proposal was before parliament until 1706, never commanding quite enough support to pass.[61] The Crown's final resort, having given up the courts and failed in parliament, was to negotiate as many of the charters as possible out of existence or at least into a state of suspension. New Jersey became a royal colony in 1702, the Bahamas in 1717, South Carolina in 1720, and North Carolina

[59] K. B. Murdock, *Increase Mather: The Foremost American Puritan* (Cambridge, Mass. 1925), 232.

[60] *CSPC 1697–1698*, no. 265i.

[61] A. G. Olson, 'William Penn, Parliament, and Proprietary Government', in *William and Mary Quarterly*, 3rd ser., 18 (1961), pp. 182 ff.

in 1729: a laborious process and feasible only in respect of the proprietary colonies. The chartered corporate colonies of New England were not tackled at all.

Most of the major changes after 1694 were intended to improve general management of the empire. At the centre a new body, the Commissioners for Trade and Plantations (Board of Trade) was instituted in 1696 for collecting and storing information about the colonies and for advising the Privy Council and parliament on matters referred to it. On the subject of most general interest to the colonies, the Acts of Trade, William's reign saw no relaxation but rather measures for better enforcement. In 1696 a new Navigation Act was passed codifying and clarifying the existing laws and strengthening them in some particulars. In 1697 vice-admiralty courts, which had proved their effectiveness against illicit trade in the time of the Dominion, were ordered to be established in every colony, the intention if not the effect being to eliminate the chief saboteur of British commercial policy in America, the colonial jury.[62] In England the revolutionary settlement may have curbed the royal prerogative, but in the colonies there was perceptible movement in the opposite direction.

England and the colonies were not brought closer by common suffering at the hands of James II; nor were they united by equally shared benefits from his departure. The entrenchment of parliament in English constitutional practice did not mean a like entrenchment of representative assemblies in the colonies; and the English parliament, given time, showed itself to be almost as great a threat to American independence as the Stuart monarchy. Lords and Commons in England gained complete control over the making of laws, the Crown not only losing what right it may have possessed to suspend law, but eventually ceasing to exercise its veto on bills passed by both houses. Nothing like that happened in the colonies: bills passed by both houses were frequently vetoed by the governor; and should the governor, as sometimes happened, be bribed or browbeaten into consent, the Privy Council was there to disallow offensive Acts. Outlawing a standing army in peacetime without parliament's consent did nothing for

[62] In 1680–2 in New England Randolph commenced suits against 36 ships for breach of the Acts of Trade: 2 were won, without jury; the rest were lost, with jury. In the time of the Dominion of New England, when a vice-admiralty court was available, the success rate was better. See Hall, *Edward Randolph*, 57–60, 101.

the House of Burgesses in Virginia or the House of Representatives in Massachusetts; the redcoats would be stationed anyway. The Triennial Act of 1694 had no application to the colonies: American assemblies had to struggle for their own rights and privileges. That they were successful in learning how to outwit royal governors owed no more to the English revolutionary settlement than that it set new marks for the Americans to aim at.

It would be presumptuous to think that William invaded England to save parliamentary institutions or the rule of law; doubly so to think that he came to rescue New England from James's despotic Dominion. Not even the Americans can have believed that: their joy at the event had at least as much hope in it as confidence. As David Ogg wrote: 'In the years 1678–1688 William was an absolute monarch in all but name.'[63] Such experience and the dispositions formed by it did not fall from him like an old suit of clothes when he became a king in England. Never a champion of the rights of his colonial subjects, when New York recovered its elected assembly and re-enacted something like the Charter of Liberties of 1683, William left it unconfirmed for five years, then disallowed it just as James had done before him.[64]

An eyewitness of the revolution in Massachusetts, writing two months after the event, deplored the resort to violence: 'Had we truly regarded our Country and the enterprise of the Prince of Orange we should have remained satisfied, and not have anticipated by force and violence what might have been given us with mildness and justice.'[65] But would it have been given? The revolutions in America proved to be without relevance to much of what came after; but not necessarily to all. There was little predetermined about William's colonial policies in the months after he became king. The possibility cannot be ruled out of features of the Dominion of New England being left in place. Had Boston stayed quiet, Andros would have had the chance to make an early peace with the new government, and might have retained his appointment. Boston's uprising on 18 April 1689 did not exactly present the king with a *fait accompli*, but it served some kind of notice that, while Massachusetts could help the

[63] D. Ogg, *Europe in the Seventeenth Century* (4th edn., 1946), 434.
[64] Lovejoy, *Glorious Revolution in America*, 354–63.
[65] *CSPC 1689–1692*, no. 181.

cause of war with France (and did so), it could also be a perfect nuisance. The prudent course for the colony was to trample on the Dominion when the opportunity was there; the prudent course for the king was to effect a compromise between his own requirements and the expectations of his new subjects. In Massachusetts, as elsewhere, William gave notice that the difference between his predecessor and himself was more in political understanding than in political ideology.

8

The Significance of 1688: Some Reflections on Whig History

J. G. A. POCOCK

I

'WELL, doctor,' William of Orange is said to have remarked to Gilbert Burnet, as they stood on Brixham beach on 5 November 1688, 'what do you think of predestination now?' The jest, if it was one, might be taken as referring to the extraordinary series of physical events which had brought them where they were—to the multiple changes of the Protestant wind, blowing them east, west, and east again; or it might refer to the no less extraordinary series of contingencies in Church, State, and dynasty which had led to William's being invited to England and had made it worth his while to set out thither; or finally, it might be taken as indicating that neither William nor Burnet at that moment could have had the least idea what was about to happen. With the benefit of hindsight, we know; and we know also that William had done his best to ensure that some things should happen which did in fact happen. We are therefore tempted to see the outcome of William's expedition as a foregone conclusion, which is to know more about predestination than William or Burnet did. A warning against 'Whig history' in a very crude sense may therefore be uttered at the outset. William was a careful planner, but careful planners in military and political affairs are at the same time very daring gamblers, and he was engaged on a gamble of a quite breathtaking nature.

He was in Tor Bay at the head of a powerful military expedition, involving a number of the regiments which he commanded as captain-general of the United Provinces. He was there because a group of powerful English magnates had asked him to come; he was there in pursuit of his wife's dynastic interests and his own;

and he was there in pursuit of reason of state, as this declared the interests of the House of Orange and the Republic of the Netherlands—which might be, but were not necessarily regarded as, identical. In this last respect, the descent upon England was, or turned out to be, an enormously dangerous but successful fling in the political and military struggle against the king of France; the Sicilian expedition of the wars of the Grand Alliance, which transformed their nature by extending their scope and succeeded where its analogue had failed. But the first and second sets of reasons for William's presence in Tor Bay might well have moved a French statesman, on hearing that the Prince of Orange intended to set out for England, to the thought that if the prince meant to involve himself in the affairs of the wild and unmanageable kingdoms beyond the Channel and the North Sea, he should by no means be prevented from doing so. These reasons were such as to create a strong probability that William would involve himself in an English civil war, swelling into another war of the three kingdoms of Britain and Ireland, which would absorb and destroy his resources and from which he might never return.

England in 1688 had not emerged from the conditions which had produced one such series of civil wars between forty and fifty years previously, and had nearly renewed them on two occasions in the most recent decade. These conditions arose from instabilities within the ruling structure of the Established Church, which compromised the role of the monarchy and the lay and clerical governing élites. Some of these problems were constitutional in character, recognized as problems in the relations between monarchy, law, and parliament; others, while inseparable from the former, were rather problems in the location of sovereignty, and had come to pass in the grim realities of civil war in 1642 and temporary dissolution of the historical structure of government in 1649—two memories which did more than anything else to determine the political consciousness of the governing classes (to look no further) in 1688. All knew that there had been a civil war which nobody had desired; all were determined that it should not happen again, but were at the same time aware that such a determination might not be enough to prevent it recurring; and in 1688 matters were in such a state that civil war was being risked again.

The restoration of the monarchy in 1660 had been followed by a restoration of the royal and episcopal church in 1662, but the relation between the two had not been stabilized. As well as a small Catholic minority in England, a rather larger one in the Highlands of Scotland, and a partly subjugated Catholic majority in Ireland, there was in England a significant group of semi-organized Dissent; and though this last was far from militant in its politics, the sons of Charles the Martyr—who were not reliable witnesses to the church for which their father had died—were tempted to exploit the opportunities which they saw in this degree of ecclesiastical fragmentation. Alliances between clergy and parliamentary gentry had on occasion been formed to pull the monarchy back into its necessary alliance with the Church; but these had forced groups active in politics to choose between their visceral Anglicanism, which presented Church and king as the sole guarantors of the ruling order, and the equally visceral erastianism which impelled them to reject the clergy as arbiters in matters of state. Some had carried mistrust of both monarchy and clergy so far as to attack the alliance between the two, and this tension had been vastly exacerbated by the prospect that the successor to the crown and its headship of the Church might himself be a Catholic. Though the attempt to force the Crown to review its relationship with the Church was known to be a recipe for civil war, the prospect of a Popish successor had carried England within recognizable distance of such a war in 1679–81 and had led to an actual attempt to renew it in 1685. Each time, however, the prospect of civil war had brought about renewed support of Church and king even under a Popish successor, and this had been reinforced by the assurance that the succession to James II was guaranteed to his Protestant daughters and their consorts. Threatening as the actions of James appeared, therefore, they were endurable until a major breach between the king and the bishops coincided with the birth of a male heir to the throne. The public causes professed in the invitation to William to present himself in England, and in his printed Declarations on doing so, were therefore dynastic, in the sense that the heir (being intolerable) was supposed to be spurious and the interest of William's wife in the succession at risk; ecclesiastical, in the sense that the monarchy was seen to be engaged in an attack on the Church of which it was head; and political, in the sense that William was calling for the meeting of a free parliament to settle these and other issues, including James's attempts to pack parliaments so that they would obey him.[1] Any one of these problems might have to be resolved by the sword in civil war, and here were sufficient reasons why William should bring an army with him; but his mind was engaged, so far as we know it, by thoughts of European, not English, war, and the exact calculations of his reason of state are a fascinating enigma. Perhaps he was placing his reliance on predestination; which would be to say, in other words current at the time, that he was making an appeal to heaven.

John Locke had written the scenario of such an appeal a few years before, and it had been a scenario of civil war. The concluding chapters of his *Treatises of Government*, written when desperate associates of Shaftesbury were turning to thoughts of violence after their defeat in parliament, envisage a people determining that their government is in a state of war against them, decreeing that government to be dissolved, making their appeal to heaven, and resuming the power to place the government in new hands or continue it in old, as they should see fit. Every one of these phrases—dissolution of government, appeal to heaven, reversion of power to the people—carried as its normal connotation the kind of thing that had happened in 1642, when the subjects had been obliged to draw swords against one another, and in 1649, when they had been obliged by the collapse of the main structures of government to face the dreadful necessity of constituting a new régime by deciding where to yield their submission and give their allegiance. Locke was exposing himself like Sidney to the penalties of treason, by imagining and compassing a civil war that had not happened yet; and this aside, he was inhabiting the world of Thomas Hobbes—of the frontispiece to *Leviathan*, in which dissent over the location of authority in Church and State can plunge a kingdom into civil war, and this condition can be ended only by replacing the appeal to heaven by the yielding up of the subject's sword to a sovereign who can exercise it for him. But it took more than the free gift of the sword to constitute a sovereign who could keep it in his hands. The English had attempted the Hobbesian solution in 1660, when they solemnly declared that power over the militia was forever vested in the

[1] For these see J. R. Jones, *The Revolution of 1688 in England* (New York 1972) and *Country and Court: England 1658–1714* (1978).

king; Charles I had posthumously triumphed in one of the things he had chiefly fought for in 1642; but a Leviathan who fumbled with the crozier he held in his left hand might press back upon his unwilling subjects the sword he should have retained in his right. That was the menace of a Popish successor, and it was nearer happening in 1688 than when Locke was writing in the early 1680s. And Hobbes's readers in 1651, when *Leviathan* was published and Charles II was leading his army towards Worcester, had known that Hobbes offered no advice on what was to be done when two rivals for the role of Leviathan were claiming the subject's allegiance with their swords drawn. That too was the condition of England from 5 November 1688, when William of Orange landed his army, to the second flight of James II at the end of December.

The success of William's expedition must be measured by the proposition either that what happened between those dates was not an English civil war; or that if it was one, as Edmund Burke contended a hundred and one years later, it ended without battle on English soil and without the disintegration of the ruling élites into groups compelled to draw sword against one another, as had happened in the well-remembered catastrophe of 1642. I have tried in another place to emphasize how very narrowly we must see civil war as having been averted;[2] how very easily James II, by fighting one inconclusive battle, might have rendered the military issue uncertain and compelled his subjects to take decisions about an armed contest for sovereignty. When his father left London and Westminster for York in 1642, when he exposed his person in battle at Edgehill, when he left Oxford for Newcastle in 1646, when he left Hampton Court for Carisbrooke in 1647, he was on every occasion dramatizing the fact of civil war; he was dramatizing his own indispensability to legitimate government and finding men willing to hazard war in his support. The tactic had proved disastrous but in the end effective; the monarchy had won the civil wars. But when James abandoned his capital in 1688, he did not throw himself into the heart of his

[2] J. G. A. Pocock, 'The Fourth English Civil War: Dissolution, Desertion and Alternative Histories in the Glorious Revolution', *Government and Opposition*, 23 (1988), 151–66. It is conventional to count the Worcester campaign of 1651 as a civil war, but not the Sedgemoor campaign of 1685; if this were disregarded, William's campaign would become the fifth.

own kingdoms or yield himself with conscious dignity into the hands of his adversaries. He took refuge at the court of the king of France, thus going far towards converting a civil war into a foreign one; and by such actions as the jettisoning of the Great Seal, he did much to declare that he had tried but failed to dissolve a government capable, since he compelled it to the necessity, of functioning without him and replacing him.

What may be Whiggishly asserted about these events is that they expelled the reality, though not by any means the threat, of civil war from English experience, and in so doing went far to constitutionalize English perceptions of drastic political change. Civil wars are fought among those who know what civil sovereignty is, but are in conflict over where it is located and how it is to be exercised; they may find that they have destroyed it and are in disagreement over how it is to be restored. The English of the 1640s had faced themselves with these terrible questions, and John Locke was envisaging that they might confront them again. When James II fled to France he kept the location of sovereignty an open question; he retained a very good case for claiming that he was lawful king and his son his lawful heir, and that the dispossession of both was deeply fraudulent.

We used to hold that his case was so good that it could be answered only by a revolutionary restatement of the nature of kingship, though the great Whig writers Burke and Macaulay were at pains to point out that no such restatement was ever promulgated. But James abandoned, or never exercised, the weapon of civil war; by not waging war within the kingdom he lost the power to oblige his subjects to choose between two claimants to sovereignty, each with his own definition of what it was and each at the subject's door to demand his allegiance. In consequence the English of 1688 did not re-enter, and as things turned out they had forever left, the world of politics as Hobbes and Locke had known it.

In 1642 the powerful sovereignty built up by the Tudors had split apart, but retained the strength to force subjects into civil war against their wills. In the new year of 1689 the English found the edifice of sovereignty deserted by its king, but themselves possessed of most of the resources for continuing it in existence. There had been a desertion but not a dissolution; the people had neither declared nor discovered the government to be dissolved, and if they had done anything it had been to frustrate the king's ineffective attempts to dissolve it. 'Government' could therefore be defined less as 'sovereignty' than as 'constitution', and those few who took notice of the *Treatises of Government* which Locke now anonymously published could respond that there had been no dissolution of government because the constitution retained its ancient form and force, so that all which had been done was authorized by the necessity of preserving it. This view of the significance of 1688 was that retained by aristocratic Whigs and Revolution Tories thereafter; the only question contested by a few was whether the constitution reserved to the people or their representatives a power, not to dissolve the government, but to divest of power those guilty of seeking to dissolve it.

We have reached a point where it is necessary to walk carefully; paths lead from it in a number of directions, and we may construct either Whiggish or narrowly revisionist histories if we follow one of them to the exclusion of the rest, or presume that one of them is the main road and the others mere by-paths. The flight of James reinforced constitutionalism, in the sense that it left the parliamentary and legal fabric in a position to remedy its own predicament; and for this reason it came to be held that the Revolution of 1688, precisely because it was not a dissolution, was a victory for the ancient constitution, that James's misdeeds could be defined as transgressions against it, and English history before and after 1688 could be written in terms of the constitution's persistence in the teeth of Stuart and Cromwellian attempts to overthrow it. The Whig need to distance 1688 from 1649 produced a historiography of the civil wars which vindicated the parliamentary cause while condemning the regicide; and republican, and much of what we call 'Whig' history came to be written in these terms from Rapin de Thoyras to Macaulay, with some notable dissents from David Hume. But though there came, rather momentously, to be a reading of English politics which was both constitutionalist and consensualist, to say this is not to say that there came to be a consensus about either the workings of the constitution or the claim that the problems of the kingdom had been solved in constitutionalist terms. There is plenty of evidence to the contrary, and all I am claiming here is that the non-recurrence of civil war and armed conflict over sovereignty made it massively more possible than it had been before to interpret English politics and history in these terms.

There continued to be a radical Whig reading of the events of 1688, though if we are to say so we shall have to decide what significance to attribute to its survival. Few if any argued that the Revolution had constituted a Lockean dissolution of government and reversion of power to the people; this scenario of revolution, though invented in England, has never been practised there—except in the deeply counter-revolutionary cases of 1649, or perhaps 1659—and this is one reason why it is difficult to put forward a populist theory of British as opposed to American democracy. But we can find those—and Locke may have been one of them—who thought that such a dissolution ought to have occurred in 1688 or 1689, and regretted the lost opportunity to conduct one. There were the originals of the eighteenth-century commonwealthmen, who thought the opportunity should have been seized to institute frequently summoned parliaments and lessen the patronage powers of the Crown. Locke does not seem to have been among these, but he did publish the *Treatises* to promote the view that William III (he does not here mention Mary) owed his crown to the choice of the people, the only foundation of all lawful government. This may or may not make the monarchy as elective or conditional as it sounds; it need not entail a dissolution by the people of the entire fabric of government (which is what the text of the *Second Treatise* necessarily envisages) but merely a power reserved to the people to 'cashier' (as Richard Price was to put it) a monarch guilty of misgovernment and choose another in his place; so that any monarch ruling with the support of his people may be said to rule with their consent and by their approbation and election. What is paradoxical about this assertion—voiced recurrently by a minority throughout the century, beginning with the publication of Locke's *Treatises*—is that it rests on an implicit denial that there had been civil war in 1688. The flight of James had irretrievably constitutionalized the English perception of revolution itself; the deposition of a king and the substitution of his successors, the dissolution of a régime if not of a constituted form of government, could now be seen as taking place bloodlessly, within the fabric of an ancient constitution, and without imposing on the people the savage choices about allegiance and sovereignty, violence and submission, under which they had suffered in 1642 and 1649. It now became by degrees open to the English to believe that they could have revolution but have it painlessly; a belief so remote from their experience in the seventeenth century that it took another hundred years to form it after 1689.

There is a posturing theatricality about Wilkes and even Paine reminding George III of the fate of his predecessors, and Burke poured out his wrath on Richard Price because he could see that revolution had become, as it has remained, a spectator sport for middle-class intellectuals, tempted to believe that they can proclaim governments illegitimate without anyone getting hurt in the process. It took a long time for this sort of left to take shape in British political culture, but 1688 is among its preconditions.

From the existence of a commonwealth left, populist and quasi-republican, operating on the flank of a rather complacent constitutionalism, we now move right, into areas where there was nothing to be complacent about, because the legitimacy of the régime traceable to 1688 was far from being clearly accepted. Much emphasis is now very rightly given by historians to two persistent instabilities in post-Revolution England: the inability of a great many churchmen to accept that the secular power could change the Supreme Governor of the Church of England even when that governor was an aggressively Popish successor; and the consequent survival of a Jacobitism which held at the least (and it sometimes held a good deal more) that the Williamite and Hanoverian régimes were a government *de facto* and that authority *de jure* resided with the exiled family, against the day when it should please that family to return to the Church of which they were lawfully at the head.

Let us accept, then, that the tensions and cleavages left behind by the Revolution were extraordinarily deep; that they included a succession of rulers insecure on their throne and a Church unsure about its establishment; that what has been called 'the rage of party', persisting through the Hanoverian accession and beyond it, can quite rightly be described as the continuation of civil war by other means. Civil war did not break out again, in the sense that Englishmen did not again draw swords against one another in a dissolution of effectively sovereign government; to use Roman language in an Anglocentric perspective, the wars in Ireland and Scotland down to 1745 were not civil but social wars, taking place in associated but inferior provinces of the English imperium. It is of course true, as Thomas Hobbes pointed out, that the state of war is not identical with the day of battle, but consists in 'a known disposition thereto', present all the time 'in the nature of weather';[3] and in that sense a disposition to civil war existed in England as long as there was a potentially active Jacobitism, which we now know was longer than we used to think. But Hobbes's formula does not go to the heart of the seventeenth-century experience of civil war, which was that men fight each other not merely because there is no sovereign to stop them, but because an existing sovereignty has disintegrated and they must fight each other in the effort to reconstruct it. Englishmen had fought each other in this setting in 1642 and 1648; they had not had to do so in 1688.

One reason widely recognized why they had not had to do so was the rise of what was known as the standing army, consisting of permanently embodied regiments financed and controlled by a state. The first English civil war had been fought the way it was because no such army then existed in England, and the relations between king and parliament had reached a point where each set out to mobilize the county militias against the other; Leviathan could not draw the sword without returning it into the hands of the subject. But in 1688 William landed at the head of a force of professional regiments and James advanced to meet him at the head of another. Because they did not come to battle, the warlike activity of the southern élites was limited to giving political support to one army rather than the other. In the Midlands and the North the Earls of Devonshire and Danby were in rebellion, but there too the sword was not drawn in civil war. In the frontier kingdoms of Scotland and Ireland the sword was drawn and battles were fought; but with our eye on the structure of the English state—which held together in 1688 as it had not done in 1642, and so determined much of what happened elsewhere—we may be tempted to suppose that the advent of the professional army had rendered impossible a recrudescence of the initially amateur civil war the militias had fought in 1642. The matter was not put to the test. What actually happened is that because James fled without fighting there was no civil war in England, and

[3] Hobbes, *Leviathan*, ch. 13.

William was called to exercise the sword of Leviathan. What he did with it was to proceed, once the campaigns in Ireland were over, to reorganize a force of English and Scottish regiments capable of assisting him in his wars in the Netherlands. Perhaps it was with this aim and no other that he had come to England, though how he thought he was going to achieve it when he went on board ship in 1688 defies our imagining.

There followed during the Nine Years War that reorganization of the fiscal and military structures of the English state which would transform it into Britain and render it capable of a major role in the wars in Europe and the European presence in America and India. If there is a revolutionary change in the course of early-modern British history it is to be found here; at least, this was the point at which observant contemporary intelligence became capable of saying that such a transformation was going on. They identified the reorganization of politics as consisting of two innovations: the institution of a standing army, and the institution of a system of public credit capable of maintaining such an army, both during long campaigns in the field and during periods of peace—which was what made it a standing army—without beggaring the state in the process. A few years later, Marlborough could march from Flanders to Bavaria and back again, fighting a major battle on the way, without seeing his army dissolve into plundering hordes, because he paid his way with letters of credit on Dutch and English bankers; a feat which would have been beyond the capacity of Wallenstein or Turenne. England was leaving the world of civil and social war and entering that of European reason of state; was passing out of the age of the Wars of Religion and entering that of the Enlightenment, in which states were capable of controlling their armies and their own fissiparous tendencies towards religious and civil war. It was the end of Hobbesian politics; or rather, it was the victory of Leviathan.

Because there was no more civil war in England, England became capable of imperial power; of fighting major wars in Europe and beyond. Figurative language such as I have just been using is the necessary consequence of our speaking of long-term processes in structural history; but it comes to be justified when we think there are such processes to describe, or when we are dealing with the emergence of a discourse in which they are supposed and depicted. Within a decade of 1688, observing intelligences—whose existence and activity are a part of history if they are not the key to it—thought that they were in a process of long-term yet rapid structural change. They held it to be one involving the rise of the standing army and the preconditions of its existence, and they were aware of it precisely because the conditions making civil war a possibility had by no means disappeared. The standing army and public credit had been instituted in England both to confirm the Revolution régime and to make it capable of defending itself by extending its power abroad; and whenever in the next half-century country politicians and republican ideologues sought to reduce the standing army and lessen the public dependence on credit, they were suspected —sometimes with reason—of a design to weaken the régime and facilitate a restoration of the exiled family. One such moment occurred in 1698, when the wars in Europe had ended and the English parliament set about compelling William to reduce his armies. In the printed discourse of the time, we find an interesting debate between the Scot Andrew Fletcher, the Anglo-Irishman John Trenchard, and the Londoner Daniel Defoe, about the history of standing armies.[4] All three are writing Whig history in one of the accepted senses of the term; that is, they agree on the existence of a process of change in the structure of society, to which the political structure cannot refuse to respond; they differ on the extent and character of the response required. It is common ground between them that a growth in commerce and culture has made it possible, desirable, and perhaps unavoidable that the subject shall cease to be the proprietor of the sword, letting it pass out of his hands into those of a professional paid by a state in which the subject is active, and controls the sword, only through his representatives. Fletcher (writing from a point of view both Scottish and British) wants the militia preserved as a remedial device, in order to institutionalize and preserve the subject's control of his own sword and his own liberty. Defoe (whose stance is English, but at the same time British) thinks it pays the subject to let the process go all the way, retaining only parliamentary control over the taxes which pay the soldiers.

[4] J. G. A. Pocock, *The Machiavellian Moment: Florentine Political Thought and the Atlantic Republican Tradition* (Princeton 1975), ch. 12, and J. Robertson, *The Scottish Enlightenment and the Militia Issue* (Edinburgh 1986).

Here are the makings of a Whig interpretation of history, in the sense of a perceived long-term process which was to make sense to both Hume and Macaulay in providing the civil wars with a history; but it was not the product of any sudden slide into complacent ancient-constitutionalist consensus. The debate over the role of arms in history was to continue down to the Scottish Enlightenment and the American Revolution, and it was formed by a period during which the continued existence of the Jacobite possibility determined the character of the militia debate which lay at its core. The turning-point I have detected in 1688 continued to hold significance.

The debaters of 1698 had been supplying a social-change explanation of the conditions under which a final transfer of the sword from the individual's hands into those of Leviathan had become possible. As long as he retained the property of his sword, the individual could not yield it up to Leviathan without the risk that Leviathan would thrust it back into his hands; no mere act of will would get him out of the state of nature. But once he ceased to be merely the proprietor of his own land, his own sword, and his own right and duty to use it, and became instead the generator of wealth and credit which could be used to pay soldiers and to multiply culture, the sword might be borne by an agent other than himself, whom he could pay Leviathan to pay for him. There was resistance to this process; the classical rhetoric of the militia as necessary to the security of a free state is found in Jacobite mouths as well as republican, and there were many Whigs who feared for the consequences to the individual; but by the time of the Seven Years War, the Hanoverian line felt strong enough to mobilize a national militia, and to keep it under canvas for two years as a standing army for home defence, to guard against a landing of French troops and any pretender (if there still was one) they might have brought with them. It was service in this militia, wrote the historian Edward Gibbon, combined with 'the accession of a British prince' brought up in the Church of England, which finally reconciled Jacobite families like his own to the Hanoverian Succession and the Septennial Act.[5] Opposition to that prince's policies, expressed in a medley of commonwealth and Scottophobe language, began in a very

[5] E. Gibbon, *Memoirs of My Life*, ed. G. A. Bonnard (New York 1966), 111.

few years; but Leviathan retained his grip on the crozier as well as the sword, and it became apparent that the urban factions and the great men who might promote them were no longer parties capable of pushing the realm into civil war. The Sacheverell riots had threatened a régime; the Gordon riots threatened only the public peace.

A process of structural change, in the character of property, the technology of warfare, and the production of wealth—it was now possible for those interested in the history of justice, police, revenue, and arms to say—had done in history what Hobbesian man could not do for himself in the emergence from the state of nature. The perceived macro-process was an enlargement of a micro-process by which civil war was becoming less probable in England. Hobbesian politics, and the Hobbesian solution from which Locke had not much departed in his writings before 1688, had been rendered less immediate by the events of that year and the next; and the rapid-seeming transition from the state perpetually lapsing into civil war to a state capable by its new military and financial structure of evading civil war and exercising imperial power, could be and was envisaged in terms of an historical process. Neither Hobbes nor even Locke had done much to describe the process, and there is no need to invoke it in order to explain the events of 1688—or indeed the actions of those in high politics at any moment thereafter. Long-term processes, it is worth remarking, seldom explain what political actors do; they only explain what they turn out to have done. The significance of 1688 which we are here considering was not immediately operative, but took time to become apparent. That is a statement in Whig history; it exercises hindsight and renders the event significant in terms of its consequences. It is also a statement about Whig historiography; it begins to show how the event generated its own history, and became significant in terms of both constitutional persistence and structural change. We can choose for ourselves whether to accept such historiographies as providing explanations of the event or as rendering it significant; we cannot deny the historical fact that they were generated by the event and by those reflecting on its consequences, or that the event was an agent in producing its own significance. Whig historiography, to that extent, is a product of Whig history.

II

There is a sense in which the processes just described can be characterized as belonging to what we call Enlightenment. That is, it is useful to say that Enlightenment denotes a series of occurrences whereby England, Scotland, and other states of western Europe passed out of a period of religious and civil war, in which sovereigns could not adequately control their churches or their armed men and were consequently threatened with dissolution, and entered a period of more settled government and interactions between states, which lasted until the French Revolution and was partially renewed after it. There are historians who prefer to call this the period of the *ancien régime*, but there seems no reason why the two terms should not be used interchangeably. The process involved a certain dissociation of the individual from activity in political and religious conflicts, which he was encouraged to allow the sovereign to manage for him; he was encouraged to think these conflicts less urgently important than he had, and to think that he had other ends and values to pursue. The individual described by both Fletcher and Defoe, interested in commerce and enquiry to the point where he is content to let the sword which protects his liberties be managed for him, is a type of what I am here calling the individual of the Enlightenment; and we have seen that he was encouraged to see himself as produced by a process of historical change, which rendered him modern as distinct from his predecessors. His 'modern' characteristics, both cause and effect of his transfer of the sword into the hand of Leviathan, were defined by theorists following Defoe as 'manners', 'politeness', 'taste', and other terms denoting an increased capacity for civilized intercourse in a society increasingly commercial, urban, and reliant on the exchange of goods, ideas, and cultural traits. This was to be a major theme of Enlightenment historiography.

A not dissimilar development can be detected in the religious field. Leviathan, we know, wielded a crozier as well as a sword, and his left hand might impair the strength of his right. The most delicate area we have to treat, in assessing the significances of 1688, is the Revolution's impact on the Church; even today when Anglicans probe the foundations of authority in their communion, terrible things can still happen. Since the Restoration and even before it, the Anglican clergy had been propounding a doctrine in which the Word and the Spirit acted in the world without departing from the forms of civil society, of which the authority of the magistrate was necessarily one. This made it difficult—though for many it also made it necessary—to submit to the replacement of the Church's supreme governor by a civil process which the clergy found understandably questionable. We may emphasize both the continuing restiveness and Jacobitism to which this gave rise, and the thoroughness with which the majority of clergy who took the oaths to William and Mary succeeded in transferring their doctrines of divine and apostolic authority into the new framework of allegiance; though to emphasize both with equal rigour points towards a revisionist posture of affirming that authority persisted without consensus.

But it is also important that the Church's problem of allegiance be seen as part of an enterprise in which the clergy had been engaged ever since the disintegration of the Commonwealth's godly rule: that of exorcizing rebellious enthusiasm and antinomianism by insisting that the Spirit never rebelled against the Law and teaching a civil piety which was by no means the same as a civil religion. If the Spirit was to be mediated to humanity through the forms of civil order, with which the Church was to be congruent, it was necessary to dismiss all claims that the Spirit's presence might be recognized by those acting outside those forms—whether a priesthood claiming the authority of Christ really present in the sacraments, or an anarchy of sects claiming the authority of the Spirit immediately present in the congregation or the prophetically illuminated individual. Ecclesiastics inclined to this way of thinking might not be ill-disposed towards John Locke's argument that the mind knew not things but the ideas which it had of things, not God but the reasons which it had for believing in his existence. As a polemic against enthusiasm, the *Essay Concerning Human Understanding* is part of an enterprise in which the Church had been long engaged, and it may have been by publishing this work (and owning it as his) in 1690 that Locke began moving away from the subversiveness of the writings which he published anonymously in the same year.

It was the aim of much that we call Enlightenment to increase the powers of reason by limiting its range; by redirecting it from metaphysics towards experiment. This enterprise was highly congruent with the endeavours of both states and established churches to reduce the danger of religious civil war by combating the various forms of fanaticism which had claimed authority from the certainty of spiritual knowledge.

There arose—I am compressing the story here—an Anglican probabilism which tended to replace theology by the history of theology; by the discussion of beliefs which had been held and of the grounds there had been for holding them. It was both an Anglican and an Enlightenment belief that the human mind did what it was capable of doing; this could be used to suppress doctrinal challenges to the authority of the magistrate as well as to deter the magistrate from imposing restraints on the freedom of enquiry.

There could thus be a history of religion written as a history of opinions held, or by more sceptical and scientific intellects as a history of the belief systems which the human mind was capable of generating. It could coexist with a history of social and governmental systems written as a history of manners, by which was meant not only codes of behaviour but the intellectual, aesthetic, and ethical systems generated by human minds in interaction with one another, often on the foundation of property systems increasingly geared to exchange. Both historiographies depicted humans as moving from ancient to modern: from ancient metaphysics to modern experimentality, from ancient virtue to modern politeness, from ancient autonomy to modern sociability; and each was explicitly connected with the emergence of sovereign government over settled societies free from the dangers of religious civil war. Enlightenment grew under the sword and crozier of Leviathan.[6] The first history of England written entirely in the enlightened mode is that completed by David Hume between 1754 and 1762; it ends in 1688 because Hume considered the Revolution to have ended the civil wars of the seventeenth century and did not wish to enter on the turbulent history of the régime which had succeeded them. His history is in our eyes deeply revisionist in its refusal to see constitutional rights and wrongs at issue in the civil wars, and at the same time deeply Whig in its willingness to see both political and religious

[6] See further, J. G. A. Pocock, 'Clergy and Commerce: The Conservative Enlightenment in England', in R. Ajello *et al.* (eds.), *L'Età dei Lumi: studi storici sul settecento europeo in onore di Franco Venturi* (Naples 1985).

fanaticism as the products of a process of social change—a 'revolution in manners' at work in both England and Europe with changes in the character of property as its infrastructure.

Hume can be seen as taking English historiography in an altogether new direction, but it is as well to remember that he was a Scot, and that his *History* was a companion to his friend William Robertson's *History of Scotland*, published as he began work, and was in some sense a precursor of the great conjectural histories of the progress of society which the Edinburgh literati began producing during the 1760s and 1770s. The Scots were writing enlightened history: their works were histories of manners and modernity, in which the redistribution of arms and the changing nature of property played a large part, and the supposed progress of mankind from fanaticism to politeness allied the moderate Robertson with the irreligious Hume—though the latter's deeper pessimism foresaw the replacement of religious fanaticism by political. They were writing in this way because, though their strong emphasis on military virtue is a response to the Highland incursion of 1745,[7] they believed that Scotland—merged with England in the extensive monarchy of Britain—was now living under strong and settled government and free from religious civil war. The modernity of Leviathan was upon both nations.

Belatedly in this essay, I have reached a point where we may consider the significance of 1688 for British realms and dominions other than England. I have a better than ethnocentric reason for postponing it so long. Between 1638 and 1642, rebellions in Scotland and Ireland imposed strains upon the English polity it was in no condition to bear, and precipitated its disintegration in civil war. In 1688—though we might do well to ask how far the invitation to William of Orange was a product of what was happening in Ireland—there was no civil war in England, the English polity did not disintegrate, and as reorganized by William for his wars was able to impose solutions immediately on Ireland and after twenty years on Scotland. The wars fought in both associated kingdoms as a result of 1688 were not civil wars in the English sense. The Highland war from Killiecrankie to Glencoe was momentous in the history of British intercommunal conflict,

[7] Robertson, *Scottish Enlightenment and Militia*; R. B. Sher, *Church and University in the Scottish Enlightenment: The Moderate Literati of Edinburgh* (Princeton 1985).

but was not a civil war to those many Scotsmen who did not consider Highlanders members of a shared civil polity, but in Roman terms rebellious barbarian *federati* who might be subjugated or exterminated if the means were at hand.

Nevertheless, Leviathan, that very English figure, is at his least imposing in his outer realms and marches, where he must wield his sword over those who are not incorporated in his body and may have little respect for his crozier. Even in Scotland, where incorporation was carried out and has endured, it was no light matter to create a unified realm with two national churches; and outside the island of Britain there were two frontiers of conquest where it is reasonable to ask whether Leviathan obtained the victory or wrote a new history. If in England 1688 was the year of the civil war that did not happen and the end of a cycle of such wars, in Ireland it marked the last of a series of wars which were less civil wars than wars of conquest: a series that had begun in the reign of Elizabeth I and consisted in collisions between older Irish and English communities and new patterns of English and Scottish settlement and sovereignty. William's Irish war ended at Limerick, and the harshness of its settlement marked the beginning of the longest period of peace in modern Irish history. During this hundred and more years various forms of settler nationalism took shape; these are ideologies in which settler communities appropriate to themselves the authority by which settlement has been carried out, and seek to use it in governing themselves and determining their own identity. In Ireland this claim was prematurely made by William Molyneux in 1698, claiming that the right to rule Ireland by conquest belonged not to the English Crown and Parliament, but to the Anglo-Irish settlers as a community of conquerors.[8] The claim, made in Lockean language, was repudiated by Locke and little heard of again until the Volunteer movement of 1780; but the events of the Irish war following 1688 also provided heroic myths which were to be used in furnishing the Protestants of Ulster with their own militant identity. That formidable people, however, remained for a century radical, emigrant, and rebellious, and did not till after 1798 become the loyalist sub-nation which, to the discomfiture of British and Irish alike, they remain. But where Leviathan

[8] J. G. Simms, *William Molyneux of Dublin: A Life of the Seventeenth-Century Political Writer and Scientist*, ed. P. H. Kelly (Blackrock, Co. Dublin 1982).

was thus imperfectly corporate, it was understandable that there should not develop a Whig history of Ireland. From the Scottish parallel we know that one could have been written; it would have traced a passage from pastoral, warrior, and monastic antiquity to commercial and Protestant modernity. It may very well be that histories pointing in this direction were attempted, and the phrase 'an Irish Enlightenment' has been applied to intellectual developments in Dublin and Belfast; but there did not take shape, as there did in Edinburgh and Glasgow, an authoritative élite promoting Whig history in furtherance of their image of national identity and the state. Scottish enlightened history contributed powerfully to form the Whig historiography of Macaulay.

The colonies established by the English Crown and its grants to proprietors beyond the Atlantic constituted a further border area: a frontier of conquest and settlement, which was described as an 'empire', but only in part juridically organized as one. Leviathan, being English and invented in the struggle to avert civil war, knew better how to be king than Caesar; his sword and crozier did not extend readily to the creation of provinces beyond his realm. Ireland was defined as a subordinate kingdom, conquered and ruled by the Crown of England in its parliament, but this concept was not systematically extended to the settlements in America. It is tempting to suggest that the significance of 1688 in American history lies in the abandonment of whatever attempts James II had been making to reorganize Virginia and New England into dominions ruled directly by the Crown.[9] This enterprise was imperial; had the colonies become subordinate states within an empire, they would not have found it necessary to begin a revolution by declaring themselves states, which is what they did in 1776. The American secession of that year may be considered as a response to the incoherence of empire, which had left room for the growth, in the course of human events, of a settler nationalism in which the colonists took the authority of empire to themselves and claimed the right to wage war, to conquer others, and to conduct their own government. What is

[9] I have ventured to do so: J. G. A. Pocock, 'States, Republics and Empires: The American Founding in Early Modern Perspective', *Social Science Quarterly*, 68 (1987), 703–23, and *The Politics of Extent and the Problems of Freedom* (Colorado College Studies, 25, Colorado Springs 1988).

remarkable is that they drew in doing so upon arguments which had put forward an alternative interpretation of 1688 and criticisms of the régime founded upon it; a Lockean doctrine of emigration and dissolution, which they employed first to declare the relations between Crown and colonies a confederation between states and then to declare that confederation dissolved;[10] a republican doctrine of the relations between the powers composing a government and between the state and the arms borne by its citizens; a sectarian, and increasingly unitarian, doctrine of the separation of the State from the Church. They were about the creation of a congregational polity in which the crozier would have little place, though before Leviathan could lay it down the authority of his sword must be established.[11] They made no attempt to promote a British revolution or dissolve the authority of George III over his kingdoms; they separated themselves from the state of Great Britain by declaring their ties with it dissolved; but their perception of themselves and the governments they would have was shaped in the first instance by the radical Whig critique of the Revolution, which was as old as the Revolution itself and was now being revitalized by the English enemies of George III and the aristocratic and Anglican régime.

On both sides of the Atlantic an anti-Georgian Whig historiography took shape, which tended towards both a radical reading of 1688 as a deposition—the better to threaten George III with the fate of his predecessor—and a radical critique of 1689 as an insufficient remedy for political abuses. The commonwealth and republican rhetoric on which it drew offered means of criticizing the enlightened moves towards modernity which I have considered in this essay; but at the same time it appropriated many elements of that progressive programme, presenting both aristocracy and established clergy as medieval and archaic, instead of the powerful modernizing forces which the English and Scottish Enlightenments had shown them to be. The Enlightenment of the *ancien régime* had been a direction of modernizing processes

[10] Y. Ohmori, 'The Artillery of Mr Locke: The Use of Locke's *Second Treatise* in Pre-Revolutionary America', unpublished Ph.D. dissertation (Johns Hopkins University, 1988).

[11] J. G. A. Pocock, 'Religious Freedom and the Desacralization of Politics from the English Civil Wars to the Virginia Statute', in M. D. Peterson and R. C. Vaughan (eds.), *The Virginia Statute of Religious Freedom: Its Evolution and Consequences in American History* (Cambridge 1988), 45–73.

by the established élites; the democratization which followed was both an annexation and a criticism of progress. It is against a secularizing and democratizing progressivism, still very much part of our thinking, that the contemporary polemic against Whig history is for the most part directed; with the effect that a democratized and secularized society, which certainly exists today, is being commanded to do without a history that guarantees it.

Starting with a deliberately non-Whiggish reading of the events of 1688, I have tried to show how they can be situated in the context of continuing historical processes which can still be used to invest them with significance, and at the same time to show how they acquired the kind of significance which goes with the construction of Whig interpretations of history. That is, it has been my aim to show how Whig histories—I use the plural because there have been several—have been themselves the product of English, British, and American history, ways of investing it with significance which it has itself generated.

It is therefore a problem that the demolition of Whig history is a programme for asking the present to live without a past that justifies it. To do so vastly enriches our understanding of both the past and the present; but we need to know whether this is other than a programme for the owl of Minerva, for mood being the more as our might lessens. Historiography has been so much a matter of the construction of usable pasts that it is desirable for the historian engaged in denying the past usability to ask himself what demands he is making on the present. Given the world-wide failures of revolutionary dialectic, it should seem that the destruction of history as a process justifying the present is a programme for emphasizing irony and contingency, for inviting the inhabitants of the present to conduct their affairs in the knowledge of how very easily things might have been otherwise, and of how complex and contradictory were the processes that have made them what they are. David Hume, the first truly great historian of England, clearly thought it good for a people to learn to live in the ironies of history; but he also thought the English too self-centred, philistine and faction-ridden a mob to sustain such an awareness very long, and he was not sanguine about their political future. Two hundred and more years later, here we are. 'Well, doctor,' a modern William might say 'what do you think of demystification now?'

Index